Ocmulgee Archaeology, 1936–1986

OCMULGEE ARCHAEOLOGY 1936–1986

EDITED BY David J. Hally

The University of Georgia Press

Athens and London

© 1994 by the University of Georgia Press
Athens, Georgia 30602
All rights reserved
Designed by Louise OFarrell
Set in 10/12 Ehrhardt by Tseng Information Systems, Inc.
Printed and bound by Thomson-Shore, Inc.
The paper in this book meets the guidelines for permanence and
durability of the Committee on Production Guidelines for Book
Longevity of the Council on Library Resources.

Printed in the United States of America

98 97 96 95 94   C   5 4 3 2 1

Library of Congress Cataloging in Publication Data
Ocmulgee archaeology, 1936–1986 / edited by David J. Hally.
p.   cm.
Includes bibliographical references and index.
ISBN 0-8203-1606-7 (acid-free paper)
1. Ocmulgee National Monument (Ga.)   2. Indians of North
America—Georgia—Macon Region—Antiquities.   3. Indians of
North America—Southern States—Antiquities.   4. Macon Region
(Ga.)—Antiquities.   5. Southern States—Antiquities.   I. Hally,
David J.
E78.G3036 1994
975.8′01—dc20   93-2482

British Library Cataloging in Publication Data available

To Arthur Randolph Kelly and the thousands of men and women who labored at Ocmulgee during the Great Depression

CONTENTS

ILLUSTRATIONS

TABLES

PREFACE

Early in 1986, Sibbald Smith, superintendent of the Ocmulgee National Monument, asked me to organize a conference to commemorate the fiftieth anniversary of the founding of the Ocmulgee National Monument. The resulting conference was held at Mercer University in Macon on December 13, 1986. Fourteen papers dealing with various aspects of Ocmulgee archaeology were presented in morning and afternoon sessions. In the evening, following a reception and banquet, Jesse D. Jennings spoke about his experiences as acting superintendent of the Monument in 1938 and 1939.

The chapters in this volume are derived from the papers delivered at the conference. Two papers by Walker and by Hally and Williams on important aspects of Ocmulgee archaeology that were not covered in the conference are also included, as is the speech that Gordon R. Willey, assistant archaeologist at Ocmulgee from 1936 to 1938, prepared for the banquet but was unable to deliver because of illness.

A number of people contributed to the success of the fiftieth anniversary conference and to the publication of its proceedings. The Ocmulgee National Monument Association, a citizens support group in Macon, sponsored the conference and provided travel funds for Griffin, Jennings, and Willey. Mercer University and its president, Kirby Godsey, served as host for the conference. Don Evans handled local arrangements with the assistance of Sibbald Smith. Sylvia Flowers provided assistance and, more important, encouragement to me on numerous occasions prior to, during, and after the conference. John Walker selected a number of photographs from the Southeast Archeology Center archives for reproduction in this volume. Prints of these photographs were provided by the Center. Gisela Weis-Gresham drafted many of the figures. I am grateful to all of these people and institutions.

Of course, nothing would have been possible without the participation of the contributors to this volume. I appreciate their efforts and their tolerance of my demands and shortcomings as editor of this book.

Ocmulgee Archaeology, 1936–1986

INTRODUCTION

David J. Hally

On DECEMBER 23, 1936, President Franklin D. Roosevelt signed a proclamation establishing the Ocmulgee National Monument. Fifty years later, on December 13, 1986, a conference commemorating this event was held at Mercer University in Macon. This volume and the essays in it are a direct outgrowth of that conference.

As part of the federal government's effort to reduce unemployment during the Great Depression, truly massive archaeological projects spanning many years and involving hundreds of workers were conducted in several locations across the southeastern United States. One of the first projects to be initiated, and one of the largest in terms of work force and duration, was conducted in the Macon, Georgia, area between December 1933 and March 1941. Administered by the National Park Service and funded at various times by the Civil Works Administration (CWA), Works Progress Administration (WPA), Federal Emergency Relief Administration (FERA), Emergency Relief Administration (ERA), and the Civilian Conservation Corps (CCC), these excavations involved more than a dozen sites and employed at their peak in 1935 almost 800 workers.

The most extensive and probably the best-known excavations were conducted at the Macon Plateau site (9BI1) in an area that ultimately became part of the Ocmulgee National Monument (Figure I.1). Excavations also were conducted at a number of other sites in the vicinity of Macon with those at Lamar (9BI2) (H. Smith 1973a), Swift Creek (9BI3) (Kelly and Smith 1975), Brown's Mount (9BI5), Napier (9BI9), Mossy Oak (9BI11), Stubbs (9BI12) (M. Williams 1975), and Cowarts Landing (9BI14) (Hamilton et al. 1975) being the most extensive and productive. Excavations involving personnel from Macon also were conducted at several sites located some distance from Macon; those at Carroll (9PM85) (Kowalewski and Williams 1989) and Lawson Field (9CE1) (Willey and Sears 1952) are the best known.

A certain amount of confusion surrounds the manner in which sites and excavations in the Macon area have been referred to in the archaeological literature. The term "Ocmulgee," which derives from the Ocmulgee Indians, their Old Fields, and the river that flowed past those fields, is often used to refer to any or all federal relief program archaeological activities that took place in the vicinity of Macon. The Ocmulgee National Monument, where most of this activity occurred, includes two geographically separated tracts of land: one located in the floodplain of the Ocmulgee River and containing the Lamar site; and the other located 3 km to the north on the Macon Plateau and containing the Macon Plateau site. The Macon Plateau is a relatively flat area of Piedmont uplands bordered by the Ocmulgee River on the southwest and Walnut Creek on the southeast (see Figure 8.1 and Chapter 8, this volume). It was divided into four segments by two railroad cuts in the nineteenth century, and these were referred to as the Southeast, South, North, and Middle plateaus by archaeologists working there in the 1930s (see Figure 8.2). These areas were also given National Park Service designations: 1Bi1, 1Bi2, 1Bi3, and 1Bi4, respectively.

Federal relief program excavations at Ocmulgee were conducted under difficult conditions: The work force generally numbered in the hundreds; there was a minimum of trained supervisory personnel; funding came from a variety of government programs and seems to have fluctuated widely in availability over time; funding for nonwage expenses was minimal; and little provision was made for analysis of recovered materials or for report writing. These conditions and the people who struggled under them to conduct research and to develop and administer the Ocmulgee National Monument are described by Walker in Chapter 2 of this volume.

Archaeological investigations in the Macon area during the 1930s raised a number of important questions, most of

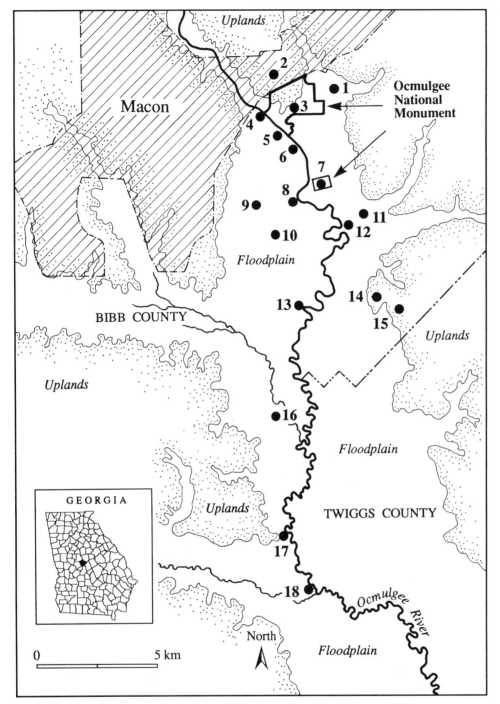

I.1. Location of sites in the Macon area investigated as part of the federal relief archaeological program.

1. Scott (9BI16)
2. Ft. Hawkins (9BI21)
3. Macon Plateau (9BI1)
4. Deer Park (9BI8)
5. Mile Track (9BI7)
6. Napier (9BI9)

7. Lamar (9BI2)
8. Horseshoe Bend (9BI0)
9. Tuft Springs #2 (9BI19)
10. Tuft Springs #1 (9BI13)
11. Swift Creek (9BI3)
12. Adkins Mound (9BI4)

13. Mossy Oak (9BI11)
14. Brown's Mount (9BI5)
15. Shell Rock Cave (9BI6)
16. Stubbs Mound (9BI12)
17. Cowarts Landing (9BI14)
18. Hawkins Point (9BI15)

which were not satisfactorily answered at the time. Some of these—for example, the functional identification of the "prehistoric dugouts"—were primarily of local or site-specific significance. Most questions—the existence of platform mounds in the Woodland period and Plains-style earth lodges in Georgia, the spread of Mississippian culture by migration, and the prehistoric identity of the Creek Indians—related to issues that were at least pan-southeastern in significance.

In the years since the termination of federal relief program archaeology, considerable progress has been made in answering many of the questions raised at Macon. Ironically, little of this progress has been the result of research involving the collections recovered in the 1930s or subsequent fieldwork in the Macon area. Archaeological research in the Southeast has increased significantly in both quantity and quality during the last 50 years, but little research has been conducted in the Macon area during that period, and archaeologists seldom refer to the archaeology that was conducted there prior to 1940.

I suspect that the moribund condition of Macon-area archaeology during the last several decades is due in large part to the nature of the artifact collections and field records generated by the 1930s excavations and to the lack of widely available published reports on that archaeology. Researchers (Ingmanson 1965; Prokopetz 1974; H. Smith 1973b) who have worked with the Ocmulgee material curated at the Southeast Archeological Center in Tallahassee, Florida, report that critical fieldnotes and drawings are often missing or vague and inconsistent in content, while artifact provenience is frequently poorly documented. There are only six widely available publications that contain much useful information pertaining to Macon-area sites (Fairbanks 1946b, 1956a; Kelly 1935b, 1938c, 1939; Willey 1939). In addition, there are 16 reports and one dissertation (Mason 1963a) dealing with specific sites or features of sites located in the Macon area. The reports were written by National Park Service personnel or under National Park Service contract and published in limited numbers in the mid-1970s (Hamilton et al. 1975; Ingmanson 1964a, 1964b, 1965; Kelly and Smith 1975; Nelson, Prokopetz, and Swindell 1974; Nelson, Swindell, and Williams 1974; Prokopetz 1974; H. Smith 1973a, 1973b; Stoutamire et al. 1977, 1978, 1983; M. Williams 1975; Williams and Henderson 1974; Zierden 1978). They generally contain descriptions of the excavations, recorded archaeological features, and recovered artifacts, but beyond artifact counts they contain little additional information that is of use to archaeologists today. This is mostly because contracts provided insufficient funds for more complete analysis.

The fiftieth anniversary of the founding of the

Ocmulgee National Monument provided an appropriate opportunity to bring the archaeology of the Macon area up to date and back into the mainstream of southeastern archaeology. In organizing the conference, I decided to solicit papers that dealt with the important questions that were raised in the 1930s at the time the Monument was established. I urged authors to describe the archaeological material that originally gave rise to these questions and to interpret it in light of relevant research being conducted elsewhere today. Approximately half the chapters in this volume follow this format. The remainder deal with various aspects of the federal relief project excavations and should provide the reader with a fuller understanding of the historical context and scientific significance of those excavations.

Stephen Williams's chapter is the first of five in this volume that take a historical view of the federal archaeological program at Macon. Williams is concerned with the development of southeastern archaeology during the latter part of the nineteenth century and the early decades of the present century. His discussion provides the broader historical context within which the research effort at Macon should be viewed and understood. One point clearly emerges from his discussion: when research began, the people responsible for its conduct—Arthur Kelly and James Ford—were working largely in a culture-historical vacuum. The broad outline of eastern North American prehistory—preceramic, mound builder, and historic type cultures had been distinguished—was beginning to emerge, but few archaeological cultures in the interior Southeast had been investigated and characterized in a systematic fashion, and there was nothing resembling a culture sequence for the region. Given this fact and the considerable problems posed by the exigencies of managing a large fieldwork force and inadequate time for analysis and interpretation of completed fieldwork, the scientific accomplishments of the project were rather remarkable.

John Walker's chapter is a "day-by-day" account of the history of Ocmulgee National Monument and is based in large part on personal correspondence, administrative documents, and newspaper stories from the archives of the Monument and the Southeast Archeological Center in Tallahassee, Florida. Walker's style of presentation effectively conveys a sense of the hectic conditions under which archaeological research was conducted at Macon in the 1930s. The number and variety of investigations undertaken by Kelly and his assistants, the rapid pace with which they were initiated and completed, and the geographical extent of the area over which they were distributed are indeed impressive. Equally impressive is the list of eminent and soon-to-be eminent scholars who visited and in some fashion contributed to these investigations.

It is, of course, fitting that Gordon R. Willey, Jesse D. Jennings, and James B. Griffin should be represented in this book. Gordon Willey was a research archaeologist at Ocmulgee from 1936 to 1938. During this period, he directed excavations at the Stubbs Mound, conducted test excavations at a number of sites across central Georgia, and developed a dendrochronology sequence for the region. As Kelly's assistant, he also had a significant influence on the direction that archaeological research took at Ocmulgee during the latter part of the decade. Jesse Jennings served as acting superintendent of the Monument from 1938 to 1939. As the first National Park Service employee assigned to Ocmulgee, he began the process of transforming the Monument from a Depression-era make-work archaeological project to a visitor-oriented archaeological preserve. Years later, he helped develop the exhibit plan for the museum that opened in November 1951. Willey's and Jennings's highly personal reminiscences of their experiences at Ocmulgee are certainly the most readable and in many respects the most valuable contributions to the present volume.

In his role as discussant for the 1986 conference, Griffin is once again an outsider looking in. (He visited the excavations at Macon, and he had an impact on their conduct, but he did not participate directly in them.) From this vantage point, he is able to look with equal objectivity (and humor) at the nature and significance of the Ocmulgee research carried out fifty years ago and today.

Federal relief program excavations on the North Plateau resulted in the discovery of the first recognized Clovis point from an excavation in the southeastern United States and in the recognition of the relatively great antiquity of lithic material that is today identified as Early Archaic. Early man studies in Georgia languished for the next four decades despite this auspicious beginning and despite the fact that several neighboring states were making considerable progress in the development of Paleoindian and Archaic period artifact typologies and chronological sequences. Fortunately the pace and quality of early man research in Georgia has increased dramatically in the last decade.

In their paper, David Anderson and his colleagues review the history of early man studies in Georgia and South Carolina. They also provide a thorough and very timely synthesis of recent research. Of particular interest is their review of several Early Archaic settlement models that have been proposed recently. These models present quite different pictures of Early Archaic band size, mobility, territory size, and population density. The contrasts between them will undoubtedly influence research effort and debate for years to come.

The 1937–38 excavations of Mound A at the Swift Creek site had great potential significance for the devel-

opment of southeastern archaeology. As reported by Kelly in 1938, Mound A represents the first recognized example of a pre-Mississippian platform mound in the eastern United States. Today more than a dozen such mounds have been excavated and reported, and their existence as a distinct type of Middle and Late Woodland ceremonial construction is accepted by most archaeologists.

Unfortunately, widespread acceptance of Woodland platform mounds has come about only in the last 10 years. Why the discoveries at Swift Creek had so little impact on contemporary archaeologists is unclear. Had it stimulated interest among researchers, we would probably know much more today about the cultural and historical significance of this type of mound construction, and our perception of Woodland ceremonialism and its relation to Mississippian ceremonialism would probably be quite different.

Dick Jefferies's chapter presents a useful overview of the currently available information on pre-Mississippian platform mounds. Beginning with Swift Creek and concluding with hitherto unpublished information on the mounds at the Cold Spring site (9GE10) in north Georgia, he describes the major known examples of Woodland platform mounds in the Southeast. He concludes with a number of generalizations about the nature of these mounds.

More effort was devoted to the investigation of the early Mississippian Macon Plateau phase occupation at Ocmulgee than any other component. Unfortunately, despite the intensive excavation, very little is known about the nature of the site occupation or the people responsible for it. In response to this situation, six papers in this volume address various aspects of Macon Plateau phase archaeology.

The first of these papers, by Hally and Williams, looks at the architectural features and internal chronology of the Macon Plateau occupation. There exists an extensive literature pertaining to these subjects (Fairbanks 1946b, 1956a; Ingmanson 1964a, 1964b, 1965; Kelly 1938c, 1939; Kelly and Smith 1975; Mason 1963a; Nelson, Prokopetz, and Swindell 1974; Prokopetz 1974; Stoutamire et al. 1983; Williams and Henderson 1974; Wilson 1964), but little of it has been published in a widely available form, and there has been no attempt to synthesize it into an overview of the site as a whole. Williams and I review this literature and conclude that site occupation was of sufficient duration that the site's settlement configuration changed through time and that the site may have ultimately consisted of several mound-plaza-residential complexes that were spatially situated so as to conform to an overarching cosmological plan.

The first recognition and excavation of a subsurface agricultural field in eastern North America occurred on the Macon Plateau in 1934. More than thirty years were

David J. Hally

to pass, however, before other examples of this type of feature were investigated. In his chapter, Thomas Riley reviews the history of research on aboriginal agricultural fields in eastern North America and considers the significance of the Mound D "cornfield" within the context of more recent work on prehistoric agricultural fields. He concludes that ridged fields may be characteristic of Mississippian societies throughout much of the eastern United States and that their widespread distribution is most likely the result of the coevolution of maize-specific agronomic techniques throughout the region from a preexisting agricultural base.

The so-called Macon Earth Lodge is probably the most widely known archaeological feature encountered on the Macon Plateau during federal relief project excavations. Reconstructed as circular in shape, with a covered passage entryway and earth-covered roof (Fairbanks 1946b), this structure stimulated comparison with Plains Indian earth lodges and lent support to the migration theory of Mississippian origins in the nuclear Southeast. Its existence, furthermore, served as justification for the identification of other Mississippian structures as earth lodges.

In his chapter, Lewis Larson argues that all claims for the existence of earth-covered structures in the nuclear Southeast during the Mississippi period are wrong. The importance of this conclusion goes well beyond the matter of clarifying the architectural characteristics of a handful of prehistoric buildings. For one, it diminishes the uniqueness of Macon Plateau culture; as an earth-embanked structure, the Macon Earth Lodge conforms more closely to the general pattern of Mississippian architecture in the region. This result is in line with current tendencies to see a greater role for indigenous cultures in the development of regional variants of Mississippian culture.

The fifty years since federal relief project excavations were undertaken at Macon have seen tremendous growth in the variety and usefulness of information that can be obtained from human burials. More than 150 burials were recovered from the Mound C and the Trading Post excavations on Macon Plateau. Mortuary, sex, and age data were published in the reports for these excavations (Fairbanks 1956a; Mason 1963a), but no thorough biological analysis of the skeletal material was undertaken until Mary Powell inventoried and analyzed the extant collections in 1985–86. Powell's chapter presents the results of this study.

As the chapters in this volume clearly illustrate, many of the research questions raised by archaeological investigations at Macon during the 1930s have been resolved or are well on their way to being resolved. This is not the case with the question of Macon Plateau culture origins. The chapters by Mark Williams and Gerald

Schroedl take diametrically opposite positions with regard to this question. Williams reviews the archaeological data pertaining to the Late Woodland and Mississippi periods in central Georgia that has accumulated in the last fifty years and can find no convincing evidence for an *in situ* development of Macon Plateau culture. Schroedl describes changes that have taken place in recent years in the interpretation of Mississippian origins in eastern Tennessee and more generally in the way archaeologists study and interpret culture change. From this perspective, he concludes that Macon Plateau culture must be the result of an *in situ* development. Neither argument is completely convincing for the reason that there has yet to be a systematic research effort designed to solve the issue. Such an effort will require additional information concerning the spatial distribution and dating of Late Woodland and Mississippi period sites and the nature of their material culture assemblages. It will also require that existing Macon Plateau site collections be restudied within the interpretative framework recently developed in eastern Tennessee and in archaeology generally.

Most of the late prehistoric and historic aboriginal inhabitants of Georgia and adjacent portions of Alabama, South Carolina, and North Carolina had a material culture that archaeologists know as Lamar. First recognized and defined (Kelly 1938c) at the Lamar site (9BI2), Lamar is today one of the most intensively studied and best understood archaeological cultures in the region. Since it was in existence at the time of first European contact in the mid-sixteenth century and many of its component societies are referred to in the early Spanish accounts, Lamar studies have the potential for providing far-reaching insights into the Mississippian way of life that has dominated the region since at least A.D. 1000.

In my chapter, I review the history of Lamar research and summarize what is known about the culture today. By taking a broad regional perspective, I am able to show how some aspects of Lamar culture changed through time and how its variability in space relates to variability in the natural environment and to the political, ethnic, and linguistic dimensions of human social organization.

One of the more important new developments in the archaeology of central Georgia during the fifty years since the founding of the Ocmulgee National Monument is the recognition that the Lamar site was probably the capital of De Soto's Ichisi province. Kelly (1938c:57) believed that Lamar culture predated the De Soto expedition. He evidently also believed that Lamar pottery evolved into the pottery characteristic of the late seventeenth- and early eighteenth-century Ocmulgee Fields component at the Macon Trading Post. By implication, Lamar culture, at least in its latter stages, would have been in existence in 1540. Whether he reached this conclusion himself or not, Kelly makes no mention of the possibility that people with Lamar culture would have been encountered by De Soto as he traversed the state. Swanton (1939:179) considered the possibility that the Macon Plateau site was one of the named towns—Cofaqui or Patofa—in the Ocute province, but rejected the idea because the site's location and size did not fit the expedition route as he was reconstructing it, nor his notion of what these towns would have looked like.

Swanton and the De Soto Commission attempted to use archaeological evidence in reconstructing the De Soto route. In the absence of reliable site distribution and chronology data, however, this effort was bound to yield inconsequential, if not misleading, results. Current efforts by Charles Hudson and his associates (DePratter et al. 1985; Hudson et al. 1984, 1990; Hudson, Smith, Hally, Polhemus, and DePratter 1985) to reconstruct the expedition route make extensive use of the archaeological evidence that has accumulated in recent decades, and it is for this reason in part that their reconstruction is so much more credible. The Lamar site is now known to have been occupied during the mid-sixteenth century. It is just one of a series of large Lamar-culture mound and village sites in Georgia and South Carolina located on southward flowing rivers at the Fall Line that we now know date to this period. De Soto was invariably drawn to the largest and most powerful chiefdoms, and in central Georgia during the sixteenth century these would have been the Fall Line Lamar-culture sites.

In his paper, Charles Hudson identifies the Lamar site as the main town of the province of Ichisi. He suggests that Ichisi and its associated towns on the Ocmulgee River may have been part of a much larger paramount chiefdom centered on the Oconee River and dominated by the chiefdom of Ocute. This latter suggestion is only weakly supported by the ethnohistorical documents. Nevertheless, as Hudson demonstrates, there is good evidence for the existence of spatially extensive paramount chiefdoms elsewhere in the Georgia–South Carolina area. Little is known about the political relationships holding these polities together nor about their duration in time. By raising the question of their possible existence, Hudson has defined an area of research that should keep scholars busy for some time to come.

Excavation of the Trading Post and associated aboriginal features on the Macon Plateau raised two issues that continue to dominate contact period archaeology to this day: the historical and developmental relationships existing between late prehistoric and historic aboriginal societies in the Southeast and the nature of aboriginal culture change as a response to European contact. The former issue, as it pertains specifically to Lamar and Ocmulgee Fields cultures, is addressed in the chapter by Vernon Knight. The latter is the focus of Gregory Waselkov's chapter.

Two of the enduring questions raised by investigations at Ocmulgee National Monument are the historical relationship between Lamar and Ocmulgee Fields ceramics and the ethnic-linguistic identity of the people who made the former. In his chapter, Vernon Knight successfully puts the first question to rest by demonstrating that Ocmulgee Fields ceramics have their greatest similarity with Blackmon phase in the lower Chattahoochee River valley and probably developed there from local antecedents. As such, Ocmulgee Fields ceramics represent a site-unit intrusion in the Macon area and are essentially unrelated to Lamar ceramics from the type site. Of perhaps greater significance for future long-term research efforts, Knight demonstrates the variability that exists among Lamar phases in eastern Alabama and western Georgia during the fifteenth to nineteenth centuries and is able to propose developmental relationships between them and specific eighteenth-century Creek communities. While Lamar culture is clearly antecedent to eighteenth-century Creek culture in this region, the relationship is complex and in need of additional investigation.

Following a review of the federal relief program excavations at the Trading Post and their interpretation, Waselkov turns his attention to the external forces that were impinging on the Creeks during the late sixteenth and seventeenth centuries and the responses that they made to them. Some native responses identified by Waselkov, such as wholesale population movements and selective adoption of European material culture, are widely accepted by scholars today. Others, such as the trend toward homogenization of aboriginal culture and the development of above ground domestic structures in response to the deerskin trade, are likely to generate some discussion among researchers.

Waselkov notes that the development of contact period archaeology as a research focus owes much to Kelly and Fairbanks's excavations at the Trading Post. Given the current growth in contact period research, we can expect that many of the questions summarized by Waselkov, and first raised by the excavations on the Macon Plateau, will be resolved in the near future.

As demonstrated by the chapters in this book, many of the research interests and questions first raised at Ocmulgee in the 1930s have been expanded in scope or answered. We now have a respectable and rapidly growing knowledge of the Paleoindian and Early Archaic inhabitants of the southeastern United States, the nature of Woodland period platform mounds, and the nature of the societies encountered by Hernando de Soto as he traveled through the region in 1540. We also appear to have resolved the earth lodge issue and identified the people who were inhabiting the Macon Plateau in the late seventeenth and early eighteenth centuries. Furthermore, historic archaeology is a well-established field of inquiry, and interest in Mississippian agronomic practices is growing.

Two major questions, in my opinion, remain to be answered: the nature of the Macon Plateau site community plan and the origin of the people responsible for its creation. Resolution of these questions will require major research efforts involving thorough analysis of field records and artifact collections from the Macon Plateau site and development of fine-grained phase chronologies for the Late Woodland and Early Mississippi periods in central Georgia.

CHAPTER ONE

The Ocmulgee Investigations in Historical Perspective

Stephen Williams

THE FIFTIETH ANNIVERSARY of the establishment of the Ocmulgee National Monument celebrated a time of great change and new development in the archaeology of the eastern United States. This site, with its time- and toil-ravaged mounds, became in the midst of the Great Depression a symbol of these new changes in the Southeast. Ocmulgee was not the most important site in the region or even in Georgia, but because it was valued and promoted by strong citizen loyalists, it became a center for a short but significant time for the "young turks" in southeastern archaeology, who were tearing up the old and seeing visions (aided by local elixirs) of Temple Mounds and messianic cults.

No, I shall not distort recent history and name Arthur Randolph Kelly as the catalyst for these important events. A gang of young archaeologists—including Ford, Willey, Holder, Waring, Jennings, Caldwell, and Fairbanks, to name the most obvious participants in the federally sponsored work, and Wauchope at the university in Athens—brought new light and exciting interpretations to the archaeology of Georgia. Art Kelly ran the project at Macon much of the time and in that position, at what would become Ocmulgee National Monument, served as titular head of the major excavations as the park was developed. He watched, slightly bemused and across a small generational gap, the innovative work of these young men.

One cannot forget the more distant past, however, when other questions and other mysterious bits of information were first wrenched from the ground to serve in the construction of the prehistoric past as it could then best be reconstituted. For the archaeology of Georgia and the greater Southeast did not spring from the foreheads of these once dauntless young turks during those shining summers of the thirties; nor did they suggest that it had. For them, and for us, too, the archaeological past was caught up in the interesting and slightly florid prose of native son Charles C. Jones (Williams 1973), the lavishly illustrated quarto volumes of C. B. Moore, and the heavy, green annual reports and bulletins of the Bureau of American Ethnology. It is to that storied past that we will first turn.

Parenthetically, I welcome this opportunity to return to Georgia archaeology, since it is now twenty years since I finished the Waring Papers, in which I first documented my affection for this area (Williams 1968:314). It is from Tono Waring's own paper on Georgia archaeology (Waring 1968b:288–99) that I have drawn much of the information that follows.

The Nineteenth-Century Background

The recording of archaeological sites in Georgia begins in the late eighteenth century with the important work of William Bartram (1928). His descriptions of a number of significant sites, including Ocmulgee Old Fields and Lamar in the Macon locality, were excellent, and his suggestion that the mounds were used in recent Creek ceremonials was unfortunately lost on, or ignored by, most Mound Builder enthusiasts of the nineteenth century (Swanton 1928a).

The great site of Etowah, near Cartersville, would understandably command archaeological attention for most of the century; beautifully located on the banks of the Etowah River, the great mounds and circular embankment and ditch were fascinating to early nineteenth-century travelers (Cornelius 1819) and historians (Haywood 1823) long before the wealth of its burial tombs had been revealed. Rafinesque, whose map of Etowah was published by Squier and Davis (1848:

108, plate 38), located the site in Alabama, but he was obviously using secondary sources that may also explain the map's other errors.

However, the most important nineteenth-century contributor to Georgia archaeology would not be an outsider; instead we find Charles C. Jones (1831–93), a native of Savannah, whose education included an undergraduate degree from Princeton and a law degree from Harvard. He practiced law much of his life but found time to write a number of important books on Georgia history and archaeology. His archaeological efforts began in 1859 and culminated in the famous *Antiquities of the Southern Indians* published in 1873. Both Charles and his brother, Joseph, were avid collectors of antiquities who did good fieldwork as well. They knew many of the sites from direct observations and dug "with a sparing hand," to use Waring's felicitous phrase (Waring 1968b:292).

Jones describes nearly a dozen sites in some detail; they are the expected ones: Etowah, Ocmulgee, Nacoochee, Hollywood, and Kolomoki. He also records his excavations at the Stallings Island shell heap, which was near his family home. His approach to archaeology was admirable (Williams 1973), in that he combined field research and direct knowledge of the artifacts with a broad historical coverage of the ethnographic sources. Jones did spread himself a bit thin on the ethnography (Waring 1968b: 290), and his rather romantic prose has put some readers off. His *Antiquities*, however, was a major contribution. On the prime topic of the period he was also forthright and correct: the Mound Builders were the ancestors of the native tribes in the area. He, like his brother, changed his mind on this important subject between 1860 and 1870. *Antiquities* also contained fine illustrations of Georgia artifacts that covered a broad temporal range: Archaic atlatl weights were thought to be ceremonial "badges of distinction"; functional uses of other artifacts were sought by well-researched ethnographic analogies.

Jones's *Antiquities* was representative of what might be called a "Golden Age of Eastern Archaeology," which temporally matched to some extent the Gilded Age of our country's history. Dozens of books on American archaeology were written between 1870 and 1900, many by well-educated gentlemen like the Joneses, Thruston, Potter, and others. But this was also to be the beginning of institutional archaeology, with the Harvard Peabody Museum, founded in 1866, and the Smithsonian Institution's Bureau of American Ethnology (BAE), founded in 1879, leading the way. These two institutions, led respectively by Frederic Ward Putnam and John Wesley Powell, put excavators in the field in a very effective manner for data collection. Powell, more than Putnam, with his Mound Survey under the direction of Cyrus Thomas, had a stated research objective: to end the mystery of who were the Mound Builders. Putnam's objectives were less

well-defined until he focused much of his efforts on early man research.

The Peabody Museum, after forays into Florida with the pioneering work of Jeffries Wyman, worked in Tennessee (Williams 1986) and in the Lower Mississippi Valley. It was the BAE that turned to Georgia in a major way. Waring (1968b:290–94) has discussed these important excavations at Etowah, Kolomoki, and Hollywood in some detail. The work at Etowah by John Rogan in 1884 produced the first well-excavated "Southern Cult" ceremonial objects, and when shipped to the Smithsonian, they "arrived as something of a bombshell," according to Waring (1968b:292).

Georgia archaeology would never be the same again, not to mention what the Etowah discovery did for southeastern archaeology as a whole. The area was then looked at, by some at least, as having real archaeological treasures. This view was held despite the fact that the killing of the myth of the Mound Builders by the conscientious work of Powell, Thomas, and the BAE, aided by some of Putnam's findings, seemed to dampen interest in the area. As it turned out, attention became focused instead on the Southwest and the exciting Cliff Dwellers (Williams 1968:5; Judd 1967).

One last nineteenth-century character appeared on the Georgia scene in 1896, at the beginning of his illustrious career in southeastern archaeology. Clarence B. Moore was a Harvard-educated Philadelphian whose contributions eventually included a shelfful of well-illustrated monographs, the contents of which tantalized and edified generations of archaeologists. Moore worked briefly but significantly on the Georgia Coast, including excavations in a number of shell mound constructions, such as the ring at Sapelo (Moore 1897).

Nineteenth-century archaeology in the eastern United States can be seen to have been concerned with three major topics: the Mound Builder question; the search for early man, mainly carried out in the north, such as in the Delaware River Valley; and the shell mound excavations (Belmont and Williams 1965; Willey and Sabloff 1980:43). Thus, in terms used by some today, the Paleoindian era was being investigated by the early man studies, and the Neoindian era covered the period of the Mound Builders. Although the nineteenth-century workers did not realize it, they were also busily taking care of the Mesoindian era (Archaic) with their work in the shell heap at Stallings Island and Wyman's prescient work in the St. John's River shell mounds, where he noted nonceramic sites. Things were off to a very good start.

The Early Twentieth Century, 1900–1930

The golden age of eastern archaeology faded with significant changes in the evaluation of the data resources by the major institutions; the Peabody looked to the Maya and the Southwest and, later, even to another hemisphere, while the Smithsonian and also the American Museum of Natural History looked westward. The East became a backwater for research by a devoted few. Clarence B. Moore followed the chimera of Etowah's rich finds with great success at Moundville, and then was completely disappointed by the Lower Valley sites of Winterville and Lake George (Williams and Brain 1983:11). To his sorrow, Moore found that all large mound sites were not equal. His instincts, however, were not all bad, and his survey and exploration of sites during this period added two unforgettable names to the East's hall of fame: Poverty Point in Louisiana and Indian Knoll in Kentucky. Neither site was full of treasures like Rogan's Eagle Warrior plates, but the enigmatic clay balls at Poverty Point and the richly endowed burials full of "bannerstones" and antler hooks at Indian Knoll were trying to tell us something about Archaic cultures, but we could not hear.

In Georgia the focus of excavations and their excavators during this period reflected the previous research in the area, and with rather marked success. Northern museums found a happy hunting ground here. First, in 1915, the Museum of the American Indian (Heye Foundation) cooperated with the Smithsonian (Hodge 1916) for excavations in the northern part of the state at the well-known Nacoochee Mound site (Heye, Hodge, and Pepper 1918), and very single-mindedly attacked the mound for its contents (Waring 1968b:294).

Then in the post–World War I period, Warren K. Moorehead led a party (1925–27) from the R. S. Peabody Foundation at Andover to the Etowah site to follow up on the BAE's earlier successes there. The excavations focused on Mound C with considerable good fortune; there were, however, also rather extensive excavations carried out in the Lamar village area nearby. The quality of Moorehead's work at Etowah has been caustically reviewed by Waring (1968b:294). Moorehead's friend, Charles C. Willoughby of the Harvard Peabody Museum, visited the site, taking useful photographs and some notes, and wrote up the artifacts for the final report (Moorehead 1932). Despite the poor digging techniques and the havoc Moorehead's party wreaked on Mound C, Lewis H. Larson found thirty years later that all was not lost.

The final important work in this period in Georgia was again done by northern visitors, but with a significantly different approach. William H. Claflin, Jr., of Massachusetts, a Harvard administrator and affiliate of its Peabody Museum, was no stranger to the Savannah River valley. His family had owned a home near Augusta for years and he had spent winter vacations there. The property abutted that of the C. C. Jones family, and Claflin had played with the Jones children as a youth. Claflin, a longtime collector of arrowheads, knew the Jones collection well,

and so it is not surprising that his interest turned to the nearby Stallings Island site, which he visited and "messed about in" from 1906 on (Claflin 1931:3–4).

Jones had dug there much earlier, as already mentioned, and Claflin and his hired team of excavators, Mr. and Mrs. C. B. Cosgrove, made their significant excavations there in 1928–29. Of course, the importance of this work is that the Stallings Island "mound" was a shell heap and not a major ceremonial construction, which had been the focus of so much earlier work in the Southeast. The characteristic fiber-tempered pottery and the tool types of the late Archaic were found here in great numbers. Although Claflin did not emphasize them, some of the bottom layers were noted as being possibly preceramic (Claflin 1931:13–14), a lead that Fairbanks (1942) was to pursue with great success.

Also taking place at the end of the decade, in 1929, was a meeting of archaeologists in St. Louis, Missouri, sponsored by the National Research Council (NRC). This body had set up a Committee on State Archaeological Surveys in 1920 (Guthe 1952:2) that worked throughout the decade to bring a higher level of professionalism to the archaeology of the eastern United States. It was quite successful in that enterprise, for which Carl Guthe should get much of the credit. The St. Louis Conference on Midwestern Archaeology, which stands as a landmark event, was but the first of three such gatherings—the others were Birmingham in 1932 and Indianapolis in 1935, which, although not essential catalysts, served to document the state of the art at those times and to bring together in one room the active participants in each area (NRC 1929, 1932, 1935).

The participants at St. Louis were a bit awkward in facing questions of public concern, especially since some of their remarks were aired by local radio stations— surely a first for the profession. Nonetheless, they deplored the wanton destruction of sites and hoped that the public would help in preservation activities, not in mindless pothunting. Matthew Stirling, chief of the Bureau of American Ethnography, echoed the call of his Smithsonian colleague, Neil Judd (1929), for historic archaeology and shied away from the early man topic as "too risky." Stirling did mention, however, that he had recently been in Macon because of a citizen's request to check on some looting there (NRC 1929:27); this event began the fruitful ties between Ocmulgee and the federal archaeologists (Fagette 1985).

The Beginning of a New Era, 1930–1942

America was changing in 1930, not easily or without great pain to thousands. The stock market crash, the agricultural decline that had begun some years earlier (especially in the South), and the dust bowl days of the Great Plains combined to bring the Great Depression to much of the nation. Archaeology, strangely enough, benefitted immensely from this national disaster. I cannot dwell at any length on the details of the history of American archaeology and the government relief programs, such as WPA, that sent hundreds of out-of-work citizens to dig on archaeological sites, especially in the Southeast, including, most particularly, Georgia. More excavation, by more personnel, in more sites was carried out in the 1930s and early 1940s than had been done in the previous century (Griffin 1976; Guthe 1952; Haag 1961, 1985; Quimby 1979; Schwartz 1967; Setzler and Strong 1936; Stirling 1934; Stoltman 1973; Willey and Sabloff 1980).[1]

The questions of the earlier decades would, in many cases, be answered by this new work, if not in quite the expected manner. On a national level, things had started off rather quietly in the thirties, as if, quite rightly, the people were waiting for a chance to speak, and speak they did with a landslide victory for Franklin D. Roosevelt in the fall of 1932. In late December of that year, the second archaeological conference sponsored by the National Reserach Council was held, focusing on southern prehistory. Meeting in Birmingham just before Christmas, a small band (forty in number) of professionals, amateurs, and a few students toured the local sites, such as Moundville, and saw the facilities at the University in Tuscaloosa. The weather was cold and stormy, and John R. Swanton gave two long lectures in one day.

Among the participants at the Birmingham conference were: the NRC representatives, such as Cole, Linton, and Guthe; the BAE crew, including Stirling, Strong, Swanton, and Walker; and the National Museum people, Collins and Judd. Then the logical state representatives were there, such as DeJarnette and Jones from Alabama, Dellinger from Arkansas, Kniffen from Louisiana, Pearce from Texas, and Webb from Kentucky. Wissler was there from the American Museum of Natural History, and Moorehead from the R. S. Peabody Foundation, Andover, presumably because of his recent work in Georgia and the Mississippi valley.

Many states were represented, but interestingly, no one from Georgia was present. Even more to the point was the fact that two young men from Mississippi were there, James A. Ford and Moreau B. Chambers, both acquaintances of Henry Collins, with whom they had done some digging. The former were two "very young" turks, to be sure.

The papers presented ranged from topical to geographic. Wissler was very candid and decried the fact that most archaeologists worked elsewhere, not in the East; he said there were forty archaeologists working in Arizona and New Mexico at this time. Matthew Stirling gave an interesting paper that included a map (NRC 1932: figure 7) showing cultural distributions in the Southeast,

a modern-day first. The paper stressed the importance of learning about the historic tribes and going from the known to the unknown—by now a familiar approach. His attitude on another subject had not changed: "The problem of ancient [read early] man in the Southeast is one which had perhaps best be avoided at this time" (NRC 1932:30). Cave research was still being suggested as the most logical method; all this at a time when Stirling's colleague, Frank Roberts, would soon lead his important expedition to Lindenmeier in Colorado and find the first Paleoindian living site on the dissected High Plains.

Henry Collins was not afraid to speak his mind, and in a paper that was surely the most intellectually challenging of the lot, he said the major task was that of establishing a chronology. The "lowly potsherd" would bear the main weight of this task: "we must seize upon every clue, no matter how small, that throws light upon their [the sherds'] respective chronological positions" (NRC 1932:41). He also believed that village site excavations might provide valuable evidence on house remains and other neglected classes of materials. He, like the rest of the Washington group (including Swanton), reiterated the direct historical approach.

Winslow Walker, also with the Smithsonian and hardly known to most southeasterners, provided a very detailed discussion of Louisiana that evidenced an uncommonly broad knowledge of artifact distributions, including pottery and projectile point types. Today such a paper would be quite painfully common; in 1932 it was the exception. Another first for Walker was the suggestion that sites be dated by river channel correlations, something that Fred Kniffen would soon try and that would be quite suggestive to researchers such as Philip Phillips many years later (1950s) in the pre-Carbon-14 days.

The legacy of the Birmingham meeting, held just before Roosevelt's inauguration, was to set some guidelines for further research in the area. Not surprisingly it was Collins's own "student," James A. Ford, who followed every word of Henry's prescription and, less than four years later, proved the efficacy of the advice in his "Indian Village Sites" monograph. Ford (1936) looked at every clue on every potsherd and, following from the known to the unknown, he set up four cultural complexes named for historic tribes in the area of Louisiana and Mississippi. No one else would make such progress so fast.

But Ford was to have a part in another history-making adventure even sooner. During 1933, with Harry Hopkins running the relief programs, efforts were made to find jobs that would take care of the unemployed quickly and without a lot of expensive equipment or a long training period. It was suggested that archaeology might fill the bill, and since the South was an area that could be worked in during all times of the year, a trial project was set up at Marksville, Louisiana, with Frank Setzler from the Smithsonian in charge. His field assistant was James A. Ford.

The innovative excavations at Marksville began in the late summer of 1933 and were continued into the fall by Ford after Setzler returned to Washington. It was found that large crews of men could be managed without too much difficulty and that they could be trained quite easily as well. Important work was done at Marksville then, but tragically Setzler never wrote it up. Years later Ford tried unsuccessfully to complete Setzler's manuscript for publication. Indeed, Ford spoke of it with Neitzel just before his death, so the unfinished work remained a concern of his to the very end.

This serious problem surrounding write-up and publication of fieldwork associated with the federally supported relief excavations was a recurring one. The emphasis was quite obviously on keeping those on relief busy digging, without any regular, planned opportunity for write-up. Most of the basic washing and cataloging of specimens was done, since these tasks were ones that could make good use of the unemployed.

In December 1933 a broad program of relief-supported archaeology was started, with the Smithsonian having overall control. Also in this same year the Tennessee Valley Authority was established to build hydroelectric dams on the Tennessee River. This project saw the first federally sponsored salvage archaeology of soon-to-be-flooded sites. The excavations were under the control of William S. Webb of Kentucky (Schwartz 1967).

Almost a decade of federally funded excavations followed, until World War II closed down all the projects in early 1942. The methodology of this research with regard to site selection and research strategy was quite simple. Sites were found near areas of high unemployment, and in the South the work was carried out on a twelve-month basis. In some cases surveys were done first, and some selectivity was used. But if site selection was any problem, it seems as if the largest and most impressive ones were chosen.

Even then it was sometimes difficult to keep all the crews busy. I do not believe that it was an apocryphal story that Art Kelly at Macon sent a large crew out to an unlikely location in some nearby bottomland to do some random testing, with the hope that nothing would be found, since their laboratories were already overflowing with materials to be washed and cataloged. Unfortunately, under lots of sterile overburden, these careful diggers found buried archaeological materials, which they dutifully recovered, only to swell the lab backlogs even further.

If site selection criteria were not exactly new, the use of these large crews was. Huge areas could be opened up and carefully cleared. Large mounds could be gently peeled and dug thoroughly; then they could be restored. Not till the seventies and with the use of large power equipment in some highway salvage projects, such as in the American Bottom in Illinois (Bareis and Porter 1984), would similarly broad-scale excavations be attempted again. Technically, much of the work was first-rate. Slow careful clearing of burials was the order of the day, and the results were excellent. Recording was generally quite good, too.

As I have indicated, it was in the write-up stage that problems arose. As many have found, however, these materials, well-excavated and quite well-cared for curatorially, have proved to be real archaeological treasures. The work of Peebles (1979) and Steponaitis (1983) at Moundville with relief-excavated materials is just one good example; George Milner (Milner and Smith 1986) has recently published a description and a well-documented listing of the comparable data sources on Kentucky archaeology that derived from relief archaeology in that state. The situation in Georgia was quite similar and has been discussed by several authors who participated in this work (Waring 1968b; Wauchope 1966).

Let me only say, to put closure on some of the topics that we have been following since 1800, that results of the work of these "young turks" at Macon did cover, rather miraculously, most of the cultural sequence of the Southeast as we know it today (Williams 1968:315–24). Starting with a single Clovis fluted point, we then have Kelly's enigmatic Early Macon flint industry, heavily patinated (Kelly 1938c), which is now seen as early Archaic (see Chapter 6, this volume). Other, more recognizable Archaic lithics also occurred at Macon in small quantities, especially those later varieties that are found with fiber-tempered pottery. Most of the well-known pottery types are also known from the Macon Plateau, as Fairbanks (1956a: table 1) has indicated.

There were, of course, some surprises and missing links. We are still arguing about whether or not there was an invasion of outsiders around A.D. 900 to account for Mississippian influences that appear then. Gordon Willey (1953) is most often associated with this hypothesis; Bruce Smith (1984) has recently discussed the question at some length. The issue was made an important part of the general archaeological literature when Willey and others used it as an example of "site-unit intrusion." In a review of Fairbanks's (1956a) monograph on Ocmulgee, I suggested (Williams 1958) that the sherd distributions from Willey's test excavations (Fairbanks 1956a: figure 3) did not seem to show this cultural disjunction very clearly. Nonetheless, I feel that significant changes do occur at that time; perhaps the early Mississippian sites have just not been found or recognized in this area.

But there were a lot of real breakthrough discoveries

by this gang of young archaeologists that were much more clear-cut. The establishment of the Swift Creek culture by the excavation of its type site was one such important event, as was the work at Lamar with some of Jesse Jennings's exciting insights (Jennings 1939).[2] Gordon Willey (1937a, 1937b) did innovative research into dendrochronology; unfortunately it did not work well in the Southeast. More important, the cultural sequence that was established at Macon did not stop with prehistoric arrowheads and complicated stamped pottery; there was the careful excavation of the Ocmulgee Trading Post, too. Thus that concern for the Historic period, so often voiced earlier, was significantly followed up on as well.

With regard to excavation techniques, one must also mention the exciting contributions that the broad horizontal excavations made: nowhere else in the Southeast have we yet found ridged agricultural fields so clearly delineated, although some have been noted north of the Ohio River (see Chapter 9). The mound stratigraphy as delineated and exhibited at Ocmulgee does not get much better than that. So, they were very good field technicians, as the work of Ford and others showed in the excavations in the Council Chamber (Fairbanks 1946b).

But there were triumphs of the mind as well. By 1935, things had progressed both intellectually and in the field, so that when the third and final NRC conference was held in Indianapolis, the most important contributions were to record the progress in the ordering of archaeological data by the use of the Midwestern Taxonomic System, also known as the McKern Classification. Although it did not have too much direct use in the southern states, Fairbanks (1942) did put it to the test at Stallings Island. Some other important northern practitioners of the McKernian art, such as James B. Griffin, had immense impact on the way all workers, North and South, dealt with their ceramics. That number even included strong-willed James A. Ford, who gave up his earlier numerical system for the binomial nomenclature that he had first run into during a summer at Chaco Canyon. Ford and Griffin (1960b) ultimately worked together on this topic, to the benefit of all.

Griffin, whose doctoral dissertation was on Norris Basin ceramics recovered by the TVA researchers under Webb's direction, came to know the ceramics of the Southeast very well indeed. Although first known for his "Fort Ancient Aspect," a lengthy exposition of the McKern Classification, Griffin made his most important contribution of the pre–World War II period by working on a synthesis of eastern archaeology, which was first presented at the American Anthropological Association meeting at Andover in December 1941. Also coming out in 1941 was another valuable synthesis by Ford and Willey. The two had met at Macon and then later worked together

in Louisiana. These two papers (Griffin 1946; Ford and Willey 1941) were distillations of the work done in the climactic days from 1937 to 1941, when relief archaeology was at its highest level of activity at Macon and elsewhere.

Taking off from the Southeastern Ceramic Conference (Ford and Griffin 1960a, 1960b) held at Ann Arbor in May 1937, where Griffin was running the Ceramic Repository and Ford was a graduate student, there was a series of Southeastern Archaeological Conferences, beginning in Birmingham in the fall of 1938 (Williams 1960). At first two a year were held, so that the workers could share the wealth of data from the WPA excavations all over the South. They started to put sequence charts for the various areas up on the blackboards; the cultural coordination that Judd had called for in 1929 could finally be done. It was from these data that Ford, Willey, Griffin, and others drew their chronological inferences.

Also at these regional get-togethers Waring and Holder and others hashed over their new data, comparing it to the new finds coming out of the fantastic looting of the Spiro mounds in Oklahoma (Williams 1968: 6–8). At last they had enough comparable material to erect hypotheses such as the spread of the Southern Cult. Yes, their chronology was wrong and terribly foreshortened, but there was real excitement in the air then for these young diggers (Jennings 1938c), and a lot of it was generated at Macon. That feeling even continued in some wonderful postwar meetings that I took part in, when the Southeastern Archaeological Conference used the Ocmulgee National Monument as a regular meeting location.

Thus Ocmulgee was a focal point for these people, ideas, and research. The "young turks" have now turned gray or balding, and some are gone forever, but the dreams of those stalwart members of the Society for Georgia Archaeology (Dr. C. C. Harrold, Gen. Walter A. Harris, and Linton Solomon), who had so much to do with the establishment of the National Monument that we honor in this collection of papers, were fulfilled, I believe. It was not to be quite as Arthur Kelly had hoped in his own dream of a "Pecos" in the Southeast that would solve all the area's archaeological problems. But then, as I have outlined above, investigations in the Macon area did produce significant results and insights that hold firm today. And it gave those "young turks" a fine place from which to take off. So I salute those diverse men of good spirit, of this place and at that time, who dared dream of something that had never been, and who were not denied.

Notes

I would like to thank my Lower Mississippi Survey (LMS) colleagues, Jeffrey P. Brain, Ian W. Brown, and T. R. Kidder for their helpful comments on earlier drafts of this chapter.

1. WPA archaeology is a huge topic that these citations only begin to suggest. There are two recent unpublished doctoral dissertations on the topic, both by historians (Lyon 1982; Fagette 1985), that are little known quite naturally to most of the archaeological profession. What really needs to be done is a book-length treatment of this "revolution" in American archaeology, as Haag has called it.

2. The restoration drawings of Lamar are especially fine (Fairbanks 1941d).

CHAPTER TWO

A Brief History of Ocmulgee Archaeology

John W. Walker

THE ARCHAEOLOGICAL REMAINS located in the Ocmulgee River bottomlands and on the adjacent hills near Macon, Georgia, have interested laymen and scientists for more than 250 years. It was not until the 1930s, however, that local efforts led to their investigation and to the preservation of a portion of them as Ocmulgee National Monument. This chapter discusses the archaeological investigations conducted at Ocmulgee during the 1930s and early 1940s under federal relief agency sponsorship and related activities occurring prior to and after that period.

Historical Background of Ocmulgee

When first mentioned in 1675, "Ocmulgee" referred neither to the river nor the archaeological site by that name but to an Apalachicola (Lower Creek) town on the Chattahoochee River (Wenhold 1936:9). The town remained there in 1685, when Spanish troops twice ascended the river (Bolton 1925:121), but by 1690 it and most other Lower Creek towns had moved to central Georgia.

The "Okmulgees" were on Ochese Creek (now the Ocmulgee River) in 1696 when the governor of South Carolina wrote of them (Crane 1956:38). They were still there in 1703 when Colonel James Moore left "Ockomulgee" to raid the Apalachee Indian settlements (Swanton 1922:121) and in 1710 when trader James Lucas wrote a letter from "Oakmulgas" (McDowell 1955:6). They returned, however, to the Chattahoochee in 1715, for James Adair reported that Carolinians destroyed the town in that year (Adair 1775: 39), and the Spanish listed "Ocmulque" as an Apalachicola town on the Chattahoochee in 1716 (Boyd 1949:25).

The earliest known description of mounds within the Ocmulgee National Monument was written in 1739 by a ranger who accompanied General James Oglethorpe to the Lower Creek towns on the Chattahoochee. He stated that the Oglethorpe party "camped at Ocmulgas River where there are three Mounts raised by the Indians over three of their Great Kings who were killed in the Wars" (Ranger's Report 1916:219). Most probably these were Mounds A, B, and C of the Macon Plateau site (9BI1).

It was some 40 years later before William Bartram wrote a more detailed description of the site:

On the east banks of the Oakmulge, this trading road runs nearly two miles through ancient Indian fields . . . called the Oakmulge fields. . . . On the heights of these low grounds are yet visible monuments, or traces, of an ancient town, such as artificial mounts or terraces, squares and banks, encircling considerable areas. . . .

If we give credit to the account the Creeks give of themselves, this place is remarkable for being the first town or settlement where they sat down (as they term it) or established themselves after their emigration from the west. (Bartram 1928:68)

That the Creeks continued to consider Ocmulgee Fields important is shown by the Treaty of 1805, which ceded all their lands east of the Ocmulgee except for a 15-square-mile tract including both the Macon Plateau and Lamar (9BI2) sites (Kappler 1972:85). That they wished these areas preserved seems corroborated by an 1806 survey of the reserve made "to fix some points for the Secretary of War" (Hawkins 1916:428–29), for 10 of them were Indian mounds. Seven of the 10 are in the Macon Plateau section of the Monument; and although Mound E (Southeast Mound) was omitted, Mound X (not recognized as a mound in the 1930s) was included.

By 1828, when the Creek Reserve was sold, the mounds had been romanticized and their origins questioned:

The one most noted, called the *Large Mound,* is on the East side, about half a mile below the Bridge. . . . The top of the mound is about 120 feet above the bed of the river . . . and not over 50 feet above the plain on the north. . . . Other mounds of a small size are near. . . . General opinion is that they are artificial. . . . They are undoubtedly of very remote antiquity as they exhibit in general too much labor to have been achieved by any race of modern Indians. (Bartlett 1828)

In central Georgia, however, the idea of mound builders being other than Indian was short-lived. This is evidenced by the description of artifacts found when the Central of Georgia Railroad cut across the plateau in 1843, destroying a large portion of Mound B:

[In] . . . cutting through the edge of the mounds . . . a number of Indian relics were exhumed, consisting of a large earthen pot, capable of holding eight gallons, in which was contained a considerable quantity of burnt corn which appeared to have been reduced to charcoal; also a number of skeletons and human bones; a variety of spoons; a single formed stone, translucent, and resembling amber, and a stone axe; also, five feet below the surface, a brass spoon in a bowl of Indian earthenware. (Butler 1960:160)

At least two, and more likely four, of the mounds within the Monument were mentioned by George White in an account published in 1849:

About three miles above Lamar's Mount [Brown's Mount, 9BI5] commences a chain of five artificial mounds. The first two are on the plantation of John B. Lamar, Esq. [Lamar site]. The remaining three are at regular intervals, the last one situated near the old blockhouse at Fort Hawkins. . . . The two on Mr. Lamar's plantation have had the forest growth recently cleared from about them, and present a very distinct outline of circumvallations and other such works connecting them (1849: 113–14).

The earliest accurate description of the archaeological remains in the Macon area was published by Charles C. Jones, Jr., in 1873. Included in his *Antiquities of the Southern Indians, Particularly of the Georgia Tribes* are: a map showing the locations of Macon Plateau Mounds A, B, C, and D in relation to one another, the railroad, and the Ocmulgee River; descriptions of the sizes and shapes of these mounds and statements regarding their construction and probable uses; a mention of the Lamar site mounds; and a rather detailed description of the Brown's Mount site fortifications (1873: plate 4, 158–65).

Illustrating the accuracy of Jones's observations was his conclusion that Mound C contained both prehistoric and historic burials. This he deduced from study of two burials exposed in 1871 when railroad construction destroyed almost half of the mound. Having noted placement of the burials—with one in the side of the mound and the other

under the mound—the association of glass beads and copper bells with the intrusive burial and their absence from the other, and the lack of cranial deformation in the intrusive burial and its presence in the other, he concluded that "these ancient tumuli were, in turn, used by tribes who had no knowledge, the one of the other" (1873:161).

During the Bureau of Ethnology mound exploration that began in 1881, ten Georgia sites were investigated (Thomas 1894:292–93), but no work was done at Ocmulgee or other central Georgia sites. The Bureau's 1891 *Catalogue of Prehistoric Works East of the Rocky Mountains* (Thomas 1891) did include brief descriptions of the Macon Plateau, Lamar (Patterson's plantation), and Brown's Mount sites; however, they were taken from Jones (1873) and White (1854).

The Beginning of Federal Relief Program Archaeology at Ocmulgee

Federally funded archaeological research began at Ocmulgee in December 1933. The complete story of Ocmulgee's selection for archaeological investigation under federal relief program sponsorship and of its subsequent designation as a national monument may never be known. It is clear, however, that it took the combined efforts of Macon citizenry to bring these ideas to fruition.

In February 1922, General Walter A. Harris, a prominent Macon attorney and the author of credible papers on Creek history (1935, 1944, 1958), wrote to the Bureau of American Ethnology expressing an interest in public acquisition of the Indian remains located in Ocmulgee Old Fields to ensure their preservation. The letter was acknowledged, but no further action was taken (Marsh 1986:7).

General Harris wrote to the Bureau again in April 1929, suggesting that the City of Macon fund excavations directed by Smithsonian archaeologists. This idea interested Matthew W. Stirling, the new chief of the Bureau, and soon thereafter he "visited the large mounds on the site of Old Ocmulgee Town, traditional founding place of the Creek Confederacy" (Stirling 1930:2).

The visit had no immediate effect. Three years later, however, public interest was aroused when General Harris, then president of the Macon Historical Society, spoke on Ocmulgee's significance. As reported in the *Macon Telegraph* of May 4, 1932, after stating that the South is English instead of Spanish because of the Creeks, whose "mounds stand beside the Ocmulgee River," he asked, "Is it too much to ask of white men that, . . . when the . . . mounds . . . attract their attention, they pay tribute to the red men who held the . . . frontier for the English?"

A year later, the *Telegraph* of June 7 reported that

through the efforts of General Harris and other Historical Society members, "ably assisted by [Georgia] Congressman Carl Vinson," the Smithsonian was seriously considering investigation of the site. Also mentioned were "thrills [that] might be in store . . . as the Government lends its aid to the development of the . . . story of the Old . . . Fields." This reference to federal sponsorship proved somewhat premature, for the first federally funded archaeological investigations, those at Marksville, Louisiana, did not begin until August, and no others began before December.

In the meantime, encouraged by Walter B. Jones, the director of the Alabama Museum of Natural History and the person responsible for purchasing the Moundville site, General Harris invited Georgians interested in organizing a state archaeological society to meet in Macon on October 13. This resulted in the formation of the Society for Georgia Archaeology and the election of: Dr. Charles C. Harrold, a leading Macon surgeon and an amateur historian, as society president; Linton M. Solomon, a well-known Macon businessman, as secretary; and General Harris as executive committee chairman (Smith 1939:13–14). It appears that the Society members chose wisely, for these are the men credited with the establishment of Ocmulgee National Monument.

Heightened local interest in archaeology was reflected by the November 17 *Telegraph* report that, at the urging of General Harris and Dr. Harrold, the Macon Junior Chamber of Commerce had obtained options to purchase Mound A and other nearby mounds. Three weeks later, on December 7, 1933, Dr. Harrold was notified by Matthew Stirling that Ocmulgee was one of 11 archaeological projects approved for Civil Works Administration (CWA) funding.

Federal Relief Program Archaeology at Ocmulgee, 1933–1942

Archaeological investigations under federal relief program sponsorship began in December 1933 and continued with only brief interruptions for more than eight years. These excavations, which were conducted on a massive scale not seen before or since in Georgia, had impacts, both economic and scientific, that cannot be overestimated. They provided jobs for literally thousands of unemployed workers and for a number of the nation's most promising young archaeologists. Perhaps of greatest importance, they helped to define the direction of archaeological research in the region for decades to come.

Arthur Randolph Kelly, a 33-year-old anthropologist trained at Harvard University, was selected to direct the project. Although his doctorate was in physical anthropology, he had a creditable background in archae-

ology. He received a bachelor's degree in 1921 from the University of Texas, where J. E. Pearce, who founded the anthropology department in 1917, had conducted archaeological investigations in conjunction with Smithsonian archaeologists since 1919. After graduation, Kelly remained on the department staff until 1925, when he entered Harvard. There he was a Hemenway Fellow in American Archaeology, 1925–27, and a teaching/research assistant, 1927–29. After receiving a doctorate in 1929, he became an assistant professor in anthropology at the University of Illinois, where he taught for four years, 1929–33. For two of these years, 1929–30, as director of the Illinois Archaeological Survey, he conducted fieldwork at Cahokia, Starved Rock, and Fountain Bluff. Based on this research, he published two papers, one with Fay-Cooper Cole as coauthor (Kelly 1933, Kelly and Cole 1931). When archaeological research was halted in Illinois because of lack of funding, however, he returned to Texas and began a study of Alibamu Indian physical characteristics for Earnest A. Hooten, who had been his major professor at Harvard.

Stirling wrote to Kelly on December 9, notifying him of his selection, sending him government transportation requests to cover train fare from Texas to Macon, and instructing him to confer with the Georgia CWA chairman in Atlanta and with Dr. Harrold upon arrival in Macon. This letter explained that Kelly would receive a salary of $50.00 a week once his name was on the CWA rolls and that James A. Ford, who was to be his assistant for the nine-week project, had been instructed to report to him in Macon.

James Alfred Ford was a 22-year-old undergraduate who had begun fieldwork upon graduation from high school in 1927. His archaeological experience included: three summers (1927–29) participating in an archaeological survey of Mississippi jointly sponsored by the State of Mississippi and the Smithsonian; one summer (1930) assisting Smithsonian archaeologist Henry B. Collins, Jr., with investigations on St. Lawrence Island, Alaska; 18 months (1931–32) as a Smithsonian employee excavating near Point Barrow, Alaska; seven months (1933) conducting an archaeological survey in Mississippi and Louisiana under a National Research Council grant; three months (August–October 1933) assisting Frank M. Setzler, Smithsonian archaeologist, in excavating and restoring the Marksville site in Louisiana; and one month (November 1933) supervising the Marksville project following Setzler's departure (Ford 1934:74–75). The latter project was the first involvement of archaeology in the relief effort, and its successful use of more than 100 unskilled laborers convinced CWA officials to fund similar projects (Setzler 1956:1; Haag 1985:274). Of course, Ford's Marksville experience made him uniquely qualified for the Macon project.

2.1. Arthur R. Kelly teaching night school archaeological class. (Photograph courtesy of the National Park Service, Southeast Archeological Center.)

Both Kelly and Ford arrived in Macon on December 14. The next day, the *Telegraph* reported that the CWA had authorized the employment of 205 men until February 15, 1934. Actual work began on December 20, with one crew of 100 CWA workers clearing Mound A and another crew of 100 improving the road to it. The need for knowledgeable personnel was immediately apparent; and within a few days Kelly and Ford had selected 45 of the more highly trained workmen and begun a three-month archaeological night school designed to train them for positions as trowel men, engineering assistants, laboratory technicians, and excavation foremen (Kelly 1935b:119) (Figure 2.1).

Work on the disturbed northern section of Mound C began on December 26. It was not until December 29, however, that the sixth excavation trench exposed an undisturbed mound surface. Work also began on Mound D (Cornfield Mound) on the twenty-ninth.

By January 2, 1934, with 157 employees split between them, Kelly and Ford were heading what were in effect two separate field organizations. Kelly was directing excavations at Mounds C, D, and A on the Macon Plateau; and Ford was excavating Mound A, the truncated pyramidal mound, and a low house platform at the Lamar site (Kelly 1935d).

Though they differed in education, experience, and age, Kelly and Ford seem to have had a good working relationship and genuine respect for each other's abilities. Statements from personal correspondence seem to corroborate this: Ford wrote to Collins that he liked Kelly,

whom he described as having "substantial ideas on the subject of archaeology and . . . not . . . too much perverted by his Harvard training"; and Kelly wrote to Stirling that "Ford's technique in exploring house sites is one of the finest examples of workmanship I have seen" (Lyon 1982: 35, 37).

By January 11, 243 workers were employed, and one week later the number reached 274. In order to supervise so many workers, two unorthodox steps were taken: (1) the project was run on a two-shift day, six-day week schedule; and (2) workers in the archaeological night classes were placed in the positions for which they were being trained. Kelly was assisted at Mound C by "Mr. [Frank E.] Lester," who recorded postholes, and "Mr. [John T.] West," who cataloged artifacts; at Mound D, by "Mr. Lavender" and "Mr. Griffith"; and at Mound A, by "Mr. Lifesey," who kept fieldnotes. "Mr. Napier" was the engineer for the Macon Plateau; and at Lamar "Mr. Cawthorne" and "Mr. Hulgan" assisted Ford.

Both Kelly and Ford used the photographic services of Joseph B. Coke, a 24-year-old Macon resident who had earned part of his college costs by photography, was agile and daring enough to climb Ford's makeshift photography tower, and owned an 8-by-10-inch camera. He was assisted by his 18-year-old brother, Cecil R. Coke, who developed the film and printed the negatives. It is their photographs that so well document Macon archaeology of the 1930s and are reproduced in several places in the present volume.

John W. Walker

Small blue glass trade beads were found with burials in Mound C, and Kelly wrote regarding them to John R. Swanton, preeminent authority in Creek ethnohistory. His interest aroused, Swanton asked that the beads be sent to the Bureau for identification. Some time later, he wrote Kelly stating that the beads dated from the period of 1700–1730, dates in keeping with Creek abandonment of the site in 1715. This must have pleased Swanton, for he, along with General Harris and Dr. Harrold, hoped that a historic Creek settlement would be found. However, because of artifact content and the use of "archaeological trenching with straight, vertical profiles [that] brought out [stratigraphic detail] in sharp relief" (Kelly 1935b:119), Kelly and Ford recognized that the historic burials were intrusive into the prehistoric mounds on the Macon Plateau; but they were not certain as to Lamar's chronological position.

On January 16, Kelly noted that in excavating Mound D he had the "squares . . . dug so as to preserve partitions of earth [i.e., balks] and so afford a record of stratigraphic changes from the surface down."

Excavation of a 10-by-15-foot trench atop Mound A was begun on January 26. It was intended to reach mound base so that the mound's internal structure could be recorded, but the walls of the trench collapsed at a depth of 28 feet and almost buried Ford. Detailed notes were not kept on mound construction, and no profiles were drawn; hence little was learned except that it was of composite construction.

Georgia Congressman Carl Vinson introduced a bill on February 5 seeking appropriation of $50,000 to acquire 2,000 acres near Macon for development of a national park known as Old Ocmulgee Fields. At that time 343 workers were employed in the excavations, and local civic groups saw archaeology and the proposed park as a way to combat the Depression.

The initial CWA project ended February 15, and all of the workers were laid off. However, the city's request for continuance was approved, and work resumed on February 19.

The *Macon Telegraph and News* of February 25 carried an article entitled "Smithsonian Authorities to Lead Study and Inspection of Macon Indian Mounds." It stated that Swanton and Stirling were to visit the investigations and that both would speak to groups interested in archaeology. It also stated that newsreel cameramen would be present on February 28 to photograph 500 school girls in white dresses lined in single file up the spiral rampway on Mound B at Lamar.

Stirling soon returned to Washington, but Swanton, who as chief of the United States De Soto Expedition Commission (Swanton 1939) was trying to trace the expedition's route, stayed to visit central Georgia archaeological sites.

Early March saw work resumed on the Macon Earth Lodge (Mound D-1 Lodge), where only limited testing had been done following its discovery on February 21. By March 17, enough of the structure was uncovered for its significance to be recognized, and construction of a protective roof over the "circular council house," as it was then called, was begun.

Two days later Swanton left Macon, having concluded that De Soto had crossed the Ocmulgee at Abbeville more than 50 miles south of Macon. With him he took a detailed description of the Earth Lodge.

Work funded by the CWA ended on March 31, but it began again under Federal Emergency Relief Administration (FERA) sponsorship on April 4. By that time Ford was supervising work in the Mound D/Earth Lodge area. On April 5, his assistant, Mr. Hulgan, reported finding burned corncobs in the mound area. The next day, after studying the undulating surface under the mound, Ford suggested that it might represent "garden beds, cultivation rows, or hills."

Interest in both the field and the Earth Lodge grew. By April 19, it was decided that a replica of the lodge would be displayed in the Georgia booth at the Chicago World's Fair. Another display arousing interest at that time was an oil painting of the multicolored profile of Mound C. Kelly, who was intrigued by the mound's multistage construction and the presumed symbolism of the colors of those stages, asked the Cokes to photograph the mound. When they were unable to find film that would accurately reproduce the colors (Cecil R. Coke, personal communication 1987), Kelly asked Carolyn Smith Meriwether to paint the mound profile. Her painting, which was completed in mid-April, was shown for a short time in Macon and then sent to the Smithsonian for exhibit. (It now hangs in the Ocmulgee Visitor Center.)

Ford left Ocmulgee on May 26, having been employed by the State of Georgia to test a coastal tabby ruin. Romantics, who believed the ruin to be that of a Spanish mission, were most disappointed when Ford determined it was the ruin of a nineteenth-century sugar mill (Ford 1937).

In keeping with the National Park Service's suggestion that the people of Macon purchase the lands for the proposed park, a city-wide campaign to raise $25,000 for the purchase of the required 2,000 acres was begun on June 5. Nine days later the act authorizing the establishment of Ocmulgee National Monument was passed. It stated that the area would be made a national monument by presidential proclamation when adequate lands were donated.

From June 21 until August 17, excavations were carried out at Mound E (Southeast Mound); and in October, intensive testing of the series of linked pits or "dugouts" enclosing much of the central ridge top of the Macon

Plateau was begun. The previous spring when the first of these was encountered, Ford thought it was a subterranean house similar to one excavated at Marksville (Ford 1934), and Kelly accepted the idea for some time. He referred to a "village of subterranean house sites" in an unpublished article written in 1935 (Kelly 1935a), and even three years later he mentioned this as a possible explanation for the dugouts, although he did say that a more logical explanation would be borrow pits and/or fortification trenches (Kelly 1938c:13).

On December 2, a new FERA-funded project began at Mile Track (9BI7) in Central City Park across the river from Ocmulgee. This work continued until April 1935, whereas work on the dugouts ceased in March. Excavations at the Napier site (9BI9), which began in February, continued until June.

In March, the first of three articles by Kelly on the first six months of archaeological investigation at Ocmulgee appeared in *Scientific American* (Kelly 1935b), one of the few journals publishing papers on American archaeology at that time. It was also during that month that National Park Service officials began laying out the boundaries of the proposed monument and that deeds to 435 acres of land for inclusion in the park were mailed to Washington.

From April 8 through August 2, investigations on the summit of Brown's Mount were carried out. This work led to the discovery of a collapsed earth lodge, which was very similar to the Mound D-1 Lodge on the Macon Plateau (Fairbanks 1946b).

The Deer Park site (9BI8) in Central City Park was tested between April 10 and June 6. Work, which began at the Horseshoe Bend site (9BI10) near Lamar on May 3, continued until July 29.

On June 6, 1935, General Harris, Macon Historical Society president; S. Gus Jones, Macon Junior Chamber of Commerce Indian Mound chairman; and W. E. Dunwoody, Citizens Committee chairman, announced that the $8,500 to purchase the remaining acreage required for establishment of the Monument had been raised. However, due to difficulties in acquiring some properties and clear titles to others, it was several months before the park was established.

Stirling and Setzler returned to Macon on June 19. Stirling stayed only a short time; Setzler stayed for two weeks. While examining the field collections with Setzler, Kelly recognized a "Folsom projectile point" (Kelly 1935c). This point (better described as an eastern Clovis) was recovered on March 23, 1935, a short distance west of Mound D. It was found eight inches below the plowzone in tan weathered sand. Neither Kelly nor Ford had seen the point, and understandably it was not recognized by supervisory personnel who were trained in the archaeology night school.

Of this find, Antonio J. Waring, a frequent visitor to the excavations, later wrote: "Georgia's first fluted point was fortunately found in good archaeological context. . . . I personally just missed the discovery and then spent the summer sitting on the edge of the excavation watching each shovelful of dirt and every spall of flint in the forlorn hope that more fluted points would be found" (1968a:237).

In July approximately 700 laborers working in shifts were employed in the excavations being conducted in the Macon area. Yet Kelly still remained without any professionally trained assistants.

Work at the rockshelter known as Shell Rock Cave (9BI6) began July 30 and continued through September 11. During that period, on August 6, the *Macon Telegraph* announced approval of a WPA allotment for further Ocmulgee excavation. This funding allowed for a larger research program, which was reflected some months later by a full-page *New York Herald Tribune* article by Setzler stating: "the Macon project . . . [which employs] as many as 800 workers [is] easily . . . the largest and most significant effort of that sort . . . in this country."

Swanton, William S. Webb of the University of Kentucky, and T. M. N. Lewis of the University of Tennessee visited Ocmulgee in mid-August. Webb, who headed the Anthropology Department at Kentucky and the Tennessee Valley Authority's archaeological salvage program, later wrote to Kelly in regard to one of the Macon Plateau site houses, that "you have a 'small log town house' as we have denominated the structure in Norris Basin" (1935).

By late 1935, Kelly recognized the presence of four "cultural complexes" at the Macon Plateau and Lamar sites. These were: a complicated stamped complex (Swift Creek) predating the Macon mounds; a Macon Plateau complex; a Lamar complex; and a historic Creek complex. He also recognized two other pottery types, Delta (Napier Complicated Stamped) and checkerboard stamped (Deptford Check Stamped), but was unsure of their chronological positions.

Philip Phillips, then a Harvard University graduate student, spent some time at Ocmulgee in January 1936. He was primarily interested in ceramic classification; and after returning to Harvard, he sent copies of volumes 1 and 2 of *The Pottery of Pecos* (Kidder 1931; Kidder and Shepard 1936) to Kelly and laboratory supervisor West.

Fieldwork was concentrated on the Middle Plateau, especially in the Trading Post area, in January and February; and it continued there through early November (Kelly 1939). Work also began on the McDougal Mound in mid-February and on the Dunlap Mound in early March. During the latter period, James B. Griffin, who had just completed a graduate fellowship in aboriginal North American ceramics at the University of Michigan Museum of Anthropology, spent several days with Kelly and West working on a pottery classification system for central Georgia ceramics. This system appears to have been based largely on the classification code that Griffin used in analysis of ceramics from the Norris Basin in eastern Tennessee (Griffin 1938). Of course there were differences between the two codes, reflecting differences in the ceramics of the two areas. The central Georgia code also differed in that it put forth an incipient pottery typology based on surface decoration. It recognized four "specialized stamped or paddle marked" decorative techniques, which were termed: Alpha, or curvilinear complicated stamped; Sigma, or simple stamped; Delta, or "fine line cameo effect" (Napier Complicated Stamped); and Pi, or check stamped (Griffin and Kelly 1936). That the latter designations were Kelly's idea, and not Griffin's, has been emphatically stated by Griffin (personal communication 1988).

West immediately began a test of the ceramic code. It was completed by April 10, and Kelly reported the results: "We have . . . [studied] 5,000 Lamar sherds . . . using the . . . code . . . Griffin and I worked out. . . . There is more homogeneity at Lamar than I . . . suspected. Now I consider that the Lamar type site establishes a horizon duplicated at Nacoochee, Etowah, Oconee, Neisler, Toa and Kolomoki . . . sites . . . in their prime at the time of De Soto or preceding him" (1936b).

The previous November, eager for park development to begin, Kelly had asked that H. Summerfield Day, a National Park Service archaeologist working at Jamestown, Virginia, be transferred to Ocmulgee to oversee reconstruction of the Earth Lodge and erection of exhibit shelters at Mounds C and D (Kahler 1935; Kelly 1936a). His request was denied, as the park had not been officially established; however, it was agreed that Day would visit the area. The *Macon Telegraph* of March 1 reported that Day had arrived and was examining possible field exhibits. His report on the visit discussed the major prehistoric features of both the Macon Plateau and Lamar sites and made recommendations for their development. Chief among these were: (1) reconstruction of the Earth Lodge, five or six of the "pit houses" (dugouts) and the stockade of the Trading Post; (2) building shelters to cover the exposed Mound C profile and the field under Mound D; (3) construction of a museum; and (4) assigning a Park Service archaeologist to the park (Day 1936).

On March 4, shortly after Day's departure, Kelly wrote to Swanton regarding the Trading Post site. He described the evidence for a horizontal log palisade and mentioned the recent acquisition of a brass weight dated 1712 that had been found on the site some 55 years earlier (Kelly 1936b). Ten days later Swanton replied: "You have . . . the site of the English trading house . . . [located there] between 1690 and 1715. . . . [Then] there were . . . two main

centers among the Lower Creeks, one at . . . Coweta . . . higher up the river and the other at Ocmulgee" (1936). Also included in his reply was a preliminary outline of Lower Creek history:

1565–1647 Period when the Ocmulgee [River] Indians traded with St. Augustine.
1647–90 Period when the Lower Creeks lived on the Chattahoochee and traded with the Spanish in the Apalachee province, probably beginning after the Apalachee rebellion of 1647 and extending to 1690.
1690–1715 Period during which most Lower Creek towns were on the Ocmulgee and the English were paramount.
1715–1836 Later period of occupancy of the Chattahoochee by Lower Creeks. (Swanton 1936)

Worth noting is that this chronology appears in later publications (such as Fairbanks 1956a) with but minor changes.

Also during early March, the construction of an airport on St. Simons Island in Glynn County, Georgia, exposed human bones. Setzler came to investigate and uncovered several skeletons. Hearing of the find, Dr. Harrold, accompanied by Linton Solomon and Wesleyan College Dean Leon P. Smith, came from Macon, arriving just as Setzler realized that a larger-scale excavation was necessary. At Harrold's urging, Kelly wrote a proposal for a Glynn County archaeological project. The project was approved, and by June, an "'offspring' of Macon was established . . . on the Georgia coast" (Waring 1968b: 296). The archaeologist chosen to head the project was Preston Holder (Holder 1938; Chance 1974).

Excavation began at the Swift Creek site in late March. This WPA project was set up to employ 30–40 black women as an archaeological field crew working under men who had been trained by Kelly and Ford. The principal investigator was Kelly, and supervisors were Joseph Tamplin, engineer; Joseph Coke, photographer; James Jackson, artist-illustrator; and Hugh Hanna, unit supervisor (Kelly and Smith 1975:2).

In late June, six anthropology graduate students who had been selected by the Laboratory of Anthropology in Santa Fe to participate in a summer field program in archaeology, arrived in Macon to work under Kelly. The six were: Gordon R. Willey, who had a master's degree from the University of Arizona; Walter W. Taylor, Jr., a graduate student at Yale University; J. Lawrence Angel, who had a bachelor's degree from Harvard University; Joseph Birdsell, a Harvard University graduate student; Charles Wagley, a Columbia University graduate student; and Han-Yi Feng, who had a doctorate from the University of Pennsylvania (Figure 2.2).

Their first assignment was hands-on training in civil engineering. They then recorded and removed the charred timbers from the Earth Lodge. On July 22 they began work at the so-called Adkins Mound (9BI4), an erosional remnant near the Swift Creek site. The site, however, was not considered productive, and work there was stopped. Lastly, beginning on August 6 and continuing through August 28, when the training program ended, the group conducted excavations at Stubbs Mound (9BI12) in the Tobesofkee Creek drainage south of Macon (Kelly 1938d:34, Williams 1975).

When time came for the students to leave, Kelly asked Willey to stay on as his assistant, and Willey agreed. Initially he continued work at Stubbs Mound; but beginning on September 8, he supervised test excavations at the site of Fort Hawkins (9BI21), a U.S. Army fort built in 1806 on the reserve retained by the Creeks until 1828

(Willey 1936). The project was soon completed, and by late October, with the assistance of Linton Solomon, he was involved in obtaining dendrochronological specimens from living trees, structural timbers, and charred wood from archaeological contexts.

Encouraged by Antonio J. Waring and other Savannah residents, Kelly submitted a proposal to the state WPA office on September 16, 1936, for archaeological excavations at the Irene site. Kelly intended for Preston Holder to head the investigations (as he later did) and for Walter Taylor to serve as his assistant. Understanding that approval of the project was imminent, Taylor left New York for Macon on September 23, planning to visit there until the work began (Taylor 1936). Before he reached Macon, however, it was learned that the project's approval would be delayed for some time, so he left after spending a few days (Gordon R. Willey, personal communication 1988).

2.2. Anthropology graduate students removing charred timbers from Mound D-1 Lodge. Foreground left to right: Joseph Birdsell, Charles Wagley, Lawrence Angel, Arthur Kelly; Background left to right: Han-Yi Feng, two unidentified workmen, Gordon Willey, and Walter Taylor. (Photograph courtesy of the National Park Service, Southeast Archeological Center.)

2.3. Ceremony initiating reconstruction of the Mound D-1 Lodge. Foreground left to right: Hugh Hanna (foreman), Linton M. Solomon, Arthur R. Kelly, Charles C. Harrold, Walter A. Harris, and James T. Swanson. (Photograph courtesy of the National Park Service, Southeast Archeological Center.)

The park, for which the citizens of Macon had raised the funds to purchase the lands, came into being on December 23, 1936, when President Franklin D. Roosevelt proclaimed the establishment of Ocmulgee National Monument. James T. Swanson, the National Park Service architect under whose direction restoration of the Earth Lodge had begun two days earlier (Swanson n.d.), was named acting superintendent (Figure 2.3). Kelly was then made archaeologist for WPA Projects, and Willey, assistant archaeologist for WPA Projects.

In January 1937, Philip Phillips visited Ocmulgee again. After several days of "talking pottery" with Kelly and Willey, the three of them drove to the Georgia coast to visit Holder's excavations (Gordon R. Willey, personal communication 1988). Throughout the rest of the winter and into early spring, Kelly was primarily occupied with excavation between Mounds A and B on the South Plateau, where he uncovered a complex series of earth lodge floors located one above the other. Willey, with Solomon's continued assistance, remained involved with dendrochronology.

On March 6, it was announced that a 250-person Civilian Conservation Corps (CCC) camp would be established at Ocmulgee, with park development as its primary purpose. Another announcement stated that the WPA force had been cut from 200 to 65 workers, most of whom were to work in Earth Lodge restoration under Swanson's direction. When the camp was established in May, the enrollees were assigned to three major duties: park-related construction, restoration of the Earth Lodge, and archaeological investigations. The number assigned to the latter was quite limited.

James Ford, who uncovered the Earth Lodge in the spring of 1934, returned to Ocmulgee in late May as consultant for reconstruction of the lodge interior. Except for six weeks at a University of New Mexico field school in Chaco Canyon, he remained in Macon until September, when he went to the University of Michigan to work on a master's degree.

Learning that the WPA work force would be withdrawn on June 1, 1937, and knowing that few CCC enrollees would be available for archaeological research, Kelly realized that large-scale excavations could not be continued. Instead, he and Willey decided to carry out stratigraphic testing at numerous sites in order to obtain better data on cultural stratigraphy. Kelly, who was named project superintendent for the CCC camp, assigned Willey, now CCC senior foreman archaeologist, to carry out these projects. The first of the tests were conducted on June 7–10 in the Ocmulgee River bottoms southwest of Mound A. They produced evidence of historic Creek occupation but none for earlier occupations (Walker 1961:8–9).

Among the other sites tested that year were: Mound C Village, Lamar, southeastern spurs nos. 1 and 2 of the Macon Plateau, Mossy Oak (9BI11), Hawkins Point

(9BI15), Napier, Tuft Springs no. 2 (9BI19), Cowarts Landing (9BI14), and Scott (9BI16), all in Bibb County; Big Sandy no. 1 (9BS1) in Butts County; and Lords Ridge (9WK4) in Wilkinson County. It might be noted that methodology used at two of the sites departed from that in general use at the time. Finding the cultural deposits at the Big Sandy no. 1 and Scott sites confined to the plowzone and realizing that only horizontal stratigraphy was present, Willey devised an archaeological surface collection strategy that he termed "Recorded Surface Areas." The collection areas were established by laying out a line of circles (of 200-foot diameter at Big Sandy no. 1 and 100-foot diameter at Scott). Then surface materials were gathered from each of the circles and percentage studies made.

Willey later reported that in the Cowarts Landing tests, Lamar ceramics were found above Swift Creek ceramics in good stratigraphic context (1939). This was a significant find, for although their relative chronological positions were known by 1935, they had not been found together in a stratified site.

Kelly submitted a report entitled "Glimpses of a Macon Chronology: A Statement of Progress at the End of Three Years of Field Work" (1937a) to the National Park Service and the Smithsonian on July 30, 1937. It was published in 1938 as *A Preliminary Report on Archaeological Explorations at Macon, Georgia* (Kelly 1938c).

Preston Holder began excavation at the Irene Mound on September 10, 1937, under the proposal submitted by Kelly the previous year. The field crew for the project, like the Swift Creek crew, was made up of black women (McIntyre 1939).

Early the next month, Kelly acquired some sherds from a Houston County site located at the confluence of Big Indian Creek and the Ocmulgee. These sherds interested him, for he saw them as being "Late Swift Creek" and as related to ceramics from the Evelyn Plantation on the Georgia coast and the Kolomoki site in southwestern Georgia, which had been acquired by the State of Georgia in 1935 largely through the efforts of Dr. Harrold (Kelly 1938c:44–45, Sears 1948:vii). On October 23, Kelly wrote to the property owner asking that Willey be allowed to test the site, but the owner refused. Reexamination of material from the site some 25 years later disclosed a Weeden Island component. As the Weeden Island complex of the Florida Gulf Coast was not defined until 1945 (Willey 1945) and as its presence on Georgia streams flowing into the Atlantic went unrecognized until 1965 (Nielsen 1967), it is interesting to speculate how this segment of southeastern prehistory might have been interpreted had permission to investigate the site been given in 1937.

Reconstruction of the Earth Lodge was completed in early November, and on November 27, it was opened to the public.

Beginning in late 1937 and continuing into early 1938, Kelly directed archaeological testing of the area around the Rock Eagle effigy mound (9PM80) in Putnam County with an Ocmulgee field crew supervised by Joseph Tamplin (Patterson n.d.:13). Regrettably, the tests revealed "an absolute sterility" (Petrullo 1954:10).

In December 1937, Kelly and Willey attended a regional meeting of the Society for American Archaeology held in New Haven, Connecticut. Both gave papers: Willey's was entitled "Preliminary Dendrochronological Studies in Central Georgia" (1937b); Kelly's, "Lamar and Related Site Exploration in Georgia." Later that month Kelly accepted a National Park Service position as associate archeologist. However, his duty station continued to be Ocmulgee. On January 18, 1938, he wrote to Ford complaining that no provision had been made for office assistance in line with the additional duties; but he did express pleasure that "the Regional Office . . . is sending sherds from all over the southeast. . . . Today we received sherd collections from . . . 6 different states" (Kelly 1938a).

Willey continued conducting stratigraphic surveys into 1938, testing areas of the Southeast Plateau not tested previously and the Swift Creek, Stubbs Mound, and Oconee Town (9BL16) sites, the latter in Baldwin County. Fieldwork ended in April, and he began analysis of the data that had been recovered. Later that spring, he visited Panama City, Florida, where he became intrigued by the association of stamped ceramic wares similar to those of central Georgia with incised and punctated wares resembling those found in the lower Mississippi Valley. "Here," he later wrote, "on the Florida Gulf were the means of relating the Louisiana and central Georgia sequences, in 1938 the only ones known for the lower Southeast" (1949:xix).

At the ninety-ninth annual meeting of the Georgia Historical Society in Savannah on February 16, 1938, Dr. Harrold presented a paper entitled "Georgia Archaeology with Especial Reference to Recent Investigations in the Interior and on the Coast" (1939). This paper dealt largely with Ocmulgee and related investigations. It was also on that day that Swanson was replaced as acting superintendent by Frank Lester, so that all of his time could be spent in design of the park visitor center. In turn, Lester was replaced as acting superintendent on April 10 by Jesse D. Jennings, who transferred from Montezuma Castle National Monument in Arizona.

One hundred fifteen WPA workers were assigned to Ocmulgee on March 13, 1938, for a three-month period and were put to work under Kelly's supervision on the South Plateau between Mounds A and B. Nine days later, twenty more WPA workers were assigned to the project. They were placed in the laboratory, where West put them to cataloging.

Archaeological data recovery began April 19 at Lamar in areas that would be affected by construction of a levee to protect it from flooding. This work, which was supervised by James H. Jackson, continued for the rest of the year.

At the Society for Georgia Archaeology meeting held on May 6, Willey gave a paper entitled "Time Studies: Pottery and Trees in Georgia" (1938b). Kelly also presented a paper. His paper, entitled "The Need of a Museum of Southeastern Archaeology" (Kelly 1938b), prompted the Society to pass a resolution stating that "the Society . . . strongly urges the establishment, at Ocmulgee National Monument . . . , of a central museum and research institution for Southeastern archaeology under the cooperative sponsorship of the Smithsonian Institution, the National Park Service, and other interested organizations" (Smith 1938:13).

After Ford's arrival at the University of Michigan in September 1937, he and James B. Griffin began discussing the need for a ceramic typology for the southeastern United States. Soon they had agreed that they would organize a meeting of archaeologists to formulate a framework for use in establishing pottery types. Throughout the winter and into the spring they corresponded about this concept with a number of archaeologists, including Kelly, Willey, Holder, and William G. Haag.

Because the Society for American Archaeology's third annual meeting was to be held in Milwaukee on May 13–14, 1938, Griffin and Ford selected May 16–17 as the dates for the ceramic typology meeting, which was to be held at Ann Arbor. Accompanying the meeting announcement was a six-page statement that included suggestions that they had received and requested that participants bring provisional pottery type descriptions to the meeting (Ford and Griffin 1960a).

Both Kelly and Willey planned to attend the Milwaukee meeting and to participate in the ceramic typology discussions. At Griffin's suggestion, Joffre L. Coe, then a 21-year-old undergraduate at the University of North Carolina, arranged to ride with them to the meetings. "Coe did attend with Kelly" (Griffin 1985a:296), but at the last minute Willey was unable to make the trip. For this reason, Kelly read Willey's paper on Cowarts Landing, "Ceramic Stratigraphy in a Georgia Village Site" (Willey 1939:140–47), as well as his own paper, "The Southeast as an Archaeological Area" (1938d).

Among the 15 archaeologists attending the ceramic typology meeting at the University of Michigan Museum of Anthropology's Ceramic Repository were Griffin, Ford, Kelly, Coe, and Charles H. Fairbanks, then with the University of Tennessee. Like Willey, Holder was not able to attend this meeting (Ford and Griffin 1960b), which is now regarded as the first Southeastern Archaeological Conference.

From May 23 through June 10, 1938, Willey tested the Lawson Field site at Fort Benning, Georgia. This was the site of the Lower Creek Kasihta Town from 1715 until the Creek removal (Willey 1938a; Willey and Sears 1952).

On June 1, 1938, a ceremony was held to mark the beginning of construction on the park visitors center. Among those who took part in the ceremony were Dr. Harrold, General Harris, Linton Solomon, and acting superintendent Jennings. Kelly was in the Region One (now Southeast Regional) Office, then in Richmond, on that day.

Later that month, Jennings issued the report "Ocmulgee Archaeology: Summary Through May 1938," which contained a brief history of the previous investigations and the following plans for future research: "it is hoped that Dr. Kelly will . . . get out a series of manuscripts each dealing with a particular . . . unit of the vast Macon site. . . . Mr. Jennings [who wrote his master's thesis on the Lamar-related Peachtree Mound site] hopes . . . to carry on explorations at Lamar and write the wind-up report for this important type village" (Jennings 1938b:11).

In August 1938, an adjunct faculty composed of Kelly, Ernst Antevs, Clyde Kluckhohn, and Donovan Senter joined regular faculty members Donald Brand and Florence M. Hawley in conducting the University of New Mexico field school at Chaco Canyon. Kelly had left Macon intending to return and prepare reports on his excavations, beginning with a Swift Creek site report. For this reason, Jennings set an office adjacent to the laboratory aside for him, and he instructed West to have all site data ready for analysis. Except for brief visits, however, Kelly did not return to Macon for six years.

While at Chaco Canyon, Kelly accepted the position of assistant chief, Branch of Historic Sites and Buildings. This Washington office position also bore the title of chief, Archeologic Sites Division (the title Kelly used). The major duty of this position was the initiation of a nationwide survey of prehistoric sites to determine which were of national significance (Kelly 1940). It was in this way that Kelly later obtained National Park Service funding to assist with archaeological research projects such as the Lower Mississippi Valley (Phillips et al. 1951:v–vi) and the Florida Gulf Coast (Willey 1949:xxi) surveys.

Willey left Macon on September 15. Two days later he married Katharine Whaley (a Macon resident) in Alabama. They then moved to New Orleans, where he was to head the WPA archaeological laboratory at Louisiana State University. The project director was Ford, who had returned to Louisiana after one year at Michigan.

Replacing Willey as CCC senior foreman archaeologist was Charles H. Fairbanks, who had been assistant to field supervisor Charles H. Nash in the Hiwassee Island excavations sponsored by the University of Tennessee and the Tennessee Valley Authority. Reasonably enough, Fairbanks's interpretation of Ocmulgee archaeology was to be influenced by this experience. Upon his arrival shortly after Willey's departure, he was placed in charge of the laboratory, which then had a staff of 35.

Late in October, a National Park Service Recreation Study team made recommendations for development of Kolomoki as a state park. These included a statement by Jennings on the site's archaeological significance (1938b). It stated that 90 percent of the pottery in surface collections was Swift Creek but noted the presence of a small percentage of a pottery type that he called "Coles Creek"—Weeden Island types not having been defined at that time.

Jennings chaired the second Southeastern Archaeological Conference held at the Central Archaeological Laboratory in Birmingham on November 4–6, 1938. Like the first meeting, its major concern was pottery typology. Shortly after his return to Macon, Jennings received authorization for Fairbanks to begin his first laboratory research project, an analysis of materials from Mound C on the Macon Plateau.

Lamar levee data recovery, which began in early 1938, was halted on January 25, 1939, because of flooding. The crew was temporarily put to work on the Middle Plateau in search of burials for *in situ* display, however, the water soon receded, and the crew returned to Lamar on February 1. Work there continued for the remainder of the year.

On March 9, 1939, the *Atlanta Journal* reported that Congress had approved an $8,760 budget for the Monument and quoted Congressman Carl Vinson as stating that the funds would provide for employment of a superintendent, a ranger, a clerk, and a junior archaeologist, as well as for purchase of supplies.

Later that month, pottery descriptions for five central Georgia wares were published in the second issue of the *Newsletter of the Southeastern Archaeological Conference.* These descriptions, which were prepared by Jennings and Fairbanks (1939), were for Mossy Oak Simple Stamped, Swift Creek Complicated Stamped, Lamar Complicated Stamped, Lamar Bold Incised, and Ocmulgee Fields Incised.

The Society for Georgia Archaeology's tenth meeting was held in Macon on April 14–15, 1939. At the meeting, Jennings presented a paper, "Recent Excavations at the Lamar Site," which was of significance to Georgia archaeology because it contained the first report of Lamar ceramics being found above Macon Plateau wares in stratigraphic context (1939).

One month later, Jennings transferred to an associate archaeologist position on the Natchez Trace Parkway, where he began excavation of a Parkway unit now designated Chickasaw Village. Artifacts recovered from this

and later Parkway excavations were sent to Macon for processing and curation.

Following Jennings's departure, Lester again was appointed acting superintendent until the arrival of John C. Ewers on June 18, 1939. Ewers was most interested in interpretation, and while he was acting superintendent, he began preparation of an exhibit plan for the visitor center museum (1940a).

For several years, Kelly's wife, Rowena, had tried to develop a scheme for classifying Swift Creek Complicated Stamped pottery on the basis of design motifs. In early July, she spent several days in the laboratory studying sherds from the type site. For two days she was joined by Kelly, who was working on a Swift Creek site report. By the end of the month, Fairbanks completed the first draft of his report on Mound C.

The fourth Southeastern Archaeological Conference, chaired by J. Joe Finkelstein (later known as J. Joseph Bauxar), was held at Ocmulgee on November 10–11. "This meeting inaugurated the . . . [partially completed] Museum building and covered new developments on the local archaeological scene" (Williams 1960:3).

At the end of 1939, Ewers listed the supervisory park staff as follows:

John C. Ewers, Acting Superintendent (Field Curator, Public Works Administration, or PWA)
Charles H. Fairbanks, Senior Foreman Archeologist (CCC)
John T. West, General Foreman (Emergency Relief Administration, or ERA)
Benjamin L. Bryan, Project Supervisor (ERA)
James H. Jackson, General Foreman (ERA)

West, who was laboratory supervisor, and Jackson, who was a talented artist as well as field supervisor, had both worked at Ocmulgee for several years. Bryan, who was in charge of the park guides, had prepared a manual for their use (1940). This manual replaced a paper entitled "Old Ocmulgee Fields," which Dr. Harrold had written in 1936 as a guide for school children.

In January 1940, Ewers set up a temporary museum in the basement of the visitor center. The museum consisted mostly of artifact displays and drawings by Jackson representing the cultural complexes recognized at that time.

Two months later, the Southeastern Archaeological Conference newsletter published nine other central Georgia pottery type descriptions that were also prepared by Jennings and Fairbanks (1940). These pottery types included Bibb Plain, Halstead Plain, Macon Thick, Hawkins Fabric Marked, McDougal Plain, Dunlap Fabric Marked, Napier Complicated Stamped, Kasita Red Filmed, and Walnut Roughened. At that time, these types, together with the five previously published central Georgia types (Jennings and Fairbanks 1939) and three types (Deptford Simple Stamped, Deptford Linear Check Stamped, and Deptford Bold Check Stamped) defined by Joseph R. Caldwell and Antonio J. Waring (1939), made up the ceramic wares recognized in the Macon area.

Later that month, on March 24, William W. Luckett was named Ocmulgee's first superintendent. However, Ewers stayed on in Macon for three months to complete the exhibit plan for the visitor center museum (Ewers 1940a).

On April 2, Fairbanks, accompanied by Ewers and Linton Solomon, visited the Jackson site in Monroe County. This Ocmulgee Fields site had recently been tested by Sam Price, an assistant to Robert Wauchope in the WPA–University of Georgia archaeological survey of northern Georgia (Wauchope 1966:417–19, 470–71). Five days later, Superintendent Luckett, Dr. Harrold, Solomon, and Wauchope went with Fairbanks to visit the Turnbull site (9ST1) in Stephens County, which was thought to be the site of Tugalo, a historic Cherokee town. Shortly thereafter, Fairbanks completed a study on Macon Plateau period earth lodges and delivered the paper "The Macon Earthlodge" at the Society for American Archaeology's fifth meeting, held in Indianapolis on April 25–26 (1940a, 1946b).

Nine days after the meeting, Fairbanks and Solomon inspected the Hartford Mound site (9PU1) near Hawkinsville in Pulaski County. Fairbanks later reported that although the mound and village site had been destroyed by road building, he had collected numerous Swift Creek sherds and many heavily patinated flints from the road fill.

It was also during May that the laboratory was moved from the Macon Municipal Auditorium to the basement of the park visitor center, then almost 40 percent completed. Subsequently, archaeological collections from a number of projects conducted in the Southeast were analyzed and stored there. From June through August, Willey and Richard B. Woodbury used the laboratory as their base of operations for the Florida Gulf Coast archaeological survey that they conducted under joint Columbia University–National Park Service sponsorship. All 25,544 items that they collected were processed and cataloged by the laboratory (Willey and Woodbury 1942: 232n). This was also true of the materials from Jennings's survey of the Natchez Trace Parkway; and he spent early July in the laboratory sorting them. Later that month, Robert Wauchope, who was primarily involved in the northern Georgia survey but at times worked elsewhere in the state, brought 30 bags of artifacts from Kolomoki to the laboratory for processing and cataloging.

Ewers and Fairbanks gave papers at the annual Society for Georgia Archaeology meeting held in Athens on June 14–15. Ewers's paper was entitled "Interpreting Archeology to the Public" (1940b); Fairbanks's, "The Lamar Palisade" (1940b). During the rest of that month and most of July, Fairbanks visited and/or prepared reports on the Lawson Field (9CH1), Oconee Old Town (9BL16), Turnbull Mound (Tugalo, 9ST1), Bussey Plantation, Abercrombie Mound (9RU61), and Neisler Mound (9TR1) sites for the National Survey of Historic Sites and Buildings.

In September, Fairbanks conducted limited stratigraphic testing at Stallings Island in the Savannah River (1941c, 1942). It was also in that month that Wauchope accepted a position at the University of North Carolina at Chapel Hill. Prior to leaving Georgia, he arranged to have the northern Georgia survey collections stored temporarily at Ocmulgee. They were delivered to the park in mid-December.

At that time, Albert C. Spaulding, the state supervisor of the WPA–Natchez Trace Parkway archaeological survey, was at Ocmulgee to discuss the classification of Mississippi ceramics with Fairbanks and to study the collections from the survey that he and Jennings were conducting. Later that month, Fairbanks was named junior archaeologist, National Park Service, with duty station at Ocmulgee.

Fairbanks and Evelyn Adams Timmerman (a Macon resident) were married on February 8, 1941; yet even that day he was called upon to give a tour of Ocmulgee to Margaret Mead, "who happened to be in the area" (Wilson and Deagan 1985:4).

The following month, Fairbanks conducted archaeological salvage at two Kolomoki mounds that had been badly damaged by construction (Fairbanks 1941a, 1946a). While at Kolomoki, he visited the Singer-Moye site (9SW2) in Stewart County, which he described as a twenty-acre Lamar culture site containing one low-domed mound and four domiciliary mounds.

Fieldwork at Lamar, which had been carried out under Jackson's supervision throughout 1940, continued until late March 1941. Then the crew was moved to the Middle Plateau to search for historic Indian burials suitable for *in situ* exhibits. This work continued into August.

The CCC senior foreman archaeologist position formerly held by Fairbanks was filled on April 16 by Karl Schmitt, who was assigned to prepare a report on the Lamar stockade excavations.

During those excavations it was found that the Lamar site extended beyond the Monument boundaries. On June 13, following donation of five acres encompassing the remainder of the site, President Roosevelt issued a proclamation adding this property to the park. Excavation of the newly acquired portion of the stockade took place from August 19 until October 20. During the same period, exhibit shelters were completed for three Middle Plateau burials, work began on an exhibit shelter to protect the entire northern profile of Mound C, and Fairbanks and Schmitt gave papers at the sixth Southeastern Archaeological Conference in Lexington, Kentucky.

Fairbanks's papers were on Lamar (1941b) and Stallings Island (1941c, 1942), and Schmitt's was on Lamar (1943).

All FERA work at Ocmulgee was halted in November. However, even following the December 7, 1941, Japanese attacks on American bases in the Pacific, work on the Mound C shelter was not stopped, although very little was done because the CCC enrollees were rapidly being assigned to defense-related jobs. No work at all was done on the shelter during January or February 1942, for by that time the enrollees were involved in the construction of Camp Wheeler, a large army post located about one mile east of the Lamar site. The Swift Creek site was included in the post, and the installation of munitions dumps there destroyed Mound B and more than half of Mound A.

On February 3, Fairbanks, Schmitt, and Solomon made a survey of the Houston County site with a Weeden Island component that Kelly was not allowed to test in 1937. They collected some 380 sherds. Most were plain wares, some with notably thickened rims; but there were also Swift Creek and Napier Complicated Stamped wares and simple stamped wares as well as two unfamiliar types. One of these was described as "aberrant incised," the other, as fingernail punctated (types ultimately recognized as Weeden Island pottery types).

One week later, a charter was granted to the Ocmulgee Auxiliary Corporation, a cooperative association organized to benefit the Monument through scientific, literary, and educational endeavors. Charter members were: Dr. Harrold, General Harris, Solomon, Hugh H. Hill, Lee S. Trimble, Luckett, and Fairbanks.

In March, the CCC camp was removed from Park Service jurisdiction, and Schmitt, who had been working on plans for reconstruction of the Lamar palisade once the war ended, resigned. At this time, Fairbanks, who had spent the first two months of the year writing an interpretive statement and an archaeological narrative for the park master plan, wrote: "Archaeological development has reached a complete and profound standstill for the duration."

The Post-Depression Era at Ocmulgee

For all practical purposes, park development and archaeological fieldwork were halted at the outbreak of World War II and the termination of federal relief program funding. Park development was not undertaken again until 1950; and until 1961 the only fieldwork conducted by Park Service archaeologists stationed at Ocmulgee was in proposed river basin reservoirs and in other southeastern Park Service areas. It should be noted, however, that analysis of the major portion of the data recovered in the 1930s had not been undertaken when the war began, and subsequently, very few detailed site reports had been written at that time.

Despite the reduction in fieldwork, Ocmulgee continued as a center of archaeological activity because of its laboratory facilities, collections, and staff. When completed, the museum was an added attraction, for it was then the outstanding archaeological museum in the South. To ensure student exposure to it was one reason for holding Southeastern Archaeological Conference meetings there at regular intervals through 1971.

A number of National Park Service personnel have served on the Monument staff in various administrative, research, and interpretive positions; and others were duty stationed there when the Archeological Research Unit (1961–62) and the Southeast Archeological Center (1966–72) occupied space in the park visitor center (Table 2.1). Some of these individuals conducted archaeological investigations, many involving sites that were located outside the Macon area and were unrelated to Ocmulgee archaeology (Table 2.2).

Throughout most of 1941 the park staff consisted of only Fairbanks and Luckett. The situation was alleviated somewhat when a clerk, Lois T. Holst, was added to the staff. Until her retirement as administrative assistant some 29 years later, she supplied valuable administrative support, helped with interpretation when needed, served as a liaison with the local community, and provided a much-needed thread of continuity for a frequently changing park staff.

Staffing did not improve in 1943. In fact, it worsened when Fairbanks enlisted in the army in March. That was also the month that Luckett's title was changed to custodian. In October of the following year, he was succeeded as custodian by Arthur R. Kelly. At that time the park staff consisted of the custodian, one laborer, one part-time ranger, and one part-time clerk (Marsh 1986:24).

During the spring of 1945, Kelly used soldiers from the Camp Wheeler Educational Reconditioning Hospital as his crew in testing the Jessup's Bluff site, a Swift Creek site on the Walnut Creek bluffs within park boundaries (Kelly 1945). Park laborer James A. Herndon, who in 1935 was a foreman at the Napier site, served as crew chief.

Historian Ray H. Mattison, the first addition to the Ocmulgee staff after the war's end, began work in October 1945. During his stay at the park, he made a study of the Creek Trading House, which operated from 1795 until 1816 (Mattison 1946). Based on evidence now available, the Trading House probably was on the Macon Plateau from 1806 until 1809.

Fairbanks was discharged in January 1946 and returned to Macon. He remained there until March, when he began work at Fort Frederica National Monument, where he was both superintendent and archaeologist until September 1948. During the time he was in Macon, Willey was also there; and they, along with Kelly, inspected the Leake

Table 2.1. Superintendents and Archaeologists Stationed at Ocmulgee
National Monument, 1941–1986

Name	Position	Tenure
Walter T. Berrett	Park Superintendent	3/76–12/79
Fred Bohannon	Archaeologist, ARU[1]	11/61–6/62
	Park Superintendent	1/67–9/69
Robert T. Bray	Senior Park Archaeologist	12/58–9/59
William Bromberg	Park Ranger/Archaeologist	12/56–6/57
Carroll Burroughs	Acting Chief, ARU[2]	12/61–6/62
Joseph R. Caldwell	Archaeologist, Region One	3/53–9/54
	Park Archaeologist	9/54–4/55
Louis R. Caywood	Park Superintendent	6/55–12/60
John M. Corbett	Acting Chief, ARU	12/61–6/62
W. Pingree Crawford	Park Management Assistant	12/69–3/71
	Park Superintendent	3/71–3/76
Donald R. Crusoe	Archaeologist/Curator, SEAC[3]	12/71–6/72
Albert Dillahunty	Acting Park Superintendent	6/55
	Park Superintendent	1/61–12/66
Charles H. Fairbanks	Junior Archaeologist, SER	1/41–3/43
	Archaeologist, Region One	6/51–8/54
Richard D. Faust	Archaeologist, SEAC	10/66–6/71
	Acting Chief, SEAC	6/71–6/72
George R. Fischer	Park Archaeologist	4/64–11/66
John W. Griffin	Acting Chief, ARU	11/61–6/62
	Chief, SEAC	6/67–6/71
H. Dean Guy	Park Superintendent	10/47–6/55
David H. Hannah	Assistant Archaeologist/Curator, SEAC	1/70–5/72
Lee H. Hanson, Jr.	Archaeologist/Curator, SEAC	6/69–8/70
Lois T. Holst	Acting Park Superintendent	9/47–10/47
		12/66–1/67
		9/69–12/69
Roc Indermill	Park Archaeologist	6/76–8/81
J. Earl Ingmanson	Archaeologist, ARU	1/62–6/62
	Archaeologist, SER[4]	7/62–9/65
Carol A. Irwin	Park Tour Leader	6/56–10/56
		7/57–9/57
		7/58–9/58
Edward D. Jahns	Park Archaeologist	5/62–2/64
Arthur R. Kelly	Park Custodian	10/44–9/47
Wilfred D. Logan	Senior Park Archaeologist	10/56–12/58
William W. Luckett	Park Superintendent	1/41–3/43
	Park Custodian	3/43–10/44
Jackson W. Moore, Jr.	Junior Park Archaeologist	10/55–8/57
	Archaeologist, ARU	12/61–6/62
Gustavus D. Pope, Jr.	Park Archaeologist	4/51–3/55
Norman R. Ritchie	Park Archaeologist	5/67–5/74
Karl Schmitt	Senior Foreman, Archaeologist, CCC	4/41–3/42
Joel L. Shiner	Senior Park Archaeologist	5/55–7/56
Sibbald Smith	Park Superintendent	12/79–12/86
Charles B. Voll	Archaeologist, ARU	12/61–6/62
John W. Walker	Junior Park Archaeologist	12/58–9/59
	Park Archaeologist	9/59–11/61
	Acting Park Superintendent	12/60–1/61
	Archaeologist, ARU	11/61–6/62
	Archaeologist, SER	7/62–12/62
	Archaeologist, SEAC	10/66–6/72
	Acting Chief, SEAC	10/66–6/67
Rex L. Wilson	Junior Park Archaeologist	8/57–9/58

1. ARU: Archeological Research Unit.
2. Acting Chief, ARU: Burroughs, Corbett, and Griffin alternately served in this position.
3. SEAC: Southeast Archeological Center (moved to Florida State University in June 1972).
4. SER: Southeast Region.

Table 2.2. Archaeological Investigations Conducted Outside the Macon Area by National Park Service Archaeologists Stationed at Ocmulgee, 1941–1972

Investigator	Site and Reference	Fieldwork
OCMULGEE NATIONAL MONUMENT ARCHAEOLOGISTS		
Jackson W. Moore	Appomattox Court House National Historic Park	3/57–5/57
	Cumberland Gap National Historical Park (Moore n.d.)	
SOUTHEAST REGION ARCHAEOLOGISTS		
Joseph R. Caldwell	Jim Woodruff Reservoir (Caldwell 1978)	3/53–11/53
Charles H. Fairbanks	Fort Frederica National Monument (Fairbanks 1953b, 1956b)	11/51–2/52
		2/53–5/53
	Fort Caroline National Memorial (Fairbanks 1952a)	10/52
	Booger Bottom Mound (9HL64) (Caldwell et al. 1952; Fairbanks 1954b)	10/53–11/53
John W. Griffin and J. Earl Ingmanson	Russell Cave National Monument (Griffin 1974)	3/62–11/62
John W. Walker	Appomattox Court House National Historic Park (Walker 1963)	7/62–10/62
SOUTHEAST ARCHEOLOGICAL CENTER ARCHAEOLOGISTS		
Richard D. Faust	Keokee Lake Basin, Jefferson National Forest (Faust 1971)	7/71
John W. Griffin	Bear Lake Mound, Everglades National Park	4/68–5/68
	Osceola Grave, Fort Sumter National Monument (Griffin 1969a, 1969b)	10/68
Lee H. Hanson, Jr.	Fort Donelson National Military Park (Hanson 1968)	4/68–5/68
	Town Creek Watershed, Natchez Trace Parkway (Hanson 1969)	9/69
John W. Walker	Upper Saluda Reservoir (Walker 1967)	6/67
	Arkansas Post National Memorial (Walker 1971a)	4/68–5/68

Mounds (9BR2) near Cartersville, which highway construction had recently destroyed (Fairbanks et al. 1946). Later that spring, Robert Wauchope, then director of Tulane University's Middle American Research Institute, arranged with Kelly to spend time at Ocmulgee reviewing his northern Georgia survey collections, which had been stored there since 1940.

Jennings, who was still at Natchez Trace Parkway, spent June 2–16 in the Ocmulgee laboratory analyzing Parkway materials. Wauchope arrived shortly after and spent the next two months in sorting and recording so as to reduce the tons of artifacts from his survey to an amount that could be shipped to New Orleans (Wauchope 1966:ix, xii).

For the remainder of 1946 and into 1947, Kelly worked on a Swift Creek site report (Kelly and Smith 1975). In June 1947, he submitted his resignation from the Park Service to become effective on September 1 (Marsh 1986: 42). On that date he became chairman of the University of Georgia's newly established Department of Anthropology.

Early in March 1948, John M. Corbett, then head of the Natchez Trace archaeological laboratory, came to Ocmulgee to study Parkway collections in storage there and to discuss southeastern pottery classification with Fairbanks. Later that month the collections from Jennings's 1939–46 work on the Parkway were transferred there at the request of John L. Cotter, then senior Parkway archaeologist.

During the summer, the temporary shelters over the historic Creek burials on the Middle Plateau were replaced with permanent structures of concrete and glass.

The 1950 fiscal year federal budget contained Park Service appropriations for structural rehabilitation but none for new construction. However, pressure applied by the Ocmulgee Auxiliary Corporation through Congressman Carl Vinson and Senators Walter George and Richard Russell convinced the Service that completing the park visitor center was rehabilitation, and $135,000 was set aside for that purpose. The construction contract was let June 2, 1950 (Marsh 1986:35).

With completion of the museum building a certainty, chief historian Ronald F. Lee recognized that Ewers's 1940 exhibit plans needed updating and asked Jesse Jennings (then at the University of Utah) to come to Washington to assist with the revision. A revised plan was completed in April (Jesse Jennings, personal communication 1988).

Two months later, Fairbanks, who in the two previous years had received a master's degree and completed coursework for a doctorate at the University of Michigan, was reemployed by the Service. He spent the next year at the Museum Laboratory in Washington as technical advisor in the planning and production of exhibits for the Ocmulgee visitor center (Wilson and Deagan 1985:6). In at least one instance (the sculpture of an Indian carrying a basketload of earth up the side of a mound), he also served as a model (Evelyn T. Fairbanks, personal communication 1983).

In early 1951, with the visitor center and the exhibits that it would house nearing completion, greater visitation and a resultant need for increased interpretation were foreseen. To fill this need, two archaeologist positions were created. One was a park archaeologist position, the other, a Regional Office position stationed at the park. On April 6, 1951, Gustavus D. Pope, Jr., began work as park archaeologist, and on June 22, Fairbanks was assigned to the Regional Office position. Besides supervising public contact, Fairbanks was to oversee the installation of the new exhibits, to write reports on the prewar excavations, and to conduct investigations at other Region One (that is, Southeast Region) parks as needed.

The building was completed in June, and installation of exhibits began. On November 7, the museum was officially opened. It contained 48 exhibits, most of which were on the area's prehistoric and historic Indian cultures. Opening ceremonies included dancing and an exhibition stick ball game by Creek Indians from Okmulgee, Oklahoma.

The ninth Southeastern Archaeological Conference was held October 31–November 1, 1952, at Ocmulgee with Fairbanks as chairman. Archaeology of historic southeastern tribes was the meeting's topic. Pope gave a paper on the Creeks of Ocmulgee Old Fields (1953), and Fairbanks presented one on Lamar as protohistoric Creek (1953a).

During early 1954, Fairbanks completed his doctoral dissertation on the excavation of Mound C (1954a) and revised it for publication in the Park Service's archaeological research series (1956a). The final revision was finished in March, and he began an analysis of the Trading Post area artifacts. Initial study of the ceramics showed that the European wares were about equally divided between Spanish majolica and English delft and salt-glazed wares. It seems likely that it was he who told John Goggin of the majolica, as Goggin was accumulating data on majolica distribution at that time (Goggin 1968: 78–79). Though Fairbanks did not complete the Trading Post study, he later encouraged one of his students, Carol Irwin, to undertake it (Mason 1963a).

Kelly spent some time at Ocmulgee that spring working on a report on the 1934 excavations at Mound D on the North Plateau (Kelly 1965). Region One archaeologist Joseph R. Caldwell's duty station was changed to Ocmulgee in March 1953, when he began an archaeological salvage project in the Jim Woodruff Reservoir (now Lake Seminole) in southwestern Georgia. In June, Fairbanks oversaw removal of the never-completed Mound C exhibit shelter and the mound's reconstruction (Fairbanks 1954c). Pope began work on an interpretive handbook intended for sale at the park in July; and in August, he and Caldwell removed a Mossy Oak period bundle burial found by amateur archaeologist John Pellew in the Central of Georgia Railroad right-of-way north of Macon.

On August 26, 1954, Fairbanks resigned to accept a position in the Florida State University Anthropology Department. Pope completed the final Ocmulgee handbook draft on March 12, 1955, and submitted his resignation on March 21. On April 30, Caldwell, who had been transferred from the Regional Office to the park staff, resigned to begin investigation of the Rood's Landing site (9SW1) in Stewart County under the auspices of the Columbus Museum of Arts and Crafts (Caldwell 1955b; Frank T. Schnell, personal communication 1987).

In July, a Society for American Archaeology seminar on the classification of culture contact situations was held at Harvard University with Willey as chairman. Eight types were recognized, with the clearest example of one type—site intrusion resulting in fusion with dominance of the resident culture—being the Macon Plateau culture (Willey et al. 1956:12).

The twelfth Southeastern Archaeological Conference, the first of nine to be held every other year in Macon with Park Service archaeologists as hosts, was held October 21–22, 1955. Park archaeologist Joel L. Shiner chaired the meeting, which was on Early Woodland cultures.

Both Pope's handbook, *Ocmulgee National Monument, Georgia,* and Fairbanks's report, *Archeology of the Funeral Mound, Ocmulgee National Monument, Georgia,* were published and placed for sale at the park in 1956. Of the latter, Jesse Jennings wrote: "the most valuable portion of the publication . . . [is a] chronology of the Macon Plateau archeological manifestations" (1957:94). This proved accurate, for with the exception of filling the Early and Middle Archaic gap, there have been few changes in the basic chronology.

Carol A. Irwin (now Carol Irwin Mason) began work as an Ocmulgee tour leader on June 14, 1956. Her interest in the park came from working on a master's degree at Florida State University under Fairbanks's direction, and she planned to write her dissertation at the University of Michigan on Creek acculturation as evidenced by the Ocmulgee Fields village associated with the Trading Post. She returned to Ocmulgee for the summers of 1957 and 1958 and completed the research for her dissertation in December 1958 (Mason 1963a).

In the spring of 1959, Macon Archeological Society members began the excavation of a small log townhouse on Brown's Mount under the direction of Robert T. Bray (senior park archaeologist), John W. Walker (junior park archaeologist), and Richard A. Marshall (Macon Youth Museum director). This excavation produced the first radiocarbon date for the Early Mississippian Macon Plateau period: 970 ± 150 years: A.D. 980 (Crane and Griffin 1962, Marshall 1971).

During the mid-fifties, plans to construct Interstate 16 from Macon to Savannah were discussed at public hearings. In November 1957, the Southeast Regional Office was informed by superintendent Louis R. Caywood that the plans called for the road to cross the park, but the Service made no public comment concerning it (Marsh 1986:44–45). This continued to be the situation through 1960, but soon after Albert L. Dillahunty became superintendent on January 27, 1961, he was embroiled in controversy.

By mid-March Department of the Interior and National Park Service officials were receiving letters opposed to the proposed routing of the Interstate through the park. These letters (mostly from Society for American Archaeology members who had been contacted by Marshall and Walker) were influential in getting the Service to take a stand against the route. This proved very unpopular on both local and Congressional levels; and in May, the Service attempted to justify it by stressing the historical, archaeological, and ecological importance of the Ocmulgee bottoms, the area that the proposed route would cross (Walker 1961). In July and August the Service put forth alternate route proposals, one of which would have destroyed both the McDougal and Dunlap Mounds; but these were to no avail.

On September 8, 1961, a final decision was reached in a meeting between Congressman Carl Vinson (who had introduced the original legislation for the park), the Bureau of Public Roads, and the National Park Service: Interstate 16 would cross the Macon Plateau section of the park but would run nearer the Ocmulgee River than originally planned (Marsh 1986:47–48). At that time it was agreed that park areas that would be disturbed would be archaeologically salvaged. Later, it was agreed that the Service would be provided with up to $600,000 of federal highway funds for data recovery.

Wilfred D. Logan, former senior park archaeologist, was chosen to head the project, and he, in turn, chose the field and laboratory supervisors: Jackson W. Moore, Jr., former junior park archaeologist, and J. Earl Ingmanson. C. Fred Bohannon, Charles B. Voll, and Walker were selected as field crew chiefs.

For guidance in planning and carrying out the project, the Service established an Ocmulgee Advisory Committee made up of: John Otis Brew, James A. Ford, Frank H. H. Roberts, Jr., George I. Quimby, and Stephen Williams (Davis 1962). This group met at Ocmulgee in November 1961 prior to the meetings of the Southeastern Archaeological Conference and the Conference on Historic Site Archaeology.

By the end of the conferences, most of the project archaeologists had arrived at the park. Because Logan became ill and could not travel, the project was alternately directed by John M. Corbett, chief archaeologist, National Park Service; Carroll Burroughs, assistant chief; and

John W. Griffin, southeast regional archaeologist. Oliver J. Cosner, U.S. Geological Survey, assisted in interpreting the complex alluvial deposits encountered (Cosner 1973).

The Archeological Research Unit was housed in the Ocmulgee visitor center basement, a space originally designed for that purpose. Work began on December 5, 1961, and continued through June 29, 1962. The average number of laborers employed was 54, or 18 men per field crew, and some 75 test units were dug. Almost all of them began as 20-by-20-foot units that were stepped down to 10 by 10 feet at a depth of 6 feet. Many of them were more than 10 feet deep.

The project produced valuable archaeological data relative to the area. Most important was a stratified projectile point sequence that began with fluted points and contained both Early and Middle Archaic types not previously found *in situ* within the park (Griffin 1964; Nelson, Swindell, and Williams 1974). There was also a relatively good ceramic sequence indicating that Etowah Complicated Stamped wares either postdated Macon Plateau wares or were introduced near the end of their usage and that there was a fairly heavy Lamar occupation of the bottoms in contrast to almost none on the adjacent uplands. Much of this was not known when the Ocmulgee Advisory Committee met again on April 28, 1962, and its recommendation that the project be closed down at the end of June was never questioned.

At the close of the "Big Dig," as the participants referred to the project, it was hoped that the Archeological Research Unit could continue operation by having the archaeologists carry out needed fieldwork on parks throughout the Southeast Region and return to Ocmulgee for analysis and report writing as Fairbanks had done in the 1950s. All but Voll, who transferred to the Southwest Archeological Center, remained in the Southeast Region. However, only Ingmanson and Walker returned to Ocmulgee after completing their fieldwork assignments, and Walker left on December 31, 1962.

Ingmanson spent most of 1963 in analyzing the materials that he and John Griffin had recovered from Russell Cave (Griffin 1974:ix). During 1964 he prepared reports covering the 1930s excavations on the South Plateau (including those on Mounds A and B) and at the Dunlap and McDougal Mounds (Ingmanson 1964a, 1964b) and also surveyed a proposed reservoir on Tobesofkee Creek south of Macon (Ingmanson 1964c). In June 1965, he completed a report on Mound E (Southeast Mound) and the Middle Plateau fortification trenches (1965). Following that, he and park archaeologist George R. Fischer made a study of Archaic projectile points from the Alligator Pond site in Dooly County (Ingmanson and Fischer 1966).

Other Ocmulgee-related research conducted during the 1963–66 period included: transcription by park tour leader Bernard Berg of an unpublished May 1798–July

1801 manuscript letter-book kept by Benjamin Hawkins, the Creek Indian agent (Hawkins 1966); publication of a radiocarbon date for the Macon Plateau Earth Lodge of 935 ± 110 years: A.D. 1015 (Wilson 1964); and presentation by Kelly (1965) of a paper on the prehistoric cultivated field under Mound D.

It might be noted that throughout the park's history archaeologists were frequent visitors. Among those visiting during the year ending June 30, 1965, were: E. Mott Davis, University of Texas; Charles H. Fairbanks, University of Florida; Lewis H. Larson, Jr., Georgia State University; James A. Brown, University of Oklahoma; Melvin L. Fowler, Southern Illinois University; David S. Phelps, Florida State University; R. Stuart Neitzel, Mississippi State Historical Museum; James A. Ford, American Museum of Natural History; and David J. Hally, Harvard University graduate student, who studied collections from Lower Mississippi Valley sites on the Natchez Trace Parkway.

After more than four years of discussion and planning, the Southeast Archeological Center became a reality on October 17, 1966. On that date Richard D. Faust, who had been in the chief archaeologist's office, arrived at Ocmulgee. One week later, Walker, who had been the archaeologist for the National Survey of Historic Sites and Buildings, followed. Faust was to oversee the River Basin Salvage Program for the Southeast Region, and Walker, archaeological research in the parks. John W. Griffin, then on academic leave at the University of Chicago, was to begin duty as center chief in June 1967. In the interim, Walker was acting chief.

In February 1967, Faust and Walker visited the Swift Creek site with Kelly, who had not been on the site since World War II began. He was pleased to find it had not been totally destroyed and that, although truncated at four to five feet, about one third of Mound A remained. The possibility of obtaining charcoal from the mound for radiocarbon dating excited him, and Walker agreed that, if the opportunity arose, he would obtain samples for him.

When Griffin arrived in June, Walker was conducting test excavations at Mound A on the Macon Plateau. This project, which continued until mid-October, was primarily intended to obtain data on the mound's construction and the amount of disturbance that had occurred. Major findings were: erosion was all but imperceptible except where gulleys had been worn by motorcycles; there had been a stepped rampway down the north and east sides of the mound during the next to last construction stage; and a curb, similar to that on Mound C, had encircled the top of the mound. Even more important, it was learned that the ridge on which Mounds A and B were built had been purposely leveled and shaped to form a very regular platform, or terrace, prior to mound construction (Walker 1969).

Early in March 1969, Middle Georgia Archeological Society members began profiling the remaining portion of Mound A at the Swift Creek site under Walker's supervision. It was hoped to obtain charcoal for radiocarbon dating and to integrate the profiles exposed with those from the 1930s excavations. Despite working weekends for more than four months, no charcoal was found, and no profiles could be matched. There was, however, enough agreement between the profiles to show that the mound began as a relatively small, low conical constructed over a prepared floor.

During the time (June 1969–August 1970) that he was the Southeast Archeological Center's curator, Lee H. Hanson, Jr., made a study of kaolin pipes from Ocmulgee and, largely based on this, presented a paper on pipestem hole diameter as a dating tool at the 1969 Conference on Historic Site Archaeology (1971b). He also made a study of gunflints from the Macon Plateau. Concluding that some of them were early nineteenth century, he proposed that these, along with the ceramics and other artifacts of the period, were likely associated with the Creek Trading House, which historical data suggest was then located on the Plateau (1970, 1971a).

The previous fall, intrigued by Weeden Island ceramics collected by amateur archaeologist Joseph A. Murciak from a site on Big Indian Creek in Houston County, Walker agreed to test the site. Only ceramics that might come from Gulf Coast Weeden Island sites were recovered from 15 shovel tests, but they produced no artifacts below the plowzone. Although Walker explained to Murciak that archaeological excavation would add little, if any, further information, this did not deter him. By June 1970, he had excavated some 300 10-by-10-foot units, recovering more than 150,000 sherds. Of these, over 99 percent were Swift Creek, Napier, and Weeden Island pottery types (Walker and Murciak 1971).

In February and March 1971, J. Anderson Comer, a senior at Middlesex School in Concord, Massachusetts, made a study of Macon Thick, a Macon Plateau phase type, under Walker's direction. This ware had been described as cylindrical jars with vertical walls and flat bases (Jennings and Fairbanks 1940; Fairbanks 1956a); but when Comer reconstructed one of these "vessels," it was found to be a conical funnel, much like some of the "juice presses" from the Wickliffe site in western Kentucky (King 1971:97–98, figure after p. 96).

That summer Walker compiled brief descriptions of Macon area archaeological sites for use by the Georgia Department of Transportation in planning road locations. In doing this, he found that instead of there being only two sites with Macon Plateau period ceramics (Fairbanks 1956a:13), there were at least seven (see Figure 12.1; Walker 1971b).

On the weekend of January 22–23, 1972, Walker, assisted by Wayne Shelley, University of Georgia students, and Middle Georgia Archeological Society members,

Table 2.3. Southeast Archeological Center Contracts for Analysis and Report Writing on Federal Relief Program Investigations Conducted by Archaeologists Stationed at Ocmulgee

Investigation	Institution	References
OCMULGEE NATIONAL MONUMENT INVESTIGATIONS		
Lamar Site	Florida State University	H. Smith 1973a
Middle Plateau	Florida State University	H. Smith 1973b
Mound D and Earth Lodge	Florida State University	Nelson, Prokopetz, and Swindell 1974
Ocmulgee Bottoms	Florida State University	Nelson, Swindell, and Williams 1974
Middle Plateau Houses	Florida State University	Prokopetz 1974
North Plateau	Florida State University	Williams and Henderson 1974
Mounds A and B	Florida State University	Stoutamire et al. 1983
OTHER GEORGIA SITE INVESTIGATIONS		
Glynn County	Florida State University	Chance 1974
Stubbs Mound	Florida State University	Williams 1975
Cowarts Landing	Florida State University	Hamilton et al. 1975
Swift Creek	University of Georgia	Kelly and Smith 1975
Tuft Springs	Florida State University	Stoutamire et al. 1977
Stratigraphic Surveys	Florida State University	Hamilton 1977
Mossy Oak	Florida State University	Stoutamire et al. 1978
Hawkins Point	Florida State University	Zierden 1978
Fairchild's and Hare's Landings	Kennesaw College	Caldwell 1978
Chatham County	University of Georgia	DePratter 1991

recovered 55 Swift Creek, Weeden Island, and Napier vessels from an east side pottery deposit in a low sand burial mound in Pulaski County. Weekend work on the mound (named the Shelley Mound for its finder), continued until June. During that period it was learned that other Pulaski County sites with Weeden Island ceramics had been found in 1965 by Georgia State University student Jerry Nielsen (Nielsen 1967; Walker 1974).

An agreement between the National Park Service and Florida State University to move the Southeast Archeological Center to the university was signed on April 12, and the staff moved to Tallahassee on June 12.

The following January, the Center initiated a contract program for the preparation of reports on federally funded archaeological investigations in Georgia, most of which had been conducted by Ocmulgee-based archaeologists (Table 2.3). The first of these, a contract for a report on the 1930–40s Lamar site excavations, was let to Florida State University with Hale G. Smith as principal investigator.

Following the report's completion (Smith 1973a), the Center held a Lamar symposium in conjunction with the university. Faust introduced the symposium and chaired the morning session; Smith chaired the afternoon session and summarized the results. Participants included: Arthur R. Kelly, professor emeritus, University of Georgia; Lewis H. Larson, Jr., Georgia state archaeologist; Ross Morrell, Florida state archaeologist; and Craig Sheldon, West Georgia College, as well as Center staff and report authors (Faust and Smith 1973).

At the Georgia Academy of Science's 1973 spring meeting in Atlanta, Kelly's colleagues presented papers on Georgia prehistory in recognition of his contribution to Georgia archaeology during the preceding 39 years (Larson 1976:vii). Three of the papers had pertinence to Ocmulgee archaeology (Schnell 1976:27–36; Hally 1976:37–52; Russell 1976:53–67). As discussant Joseph R. Caldwell pointed out: "That the work at Macon, and later Savannah, was a genuine watershed in Georgia archaeology will be apparent to anyone who will look at Moorehead's *Etowah Papers* published only a few years earlier" (1976:68).

Later that year, in discussing colonial Spanish ceramics, Charles H. Fairbanks mentioned the occurrence of olive jars "as far inland as an Indian village dating from about 1685 to 1716 at Macon . . . [and then suggested,] this . . . must clearly be the result of trade with Spanish sources" (Fairbanks 1973:142–43). Presumably the latter was in reference to the pre-1685 period when Ocmulgee was on the Chattahoochee and trading with the Spanish.

In late April and early May 1974, Carl D. McMurray, a University of Florida graduate student, attempted to salvage archaeological data from the Swift Creek site after the remaining portion of Mound A was bulldozed. Regrettably he was unable to retrieve any meaningful data (McMurray 1974).

On three occasions during the winter of 1974–75, Center archaeologist George R. Fischer (a former Ocmulgee archaeologist) monitored earth removal from around the Earth Lodge. This was done in conjunction with waterproofing and installation of climate control equipment.

In early 1975, J. Mark Williams completed a master's thesis based on data recovered from the Stubbs Mound site in 1936. His study suggested that the hiatus between the Macon Plateau and Lamar phases postulated by Fairbanks (1956a), while apparently true for the Macon Plateau uplands, did not hold true for Stubbs Mound (Williams 1975).

Later that year, under an Archeological Center contract with the University of Georgia, professor emeritus Arthur R. Kelly completed his long-awaited Swift Creek site report. He was assisted by Betty A. Smith, who had been one of his doctoral students at Georgia (Kelly and Smith 1975).

In April 1977, Roc Indermill, the last archaeologist assigned to Ocmulgee, met with Center staff members Faust, Fischer, and Walker to discuss revision of the visitor center museum. For Walker, this began six years of sporadic involvement in planning, reviewing, and revising designs, scripts, and exhibit content; meeting and talking with contractors; and selecting artifacts for display.

During the first six months of 1978, Walker conducted a survey of a proposed development corridor at Ocmulgee. Two occupation areas were found: a small Swift Creek site on the Walnut Creek bluffs near the railroad trestle, and a 10-ha Macon Plateau occupation area extending from the visitor center parking area to 100 meters north of the Dunlap house. No features were found in the latter, and the low artifact density suggested that occupation was relatively brief or of a temporary nature such as might have been associated with markets and/or ceremonies.

In a 1979 article on Creek use of the black drink, Charles H. Fairbanks discussed Macon Plateau artifacts that strongly suggest use of black drink (Fairbanks 1979: 121). The next year, he wrote an introduction for a reissue of his 1956 *Archeology of the Funeral Mound* (1981).

In November 1981, the park visitor center was closed for renovation and the installation of new exhibits. It re-opened with a rededication of the museum on March 23, 1983. The only former Park Service archaeologist to attend the ceremonies was Charles H. Fairbanks.

Center staff members Allen H. Cooper, Teresa Paglione, and Walker monitored utility line installation at the park in August and September 1984. Insofar as possible, the lines were run in disturbed areas, but recovery of historic and Macon Plateau phase artifacts between the visitor center and the Dunlap house was expected. However, the disturbance of a cache of five unworked *Busycon perversum* near the Mound C parking area was not. These shells were in association with Macon Plateau phase ceramics (Cooper and Walker 1987).

Also in 1984, Charles Hudson, Marvin Smith, and Chester DePratter reanalyzed the De Soto expedition route through Georgia. Their reconstructed route placed De Soto's province of Ichisi at the Lamar site (1984:70).

In 1985, Alan Marsh, a University of Georgia graduate student in history, prepared an administrative history of the monument (1986). That fall, Thomas H. Gresham conducted an archaeological survey of four alternative freeway routes near Macon (Gresham and Rudolph 1986). On a route running between the Macon Plateau and Lamar, he relocated three prehistoric sites earlier reported by Walker. These were the Gledhill No. 1, No. 2, and No. 3 sites from which Early Archaic and Paleoindian projectile points (including a complete Clovis from Gledhill No. 2) had been recovered (Walker 1971b).

In May 1986, Mrs. Fairbanks was present for the dedication of the Charles H. Fairbanks Memorial Lab. This combination museum and laboratory was established by the park staff to provide hands-on experience and other types of interpretation structured to fit the needs of younger school children and other special groups.

Later that year, superintendent Sibbald Smith asked David J. Hally of the University of Georgia to organize a symposium on Ocmulgee-related archaeology in commemoration of the fiftieth anniversary of the park's establishment. The symposium was held December 13, 1986, at Mercer University in Macon. Sylvia Flowers of the Ocmulgee staff and Donald Evans, Mercer faculty member, were in charge of local arrangements.

In January 1987, Hally asked Walker to write a history of Ocmulgee archaeology for inclusion in a publication of symposium papers. This paper and a much lengthier version (Walker 1989) were the result.

CHAPTER THREE

Macon, Georgia:
A Fifty-Year Retrospect

Gordon R. Willey

OCMULGEE'S FIFTIETH ANNIVERSARY celebration of its archaeology corresponds with mine. It was in Macon, in 1936, that I began my professional career, at what was shortly to become the Ocmulgee National Monument. My associations with Macon also evoke other important personal memories, as I shall explain further along. As a consequence, what I shall have to say here is a "remembrance of things past," a happy remembrance.

The year 1936 was not a propitious year for an emerging college graduate. I don't suppose it was any worse for fledgling archaeologists than for anyone else; indeed, with the newly beginning federal relief archaeological projects it might have been somewhat better for us than for others; however, when I left the University of Arizona with a master's degree in anthropology and archaeology that June, job prospects were not at all bright. In the previous winter, looking ahead, I had written to various museums and research institutions in the southwestern United States, inquiring about employment, however humble, that might keep me in the field of archaeology, but to no avail. I was lucky, however, that during that same winter my principal professor, Byron Cummings, had called me into his office one day and given me an announcement of a summer field program in archaeological training to be sponsored by the Laboratory of Anthropology in Santa Fe, New Mexico. He suggested I apply, and I had done so. When May came around, a few weeks before graduation, I had a reply from the Laboratory of Anthropology saying I had been one of those selected for that summer's session. A group of six graduate students from various universities had been chosen to go to Macon, Georgia, to work under a Dr. Arthur R. Kelly in a large Indian mound excavation there. Naturally, I was delighted. It wasn't exactly a job, but, in those lean days, I felt that my future as an archaeologist had been saved—at least through the summer months of 1936.

I was scheduled to report to Santa Fe to pick up the Laboratory of Anthropology station wagon and drive it back to Macon at the end of June. In the weeks before I left the university, I attempted to "bone up" on Georgia and southeastern archaeology. All of my previous field experience had been with Professor Cummings in Arizona. In addition, I had had survey course work in various kinds of Old World archaeology, but I knew absolutely nothing about the "mound archaeology" of the eastern part of the United States. I read Shetrone's *Mound Builders* that June, and then, moving closer to my forthcoming summer's work, I made my way through Moorehead's *Etowah Papers*, but I don't remember doing much more than that.

Later in June, I went to Santa Fe, picked up the station wagon at the Laboratory of Anthropology and began my solitary journey across the southern part of the United States. The thought of it seems awesome now, but at that time I went with a light heart and in excited anticipation. Ah, youth, there is nothing like it! By any objective standards, the trip went poorly. I averaged about one engine breakdown and tow-job per day. Although the station wagon looked pretty good, with its handsomely impressive *Laboratory of Anthropology* sign on the door, it wasn't in very good condition. It apparently hadn't had much exercise around Santa Fe—before I took it on such a grueling transcontinental trek—and it wasn't until I reached Macon, and we left it in a shop for a three-day overhaul, that it regained what must have been its onetime health. But by subjective standards it was a great trip. My ego expanded greatly as I answered questions about the sign and the meaning of "anthropology" at filling stations from Texas to Alabama. The Laboratory of Anthropology's travel expense account was a generous one for those days. I put up at the best hotels and luxuriated in air-conditioned rooms while the summer heat of the South hung oppressively outside.

I arrived in Macon late on a humid, but baking Saturday night and located the YMCA, at First and Cherry streets, the place where we were to be billeted that summer. The "Y" didn't have air-conditioning, at least in those days, but, in spite of this, I slept the sleep of the young and optimistic. Macon on the following Sunday morning was quiet. The pleasant, wide prospect of Cherry Street was largely deserted, but I located a restaurant for breakfast. Afterward, I checked back at the "Y," but none of my colleagues had as yet put in an appearance. I thought perhaps it would be appropriate if I called Dr. Kelly and let him know of my arrival. The only Kelly in the telephone book that appeared probable was an "A. Kelly." I rang that number and inquired if Dr. Kelly was there. The reply came back: "He's heah, but he ain't no doctuh." In view of this, it seemed best to forego the attempt at telephonic communication and make a ground search. I went back through what correspondence I had and found Dr. Kelly's address. It was on a Laurel Street, or a Laurel Avenue—and not the address of the "A. Kelly" who, apparently, lacked a Ph.D., or any comparable higher degree. The garage attendant, across the street from the "Y," where I had housed the station wagon the night before, gave me good instructions on how to find Laurel Street, and within a few minutes I was pulling up in front of the designated address. I must confess to some excitement, as well as trepidation, as I prepared to meet my forthcoming mentor.

The Kelly Laurel Street residence was set back some distance from and above the street level, and approached by some steep porch stairs. It must have been about 10:30 AM when I arrived. I went up the stairs and saw a figure, or a part of a figure, seated in a porch swing. Only two very long legs and two large feet were visible from beneath a section of a Sunday paper behind which an individual was deeply engrossed. I had to shuffle around and clear my throat a bit before the newspaper came down, and the reader eyed me rather gravely and, I thought, not altogether contentedly. I announced who I was and that I was seeking Dr. Arthur R. Kelly. The gentleman arose, all six-feet-two of him, and quite formally confirmed that he was, indeed, Dr. Kelly and that he had been expecting me and other members of the Laboratory of Anthropology group. For a moment, I thought I had come at a bad time. Had I introduced myself too soon, intruding on a relaxed Sunday morning? He invited me to sit down, although he still seemed rather formal. I started to make conversation by inquiring about the nature of the work. That was all it took.

Dr. Kelly informed me, with considerable enthusiasm, that he was engaged in a new project—"chronimetric

studies of flint patination" was the way he put it. He asked me if I was familiar with European Paleolithic studies. I had to say that I was not. I was also secretly ashamed that I didn't know what "patination" meant. I suppose I had heard of "patina" in connection with Classical bronzes, but I am afraid I wasn't imaginative enough to recognize the processual form of the word. Besides, I was all prepared to hear about "Indian mounds" and was "blind-sided" by the Paleolithic. He went on to tell me about lithics on the "Macon Plateau" and how these undoubtedly related to early man in the Americas. Many of these flints were heavily decomposed or patinated. The thickness of the patina held promise to being a clue to relative age. I began to wonder if I was going to enjoy the summer as much as I had thought I was.

At my first opportunity, I shifted the conversation to "Indian mounds." Dr. Kelly shifted gears swiftly and smoothly away from patination, acknowledging that the Macon site and region had many and that they were the primary objectives of his research. I felt relieved. To establish my credentials as a *bona fide* young archaeologist, I asked if the Macon mounds related to those of Ee-tow-ah (I think this was how I pronounced it). Dr. Kelly looked baffled for a minute and then said, yes, that there were some similarities between the central Georgia sites and Et-o-wah (I learned how to pronounce it then), in the northern part of the state. He went on to tell me about the problem of complicated stamped pottery in Georgia and the Southeast. I was having all I could do to keep up with this when Mrs. Kelly, a charming lady, came out on the porch, with their three young daughters—Sheila, Joanna, and Patricia, ages 8 through 4. After introductions, Mrs. Kelly said that they were having a picnic lunch that day down along the banks of the Ocmulgee River nearby and would I join them. I accepted with alacrity and great pleasure.

After our riverside lunch, Dr. Kelly suggested that we drive back into town and see if any of the others of the Laboratory group had put in an appearance. At the "Y" we found one had, J. B. ("Joe") Birdsell, a physical anthropology graduate student from Harvard who had wanted a summer's archaeology. With him, we spent part of the afternoon in the railroad station, down at the other end of Cherry Street, and met there, on successive trains, J. Lawrence ("Larry") Angel, another Harvard physical anthropologist, H. Y. ("Arf") Feng, a Chinese graduate student from the University of Pennsylvania, primarily an ethnologist, who had been studying in this country on a Kuomintang fellowship, and W. W. ("Walt") Taylor, Yale and archaeology. That evening, Dr. Kelly introduced us to Robert's Cafeteria, across the street corner from the "Y," where he had arranged for us to board during the summer. Afterward, back at the "Y," well after I had bedded down for the night, the final member of our group, Charles

("Chuck") Wagley, a Columbia ethnologist, who had been assigned as my roommate, made a midnight arrival. We were all assembled. On the morrow we would visit the Macon site, and the summer would commence in earnest.

Archaeological digging at Macon had begun with federal relief funding in December of 1933—the pit of the economic depression. It had a principal welfare purpose, which was to employ the hundreds of workers who had lost their jobs in the local textile mills, but there was also an intellectual and scholarly drive behind the enterprise. This was provided by three Macon citizens who, more than any others, are responsible for the development of archaeology there: General (ret.) Walter A. Harris, a leading Macon lawyer; Dr. Charles C. Harrold, a prominent surgeon; and Mr. Linton M. Solomon, a retired businessman. Longtime archaeological and historical enthusiasts, they were the founders and the nucleus of the Society for Georgia Archaeology. It was through their influence and intercession in Washington that the Smithsonian Institution became the official sponsor of the Macon Project and that the first federal relief grant was obtained and subsequently renewed. They were also instrumental in the formation of Ocmulgee National Monument under the National Park Service. I shall be referring to these three gentlemen again.

But to return to the beginnings of the Macon excavations in 1933, Dr. Kelly had been selected as the field director by the Smithsonian, and he was provided with James A. Ford, later to become very distinguished in southeastern archaeology, as an assistant. When they arrived at Macon, they were met by some 700 laborers. Kelly and Ford had to devise rapid strategies to put all of these men to work under some kind of archaeological supervision. Selecting those among the 700—former bank clerks, insurance agents, and other "white-collar" types—they gave "cram" courses in the fundamentals of archaeological recording. Fortunately, they had a few civil engineers, two of whom were college-trained. These later became key members of the staff for the obviously necessary mapping and surveying.

In the early operations of 1933–34, the diggers were all concentrated on the Macon Plateau site, either in long exploratory trenches in which they could be relatively easily supervised, or on some of the mounds. The "Macon Plateau," as it was called, was actually a large patch of hilly, red clay high-ground above the Ocmulgee River flats. It had been selected by its Indian inhabitants at various periods in its past history as a favorable living site. There were several mounds on it. The most impressive of these, Mound A, was a huge, rectangular, flat-topped construction, over 15 m in height. It was tested only in a superficial way. Another, Mound C, later renamed the "Funeral Mound" (Fairbanks 1956a), had been sliced by a railroad cut many years before. Taking advantage of this

old cut, Kelly cleaned and trimmed a spectacular profile through the mound, revealing a complicated layered construction of different colored clays and many elaborate burials. These mounds, and others on the Macon Plateau, pertained to what Dr. Kelly (1938c) referred to as the "Macon Plateau Culture." It was eventually to be recognized as clearly Mississippian in its affiliations and intrusive into the central Georgia region from the north and northwest.

Perhaps the most unusual structure of the Macon Plateau culture was the building known as the "Council Chamber," or "Macon Earth Lodge" (Fairbanks 1946b). On the surface this had appeared as a low circular mound, and, at first, it was thought to be a burial tumulus. Excavation, however, disclosed that it was once a circular chamber with an encircling clay wall and a timber-supported, thatched roof. There was a large fire-basin in the center of the chamber, and around the interior of the encircling wall were 50 partitioned, clay seats. Three of these seats were on a clay dais or platform, higher than the other seats, and this platform had the fascinating outline of a bird, inevitably seen as an eagle (or "iggle," as one of the WPA guides used to describe it to awestruck tourists). It was—and is, quite rightly—a tourist attraction, the prime one at the Macon Indian mounds.

The mounds, the Council Chamber, the long trenches on the Plateau—one of which was 600 m long in 1936—all of this made quite an impression on our Laboratory of Anthropology group on our first visit. The Mound C excavations were finished, and we had to appreciate its colorful stratigraphy from an artist's painting; but another mound was being excavated, and we watched in amazement as profiles were water-sprayed to bring out different colors and textures in earth strata and platform floors were carefully peeled to reveal black postholes in the red clay. None of us had ever seen archaeology quite like this nor on this scale before. The several hundred diggers toiling on the Macon Plateau reminded us of pictures of Near Eastern tell excavations. Taylor and I, who had had somewhat more archaeological experience than the others, but all of that in the Southwest, were fascinated with the soft, rockless digging and the dependence upon soil colors and textures to define structures. In saying this, I do not imply that what was going on at Macon was unique in the context of eastern United States, or "Mound Area," archaeology. Such digging, on a small scale, went back to the turn of the century and before in places such as the Ohio Valley, and in Kentucky and Tennesse, W. S. Webb and T. M. N. Lewis, at the time of the Macon project, were digging on a comparable scale to Kelly's program; but for us, and certainly for me, it was a new view of archaeology.

In 1936, the Macon Plateau operations were not the only ones under Kelly's command. With his federal relief mandate he was allowed to explore or dig anywhere in Bibb County. Early on, while Ford was still there, they carried on excavations at the Lamar site (9BI2), in the Ocmulgee River flats, a mile or so distant from Macon Plateau. The Lamar tract, with two major mounds and a deep village midden, was eventually incorporated into the Ocmulgee National Monument jurisdiction even though it was not immediately tangential to it. When we arrived, there was no digging going on at Lamar, but a sizable crew was working at the Swift Creek mound (9BI3) in another part of the county. We visited the Swift Creek dig on this first day's look-around. Swift Creek has since been immortalized in the literature as the type site for an early complicated stamped ceramic complex and tradition. At that time, the chronological position of Swift Creek with relation to the Macon Plateau culture was uncertain. Lamar, Kelly knew definitely, was later than either.

The day following our first view of all of the Macon archaeological operations, we began our serious summer "course work" by receiving instruction in the use of plane table and alidade, transit, and level from J. B. ("Joe") Tamplin, a Georgia Tech graduate who, in those Depression times, was doing archaeological engineering. He befriended us and gave us exercises in mapping, running lines of levels all over the Macon Plateau, and taking level shots on mound excavation strata. This two weeks of engineering training was interrupted for one day when, in the wake of a hurricane-force storm of the night before, we went around Macon and the immediate countryside taking cross sections from fallen trees. I had indicated to Dr. Kelly that I had had two seminars with Professor A. E. Douglass while I was still at the University of Arizona, and Kelly was interested in pursuing the possibility of dendrochronology in Georgia. In gathering these living tree samples we were making a beginning toward developing a growth-ring master-chart that, we hoped, might eventually take us back into prehistoric timbers.

One immediate effect of this tree-ring foray was to take the whole class back to the Macon Council Chamber structure after our engineering stint was over. The six of us spent a week there removing the charred logs and timbers that had been left *in situ* where they had fallen when the building had burned down in prehistoric times. All of these charred specimens were carefully dunked in a solution of kerosene and paraffin and tied up in cotton—the procedures that Douglass and his colleagues had used in preserving burned archaeological timbers in the Southwest. How was I to know that every scrap of this charcoal was being made worthless for radiocarbon analysis when that method appeared about 15 years later? I might add that my fellow students were less than enthralled at this project of mine, often muttering that they had devoted a week of their summer to what they

referred to as my "doctoral dissertation." Needless to say, such a thesis never materialized, but I'll come back to Georgia dendrochronology later.

It had been Dr. Kelly's summer curriculum plan to shift us onto site excavation following our engineering training, and after our "tree-ring interlude," that is what he did. Along with a crew of 12 WPA workers, we began our Georgia digging on what came to be known as the "Swift Creek-Adkins Outlier Mound" (9BI4), a small tumulus about a half-mile away from the Swift Creek site proper. Although we found some pottery and artifacts, the mound proved to be no more than a small natural bump, or erosional remnant, in a swamp. As such, it had been lived on in the past, but there was nothing in the way of artificial mound structure to study to make it very interesting, so we were transferred after a week to what was proved later to be a much more interesting site.

This new site was given the official name of "Stubbs Mound" (9BI12), although it was better known locally as "Old Man Stubbs's Mound." It was located in the Tobesofkee drainage of the Ocmulgee, in the extreme southern tip of Bibb County. To reach it, a 12-mile trip from Macon took one to a shabby roadhouse with the arresting name of "The Seven Bridges." "Jook-joint" was the classical local term for such places in the thirties. Here, you left the paved highway and uneasily followed a narrow dirt road for about a mile. About halfway on this course, the road traversed about 50 yards of a putrid and exceedingly foul-looking swamp. I always said a prayer as we pointed the station wagon through it, going or coming. Our percentage of free passage was only about .500, which meant that on the average of once each trip, at least five of us had to get out and wade through the odorous, blue-black mud to push. After emerging from this Spanish-moss–festooned and mosquito-ridden hellhole, one came up a low rise into a small, sequestered, and singularly airless cornfield, enclosed on all four sides by the close-growing trees of swamp forests. Going down this rise, and at the opposite end of the field, was Stubbs Mound. It was located at the edge of a forest line and another arm of the same swamp that one had become acquainted with farther back. That summer, we had permission from the living owner and resident farmer— the same "Old Man Stubbs" who was to be immortalized in the literature of archaeology for having given his name to the mound—to dig away to our hearts' content. And so we did.

As I remember Stubbs Mound, it first appeared as vaguely circular, with a more or less rounded but lopsided summit. I suppose it was about 30 m in diameter and 1 m high at its highest point. Fragments of burned clay were mixed through the plowed loam, and the corn on the mound presented a slightly stunted appearance to that growing in the flats around it. These signs suggested that the mound covered, or had been formed by, a structure, a suggestion that was borne out by excavation. Once out at Stubbs, the six Laboratory fellows spent much of the morning of the first day arguing about the staking out of the mound, what system of controls we were going to use, the degrees to which we would combine a vertical profiling technique with one of horizontal stripping, and other technical and highly professional matters. Numerous votes were taken; sometimes these resolved arguments; but often the best we could do was a 3-to-3 tie. I should explain there were no very set lines in such electoral divisions; we seemed randomly contrary. Dr. Kelly was extraordinarily tolerant during all of this archaeological parliamentarianism. While he offered suggestions, he left most of such weighty decisions up to us. Eventually, by late morning, we were ready to start digging.

Meanwhile, the WPA crew, the same 12 worthies who had been with us at the Swift Creek–Adkins site, had grown quite used to—perhaps even fond of—us. They leaned on their shovels, chewed tobacco, and didn't say much, although one of them, "Popeye," so-called because of a spectacularly undershot jaw and corncob pipe, was heard to mutter that he wished "Old Man Stubbs" had his mound in an obscene place. As digging progressed, "Popeye" was heard to make this observation again and again. Dr. Kelly, who was a very gentle man, nevertheless had a formal comportment in the field, especially vis-à-vis "the men." We, as "officers" of the expedition—I suppose we of the Laboratory group rated as some sort of "officer cadets"—expected certain behavior from "enlisted ranks." "Popeye" was seriously reprimanded, even threatened to be banished from archaeology and sent to the Bibb County "Siberia" of WPA enterprises, the "Malarial Drainage Project." He almost got there, too, for after Dr. Kelly's reprimand, he went on explaining that he didn't mean anything against Dr. Kelly nor any of us. All it was, was that "he just wished that Old Man Stubbs had this here mound —— —— ——!" I suppose we were all secretly sympathetic with "Popeye." The swampside setting of Stubbs Mound in August was not exactly a dream spot. Anyway, we all put in a word for him, and Dr. Kelly undoubtedly thought that "archaeological-military discipline" should not be carried too far, so "Popeye" was saved for archaeology, at least for then. This Stubbs Mound incident, however, may have presaged a deep-seated indiscipline, for I am told that although "Popeye" remained loyal to archaeology, and even continued on the Ocmulgee National Monument staff in post-WPA years, he was eventually cashiered for operating a still on the Macon Plateau, somewhere in the undergrowth down in back of Mound A. Not even Dr. Kelly could save him then.

Those experiences at Stubbs Mound still stay with me, and among them were my associations with "Popeye"

and his cohorts. All of the workers on the dig with us were, obviously, poor men, and most of them were old men. They had sweated in the early years of their lives as "Georgia Cracker" tenant farmers. From this marginal existence they had gone into the cotton mills in the 1920s and had been dismissed from these in economic hard times and in the anger of the strikes of the 1930s. Yet they maintained a dignity and a good humor. I can remember one, perhaps the oldest of all of the crew, a Mr. Trueblood, who dug steadily and carefully and followed instructions well. I asked him once how he liked archaeology. "Mr. Willey," he replied, "I'm as happy as a dead pig in the sunshine here on the W.P. & A." Irony? Perhaps. I deserved it for such a fool question. I must admit that as a 23-year-old Californian—brought up on sunshine, orange juice, and hope—the poverty level of Georgia in the 1930s was a new experience for me. True, there was poverty in many places, including back in California, but here I was seeing and knowing about it face-to-face for the first time. On another occasion, an old man had come with no lunch. I shared mine with him, but I noticed he threw away the bread of the ham-on-rye sandwich and ate only the ham. When I inquired why, he told me that the ham was fine but the bread was full of "little black weevils."

We stuck to our task throughout the long August days, listening to the drone of the cicadas and slapping the mosquitoes. As one edge of Stubbs Mound was about 3 m from the swamp, that swamp odor pervaded these days. The heat was stifling. Our colleague Feng seemed particularly annoyed by the insects. I can still see him, masked like a bandit with a handkerchief tied around his face, busy fanning mosquitoes. One day he said to me: "Gord, this is terrible. Back in China we have high school boy do this. We be back in city." He had a point. As the summer wore on, we all grew a bit restive. Chuck Wagley was heard to say that he was glad he was going into ethnology, not archaeology. Larry Angel and Joe Birdsell, the two physical anthropologists, were, as was fitting, most industrious in uncovering and cleaning off burials, but were less than enthusiastic about some of the other aspects of archaeology. Walter Taylor and I, who considered ourselves the only truly serious archaeologists of the squad, kept a pretty good face on it, at least to each other, our colleagues, and Dr. Kelly. We all got a break, too, sometime during the Stubbs ordeal. We talked Dr. Kelly into letting us have dinner every night in the basement grill of Macon's leading hotel, the Dempsey. The air conditioning there felt mighty good after a hard day in the field; the food was a little closer to *haute cuisine* than that of Robert's Cafeteria; and we were regaled by a band and a beautiful singer.

In reflecting on our Stubbs adventure of 1936, I think one of the things that made our spirits flag under the strains of heat, swamp, and mosquitoes was that we were not sufficiently motivated by archaeological or, I should say, culture historical or problem interests. We were motivated by learning field techniques, to be sure, but we had no real conception of what we were digging up. None of us knew one Georgia pottery type from another. We had no adequate frame of reference to fit it all into. It was not until over a year later, after I had begun to learn the local ceramics, that I realized that Stubbs might be a very important site. Among other things, it had not only the Swift Creek and Lamar complicated stamped wares, but it had Macon Plateau pottery as well. If I had gone back and worked with the Stubbs collections then, and published on them, I could have produced a very key article or monograph. I didn't, and this was not done for almost another 40 years (Williams 1975). What Stubbs offered is a nice, small site example of the intrusion of Macon Plateau type culture into Swift Creek and a developmental sequence leading out of this fusion into Lamar. As such, it is a major datum in central Georgia archaeology. Given our inexperience at the time, I think our Laboratory of Anthropology class did well to do the digging and to provide the record of that digging that enabled J. M. Williams, the author of the monograph, to pull together what he did so long after the fact.

Not all of our days were spent in the pits and trenches of Stubbs Mound. Dr. Kelly wanted us to see something else of Georgia archaeology, and we took to the highways in the station wagon over the weekends. There was a sojourn to Columbus, Georgia, where another engineer, Frank Lester, was helping a local archaeological enthusiast, Mrs. Wayne Patterson, excavate a Mississippian horizon site known as Bull Creek. Similar trips were made north to Etowah and south to Kolomoki, although no excavation was then going on at either of these two impressive mound sites. Best of all, we spent two days and two nights at St. Simons Island on the Georgia Coast, where Preston Holder was doing WPA digging under Kelly's general supervision. This was the first time I had seen any shell mound archaeology, and it was there that we became acquainted with fiber-tempered (Spanish moss being the fiber) pottery, shortly afterward to be identified as the earliest ceramic in the southeastern United States. And to mix high life with archaeology, we were fortunate enough to be wined and dined one night on this trip at the famed Cloister Hotel; Dr. Harrold of Macon, whom I have mentioned, was our host.

It was only a week or so after this coastal trip that the summer fellowship program came to an end. All of my colleagues were returning to graduate school; I had no plans to do so. Fortunately, for me, Dr. Kelly agreed to take me on as his assistant. I was to continue with the Stubbs Mound excavations, and after that I was to be given a free hand in seeing what I could do with

dendrochronology in Georgia. After a farewell to my summer companions at the Macon railroad station, I began my professional career—with a salary, small as it was—on September 1, 1936. For a while, I continued to room at the Macon "Y." The Laboratory of Anthropology staff was extremely nice about the station wagon. They let me use it for another month or so, driving back and forth to Stubbs Mound, but eventually sent Sid Stallings to pick it up and drive it back to Santa Fe. This was an additional break for me, as Stallings was a leading tree-ring expert, and I wanted him to look over the tree specimens I had collected and advise me on the future of dendrochronology on the Georgia scene. After Stallings had come and gone, I rode out to Stubbs each day in an ancient vehicle with my WPA crew. I continued this until well into November. We gradually uncovered a burned wooden post structure that was quite nicely preserved (see Williams 1975), but I am afraid that the charred specimens from this went the same way as those from the Council Chamber—into the kerosene solution for that hoped-for day when dendrochronological dating would be possible. By mid-November, Dr. Kelly felt that the Stubbs job was far enough along and under good enough control that I could turn it over to a WPA foreman with only semiweekly visits on my part. He wanted me to get started in earnest on the dendrochronology.

This is a good place to pause in the narrative and say something about my boss and our relationship. I think that Arthur Kelly was one of the kindest men I have ever known. He was a great ego-builder for others, particularly young ones such as myself. He was invariably most considerate of me when distinguished dignitaries visited Macon, and a number of these came and went in late 1936 and early 1937. Some were National Park Service officials. Others were archaeological colleagues, such as Matthew Stirling, then chief of the Bureau of Ethnology of the Smithsonian Institution, or Philip Phillips of Harvard, or James Griffin from the University of Michigan. Dr. Kelly always introduced me as his "assistant"—to my mind fully establishing my professional status—and he always included me in parties and archaeological discussions— "bull sessions" might be the more appropriate term. Kelly had a style about him. It didn't matter that we received poor salaries and, for all practical purposes, if not so classified officially, were on federal relief along with the WPA workmen. He maintained a decorum, indeed almost an inner hauteur, that was unassailable.

On one occasion, a local rich man, a well-known millionaire in another part of the state, invited us to his palatial residence for lunch. He had called Dr. Kelly long-distance and said that he was very much interested in archaeology. After a long morning's drive over, we were ushered into the impressive country residence of this magnate—a textile prince as I remember—and handsomely treated to drinks and a fine lunch. Dr. Kelly had high hopes. Perhaps our archaeological research was going to be endowed in some special private way that could function in tandem with the government-supported operations. Our host "tut-tutted" at the way archaeologists were forced to grub about on federal relief. In fact, it became pretty clear that he disapproved of federal relief in general. But we were in for a letdown, for what he wanted was Kelly's advice on assembling a private collection of antiquities through purchase. A large "pothunter" collection was available for sale somewhere. Should he buy it? It was clear that he was willing to pay quite generously for professional aid in advising him on the collection and its pieces and in preparing a catalog or an authenticated list of the materials. No, he didn't want to give it to any museum or university. He wanted his own collection right here in his own house, where he could show it to the proper people and enjoy it himself. What did we think? Dr. Kelly told him in no uncertain terms. This was not the way to go about archaeology. Kelly, in an attempt to convert this tycoon to "civilized archaeology," made a counterproposal. Why not establish a private research foundation, an institution that might very well be named after its donor and would be a credit to him. Such a foundation could begin by hiring a young archaeologist. Kelly looked over meaningfully toward me. They might even hire two or three young archaeologists. Survey and excavation could be conducted in this part of Georgia, where relatively little was known as yet about its prehistory. But our host's attention and patience had begun to flag with such a scenario. It was obviously not what he had in mind. After a decent interval, we were politely but firmly dismissed. As we drove away from this baronial lodge, Dr. Kelly was silent for a long time, during which he lit his underslung, Sherlock Holmes–style pipe and puffed a few times. "Well, Gordon," he finally said, "we mustn't encourage that sort of thing. Archaeology is not to be commercialized. As officers of this expedition it is our duty to adhere to proper professional standards." I didn't answer, but I was thrilled with pride at being so "included" as "an officer of the expedition" and proud of my boss for standing up in such a manner for, what seemed to me to be, "the honor of archaeology."

Kelly had a wonderful way with words and phrases. His names for things and places somehow charged them with mystery and excitement. So it was with "the 2000 foot correlation trench," one of the long trench excavations on the Macon Plateau in the early days. There was a grandeur and sweep to the term. Another favorite was "the 9 foot level," a designation for a deep stratum that was reached, identified, or simply measured in some digging that had been done in deposits between Mounds A and B, and where some extraordinary things—I can't now remember what—had been found. "Fossil soils," a term that, in his

mind, seemed to refer to deeply buried midden strata, was still another name that managed to pack into it the idea of antiquity and the magic of discovery. This flair for nomenclature extended to other areas and was often combined with the decorum that I have already remarked upon. In relating the course of the Macon work, Dr. Kelly often detailed the duration of it in an impressive manner. Rather than making an offhand remark such as, "I've been working here for almost three years," he would say, "I have been conducting intensive research here for 34½ months." He had his lighter side, too, which often combined perfectly with the heavier pronouncements. Once, shortly after I had been taken on as his assistant, we were driving along in the still-borrowed station wagon. Kelly had been solemn, pipe-puffing for a long time. I wondered what was on his mind. Perhaps I had not been performing up-to-snuff in my new position. He finally said, "Lad, just up the road here is a little restaurant and bar. I wonder if you would mind pulling in there and we'll have a beer. After 34½ months of intensive research, a man needs a little relaxation." I had no hesitancy in doing so. After only 2½ months of intensive research, I wanted a beer too.

Dendrochronology got under way in that late fall of 1936. Prime assistance was provided by the Harris-Harrold-Solomon team referred to earlier. General Harris used his political clout to install me in a large room in the Macon City Hall building that I turned into an office-lab. Dr. Harrold sent away to Keuffel and Esser and purchased a Swedish increment borer for me. Linton Solomon gave freely of his time in taking me around the countryside to places he knew where there were stands of large, and presumably very old, trees. Actually, I had never made a tree boring before—although I had not informed Dr. Kelly of this when I presented myself as a "dendrochronologist." All of my time in Professor Douglass's seminars had been taken up in learning how to read tree-ring sequences from Pueblo Bonito archaeological borings that had been collected by others. This was good training in plotting ring-growths, but it didn't have much to do with collecting samples. But armed with the new borer, and with Lint Solomon as my interested audience, I set to work like an old hand, boring into tree trunks and extracting the small, resinous core with ease. There was nothing to it. We scouted Bibb and neighboring counties for the next three months. A lot of the Georgia pines, although of substantial girth, were of the shortleaf variety and not over a century in age; but some longleaf pines had real antiquity, often being as much as 300–400 years old. The rings showed some size variability, although not nearly as much as southwestern conifers. I suppose the ring sequences averaged only about one good "checking" ring per decade, or not really enough. I remember 1899 as such a "checking" ring. It was very narrow, faint, and sometimes even "missing," and it corresponded well with the local weather office precipitation records, which showed an extremely dry year in 1899. The big difficulty was that there just weren't enough dry years—either in the rainfall records, which went back to about 1840, or in the ring-sizes themselves.

I finally summed things up in March of 1937 by establishing a master-chart on the Georgia pines that went back to about 1810. This was published in the *Tree Ring Bulletin* at the University of Arizona (Willey 1937a) and was, incidentally, my very first publication of any sort. Back of 1810, some of the older pines carried through the 1700s and into the 1600s. The ring structures and patterns in these earlier centuries looked about like they did later—in a word, probably a little too "complacent," to use the damning dendrochronological term. Those examinations of what charcoal specimens we had— from the Council Chamber and the Stubbs Mound— showed the frequent presence of ring-growth patterns very similar to those of the living trees. Even if all of our material was on the "complacent" side, might there still not be a chance of linking modern trees and archaeological specimens? Could we find early Federal period or antecedent Colonial timbers that would bridge the gap? I took the Swedish increment borer and, in my ignorance and inexperience, attempted to drive it into a 150-year-old dry house-beam. This, of course, is a definite "no-no" in dendrochronological collecting. The borer broke. I communicated with my former mentors in Tucson, and although I am sure they were ashamed of me, they sent me a large, toothed borer for dry timbers. Lint Solomon had it replicated for me in a Macon machine shop, and we set about again trying to collect early dry timber samples. This was just after I had sent in my preliminary dendrochronological report to Professor Douglass in March. Douglass had responded with reasonable encouragement, suggesting that I pursue the idea of trying to link modern, historical, and archaeological ring sequences, although he had misgivings about ring "complacency." I was all set to do this, but it was just then that events at Ocmulgee National Monument occurred that changed my plans and put tree-ring research on the "back-burner," at least for me. In fact, I never went back to it. Some years later, Dr. Florence Hawley, then at the University of Chicago, sent a graduate student, Robert E. Bell, to collect samples, again, from many of the same living trees that I had bored, and to review the area for its dendrochronological potential. As I understand it, they concluded that tree-ring dating probably could not be developed for the region. I am not altogether sure that they were correct in this assessment. Perhaps someone should have another look at the possibility; however, the urge for such dating is no longer so great now that we have radiocarbon dating.

The events at Ocmulgee National Monument that caused me to drop dendrochronology were those that followed in the wake of the National Park Service's ownership of the Macon Plateau and Lamar sites and their plans to develop the area. WPA was phased out of archaeology, and a Civilian Conservation Corps camp was established on the Macon Plateau in April and May of 1937. Dr. Kelly became camp superintendent for the "using service" (in this case, the National Park Service), and for assistants he had Joe Tamplin and Frank Lester as "Senior Foremen, Engineers" and me as "Senior Foreman, Archaeologist." As a result, I went back to digging, this time with a young CCC crew and a former WPA foreman, Paul Myers, as my assistant. We needed more information on relative chronology, and this was to be my principal objective in what I designated as the "Central Georgia Stratigraphic Survey." One chronological perplexity was the relationship between Macon Plateau and Swift Creek. Ironically, as I have already indicated, we had this stratigraphy in some detail in the as yet unstudied Stubbs Mound collections, but I didn't know it. Moreover, we had an excess of CCC labor, and Dr. Kelly and I both felt that I should be digging rather than spending the next six months of my time analyzing the Stubbs Mound collections.

At that time, Kelly was of the opinion that Macon Plateau culture was earlier than Swift Creek. He realized the connections of Macon Plateau with some brand of Mississippian culture, but quite rightly, he could not easily identify it as the kind of Mississippian seen at Moundville or Etowah. We know now that Macon Plateau was an earlier, and at that time less familiar, variety of Mississippian. James Ford visited Macon early in the summer of 1937, and I had the advantage of meeting and talking with this forceful southeastern archaeological personality. He argued against Kelly, maintaining that Swift Creek was earlier than the Macon Plateau, that it was a part of an old local culture into which Macon Plateau had been intruded. I wanted to be the one to settle the argument in the field, so I began my "Stratigraphic Survey" in various village areas of the Macon Plateau, but I had no luck. Either ceramics typical of the Macon Plateau complex were extremely rare, or when I did find them, they were thoroughly mixed with the early complicated stamped wares. Numerous pits in the Lamar village site did no better for me. All the pottery I found there pertained to the Lamar complex. With the CCC ease of mobility, in trucks or pickup trucks, I began to range more widely, digging at other sites in central Georgia, both in and out of Bibb County. I found some stratigraphy at a place called Cowart's Landing (9BI14), on the Ocmulgee River south of Macon, but this was Lamar over Swift Creek, with no showing of Macon Plateau pottery anywhere in the extensive village. I eventually published an article on this site (Willey 1939), and on some other sites of the survey (Willey 1938b), the only papers on Macon archaeology that I was ever to publish; but the chronological position of Macon Plateau culture was never resolved by me—except unknowingly at Stubbs Mound. That Macon Plateau as a cultural complex was intrusive into Georgia Swift Creek and other early Woodland cultures seems to have been generally accepted by most southeastern archaeologists at least by the late 1940s, if not well before. I suppose this derived from a wider appreciation of Macon Plateau as some kind of a branch of Mississippian culture and from inferences drawn from work in Tennessee and elsewhere.

I should note here that my stratigraphic survey was greatly aided by Dr. Harrold and Linton Solomon. On Sundays they would devote the day to taking me around to various sites so that I would be all set up to take the CCC boys to a new location on Mondays. I suppose Linton Solomon knew about more archaeological sites than any other man in Macon. We would start out after breakfast and drive to and prowl around in places worse than "Old Man Stubbs's" swamps. There was a little railroad station some distance south of Macon known as "Bullard's Station." It was quite godforsaken. There was no town or village in the immediate vicinity, and while trains may have stopped there, I never saw one do so. We visited a site not far from the station about 11 AM of a hot July morning. Afterward, coming back to the car, which was parked at the edge of the swamp, Dr. Harrold suggested that we have a little refreshment. Had I ever tried any Georgia peach brandy? I said, no, but that it did indeed sound very refreshing. He took a jug and some paper cups out of the trunk of the car. I don't know quite what I expected, perhaps something with a lovely peach-cordial flavor, preferably ice-cold; but it wasn't quite like that. On looking back on it, I can say that a slug of warm peach brandy, in a paper cup, on a 100-degree morning, in a swamp near Bullard's Station, in central Georgia, is a character-building experience for any young archaeologist.

It was essential to my stratigraphic survey operations that I did learn something about the local pottery, and during the spring and summer of 1937, I acquired a working knowledge of it. In fact, if I had dug Stubbs Mound in that summer, rather than 1936, I think I would have done much more than I did to straighten out Macon archaeological chronology and ceramic typology. I had arrived at Macon, as I have related, with some familiarity with southwestern archaeological pottery types. I had imagined that Kelly and his associates would be working with similar type constructs. Informally, they tended to do so. In conversations, Dr. Kelly would often refer to pottery as "Swift Creek Complicated Stamped," "Lamar Complicated Stamped," "Lamar Bold Incised," and the

like; however, no pottery had been so recorded in any of the tabulations that were going on in his WPA pottery lab.

In 1936–37, the Macon "pottery classificatory staff" consisted of a man who was the chief, another a secretarial clerk, and a half-dozen women assistants. They sat around a long table. A potsherd would be brought in from the field; the paper in which it was wrapped like a little parcel was removed; and the chief would then read from the paper the site unit and full provenience data—trench, section, depth, strata, etc.—from whence the specimen came. The sherd would then be marked in ink with a catalog number, and after this, it would be passed around the table to the women, in serial fashion. Each would record on a card the particular feature or qualities in which she specialized. Thus, the first woman might give it a color coding; a second might tabulate it as plain, incised, simple stamped, complicated stamped, or whatever; the next might scratch it for hardness; the one after that would appraise its tempering material; and the following, perhaps, taste it for some other property. All of this information was dutifully punched on a punchcard. This was before the day of the computer. Quantitative handling of data was frequently done by punching out code numbers in the top margin of a 5-by-8-inch card. Cards or, in effect, units of the sample could then be retrieved by inserting an icepick-like implement through a co-aligned series of the punched-out holes, and then, by lifting up the pick, the desired units could be extracted from the cardfile. Dr. Kelly had been trained primarily as a physical anthropologist, and this is the way he had been taught by Hooton at Harvard to handle large quantities of data. By 1936, I suppose that at least 750,000 potsherds had been excavated by the Macon project; and by that year, or a short time later, when this kind of ceramic "classification" or "processing" was terminated, there must also have been 750,000 cards available.

Needless to say, this end result of such pottery processing was intimidating. We could not readily use the 750,000 cards in discussions of stratigraphies or contexts in the Macon or central Georgia setting, and it was impossible to use them in talking over ceramic comparisons with colleagues who were working in other parts of the Southeast. It was obvious that we needed another system—at least at that stage of Macon and southeastern archaeology.

It struck me that a type classification and nomenclature, similar to that of the Southwest might be more useful. I was strongly seconded in this belief by Jim Ford, who had returned to work at Macon, as a special consultant to the National Park Service, in the summer of 1937. The two of us collaborated on this with Preston Holder and A. J. Waring, Jr., with whom we had many long, afternoon barroom sessions on Georgia pottery typology. Waring, a Savannah resident and then a medical student at Yale, had a lifelong interest in Georgia archaeology and later was to contribute substantially to it. In our typology, a type designation, such as "Lamar Complicated Stamped," was simply a shorthand reference to a clustering of ceramic modes—surface decoration, tempering, paste, vessel form, and rim form—clusterings that repeatedly occurred on pottery vessels or sherds. Type versus modal analysis of pottery has a long history of debate in American archaeology, but without going into this, it is obvious we came down on the "type" side in our Georgia deliberations of the 1930s. A conference, held at the University of Michigan in the spring of 1938, in which Ford and James B. Griffin were among the principals, formalized and further systematized these procedures for the Southeast. As a result, ceramic type descriptions from Macon, as well as the several other federal relief or TVA financed archaeological projects in the southeastern United States, were soon being published in a new journal, *The Newsletter of the Southeastern Archaeological Conference.*

Besides continuing with the stratigraphic survey, as well as spending a good bit of time classifying my sherds in a CCC lab, I was permitted to travel around the Southeast in the fall and winter of 1937–38. These trips were made at my own expense, although Dr. Kelly kindly allowed me to take leave from the digging in central Georgia. I visited Ford in Baton Rouge, Louisiana, and looked over his ceramic collections. I also went with him to Knoxville, Tennessee, to meet W. S. Webb and T. M. N. Lewis, archaeologists who had been working in the Tennessee Valley. In addition to these trips, I was a frequent visitor to the Georgia coast to see Preston Holder's new operation at the Irene Mound on the outskirts of Savannah.

Holder and I made a number of trips to look at sites in south Georgia. I recall some of these quite vividly. Holder, a Nebraskan who had gone to the University of California at Berkeley to study anthropology, was an unusually vital character. We stopped one day for lunch in a small, interior Georgia town. I should note that, in those days at least, restaurant food in small Georgia towns was usually pretty good if you were right out on the coast, but if one went inland, the picture changed rapidly. We entered a typical restaurant in the pine barrens country. There was a lunch counter along the length of the room on one side and tables and chairs on the other. On the counter was the inevitable glass bell covering a partially cut lemon meringue pie on a pedestal plate. A surfeited fly moved lazily within the bell. A waitress was behind the counter, in hushed conversation with the only customer. This was a burly man with a toothpick firmly clenched in his teeth, an apparent testimony that he had been served before enjoying a postprandial tête-à-tête with the lady of the house. Holder and I strode in, khaki-clad and booted, a costume that suggested a "Government Man," possibly even a revenue agent. But the patron with the toothpick

and the waitress seemed unsuspicious enough as we took stools at the counter.

Holder, who was two stools down from the man, started up a conversation with him. This was to find out about local Indian sites, although Holder, who was much more outgoing than I, liked to talk to strangers about anything. I suppose I was secretly relieved, because this conversation ought to establish our *bona fides* as nonrevenue agents. The man responded in a friendly way, telling us about "some old Indian places" that were close by; and then he said that he had just been "up at Macon where them government fellers there had done hollered-out an Indian mound." Had we anything to do with that? After a moment's bafflement, I realized he meant the Council Chamber. After it had been finally restored, with a steel and concrete shell over it, the whole had been covered over with earth and sodded. It now looked from the outside like a very high, rounded mound—and quite logically, an Indian mound, given its setting. As I had had a hand in taking the charred beams out of the Council Chamber, I felt that I had in a small way helped "holler it out," so I pitched in, pedantically, and began to explain that we really hadn't "hollowed out" an Indian mound, that there were not such large chambers within the Indian mounds, that this was a partial restoration, and so forth. Holder also entered in these archaeological disquisitions, but our new friend remained unconvinced. His imagination obviously had been captured by what he had seen at Macon. He was convinced that there "were big rooms down inside all them there mounds" and that we should set about finding them just like "them fellers at Macon."

By this time, the waitress had brought us glasses of water and menus and was waiting for our order. I chose the roast beef lunch. While roast beef in such an establishment was always thin-sliced, dark brown, and overcooked, I had found it the best available accompaniment to the regimen of hashed browns, turnip greens, and black-eyed peas. "Country Ham" was the alternative listed on the menu, and Holder—I thought at the time unwisely—chose that. In due course our plates appeared. Mine looked like I thought it would. Holder's came as a surprise to him. Instead of a nice, red slice of cured ham—the only kind of ham he knew about—it was roast pork. He called the waitress over and said that he had ordered ham and that this, on the plate, was not ham. An argument ensued, heating up as it went along, until the waitress said, in no uncertain terms, "If that ain't ham then you ain't no man!" Holder responded with an equally insulting retort. Our burly companion at the counter, now aroused from his reveries of secret and mysterious chambers within the dark depths of unexplored Indian mounds by this noisy contretemps, volubly took the side of the waitress in the argument. Perhaps she was a girlfriend to whom he owed a chivalric allegiance, or perhaps he was getting damned tired of Damned Yankees who were so damned know-it-all and didn't even know what a piece of good Georgia country ham looked like! Suffice it to say, with all this shouting I was getting pretty uneasy. I somehow got the check from the waitress, paid it, and edged us out into the street, although as we departed Holder and the waitress, backed by her champion, continued to exchange insults even as the door closed behind us. Archaeological survey can be difficult at times.

I think it was late in 1937, or very early in 1938, that Dr. Kelly was promoted from superintendent of the CCC camp to superintendent of Ocmulgee National Monument. With this shift he became a fully fledged National Park Service employee. A few months afterward, sometime in the early summer of 1938, he was designated to be the chief archaeologist of the National Park Service, a newly created post in that organization. This meant that he and his family would have to move to Washington in a very short time. While I was glad and proud for him, I was also distressed at the news. Both Dr. and Mrs. Kelly had treated me almost like a member of the family since that first day on the front porch at Laurel Street. I had been a frequent guest at their house over the next year-and-a-half. I would miss him. I was fortunate, however, as was Ocmulgee and the whole Macon archaeological endeavor, in the selection of Dr. Kelly's successor as monument superintendent. This was Jesse D. Jennings, an archaeologist with previous field experience in both the Southwest and Southeast, as well as Guatemala. He and his wife, Jane, and I became good friends.

To shift to still more personal things in this narrative, I should explain that it was not until my second year in Macon that I began to meet many people in Macon outside of my own field or those who, like General Harris, Dr. Harrold, or Linton Solomon, were in some way involved with it. But in the fall of 1937, I was fortunate to be introduced to a young architect, James Stakely, and through him I met other young professional and businessmen in the city. And it was through this group of new friends that I met an older Macon businessman, Claude Lambert Whaley. I was immediately attracted to him by his sympathetic intelligence, good humor, and, I suppose, parental qualities. After all, I was only 24 years old, but then little did I know that he would soon stand in real parental status to me. Mr. Whaley was a widower, and he used to invite some of our younger group to his house for Sunday night suppers. Early in 1938, his daughter, Katharine, returned from New York City, where she had been studying for over a year at the Art Student's League. We met one night at the Macon Little Theater, through mutual friends. Both of us were in the audience, not on the stage; however, I should mention in passing, for any archaeological reader, that Jess Jennings once starred

there as the eccentric grandfather in *You Can't Take It with You*. To return to the more interesting theme of Katharine Whaley, I subsequently saw her at her father's Sunday evening suppers, and then I saw her as often as I could.

In the summer of 1938, as I was winding up the Central Georgia Stratigraphic Survey, Jim Ford invited me to come to Louisiana and become the head of his WPA archaeological laboratory in New Orleans. I had always been dazzled by Jim's force and brilliance. This was an opportunity to work with him and to learn something about another southeastern archaeological region. My long-term objective, of course, was to go back to graduate school, not at Arizona, which had no anthropological Ph.D. program then, but somewhere else. I had applied at a number of places for fall admission in both 1937 and 1938 but had been unsuccessful. In the summer of 1938 I wanted to do two things: marry Katharine Whaley and go to graduate school and get a doctorate—in that order. Katharine consented to marry me, and shortly after, I accepted Ford's offer to go to Louisiana. We would be married in Katharine's mother's old hometown, Selma, Alabama, that September. Afterward, we would set up our first household in New Orleans. Jess Jennings, despite the fact that I was forsaking him to go to Louisiana, agreed to be my best man. I left Macon and Ocmulgee on September 15, 1938, and Katharine and I were married on September 17. A few days after that, we were in New Orleans.

Although my departure from Macon marked the end of my personal involvement with its archaeology, Ocmulgee and Macon archaeology continued with strength. Jess Jennings, in spite of administrative duties as monument superintendent, pursued work there, and Charles H. Fairbanks, who arrived on the day I left to supplant me as senior foreman archaeologist, has been the one responsible for publishing the site's single most important monograph (Fairbanks 1956a).

But my departure from Macon in September 1938 did mark a very important point in my life. I look back upon Macon as the place where I came of age—professionally and emotionally. The memories that I associate with those years of 1936 to 1938 strike very deep and close. I think—at least I hope—that I have conveyed some of this in what I have written here. Viewed on a larger scale, or from a less personal perspective, the early Macon excavations of the 1930s were a landmark operation for the archaeological profession in the United States. What was discovered there is an important part of this land's prehistoric past, and the way these discoveries were made, whatever the mistakes or shortcomings of the moment, is an equally important part of the history of the archaeological discipline. I am happy to have been a part of it.

CHAPTER FOUR

Macon Daze

Jesse D. Jennings

THE PAPERS THAT were presented at the conference commemorating the fiftieth anniversary of the founding of Ocmulgee National Monument were well-conceived, high-level contributions on a variety of issues germane to the study of southeastern prehistory. My remarks that follow are of a different, less exalted genre. What I offer are entirely personal reminiscences of the busiest and most rewarding year of my life up to that time. Returning to Macon after almost 50 years flooded my mind with events and incidents of pleasure and frustration in what I can only describe as a maelstrom of confused memories. I felt exactly as I did those first chaotic few weeks there in 1938—disoriented and adrift; hence my title, "Macon Daze." I will try to show what I mean as I go along.

As I listened to the papers presented at the conference, I became aware that Ocmulgee was not only important to the people of Macon, Bibb County, and Georgia, but that it also provided yeast for a regional archaeological ferment not yet over. So I see this as an anniversary in more than one sense. It denotes half a century of archaeological progress that has delighted me; I wish I had had a larger part of it. In fact, I judge that southeastern archaeologists have made more progress in the past fifty years toward learning the prehistory of their region than anywhere else during that same period.

My role at Ocmulgee National Monument was to some degree archaeological, of course, but archaeology was secondary. My mission there was to establish not an *archaeological* presence but a *National Park Service* presence. I was, of course, fascinated by the archaeological record, but my role was to *protect*, *preserve*, and *interpret*—the three National Park Service (NPS) missions—not to extend the archaeological research.

What I will say in this chapter dwells on the highly personal story of creating a National Park Service image. I will only touch on my few archaeological efforts. I must emphasize the spotty quality of what I recall. The history I relate will be "remembered" fact, somewhat different from the godstrewth.

Now, here is how I remember it: I was new with the National Park Service, having been for about eight months stationed at Montezuma Castle near Camp Verde, Arizona, when we were transferred to Macon—this was in April 1938—where I was to be acting superintendent of Ocmulgee National Monument. As acting superintendent I was also the first *bona fide* National Park Service person assigned to the Ocmulgee area. I came complete with civil service status and "vast" (eight months) experience. Arthur Kelly had been acting superintendent before me. Kelly may have met me the first day at the Monument, but I am not sure. I do remember my first impression that no one was in charge. I was totally bewildered. There was a large work force: a 200-man CCC camp and a 200-man WPA force. None of the CCC staff was an archaeologist, a historian, or what you might call academically oriented, except Gordon Willey, whom I welcomed as a new colleague. For WPA, there had been only Kelly. I promptly fell into a profound depression, which I can only describe as a near-complete paralysis of mind and body. But I knew enough to know that development of the physical side of things was my task. It was clear that I had come into a chaotic mare's nest of misdirection, indirection, and indecision, and I felt swamped. My wife, Jane, however, recalls that during those first traumatic weeks I slept like a baby. It turns out that she meant I'd sleep a couple of hours, wake up, and sob for a while (my apologies to Pepper Martin, who used the analogy first).

Except for those I met in the restroom, of all the people I met that first week I felt that only one knew what he was doing. He was a CCC enrollee of about 18 or 19 who was the clerk for the Monument—the office was then in the old Dunlap House. That young man knew his work; he knew the Park Service paperwork, his files were in good order, and he seemed to me both stable and dependable. I came to trust his judgment. I think his name was Jacobs. Then, after about a week, a big man named Woodward (he pronounced it Wood'ard) walked into my office. He was a CCC inspector out of the Atlanta office, and very unhappy with our CCC camp. He talked a great deal about its shortcomings and seemed to be holding me accountable for all that was wrong around me.

I am deeply in his debt. He told me flatly that I was "The Boss." All that the Monument needed, he said, was action—any kind of movement, a source of clear-cut, simple instructions. Particularly needed was someone who would take responsibility and make decisions. There was confusion about the role of the WPA and the CCC, but there wasn't much overlap. But no one understood the NPS or its goals. Wood'ard simply told me to take charge. In my innocence and ignorance, I believed that I could. Accordingly, I began to confer with the older members of the CCC supervisory force, the few who had work experience. Many of the politically appointed foremen were inexperienced youths, so I ignored them. Based on my evaluation of the advice I got I did take action. And, of course, Wood'ard was right: everyone was delighted to be told unequivocally to do this or do that or not to do this or that. Except for one or two individuals at the CCC foreman level, I enjoyed one hundred percent support.

Those first two or three weeks were long days of deepening frustration, but then Herbert E. Kahler, the coordinating superintendent of the Southeastern Monuments, came to Macon. There were two or three historical monuments, as well as Ocmulgee, in the Southeast. Kahler was stationed at St. Augustine, where he was also the superintendent of Fort Marion. He had come to offer advice, sympathy, or whatever I needed. Without Kahler's encouragement and support, combined with his composure and calm, unflurried approach to any problem, I probably would not have survived that year at Ocmulgee; his stabilizing influence kept me sane. I don't recall that he was ever critical. He made casual suggestions to which I listened carefully. My affection and respect for him continue to this day.

Kahler did me a second great favor: he talked to me about the past problems of administering the Monument, that it was an eyesore and a source of annoyance throughout the entire Region One and said to me, "Just don't bother me. Don't call me every time you have a little problem. Do something about it." He further gave me instructions not to embarrass the National Park Service and not to antagonize the local backers of the project, men I had met earlier. Their names were C. C. Harrold, Walter Harris, and Lint Solomon. They were politically powerful men who had been able to get archaeological work started

at Ocmulgee. They were the driving force behind the establishment of the Monument 50 years ago, and they had strong opinions on everything related to Ocmulgee.

When I arrived, physical development, as planned and approved by the regional office, was underway. But the resources offered at the Monument for public enjoyment were limited. There was an approved road, not always in the best of condition, then being constructed. There was an approved museum plan which I thought then and believe today is the least appropriate museum structure I have ever seen. It has now been modified and improved. But the Council Chamber had been reconstructed within its concrete dome and was a most impressive display, as it still is.

As for my functioning as superintendent, I systematized things as best I could in both construction and archaeology. I conferred often with three people: Tom Winchester, an accomplished engineer and the work superintendent of the CCC camp; Frank Lester, one of the CCC foremen; and Reaville Brown, a tough engineer with largely South American railroad experience who was superintendent for the continued construction of the museum building. They were supportive and generous with their experience. Practices I initiated because of wasteful procedures I had perceived permitted me to have things operating more smoothly and toward a series of unified goals within perhaps a month or two.

So far as archaeology is concerned, the laboratory was operating when I arrived. The materials from the Macon Plateau were still being processed in the basement of the museum. By then Kelly had been called to Washington, but there was some kind of undirected piddling excavation program on the Macon Plateau under a man named Jackson—a local artist who had been trained by Kelly. The objective of the excavation was never clear to me, so I closed it. There was a mobile CCC crew doing what he called "strati-tests" over half of south-central Georgia under Gordon Willey. There was no other archaeology going on. The fact is that it looked neither like an archaeological project, nor a National Park Monument; construction scars and construction activity with raw earth exposed were nearly everywhere. There was not even a decent trail to get from the temporary parking area over to the Council Chamber. At once, I gave a training course for a large WPA guide force. I gave them some rudimentary archaeological concepts and tried to pass on the things I had learned about dealing with the public as an interpreter while I had been a ranger at Montezuma Castle.

I don't know what I should list as accomplishments while I was here. Incidental to construction, we did a small Lamar site excavation, which I reported. That project provided the first "stratified" evidence that Macon Plateau ceramics were older than those at Lamar. I was also able to discover that the site was built on an island in a swamp and had been completely palisaded. Jackson was the supervisor on the dig. I was there daily and set the full strategy of the research. I am proud of that work and the report.

At the same time the Museum construction was resumed; roads were pretty much finished with gravel surfaces. The Mound C shelter had already been designed and was being built. I tried to prevent the erection of the shelter. I thought it was a bad idea. It has long since been taken down, I'm glad to know. With Jane's help and advice, we built a nature trail. It was possible for her to make these recommendations and suggestions about the trail because she had volunteered to conduct a one-year bird census and banding program on the Monument. As a result of the bird-banding program, she knew every inch of the area. Her records of that census may well be somewhere in the files even today. She designed a very effective round trip that came out about where it started. I think it was about a half a mile in length. It proved popular and got quite a bit of use. I understand it is still maintained and used today, now called Opelafa Trail. Mound A was eroding badly where people climbed to the top. We repaired the erosion and erected a sturdy wooden stairway to facilitate access to the summit. The stairway, of course, was used. And I suppose we did other things. I don't recall.

I do recall situations I had never faced before that had to be dealt with. One that had me badly stymied was a request from a local splinter group of a well-known cult. An earnest young man came to me announcing that I was to close the Monument for 24 hours on Saturday so his group could have a great spiritual experience. They wished to camp on Mound A, praying the night through and then on Sunday greet the dawn with songs and rejoicing. "Why?" I asked. It transpired that the American Indians were central to their beliefs and that Mound A was for them also a hallowed place, and they wished to express their religious ecstasy there. I panicked. How important were their members? Crackpots or influential citizens? Did I dare refuse? Moreover, the problem was exacerbated by the regulations I had promulgated, one of which was: Close the gates at five o'clock in the afternoon and open them at eight in the morning to reduce the Monument's role as a local lovers' lane. After stalling while I frantically thought about what to do, I slowly negotiated a low-lying field as the camp site, using the mound for the rites and for the celebrants to be gone by opening time on Sunday. And I would have the gates on the back entrance open from six to eight on Saturday evening. On Friday it began to rain; it continued through Saturday, and the field of red clay became a quagmire and the rain continued all night Saturday into Sunday. No one showed up! Their fervor didn't include camping and

praying in the rain. Not all the unusual incidents were so amusing.

I should mention my experiences with the three new friends who had initiated the Macon project. Dr. C. C. Harrold was a cancer specialist; General Walter Harris an attorney and counsel for the Southern Railroad; and Lint Solomon a farmer/dairyman. The three had grown up and gone to school together. But in addition to a lifelong companionship, they shared an inordinate interest in Georgia history, Georgia natural history, and the Indian lore of the Southeast. Walter Harris was an authority on Georgia and the Creek tribes. It was, I believe, Harrold who was more concerned with natural history, and Solomon was the worst Indian relic buff of the three. After we had had a few rather tense sessions, during which they gently but firmly explained to me how they wanted things to go at the Monument, and I, no doubt somewhat *less* diplomatically, established my position (based on my long association) as "The Authority" on Park Service matters. Occasionally and slowly they came to understand that I was consistent, that I would do nothing that fell below my interpretation of Park Service standards. They also came to realize that we wanted the same things, and our relationships became much more cordial. After I had gained their confidence, they began inviting me on their monthly or semimonthly Thursday junkets. For years, they had apparently been traveling over Georgia to look at things: things as simple as one pictograph on a rock east of Atlanta or an acre of wildflowers down near Savannah or the site of the Coosa Village, wherever that was, and they invited me on many of these trips.

Since I had never seen any of these features or points of interest, they took me to the places they liked best. The expeditions would begin about 8:30. Dr. Harrold had a proper doctor's car—a heavy Buick sedan; Lint Solomon drove it fast but with great skill. Harrold and I sat in the back, General Harris and Lint sat in the front, and all three of them took turns telling me what we were seeing and why I should appreciate it. But an equally important part of those expeditions was the Shandygaff. As near as I can tell, Shandygaff is half white port and half moonshine, rye, or bourbon whisky with a dollop, I'm sure, of dynamite. These ingredients would be combined in a gallon thermos jug that had ice in it, and as soon as we were well out of Macon, say about 8:45, Lint would pull off the road, break out some Dixie cups, and we would all have a drink. They advised me, I recall, to lean against the trunk of a pine tree upon the first occasion. I asked why and they said, "Well, if you've never had this, you'll need some support for that first drink." By mid-afternoon, we had generally emptied the thermos jug. They had prodigious capacities for that vile stuff. I never equaled, and I certainly never surpassed, them. What with whatever thing we saw, the Shandygaff, and their incredible stories (all three were accomplished raconteurs), the day went fast. Time after time, we made our carefree return to Macon in the late afternoon. Mrs. Wilson, from whom we rented a small apartment, commented to Jane after a few trips that I certainly enjoyed those three men because I always came home so happy, relaxed, laughing, and enjoying life. Indeed I did, although I didn't always recall getting home.

Other things I remember were the dubious pleasures of being a pioneer in a hostile land. I was the only archaeologist in the Park Service east of the Mississippi River at that time. That meant that anything having to do with archaeology was not only not understood, but it was also neither appreciated nor taken seriously. That situation left me in constant conflict with the stream of supervisory Region One office personnel that came through saying we would do this and that. Usually it was something that jeopardized the integrity of the archaeological reasons for the preserve. A word about the regional office people at Richmond is appropriate. Almost none of them, except the regional director, had previous National Park Service experience. The staff had been assembled by hiring State Park people, because they at least had experience in the East. Even the National Park Service presence east of the Mississippi River was new, having come only in 1934 when Roosevelt transferred all the military parks (against the army's wishes) to the National Park Service. There hadn't even been a history branch until then.

So I was dealing with architects, clerks, engineers, landscape architects, and administrators who knew nothing of archaeology and but little about the National Park Service traditions of preservation, protection, and interpretation. However, Kahler, my coordinating superintendent, and Ronald Lee, assistant chief of historic sites in the Washington office, were both trained historians. They at least understood my position and helped with the regional problems. And I must say that I enjoyed outmaneuvering and outlasting the regional office personnel. Rather than argue all the time, I began conceiving and carrying on projects that the regional office knew nothing of. One was the nature trail I mentioned earlier. Another was the Palisade around the Plateau, which I built after I had read Kelly's account of the "pit houses" on the Macon Plateau that ran for hundreds of yards. I couldn't accept those as houses. I went to the lab and looked at the cross sections that Jackson, the artist, had created and read Kelly's notes. The sections were well-drawn and well-labeled, and it became very evident to me that the fill in those endless pit houses was nothing more than normal deposits to be expected from the disposal of trash and the erosion of a tall embankment on the west and north sides of the long trench. I reasoned that they were not pit houses but the trenches created when an earthen fortification, topped with a wooden palisade, was built. The Indians had dropped their garbage in the ditch and upon site abandonment, the embankment in which the palisade logs had been erected had eroded slowly into the trench until the surface of the Plateau was level. Without regional office knowledge, I rebuilt quite a long segment of the embankment that had originally encircled the Plateau and sodded it with Bermuda grass as well as the section of trench beside it. There was considerable consternation when some inspector noticed the completed but unauthorized project. By then, the "damage" was done and the embankment-ditch remained as part of the interpretive scheme. I'm afraid that I may have broken many fiscal rules and continuously ignored the chain of command. But we did accomplish a great deal.

We experienced many personal satisfactions in Macon. Gordon Willey would frequently visit us in the evening. Robert Wauchope, then at the University of Georgia in Athens, would drop down occasionally on weekends for conversation and Scotch. Willey, when he dropped by, often brought his own Scotch. We became briefly involved in the little theater movement in Macon. There I met a lot of very fine young people and established a reputation as the least talented actor ever to grace the Macon stage. About halfway through our period at Ocmulgee, Willey, over my protests and advice, left Ocmulgee to work with Jim Ford as director of the New Orleans laboratory that Ford had established as part of his ongoing WPA program there. I regretted Willey's failure to heed my advice because I needed his help.

After Willey left, we got Chuck Fairbanks as his replacement. Rather than have him continue the strati-tests, I put him in charge of the laboratory because I wanted someone with a modicum of archaeological background to be in charge. I told him to learn the artifacts and read the notes. Additionally, I assigned him (I think it was) ten hours a week to read all Georgia history and Indian history. What he did with that period of self-improvement is known to all of you. He became a well-known and respected southeastern archaeologist with particular interest in the protohistoric and historic periods.

I had hoped to help create the museum, but I was transferred out of administration to a research position at the Natchez Trace Parkway. You can imagine my excitement when in 1950 I was invited to come to Washington and prepare—based on my previous experience and thinking about it—a museum plan that was to be constructed under Fairbanks's supervision. I turned out a plan that I submitted complete with stick-figure illustrations and labels. It seems to have been followed rather closely in the creation of the first museum exhibits. Today's new displays are more effective, though.

I imagine I have left out many things perhaps more interesting than those I have included. Regardless of that, it has been an extreme pleasure for Jane and me to talk once again about our time here and remember the many fine things that happened.

CHAPTER FIVE

Early and Later Archaeology of the Ocmulgee National Monument Area

James B. Griffin

T HE EXCAVATIONS at and near Macon, Georgia, in the 1930s and early 1940s were among the most important of those conducted with relief labor and with the financial support of the federal government. Instigation of this program came about through the efforts of a group of Macon citizens who requested the aid of the Smithsonian Institution in the 1920s to preserve and investigate the prehistoric and early historic remains in the Macon area. At that time the local people had no idea of the extent, time depth, and complexity of the aboriginal remains, and neither did the archaeologists who came to supervise the work in late 1933.

One of the largest states, Georgia had not been a prime area of archaeological research in the latter half of the nineteenth century or the first quarter of the twentieth century. Clarence B. Moore had excavated along the Gulf Coast and up some of the major river valleys. The Bureau of American Ethnology mound survey had obtained remarkable results at the Etowah Mounds near Cartersville, and at Hollywood Mounds a short distance south of Augusta. In northeast Georgia, the Nacoochee Mound in White County near Clarkesville and on the headwaters of the Chattahoochee River, was excavated

by a joint Heye Foundation and Bureau of American Ethnology party in 1915. The Stalling's Island site a short distance north of Augusta was partially excavated in the late 1920s by the Peabody Museum, and a report was published shortly before the Macon excavations began (Claflin 1931). W. K. Moorehead had resalvaged the Etowah site in 1925, but a report was not available until six years later (Moorehead 1932). The only adequate attempt at wide regional coverage of Georgia was in the admirable compilations of C. C. Jones in the 1860s to 1880s with *Antiquities of the Southern Indians* as his major work (Jones 1873).

A year before the Macon relief labor program began, the National Research Council Committee on State Archaeological Surveys held a "Conference on Southern Pre-history" in Birmingham, Alabama, in late December 1932. Neither an individual nor an institution appeared at this meeting from Georgia; and while passing reference was made to Etowah and Macon mounds by M. W. Stirling in his talk on the prehistoric southern Indians, it is fair to say that Georgia archaeology was barely represented in that survey of the South. The major emphasis was on real or imagined migrations of historic tribes from their myths or oral tribal legends, place names, and early European historic references. Sites were identified to a particular tribal group by picking up a few potsherds apparently, or by a forked rod. The Smithsonian representatives emphasized a methodology of working from the known historic tribal culture back into the prehistoric past. At this conference there were few references to stratigraphy or chronology, and as Stirling (1932) said, "The problem of ancient man in the Southeast is one which had best be avoided at this time." Any archaeologist dissatisfied with the advance of knowledge in the last ten years should read this report of December 1932.

As a result of the activities outlined by Walker (Chapter 2, this volume), A. R. Kelly and James A. Ford arrived in Macon in December 1933. Kelly was aware of the cultural sequence in Illinois worked out by various individuals and the University of Chicago and which was well established in 1932 (Griffin 1976:20, 1985b:3). He also had some familiarity with the early and late Mississippian pottery, now called Stirling and Moorehead at Cahokia, and the Mississippian material from the Spoon River in Illinois. Ford had participated with Setzler in the country's first relief labor program at the Marksville site and had worked as an assistant to Moreau Chambers in

Mississippi for the Mississippi Department of Archives and History and under the tutelage of Henry Collins. Ford's participation in the first few years of the Macon program was a major factor in the important results that were obtained, even though some of his interpretations were not supported over the years. The six students supported during the summer of 1936 by the Laboratory of Anthropology in Santa Fe were valuable, as was the presence of Jennings and Fairbanks in 1938. The latter two were active members of the Southeastern Archeological Conference and prepared the pottery type descriptions that appeared in the newsletter of that organization in 1939 and 1940.

There were difficulties in conducting the excavation project and the surveys of archaeological resources in the Macon area, and those between Columbus and Savannah. Many of these were inherent in the relief labor administrations over the years, and others were from the lack of experience of the professional personnel. Kelly (1935b) published a number of short papers in *Scientific American*, but his summary of the first three years' work appeared in 1938 as Anthropological Paper No. 1, in *Bulletin 119* of the Bureau of American Ethnology (Kelly 1938c). This paper I regarded as difficult to understand when it appeared, and subsequent rereadings have not rendered it more intelligible. I presume it accurately reflects the author's interpretation of the relationships of the materials that had been obtained within Bibb County and from the sites across middle Georgia.

Fairly early in the archaeological works the earlier proposed occupation by Creek Indians and the presence of a trading post was confirmed and dated to around A.D. 1700. The preceding Lamar complex was recognized as similar to what was found at the Bull Creek site near Columbus, where the excavations of Frank Lester, one of Kelly's assistants at Macon, and Isabel Patterson were conducted in 1936. On at least two separate occasions L. H. Binford (1930–   ) has stated that he excavated or helped excavate the two negative painted dog effigy water bottles found at that site in 1936. The interpretation of the Lamar complex was that it was pre–De Soto, that many features resembled materials studied by J. A. Ford in Louisiana and Mississippi, that it represented the second movement of mound building societies from the Mississippi River, and that Lamar represented the legendary migration of Muskogean Kawita and Kasihta tribes. The indications of some continuity from Lamar to Ocmulgee Fields in the pottery complex, in spite of a pronounced shift from grit to shell temper, fit the interpretation that Ocmulgee Fields was early eighteenth-century Creek.

One of the perplexing problems of the Macon area was the considerable variety of paddle stamped pottery, ranging from simple linear impressions to intricate curvilinear and rectilinear patterns of stamps of varying sizes, and other features. It was further recognized that

some of the stamped styles seemed to represent different time periods and specific locations. One of these was called Swift Creek, from a location south of Macon Plateau on a small eastern tributary of the Ocmulgee River. At the time of the preparation of the 1938 report, the interpretation of Swift Creek was somewhat confused. It was believed to have lasted long enough to identify early, middle and late Swift Creek pottery. On his chart illustrating the "tentative chronology implications" of various ceramic complexes recognized in the Macon area, Kelly (1938c: figure 7) placed Swift Creek later than the "Macon Plateau Mound Building Period" (Macon Plateau phase) and before the "Lamar Mound Building Period" (Lamar phase). It was, however, recognized that there was no indication of a gradual shift from Swift Creek to Lamar stamped styles. It was also thought that the fiber-tempered pottery at Macon was a part of Early Swift Creek along with steatite bowl fragments and cord-marked pottery, footed vessels, simple stamping, and fabric impressions.

The major excavations from early 1934 to 1938, however, were on Macon Plateau on the platform mounds, the Macon Earth Lodge, the so-called prehistoric dugouts or pit houses and other evidence of a Mississippian culture presence. After W. S. Webb visited Macon Plateau with T. M. N. Lewis in the summer of 1934, he wrote Kelly that the houses at Macon Plateau were what he was calling "the small-log town house" in the Norris Basin (Webb 1938:366–70). It was immediately apparent from my examination at Macon in early 1936 that Macon Plateau pottery was very close to the small-log town house ceramic complex in the Norris Basin that had been the subject of my doctoral dissertation, and I told Kelly that was the case (Griffin 1938). For reasons I never ascertained, Kelly did not accept Webb's or my identification of cultural relationships. He recognized the Macon Plateau mound building activity and the Brown's Mount site as representative of an older prehistoric level in central Georgia and that they show many features similar to known complexes in the Mississippi Valley and woodland section of the northeastern United States. This was the earliest cultural movement from the Mississippi (Kelly 1938c:62). He did not liken Macon Plateau culture to Cahokia, as has been asserted (Waring and Holder 1945). Nor did he say that the Indians of the early Mississippian complex that were buried at Macon were born on the banks of the Father of Waters. He was not sure whether the mound building activity was a "natural cultural evolution as a continuous process or whether we have to do with an influx of new ideas coming from the Mississippi without marked cultural changes" (Waring and Holder 1945). Kelly and the other early participants in the Macon explorations were in agreement on the intrusive nature of the first agricultural Mississippian culture. It was Ford, abetted by Willey, who referred to Cahokia Old Village and the Aztlan (*sic*) site as Early Middle Mississippi (Ford and Willey 1941:350).

They identified the area between Memphis and Cairo as the source for the rapid movement of Mississippian people from the Tennessee Valley into central Georgia and regarded it as the early movement of the Muskogean people into central Georgia. Discussions of this general problem have been ably summarized recently by Smith (1984), who took the position that adequate research in the central Georgia area should produce evidence of a gradual shift of Late Woodland complicated stamp societies into "Emergent" Mississippian societies and that this *in situ* development would lead to Macon Plateau. This view has also been adopted by Schroedel (Chapter 13, this volume) who also recognizes the close relationship of Macon Plateau with early Hiwassee Island Mississippian. However, Mark Williams (Chapter 11, this volume) and his associates in the Macon area in the last several years have been as unsuccessful as Kelly, Ford, Willey, Jennings, Fairbanks, Sears, et al., in finding any evidence of an *in situ* development.

The only adequate presentation of the Macon Plateau complex was by Charles H. Fairbanks (1956a), which was largely prepared between the late 1940s and the early 1950s. He dealt with Mound C, the Funeral Mound, and concluded the Macon Plateau complex was the result of rapid invasion of Georgia from the west. Hiwassee Island and the Norris Basin small-log town house complexes, while closely related, were slightly later in time. They had full corn agriculture with 8- and 10-row corn and a complex politico-religious organization, as indicated by the platform mounds, large towns, fortifications, status symbols of certain male burials, and a large population. Fairbanks's doctoral dissertation was accepted in 1954 at the University of Michigan but was not published for two years.

My views of the late 1930s were that the Macon Plateau complex was an intrusive group from the west and was early Mississippian on about the same time level as Cahokia Old Village, but that they were not closely connected culturally. I was able to add in 1940–41 that the Central Mississippi Archaeological Survey, as the Phillips, Ford, and Griffin survey was then called, had not found the ancestor of Macon Plateau in eastern Arkansas or northwestern Mississippi (Griffin 1946:79).

The excavations at Macon Plateau obtained a considerable number of flint implements that were heavily patinated and decayed flint scraps. These were found below pottery-producing levels and in isolated locations interpreted as flint-knapping sites. Kelly hoped that a study of the thickness of the patination might show chronological differences. These materials are most likely the remains of one or more Archaic period societies. One fluted point was found, but an early Paleoindian lithic complex was not identified (Kelly 1938c:7).

A number of indications have been given of the attempts to integrate the Macon area discoveries into the framework of southern prehistory. W. S. Webb did not incorporate them into his major monographs, and Lewis and Kneberg referred primarily to the pottery types that had been described by Jennings and Fairbanks in the Southeastern Archaeological Conference newsletter. Kelly's work, however, appeared to justify the strong support given by the Macon community under the leadership of Harrold, Harris, and Solomon. It enabled them to gain congressional sponsorship from Carl Vinson and Richard B. Russell to establish the Ocmulgee site as the first national monument of an archaeological nature in the eastern United States in 1936. The current museum building and appearance of the Monument is perhaps the most lasting result of the archaeological work. Continuing recognition of the Macon area as a major center of prehistoric and historic Indian activity has been aided by the diligent participation of some of its citizens and their Ocmulgee National Monument Association.

The cultural sequence at Macon as expressed in ceramic complexes was incorporated into the southeastern cultural chronology at the Birmingham conference of 1938 and formed the eastern anchor of the chronology. This data was inserted by Jennings, Fairbanks, and Willey, for they were better interpreters of Macon area prehistory than Kelly. By this interaction of the young archaeologists from Georgia to Texas and from Louisiana to Kentucky and Illinois, the sequence of development in the Southeast from Archaic to the historic period was made known to all of the workers. Representative and oddball artifacts were brought to many of the Southeastern Archaeological Conferences so that others could see, compare, and inform.

At the conference commemorating the fiftieth anniversary of the establishment of Ocmulgee National Monument, the participants heard a series of papers, which are a great improvement over the information about Macon and its environs that was available when the Monument was dedicated. This is very true of the paper by Anderson and others on the Paleoindian and Early Archaic because of the great increase of data from the Georgia area on occupations that were essentially unknown when Kelly's report was written in 1937. It is unfortunate that there was no conference paper on the Late Archaic and early fiber-tempered ceramic complex that appear shortly before 2000 B.C. in the Savannah area and then spread inland, reaching the Macon area at least 500 or so years later. There was also a gap in the papers for Early Woodland and the first appearance of paddle stamping, such as Vining Simple Stamped (now dated to the Early Mississippi period [Elliot and Wynn 1991]) and Dunlap Fabric Impressed, and the associated material culture of which that pottery was a part.

Jefferies's paper reminds us that while there were flat-top mounds in Georgia and the Southeast before Mississippian times, none of them were erected as substructures for council or charnel houses. Unanswered questions that need to be addressed are: What happened to the Swift Creek–Napier societies between A.D. 700 and A.D. 1100? Are they related to the later Woodstock and early Etowah societies?

Larson's presentation of the basic data, which has been used to promote the presence of earth lodges in the Southeast, should cause others to question whether these structures really existed in the Southeast. On the other hand, the interpretation of the ridged fields as corn rows is still a moot proposal, even though similar constructs have been found or suggested for other areas, notably in the Midwest. The unfortunate absence of maize detritus, of carelessly left hoes or hoe flakes, and the hundreds of excavated Mississippian sites without evidence of such tillage practices are questions that need answers.

While A. R. Kelly's thesis was prepared under direction of E. A. Hooton, it unfortunately was not based on human skeletal material but on Hooton's attempt to determine if there were physical characteristics of criminals, at least those incarcerated in Massachusetts, that would distinguish them from "normal" or uncaught members of society. Thus we have the sad observations of M. L. Powell, who found in her examination of the Smithsonian collection of human skeletal material from Macon that a combination of soil conditions, poor excavation, and careless curation techniques made any adequate understanding of either the prehistoric or historic period populations almost impossible. This is all the more regrettable because the Funeral Mound might have provided evidence of the amount of maize in the diet and of anatomical characteristics bearing on whether Macon Plateau culture was introduced by a somewhat different group of Indians than earlier occupants of the Macon area.

One of the reasons why researchers were involved with the question: Who and from where did the Macon Plateau complex originate? is that migration legends of the Creek had been known for some time, and John R. Swanton had embraced them. Swanton's endorsement gave the stories that they had arrived from the west almost the status of holy scripture, and he also was a part of the emphasis

by the Smithsonian archaeologists that an archaeologist should begin his research by identifying the material culture of a given native group at the early white contact period and then trace that complex farther and farther back in time. Swanton was also the chief investigator for the government for the identification of the route of the Spanish expedition to the southeastern United States led by Hernando de Soto. Identification of the route and locations of Indian towns, villages, and proveniences by the De Soto Commission of 1939 was handicapped by the inadequate knowledge of the locations of Indian sites, their period of occupation, and the tendency for contemporary sites of the same culture to occur together in relatively restricted locales.

The recent studies of Charles Hudson, Vernon Knight, and David Hally represented by their conference papers, which are bolstered by the works of Chester DePratter and Marvin Smith, are a marked improvement over that of Swanton and associates. One result of their work, benefited by a more accurate knowledge of southeastern archaeology, is that no one can continue to believe that the Creek and Muskogean migration from west of the Mississippi River brought the Macon Plateau cultural complex or that of Lamar to Georgia. The identification of the indigenous regional subtraditions on the Chattahoochee River in the late sixteenth and seventeenth centuries and their probable tribal associations is an excellent step toward the secure description of several societies and their minor changes through time at least partly under the deleterious influence of the blessings of European culture and Christianity. Hally's paper is analogous to Knight's in the proposed sequences of related sites in the several river valleys of northern Georgia, but covers a longer time period. He recognizes that while Lamar societies are to a large degree ancestral Creek divisions, some Lamar sites in northwestern Georgia were Cherokee units. Their data are more comprehensive in the number of sites and the quality of information than were available even twenty years ago. Hudson adds his historical records and experience to the known archaeological locations to produce a more accurate interpretation of the Indian societies and their ancestral cultures in A.D. 1540.

CHAPTER SIX

Paleoindian and Early Archaic in the Lower Southeast: A View from Georgia

David G. Anderson, Jerald Ledbetter, Lisa O'Steen, Daniel T. Elliott, Dennis Blanton, Glen T. Hanson, and Frankie Snow

WHILE THE MACON PLATEAU site is best known for its monumental late prehistoric mounds and earth lodges, it is fitting that a discussion of Paleoindian and Early Archaic research should be included in this volume. Although it is not widely known, the first Paleoindian fluted projectile point found in secure excavation context in the eastern United States, and recognized for what it was, came from the Macon Plateau site. While fluted points had been previously described in Mississippi in the 1920s (Brown 1926:132–34), where they were called Coldwater points, at the time their great age was not known. The Macon discovery occurred in 1935, the same year that Bushnell (1935:35) drew attention to the existence of surface finds of fluted points in Virginia. The original discovery in Folsom, New Mexico, where the presence of a fluted projectile point between the ribs of an extinct form of bison had finally and incontrovertibly

demonstrated the co-occurrence of humans and extinct late Pleistocene fauna, had occurred only nine years previously, in 1926 (Figgins 1927). The Dent site excavations, where the first indisputable association of early hunters with mammoth was found, was even more recent, having taken place only three years before, in 1932 (Figgins 1933). At the time of the Macon excavations, furthermore, fieldwork was underway at both Black Water Draw and Lindenmeier, classic western Paleoindian sites further demonstrating the contemporaneity of early man with extinct Pleistocene fauna and, at Black Water Draw, the relative ages of Clovis and Folsom points (Hester 1972; Wilmsen and Roberts 1978). During stratigraphic excavations on Macon Plateau in 1935, relief workers under the direction of A. R. Kelly found a large Clovis projectile point fragment and a number of other stone tools, all heavily weathered, in the deepest levels. Antonio J. Waring, who at the time was an undergraduate student with a strong interest in archaeology, has described the discovery of the Macon fluted point, and the excitement it generated: "Dr. A. R. Kelly in 1935, back in the happy wasteful old days of WPA archaeology, was excavating the area just west of the Council Chamber at the Ocmulgee Fields site near Macon. Deep in the weathered tan sand, well below pottery, he was finding considerable evidence of an early flint industry. . . . In controlled excavation, in a pre-pottery context, he found about two-thirds of a fine, large fluted point (Kelly 1938, p. 7). I personally just missed the discovery and then spent the summer sitting on the edge of the excavations in the forlorn hope that more fluted points would be found" (Waring 1968a:237).

The early flint industry at Macon was described in Kelly's (1938c:2–8) *Preliminary Report on Archeological Explorations at Macon, Georgia.* Kelly (1938c:2, 3) noted the discovery of "several thousand worked flints" from a probable "early hunter people" in the lower levels of a number of the units that were opened. The early stone tool assemblage, in clear preceramic context, occurred over a wide area, and was characterized by large numbers of specialized scrapers and flake cutting tools and, as noted above, a single well-made Clovis point (Figure 6.1). A number of Early Archaic side- and corner-notched Bolen and Palmer/Kirk points were also found in this same horizon, however, and we now know that both Paleoindian period (ca. 11,500 to 10,000 years before present, or B.P.) and succeeding Early Archaic period

55

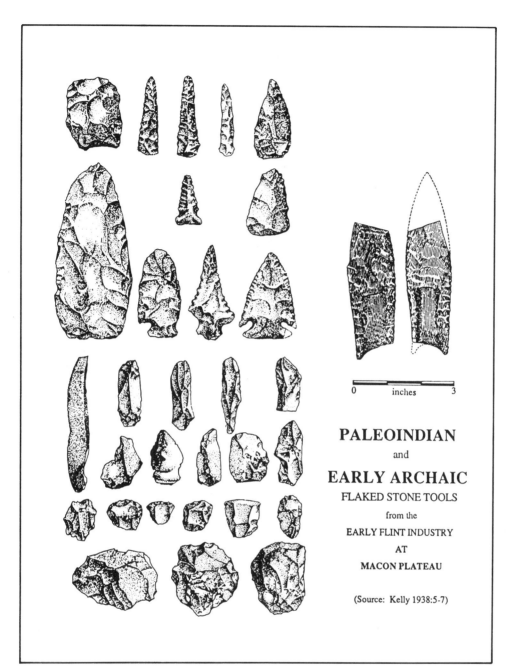

6.1. Early stone tools from the 1930s excavations on the Macon Plateau. (Reproduced from Kelly 1938c Figure 3.5.)

0   inches   3

PALEOINDIAN
and
EARLY ARCHAIC
FLAKED STONE TOOLS
from the
EARLY FLINT INDUSTRY
AT
MACON PLATEAU

(Source: Kelly 1938:5-7)

(ca. 10,000 to 8000 B.P.) components were present, mixed together (that is, conflated) on an old ground surface.

Several dense concentrations of heavily patinated chert were noted within the scatter that were interpreted as flint knapping areas. "A progressive increase in mean patination from [the] original plateau surface to the lower soil zones" (Kelly 1938c:5) was reported, although unfortunately it was not possible to separate the earlier Paleoindian from the later Early Archaic materials, which were equally heavily weathered. To this day, extensive patination on local cherts is considered a good indicator of early components in the general region (for example,

Goodyear and Charles 1984:5; Michie 1977:19). The celebrated Macon Plateau fluted point, important not only as a testament to the first inhabitants of Georgia, but also in the history of eastern North American archaeology, is displayed just inside the front door of the visitor's center at Ocmulgee National Monument. Only the one fluted point was found at the Macon Plateau site, in spite of a massive excavation effort directed to their discovery. The 1935 investigations were thus the first of many that followed documenting an apparent scarcity of fluted points on most sites of this time level in the lower Southeast. In all the years since the Macon find, only a handful of other Clovis

David G. Anderson et al.

points have been found in secure excavation context in Georgia, one each at the Muckafoonee Creek, Rucker's Bottom, Taylor Hill, and Theriault sites (see below). This pattern, markedly different from that observed in the Plains and in the Northeast, where dense kill sites have been reported, has prompted some investigators to suggest that Paleoindian populations in large parts of the Southeast were highly mobile, generalized foragers who only rarely stayed in any given area long enough to leave behind the kind of artifact concentrations that archaeologists associate with sites (Meltzer 1984:354).

Although the excavations on Macon Plateau represented some of the first modern work undertaken on eastern Paleoindian, very little follow-up research on sites or assemblages of this period was done in Georgia for over 40 years. While Kelly's preliminary statement provided some information, the early materials from the Macon Plateau site have never been fully analyzed or described, rendering them, like many of the later assemblages from the locality, shrouded in a mystery of the archaeological profession's own making. The Macon Clovis find did prompt some local interest in these early occupations, however, and after 1935 reports of Georgia fluted points did appear from time to time (Waring 1968a:237–38). In 1952, for example, Caldwell (1952: figure 167) illustrated several Georgia fluted points that were in the Smithsonian Institution collections, including a number from Big Kiokee Creek near Augusta, where a major site may have been present. In 1966 Wauchope (1966:99–100) described a number of isolated, presumably Paleoindian points found during a major WPA-era survey conducted in north Georgia. The actual age and identity of these artifacts, however, now known only from photographs, line drawings, and brief descriptions, will remain uncertain until the original materials (now apparently lost or misplaced) can be found and reexamined.

In 1968 Waring's (1968a) posthumous paper summarizing the first thirty years of Paleoindian research in Georgia appeared. Waring described in detail his nearly lifelong interest in the subject, particularly his attempt to find fluted points in private collections from around the state. The Brier Creek area in the eastern part of the state, with its rich chert quarries, was inferred to have been visited or settled quite early. At least one major site, which had yielded from ten to fifteen fluted points, was reported to have been present within this drainage, near Wrens, although unfortunately the location was never divulged by the collector who found it (Waring 1968a:237–38). Prior to 1986, however, no systematic effort at recording information about Paleoindian artifacts occurred, and any notes or other data that may have existed on most of these early point finds (save for those placed at the Smithsonian, the University of Georgia Laboratory of Archaeology or in other responsible curatorial repositories) have since been lost. Fortunately, over the past few years the documentation of Georgia's early occupants has attracted substantial interest. The multiple authorship of this paper reflects the extent of this interest. Much of this recent work, briefly recounted here, has been summarized in a monograph entitled *PaleoIndian Period Archaeology of Georgia* that interested readers may wish to examine (Anderson et al. 1990a).

Trends in Paleoindian/Early Archaic Research in the Lower Southeast Since 1938

Prior to the mid-1970s, excavations at late Pleistocene/Early Holocene sites were rare in the lower Southeast. The best-known work occurred at rockshelters such as Stanfield Worley and Russell Cave in Alabama (DeJarnette et al. 1962, Griffin 1974); at stratified floodplain or upland sites such as Doerschuk and Hardaway in North Carolina (Coe 1964) or Taylor and Thom's Creek in South Carolina (Michie 1969, 1971); or at underwater sites such as those near Silver Springs in Florida (Rayl 1974) (Figure 6.2). Since the mid-1970s there has been an explosion in both fieldwork and knowledge, much of it the result of cultural resource management (CRM)-mandated research. Large-scale excavations have occurred, not only at rockshelters but also at stratified floodplain or colluvial sites such as Rose Island, Ice House Bottom, and Bacon Farm in eastern Tennessee (Chapman 1973, 1975, 1977, 1978); at the Haw River and Baucom sites in North Carolina (Claggett and Cable 1982; Peck and Painter 1984); at Smith's Lake Creek, G. S. Lewis, and Nipper Creek in South Carolina (Anderson and Hanson 1988; Goodyear and Charles 1984; Sassaman et al. 1990; Wetmore 1986; Wetmore and Goodyear 1986); and at the Gregg Shoals, Rae's Creek, and Rucker's Bottom sites in Georgia (Anderson and Schuldenrein 1983, 1985; Crook 1990; Tippitt and Marquardt 1984). This work has led to considerable refinement of the local chronological sequence, and to well-grounded attempts to determine the kinds of activities that occurred in these settings. The contemporaneity of early human populations with extinct Pleistocene fauna in the region has been demonstrated at sites such as Little Salt Springs and Wacissa River in Florida, where perishable materials have been found that would have been lost on terrestrial sites (Clausen et al. 1979; Webb et al. 1984).

Coupled with this excavation activity, there has been a tremendous increase in site distributional data. Literally thousands of Paleoindian and Early Archaic components, identified by the presence of diagnostic hafted bifaces, have been reported from the Georgia, South Carolina, and North Carolina area in recent years (for example,

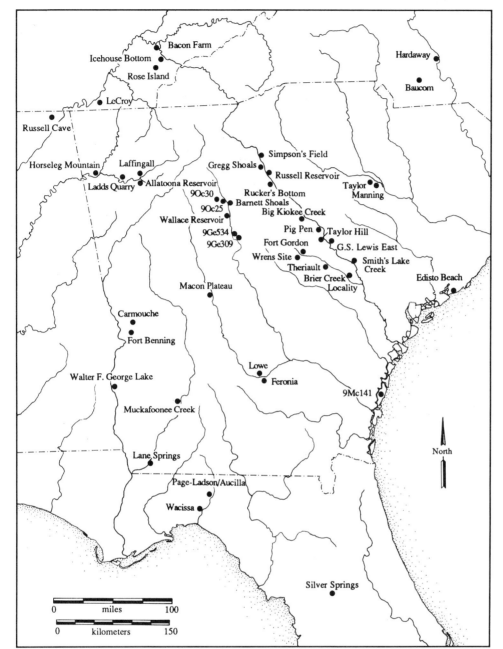

6.2. Major Late Pleistocene/ Early Holocene archaeological sites and localities in the Georgia area.

Anderson et al. 1979, 1990a; Anderson and Schuldenrein 1983; Davis and Daniel 1990; Goodyear et al. 1979, 1989; O'Steen 1983; O'Steen et al. 1989; Peck 1988; Sassaman et al. 1990). In South Carolina, for example, Hanson (n.d.) tabulated data on more than 1,000 Early Archaic components using data in the state site files and collections, and comparable numbers of components undoubtedly exist in Georgia and North Carolina. While the marked increase in knowledge in recent years is primarily due to CRM-mandated survey and excavation activity, contributing factors have included an increased awareness of the research potential of private collections (for example,

Charles 1981, 1983, 1986) and the strong interest by local avocational archaeologists in the well-made artifacts that characterize these early periods.

In recent years, furthermore, fluted point surveys have been initiated in almost every state and province in eastern North America, and a high level of amateur and professional interaction centers around this kind of effort (see Brennan 1982, Meltzer 1988, and Anderson 1990a for recent summaries of this work). In addition to large-scale excavations at major early sites, more limited survey and evaluation-related testing and surface collection has also occurred at thousands of other locations across

David G. Anderson et al.

the region, again almost all because of CRM-mandated funding. The increased fieldwork, and the strong interest in early assemblages among both the avocational and professional archaeological communities, has led to a marked expansion in our knowledge about the location and content of early assemblages in the region. In the pages that follow, the results of some of this work are presented, particularly as they relate to our understanding of the initial human occupation of the area we now call Georgia.

Paleoenvironmental Setting

The initial human occupation of Georgia is thought to have occurred between 11,500 and 11,000 years ago, during the terminal Pleistocene or Late Glacial era. Sea levels at this time were 70 or more meters lower than at present, and the Atlantic and Gulf coastal plains were much larger. The period was one of dramatic environmental change. As the continental ice sheets retreated in the north, their water returned to the oceans, inundating large sections of the continental shelf, until by 9000 B.P. sea level was within a few meters of its present stand. Over this same interval, seasonal temperature fluctuations were becoming more extreme (that is, warmer in summer and colder in winter), and precipitation was increasing (Watts 1980; Holman 1982, 1985).

When the ice sheets were retreating in the north, from ca. 12,000 to 10,000 years ago, hardwoods such as hemlock, oak, hickory, beech, birch, and elm began to replace the Full Glacial spruce/pine boreal forest that had been present earlier in northern Georgia (Delcourt and Delcourt 1985, 1987). The local vegetational matrix was thus rapidly changing, trending from a patchy boreal forest/parkland toward a more homogeneous, mesic oak-hickory forest. This transition appears to have been completed by shortly after 10,000 B.P. (M. Davis 1983: 172–73; Delcourt and Delcourt 1985:19; Larsen 1982: 208–22; Watts 1971:687, 1980:195). South of 33° N latitude, roughly the latitude of Macon, a mesic oak-hickory hardwood canopy appears to have been in place considerably earlier, and perhaps was present throughout the glacial era. The late Pleistocene and early Holocene periods in southern Georgia thus appear to have been characterized by fairly stable regional vegetational communities. The pine and scrub hardwoods now present in the interfluvial uplands and the extensive cypress swamps along the rivers emerged later, however, during the Hypsithermal Interval from 8000 to 4000 B.P. (Brooks et al. 1986; Delcourt and Delcourt 1985, 1987).

Widespread extinctions, specifically the loss of at least 33 genera of large mammals, including the *Equidae* and *Camelidae* (horses and camels), and all the members of the order *Proboscidea* (elephants) also occurred at the end of the Pleistocene (Martin 1984:361–63). These extinctions were apparently complete by ca. 10,500 years ago (Mead and Meltzer 1984:447), shortly after widespread evidence for human settlement appears in the New World archaeological record. The relationship between these human and animal populations, specifically whether the early settlers were responsible for the observed extinctions, is a matter of considerable controversy (Martin and Klein 1984). While human predation of now-extinct late Pleistocene fauna has been conclusively demonstrated at a number of locations in the Southwest and on the Great Plains, to date only minimal evidence for this kind of activity has been recovered in eastern North America (Clausen et al. 1979; Webb et al. 1984). At present, while human populations may have contributed to the demise of these animal species, the mechanisms by which this occurred, such as over-hunting, the firing of habitats, or disease, remains unknown.

Paleoindian Assemblages from the Georgia Area

Terminal Pleistocene assemblages in Georgia can now be provisionally grouped into three subperiods, the Early, Middle, and Late Paleoindian (Anderson et al. 1990a: 6–9). The Early Paleoindian subperiod is thought to date from ca. 11,500 to 11,000 B.P., and is characterized by fluted points similar to the traditional Clovis form. The points are relatively large and thick with nearly parallel haft edges, slightly concave bases, and single or multiple flutes. The Middle Paleoindian subperiod is thought to date from ca. 11,000 to 10,500 B.P., and is characterized by smaller fluted points and fluted or unfluted points with exaggerated constrictions of the haft. Some temporal overlap of these forms is probable, and it is also possible that some Middle Paleoindian forms continued in use into the Late Paleoindian subperiod, dated from ca. 10,500 to 10,000 B.P. and recognized by the presence of Dalton points. These Late Paleoindian points are characterized by a lanceolate blade outline, at least in the earliest stages of tool life, and a concave base that is usually well thinned and ground on the lateral and basal margins. Blade edges may be incurvate, straight, or excurvate, and are serrated in most examples, while cross sections tend to be flattened and biconvex. The evidence for extensive resharpening on many Daltons indicates technological differences in the use of these bifaces compared with earlier Paleoindian points (Goodyear 1974; Morse 1971, 1973).

Excavation Assemblages

Evidence for Paleoindian occupation in the Georgia area has come from both surface and excavation context. Unfortunately, while substantial numbers of early artifacts have been found in surface context, the excavation assemblages recovered to date have, for the most part, consisted of either small numbers of artifacts or else comparatively few diagnostic projectile points. This is the case even where extensive excavation has occurred. At the Theriault chert quarry site along Brier Creek, for example, a single fluted point was found at a depth of 75 to 86 cm, just above the sterile clay, in an excavation block encompassing 142 square meters (Brockington 1971:29). A single fluted point was found at the Rucker's Bottom site on the upper Savannah River in an excavation block 160 square meters in extent (Anderson and Schuldenrein 1985:289–96).

While such large-scale block excavations as those at Macon Plateau, Theriault, and Rucker's Bottom have thus far been unsuccessful and frustrating, dense Paleoindian assemblages have been found during test excavations at two locations in Georgia, at the Taylor Hill and Muckafoonee Creek sites. Taylor Hill is a stratified Archaic and Paleoindian site covering approximately 40 ha of cultivated land on an elevated portion of the Savannah River floodplain near Augusta, in Richmond County (Elliott and Doyon 1981). The site was originally documented and surface collected by George Lewis of the Augusta Archaeological Society, and a series of later visits by professional archaeologists confirmed the extreme significance of the area (Bowen 1979; Elliott and Doyon 1981; Ferguson and Widmer 1976). Although the site is very large, only a small portion has been subjected to close study, an area within a proposed railroad right of way, where testing occurred in 1980 (Elliott and Doyon 1981). This field program included the controlled surface collection of an 18,100-square-meter area and the excavation of 12 small test units totaling 45 square meters, opened using 10 cm levels and 0.25 inch mesh screens. Shortly after the testing, federal funding for the proposed railroad was cut, and excavation plans were shelved.

Well-preserved Early Archaic and Late Paleoindian deposits were found at depths of from 30 to 70 cm below the surface at Taylor Hill. The density of material recovered from the site is extremely high: 565 tools were found in the 12 test units, including one Clovis, one fluted preform, two Daltons, three side-notched Bolens or Taylors, and four corner-notched Palmers (Elliott and Doyon 1981: 149). Given the high diversity of flake tools and the variety of raw materials present, the site has been interpreted as a residential base (Elliott and Doyon 1981) or possibly a specialized camp (Anderson and Hanson 1988). The site is in an ideal location for settlement, on the Fall Line ecotone between the Piedmont and Coastal Plain. The area is rich in both biotic and lithic resources, and may have been an aggregation locus, where early populations rendezvoused periodically. Taylor Hill is perhaps the richest and best-preserved Paleoindian site now known

in Georgia and, since it is threatened by the expansion of Augusta, deserves to be either preserved or extensively excavated (Anderson et al. 1990a:29–30, 108).

The Muckafoonee site is a stratified Archaic and Paleoindian deposit situated on a terrace of Muckafoonee Creek in Dougherty County in southwestern Georgia (Elliott 1982). The site lies just north of the confluence of Muckafoonee Creek and the Flint River, and covers approximately 1.0 ha (2.5 acres). Located in the Coastal Plain, the area is underlain by the chert-rich Flint River formation, and stream sediments include materials from this geologic stratum. Major chert outcrops, in fact, occur both to the southeast, further down the Flint River, and nearby along Muckafoonee Creek.

Two deep backhoe trenches and three test units were opened at Muckafoonee. The test pits, opened in 10-cm levels and screened through 0.25-inch mesh, included two 1-m-by-1-m squares and one 2-by-2-m square. Late Archaic to Paleoindian materials were found stratified in the 90 cm of alluvial deposits that were examined, with the Early Archaic and Paleoindian artifacts occurring from 60 to 90 cm. The only diagnostic artifact recovered, an Early or Middle Paleoindian fluted projectile point, came from the 70-to-80-cm level. By far the most abundant artifact category in the lower three levels at Muckafoonee was chert debitage (6,407 specimens, or 99.1 percent of the total lithic assemblage from these levels), all of local origin. The vast majority of the debitage consisted of interior flakes, suggesting that initial core reduction occurred elsewhere, probably at the nearby outcrops. The Paleoindian/Early Archaic levels also contained 59 tools, most derived from intermediate and late-stage biface manufacture, which appears to have been the dominant activity performed at Muckafoonee. The fieldwork at the site, although limited, provides an initial picture of early chert quarry utilization in southwestern Georgia. Like Taylor Hill, this site deserves further investigation.

Minor later Paleoindian components have also been found during excavations at a number of other sites in Georgia in recent years (see Anderson et al. 1990a:26–43, for a summary of this work). At the Lowe site along the Ocmulgee River, for example, Crook (1987:51–54) found a Dalton point at a depth of 93 cm, along with several Early Archaic side- and corner-notched points higher in the deposits. At the Pig Pen site along the Savannah River near Augusta, Ledbetter (1988) found several lanceolate and Paleoindian forms, as well as a number of Early Archaic points, unfortunately most in surface context. At the Rae's Creek site, also near Augusta, Crook (1990) documented over four meters of stratified deposits, with the lowest levels dating to the late Paleoindian/initial Early Archaic periods. The Early through Late Archaic radiocarbon chronology from Rae's Creek is one of the finest ever obtained in the Southeast.

Piedmont Georgia Paleoindian Settlement— The Wallace Reservoir Locality

Several Paleoindian components were found in testing operations in and near the Wallace Reservoir along the upper Oconee River during the 1970s (O'Steen et al. 1989). The extensive fieldwork associated with the construction of the Wallace Reservoir, which was cleared and then intensively surveyed, makes this part of the central Oconee the most thoroughly examined archaeological locality in Georgia (Fish and Hally 1986). The assemblage data was used to prepare a model describing Paleoindian settlement in the Georgia Piedmont, the only model advanced to date locally for sites of this period.

The Oconee watershed has a dendritic stream drainage pattern incised into the underlying volcanic and metamorphic bedrock. Shoals and broad areas of floodplain occur at irregular intervals along the Oconee, while soils in the uplands are characteristically red clay derived from weathered granite, gneiss, and schist. The stream drainage pattern and lithic resources in the study area are essentially unchanged since Paleoindian times, although changes in the character of the Oconee floodplain have occurred (Brook 1981). The rate of erosion of the upper ridge slopes and subsequent sedimentation in the floodplains has been accelerated by historic land use, with the result that in some areas over one meter of sediment has been deposited in the past two centuries (Trimble 1974). Stone resources available within the Piedmont portion of the drainage include quartz and chert formed by nonsedimentary processes (Ledbetter et al. 1984); sedimentary cherts occur farther south along the Oconee drainage in the Coastal Plain province.

The Wallace Reservoir survey included a full surface reconnaissance of a 4,670-hectare clearcut encompassing upland and floodplain areas in the proposed floodpool (Fish and Hally 1986), plus an intensive, systematic backhoe testing program in the floodplain (Ledbetter 1978). Additional survey data from the surrounding region has been acquired from a series of subsequent upland surveys in and near the reservoir (for example, Elliott 1984; O'Steen 1986), through work by the U.S. Forest Service in the nearby Oconee National Forest (Wynn 1982:95), and from interviews with private collectors (Elliott 1978). Ninety-one Paleoindian sites yielding 141 diagnostic hafted bifaces were identified in the upper Oconee area, including 9 Early Paleoindian (N = 11 points), 14 Paleoindian (N = 24 points), 67 Middle/Late Paleoindian Dalton (N = 106 points), and 3 indeterminate Paleoindian components. Four general types of Paleoindian site were recognized, short-term camps, quarry camps, residential camps, and kill sites, based on site location, size, and assemblage characteristics.

Short-term camps are small sites with a narrow range of formal (intentionally retouched) and expedient (wear retouched) butchering and processing tools made from both local and nonlocal raw materials. Tool kits are highly curated and portable, and bifacially flaked knives manufactured primarily from locally available raw materials are common. In the absence of diagnostic projectile points, Paleoindian short-term camps are inseparable from comparable Early Archaic sites.

The second site category is clearly quarry-related. The lithic assemblages at quarry camps are characterized by quarry debris, exhausted/discarded formal tools (that is, typically bifaces and unifaces of exotic raw materials), and formal and expedient tools most typically made from the local quarry material. In contrast with quarry assemblages associated with later periods, aborted and discarded preforms are rare. There are indications that tools were not only manufactured but also used at these sites, as evidenced by the presence of bifaces that were broken during manufacture, and then modified into different tool forms. The wide variety of tools recovered from these sites indicates that a variety of activities occurred, over and above the procurement of raw material. It is possible, considering the small size of many Piedmont quartz and chert deposits, that some of these quarry sites were exploited only during the Paleoindian period, since the outcrops could have been depleted in only one or a few visits.

Paleoindian residential camps appear to be quite rare in the upper Oconee drainage, and were represented by a cluster of large sites adjacent to Barnett Shoals at the northern end of the survey area. Tool diversity at these sites is high, as is the diversity of raw materials. Tools are manufactured primarily from locally available quartz and chert, but a variety of nonlocal raw materials are also present. Formal unifacial tools are abundant; hafted, unifacial scrapers were the most common tool type in these assemblages, with most made from local Piedmont chert. Projectile points are found in a variety of manufacturing and resharpening stages, and considerable morphological variation is evident. A variety of other tool types are also present, suggesting either long-term or repeated occupation of these areas.

Kill sites, areas where Paleoindian hunters ambushed large animals, have not been conclusively identified in the Georgia Piedmont. Isolated finds of fluted points, however, are fairly common, and may represent individual kill sites or short-duration foraging camps. Large-animal kill site locations within the Georgia Piedmont would be expected near springs and along drainages, but could have been located at any place where such game was available.

Most of the 95 Paleoindian components found in the Oconee study area (N = 83) were apparently short-term camp sites (O'Steen et al. 1989:45). Residential camps (N = 4) were large and well defined, when found, but were otherwise uncommon. Quarry-related sites were also rare (N = 8), but this may be simply because the use or discard of diagnostic points may have been infrequent at such areas, precluding their easy identification. The sites were grouped by the type of landform they were found on, specifically levee, terrace, uplands edge, and uplands. A gradual expansion of land-use and settlement through time and into new areas was indicated (O'Steen et al. 1989:51). Early Paleoindian sites were located primarily in the floodplain, with the remainder of the sites at the uplands edge. Middle Paleoindian sites still appear frequently in the floodplain, but there is evidence for exploitation of the upland or interfluvial areas. A majority of Late Paleoindian sites, in contrast, were found at the uplands edge or in the uplands. These data suggest that by Late Paleoindian Dalton times populations were using upland areas more frequently. A concentration of Paleoindian sites at shoals is also evident. Although shoals comprise only about 10 percent of the river channel in the survey area, most of the Early Paleoindian sites identified along the upper Oconee were found adjacent to these features.

Another major factor affecting Paleoindian site location in the Oconee River survey area is proximity to relatively high-quality lithic deposits, particularly quartz and chert. Early and Middle Paleoindian sites consistently occur near these outcrops, a pattern not observed with the Late Paleoindian sites. The use of local as opposed to extralocal raw material increases dramatically over time in the Oconee sample. Early Paleoindian diagnostics are predominantly of extralocal materials (63.6 percent), while these materials occur with much lower incidence on Middle Paleoindian (29.2 percent) and Late Paleoindian (39.6 percent) diagnostics (O'Steen et al. 1989:53). Interestingly, Valley and Ridge cherts, whose sources lie well to the north and northwest, were observed only in the northern portion of the study area. Groups using this material appear to have had little interaction or direct movement beyond this part of the drainage.

If the upper Oconee sample is typical, Piedmont Paleoindian points tend to be small and extensively resharpened; broken points were often modified and used as scrapers, wedges, and gravers; and broken blades were often fashioned into new, but smaller, bifaces. This strategy of lithic conservation and recycling appears consistently on Paleoindian sites, but is not as prevalent in the following Early Archaic period (O'Steen 1983). The extensive reworking of these Paleoindian assemblages suggests that either locally available lithic raw materials were not as common or as prized by these groups as has been inferred or, alternatively, that the upper Oconee area may have been at the edge of one or more Paleoindian territories centered elsewhere.

Previous studies have identified areas in the Southeast where large numbers of Paleoindian points have been found (summarized in Meltzer 1988 and Anderson 1990a). These areas are hypothesized to have been the location of major Paleoindian population concentrations. Large numbers of fluted points, for example, have been documented in northern Florida, the Atlantic Coastal Plain of South Carolina, and in the Valley and Ridge province of northern Alabama (Figure 6.3). The Georgia Piedmont may thus represent a relatively unoccupied zone between two or more population concentrations whose people, when visiting this area, may have been cautious in their stone tool use. Extensive use of the upper Oconee drainage does not, in fact, appear to occur until the Late Paleoindian subperiod, although the area was certainly not devoid of settlement during the Early and Middle Paleoindian subperiods. There is some evidence to suggest that during the late Pleistocene some big game animals, such as mastodon, may have been more prevalent in the Coastal Plain and Valley and Ridge provinces than in the mosaic boreal forests of the Piedmont (Corgan 1976:17). This might help to explain the observed site distributions, if these animals were indeed targeted.

Coastal Plain Georgia Paleoindian Settlement— The Feronia Locality

Another area characterized by dense Late Pleistocene/ Early Holocene assemblages that has received extensive examination in recent years is the Feronia Locality, a concentration of 16 sites located in south-central Georgia near the Big Bend of the Ocmulgee River in Coffee County (Blanton and Snow 1986, 1989). The locality encompasses approximately four square kilometers and is centered on a prominent ridge to the south of and overlooking the broad Ocmulgee floodplain. The area, at the ecotone between the floodplain and the uplands, is characterized by reliable springs, something that may have helped attract early visitors. An extensive Middle and Late Paleoindian and Early Archaic assemblage, encompassing 960 formal flaked stone tools, has been recovered in surface context from the locality, including 2 Suwannees, 18 Daltons, and 83 Bolen and Palmer/ Kirk side- and corner-notched points. Three of the Daltons have basal protuberances, a stylistic variant that is fairly common in south Georgia (Snow 1980). The basal nipples do not appear to be platform remnants and may represent an effort to increase the surface contact in the haft. Occurring with these hafted biface types are an array of tool forms that are characteristic of Paleoindian and Early Archaic assemblages over much of eastern North America. Unifacial tools present included endscrapers, discoidal scrapers, thick oblong scrapers, thick unifaces, thin unifaces, gravers, and spokeshaves. Other, less com-

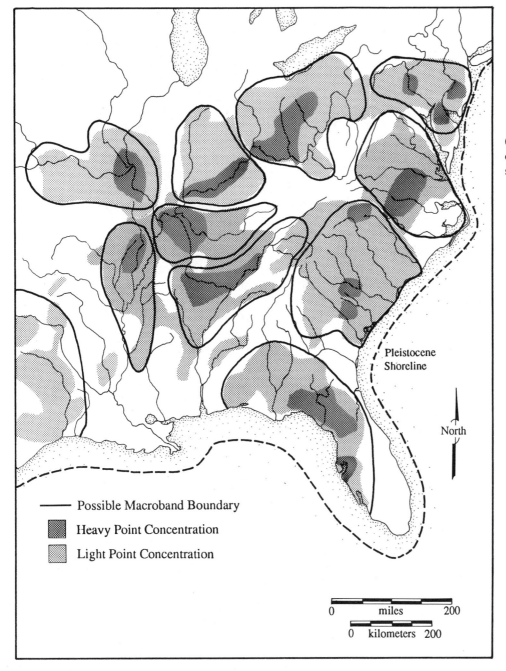

6.3. Paleoindian site concentrations in the southeastern United States.

Pleistocene Shoreline

North

—— Possible Macroband Boundary

▨ Heavy Point Concentration

▨ Light Point Concentration

```
0        miles        200

0     kilometers   200
```

mon tool forms included adzes, limaces, and Edgefield scrapers.

Two unifacial tool forms dominate the assemblages, endscrapers and thin unifaces. Eight side-notched Edgefield scrapers were recovered, a tool form that occurs in low incidence in Georgia and the Carolinas (Goodyear 1983; Michie 1968, 1972). Pecked and ground stone artifacts of ferruginous sandstone, characterized by a dimple in the smaller end (so-called "egg-stones"), were also recovered. The function of these objects is unknown, although use as bolas or throwing stones has been sug-

gested (Whatley 1986). Gravers and endscrapers appear to have been most common in the pre-Bolen Suwannee and Dalton tool kits. Edgefield scrapers and the pitted "egg-stones" appear to be associated with the Palmer/Bolen assemblages. The placement of the Edgefield scraper with the Early Archaic assemblages was largely on the basis of the side-notched haft shapes these tools share with Bolen points (Purdy 1981:29), although the tool form has been found in Early Archaic context at the G. S. Lewis site on the lower Savannah River (Anderson and Hanson 1988:277).

A noteworthy aspect of the Feronia locality setting is that there is no nearby lithic raw material source, as expected in some models of eastern Paleoindian settlement (for example, Gardner 1977, 1983). The nearest known raw material sources of any significance lie about 80 km to the north and 95 km to the south. What drew people to this locality is currently unknown. The area is very near the interface between the Atlantic and Gulf watersheds, however, a divide that may have had considerable territorial or social significance in the Late Pleistocene/Early Holocene. Almost all (99 percent) of the tools and debitage from the locality are made from Coastal Plain chert, most probably from the Atlantic watershed sources 80 km to the northeast. The remaining traces of material are of silicified coral from the sources 95 km to the south in the Gulf watershed, and traces of metamorphic and igneous materials from the Piedmont approximately 125 km to the north. This array of materials suggests a considerable range of movement and/or exchange was occurring. If the locality functioned as an aggregation locus for early populations, its presence in a non-Fall Line setting is interesting. It suggests that such aggregation sites may occur at any significant environmental interface, whether it be between the Coastal Plain and Piedmont, or the Atlantic and Gulf watersheds. The range of tool forms present suggests, minimally, that sustained occupation or a variety of activities were carried out at Feronia.

The SGA Paleoindian Artifact Recording Project

Coupled with intensive research at specific sites and localities, Paleoindian research in Georgia has also recently focused on the compilation of projectile point data. In mid-1986, several of the authors of this paper, in coordination with the Society for Georgia Archaeology (SGA), began a fluted point survey, something that, surprisingly, had not been initiated previously (Anderson et al. 1986, 1987, 1990a, 1990b). Prior to this effort, fewer than a dozen fluted points were formally recorded in the state site files. In the massive compilation of fluted points from eastern North America conducted by the Eastern States Archaeological Federation (Brennan 1982), for example, only 10 of 5,820 Paleoindian projectile points were reported from Georgia. Only Rhode Island, of all the states along the eastern seaboard, had fewer Paleoindian points. The low count from Georgia was underscored by the high totals from adjoining states, such as Alabama (N = 1,654), Florida (N = 1,392), North Carolina (N = 329), and South Carolina (N = 95). The low number of diagnostic Paleoindian artifacts reported from Georgia, in fact, represented the most conspicuous gap in the survey. The SGA Paleoindian Artifact Recording Project was initiated to correct this situation.

The reasons for recording information about Paleo-indian points are obvious. Fluted and other lanceolate projectile points are currently the only artifacts known to be unambiguous diagnostic indicators of sites of this period. Information about their occurrence is thus the only way, short of excavation and the use of absolute dating procedures, by which archaeologists can recognize these early occupations. Their locations indicate where these people lived, that is, what spots on the landscape were important to them and how they made use of these areas. Study of point styles, and raw materials, furthermore, can provide clues as to how far these people may have traveled over the course of the year and whether or not they were linked or related to groups in other areas (for example, Goodyear 1979; Sassaman et al. 1988). Georgia lies at the junction of the Atlantic and Gulf coastal regions, furthermore, and artifact and site data from the state will undoubtedly prove important to understanding Paleoindian occupations in each area and relationships between these areas. Finally, recording these artifacts provides the basic data essential to test archaeological theories about the nature of Paleoindian occupations, and perhaps in the process dispel some misconceptions (Williams and Stoltman 1965; Anderson 1990b). When the Georgia fluted point survey was initiated, for example, the authors were repeatedly told that there was little evidence for Paleoindian occupation in the state. As the results to date indicate, this does not appear to be the case at all.

Data on both fluted and nonfluted Paleoindian points of all types have been recorded, as well as on other categories of early artifacts. As of January 1992, data on over 250 projectile points have been collected, and attribute and other data on 216 of them were published in a recent monograph (Anderson et al. 1990a). Clovis, Suwannee, Simpson, Cumberland, Quad, and Dalton points have all been identified by the survey, which collects data on complete, broken, and reworked points. Examples of these artifact types are illustrated in Figure 6.4. Paleoindian points have been recorded from over 40 counties so far, mostly from the northern and southwestern parts of the state, where large numbers of collectors have been at work, or major survey projects such as the Allatoona, Wallace, and Russell reservoir projects have occurred. Much of our current evidence from south Georgia reflects the work of one individual, Frankie Snow of Douglas.

Large numbers of Dalton points have been observed in public and private collections around the state, and the survey quickly had to restrict itself primarily to fluted and nonfluted lanceolates (although attribute data on 74 Daltons has been recorded to date). The incidence of Daltons is fairly high, particularly in the central and northern parts of the state, and many of these artifacts are fluted or, more properly, basally thinned, arguing for a direct, possibly local transition from earlier fluted point

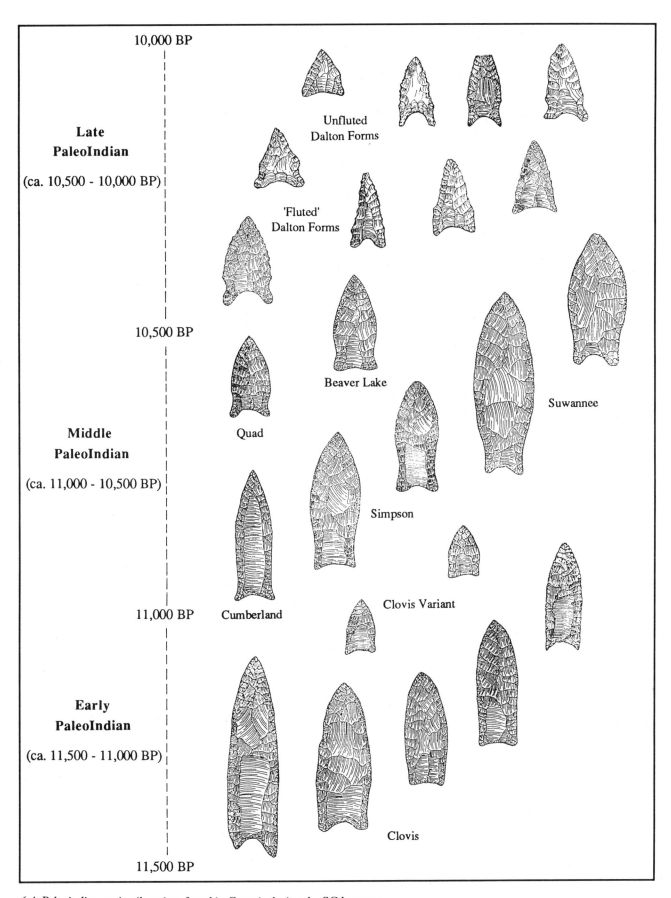

10,000 BP

Late
PaleoIndian

(ca. 10,500 - 10,000 BP)

Unfluted
Dalton Forms

'Fluted'
Dalton Forms

10,500 BP

Beaver Lake

Suwannee

Middle
PaleoIndian

(ca. 11,000 - 10,500 BP)

Quad

Simpson

11,000 BP   Cumberland

Clovis Variant

Early
PaleoIndian

(ca. 11,500 - 11,000 BP)

Clovis

11,500 BP

6.4. Paleoindian projectile points found in Georgia during the SGA survey.

assemblages. With the addition of Georgia to the fold, Paleoindian projectile point recording projects are now underway in almost every state and province in eastern North America, and as of late 1991 almost 11,000 of these artifacts have been recorded (Anderson 1991b).

Early Archaic Assemblages from the Georgia Area

The Early Archaic period in eastern North America is widely viewed as a time of initial human adaptation to Holocene, postglacial climatic conditions. Accepting the placement of the Pleistocene/Holocene boundary at 10,000 B.P., a roughly 2,000-year span for the Early Archaic period is employed in most cultural sequences. The end of the Early Archaic is usually equated with the onset of the Atlantic, or Hypsithermal episode, at about 8000 B.P. In its most common expression, the Paleoindian to Early Archaic transition is viewed as one in which the assumed predominantly big-game hunting, focal Paleoindian adaptation was replaced by a more generalized or diffuse "Archaic" hunting and gathering way of life.

In the lower Southeast, Early Archaic components are recognized almost exclusively by the presence of diagnostic side- and corner-notched and/or bifurcate-based projectile points. These hafted biface forms, from earliest to latest, include the Dalton and Hardaway-Dalton types dating ca. 10,500–9900 B.P.; the Taylor-Big Sandy-Bolen side-notched types dating ca. 10,200–9500 B.P.; the Palmer-Kirk corner-notched types dating ca. 9500–8900 B.P.; and a series of bifurcate forms, including the MacCorkle, St. Albans, LeCroy, and Kanawah types dating from ca. 8900–8100 B.P. The end of the Early Archaic in the region is characterized by the replacement of these notched and bifurcate forms by square and contracting stemmed Stanly and Morrow Mountain point forms (Anderson 1991a; Broyles 1971; Chapman 1975, 1976:2–7, 1985; Coe 1964; Daniel and Wisenbaker 1987; Dunbar et al. 1988; Goodyear 1982; Goodyear et al. 1979: 100–106; Oliver 1985).

The occurrence, relative temporal placement, and diagnostic utility of these hafted biface forms in the lower Southeast were initially delimited by Coe (1964) at the Hardaway and Doerschuk sites in Piedmont North Carolina. Subsequent excavations have provided extensive confirmation and some refinement of this sequence, which has been found to have general utility throughout Georgia and the Carolinas. Sequence refinement and component identification have tended to dominate ongoing research, although some studies have appeared that attempt to move beyond this, toward the reconstruction of prehistoric activities at individual sites and the development of formal settlement models (Smith 1986; Steponaitis 1986).

Excavation Assemblages

Until quite recently, little was known about the Early Archaic period in Georgia (DePratter 1976a). A number of Early Archaic sites have seen small-scale, spatially limited excavation in the Georgia area in recent years. Materials have been recovered from probable quarry workshop sites such as Theriault and Muckafoonee Creek in Georgia (Brockington 1971; Elliott 1982); from terrace locations in the inner Coastal Plain such as at Cal Smoak and Pen Point in South Carolina and Taylor Hill in Georgia (Anderson et al. 1979; Elliott and Doyon 1981; Sassaman et al. 1990); from Piedmont terraces such as at Gregg Shoals in Georgia (Tippitt and Marquardt 1984); and from several locations in the Wallace Reservoir in central Georgia (O'Steen 1983; O'Steen et al. 1989). In addition, extensive excavations have been conducted at several Early Archaic sites in the Little Tennessee River area of Tennessee (Chapman 1985), and at the Rucker's Bottom (Anderson and Schuldenrein 1985) and G. S. Lewis sites (Anderson and Hanson 1988; Sassaman et al. 1990:91–96), in the Georgia Piedmont and South Carolina Coastal Plain portions of the Savannah River drainage, respectively. The G. S. Lewis and Rucker's Bottom excavations, in fact, are among the largest from this time level in the lower Southeast.

Models of Early Archaic Settlement in the Lower Southeast

Many of the views that dominated professional archaeological assessment of Early Archaic settlement systems during the 1950s and 1960s and in some instances to the present day were outlined by Griffin (1952a:354–55) in a paper entitled "Culture Periods in Eastern United States Archeology." A picture of small, exogamous, probably patrilineal and patrilocal egalitarian bands moving within specific hunting territories was advanced. Seasonal population movement linked to resource procurement, as well as periodic aggregation for ceremonial purposes and information sharing, were suggested facets of Early Archaic life. While some of these views were readily adopted, notably those about small group size coupled with extensive geographic mobility, Griffin's views on the importance of ceremonial and information sharing networks at this early time level were largely ignored until quite recently.

The 1950s paper that had perhaps the most profound impact on subsequent views on Early Archaic lifeways and settlement, however, was *Trend and Tradition in the Prehistory of the Eastern United States* (Caldwell 1958). Caldwell argued that although the eastern Woodlands were rich in exploitable foodstuffs, aboriginal knowledge about the occurrence and effective utilization of these resources only slowly developed. Life prior to the establishment of what he called "primary forest efficiency" was portrayed as "unsettled, nomadic . . . almost completely wandering" (Caldwell 1958:8–11). Because the specialized nut-processing economies observed later were not in evidence, hunting was thought to be of considerable if not primary importance. This picture of Early Archaic life, as a highly mobile, predominantly hunting adaptation has continued to dominate thinking about the period.

The basic premise of Caldwell's "primary forest efficiency" argument, that it took thousands of years for local aboriginal populations to learn how to effectively exploit the eastern forest, has been severely challenged in recent years. It is no longer assumed, for example, that plant foods were a relatively minor, unimportant part of the early Holocene diet (Asch et al. 1972; Asch and Asch 1985; Meltzer and Smith 1986; Smith 1986). While probable plant processing tools have been only rarely noted or emphasized in Early Archaic excavation reports (as reviewed in Goodyear et al. 1979:104–5), recent compilations suggest that they may be more common than once thought (for example, Anderson and Schuldenrein 1983; Smith 1986). Where favorable preservation conditions occur, and where careful recovery procedures have been used, evidence for plant exploitation is common at sites dating to this time level, as Chapman's work in the Little Tennessee River Valley has demonstrated (Chapman 1977; Chapman and Shea 1981:63, 77; see also Asch and Asch 1985 and Cowan 1985 for similar examples from the midcontinent).

During the 1970s and 1980s, a number of models appeared that attempted to examine and partially explain Early Archaic settlement and land use in portions of eastern North America. Perhaps the most significant attempts in the general Georgia area have been: (1) Claggett and Cable's (1982) "Effective Temperature/Technological Organization" model; (2) O'Steen's (1983) "Wallace Reservoir" model; and (3) Anderson and Hanson's (1988) "Band/Macroband" biocultural model, each of which is discussed in turn.

THE HAW RIVER EFFECTIVE TEMPERATURE/ TECHNOLOGICAL ORGANIZATION MODEL

In the context of a major excavation and reporting program centered on two deeply stratified sites along the Haw River in the central Piedmont of North Carolina, Claggett and Cable (1982; Cable 1982) argued that changes in the technological organization of local Paleoindian through later Archaic adaptations were a direct, if delayed, response to postglacial warming. They note that the Late Pleistocene and early Holocene was a time of dramatically increasing average annual temperature in the Southeast, a situation that would have had a considerable effect on local resource structure and hence on hunter-gatherer organizational strategies.

In brief, with the onset of warmer, post-Pleistocene conditions, and increasing environmental homogeneity, a pattern of high residential mobility, or frequent settlement relocation upon the exhaustion of local resources, is thought to have developed. Archaeologically, this resulted in a corresponding shift in assemblages from highly curated tool forms characteristic of logistically provisioned collector adaptations to highly expedient, situational technologies better suited to foraging adaptations (Binford 1980). At the Haw River sites, where the study of directionality within local technological adaptations formed a primary research goal, a pronounced shift from curated to expedient tool forms was noted between the Dalton and Palmer assemblages (Claggett and Cable 1982:686–87, 764). The data from the Haw River sites thus suggest that by shortly after 10,000 B.P., at least in this part of the Southeast, a predominantly residentially mobile, foraging adaptation had become established. The increase in residential mobility and decrease in residential permanence suggested by this model thus runs counter to the traditional view advanced by Caldwell that increasing sedentism characterized the Archaic in the region (Claggett and Cable 1982:13).

A further test of the Haw River model examined assemblage data from 98 Early Archaic sites in Georgia and the Carolinas (Anderson and Schuldenrein 1983:201). Most of the Early Archaic assemblages were found to be characterized by highly expedient technologies, with only a low incidence of formal, curated tools. The variation in assemblage size and composition that was observed, it was suggested, was more likely the result of re-occupation than of major differences in site function. A high level of group mobility was further indicated, particularly along rather than across drainages, through an examination of the incidence of local versus extralocal raw materials on diagnostic projectile points (Anderson and Schuldenrein 1983:201, 205).

THE WALLACE RESERVOIR EARLY ARCHAIC MODEL

One of the more ambitious attempts to examine Early Archaic settlement in the lower Southeast in recent years was by O'Steen (1983), based on an analysis of 363 Early Archaic projectile points from 248 sites located in the floodpool of the Wallace Reservoir, on the upper Oconee River in the eastern Georgia Piedmont. O'Steen (1983: 68–69, 99) was able to demonstrate that Early Archaic site density along the upper Oconee was highest in areas of greatest resource density and diversity (major Early Archaic camps were defined as clusters of sites where more than one Early Archaic point or component were found; O'Steen 1983:106). The majority of multicomponent/multipoint sites occurred at the confluence of two or more drainages, on high terraces, and at shoals. These floodplain sites were interpreted as major spring, summer, or fall camps, while the major upland sites were interpreted as fall/winter camps (O'Steen 1983:106–8). Single point loci, the most widely scattered class of sites, occurred on all land surfaces and along both major and minor drainages. These sites, which outnumbered multicomponent/multipoint sites by a 5:1 ratio, were interpreted as transitory hunting/butchering or other specialized activity camps (O'Steen 1983:108–9).

Using population density estimates for hunter-gatherers of from 0.05 to 0.13 persons/square kilometer (taken from Jochim 1976:134), O'Steen (1983:110) argued that the area of the Wallace Reservoir could have supported between 80 and 200 people at any one time during the Early Archaic. Following this line of reasoning, she argued that a maximum band (defined by Wobst 1974:152 as "a marriage network which guarantees the biological survival of its members") of approximately 475 people could have subsisted within the overall Oconee basin, which extended over about 13,600 square kilometers (O'Steen 1983:112). In contrast to the studies conducted by Claggett and Cable (1982) and Anderson and Schuldenrein (1983) noted previously, O'Steen argued that local Early Archaic populations were comparatively sedentary, operated within smaller territories, and may have obtained their extralocal lithic raw materials through exchange with other bands (1983:115–16). The evidence marshaled in support of this position, that this type of adaptational system tended to occur among "hunter-gatherers in temperate, ecologically diverse environments" (O'Steen 1983:115), remains, however, to be demonstrated (for example, Binford 1980, 1983; R. L. Kelly 1983). Only limited data, furthermore, is available on early Holocene paleoenvironmental conditions and resource structure in the Georgia area. Overall, however, the attempt to incorporate an array of factors, including paleoenvironmental conditions, microenvironmental variability in site location, and the need to maintain viable mating networks represented an important advance.

THE BAND/MACROBAND BIOCULTURAL MODEL

The third generalized model of Early Archaic settlement to emerge in the lower Southeast in recent years is Anderson and Hanson's (1988) "band/macroband" model, which was evaluated with archaeological data from the Savannah River Basin. Four limiting factors, it was argued, strongly conditioned the structure and operation of Early Archaic adaptations in this region. These were (1) environmental structure, specifically as it relates to seasonal and geographic variation in food, lithic raw materials, and other resources; (2) biological interaction,

manifest in mating network regulation; (3) information exchange, notably for mating network maintenance and subsistence resource regulation; and (4) demographic structure, evidenced in population size and spacing.

Two levels of settlement organization were proposed, corresponding to local (band-level) and regional (macroband) organizational systems. At the band level, coresidential population aggregates of from roughly 50 to 150 people occupying individual drainages were proposed, and a hypothesized pattern of annual band mobility within the Savannah River basin was advanced. Regional social entities, macrobands corresponding to Wobst's (1974) minimum equilibrium mating networks and assumed to consist of from roughly 500 to 1,500 people, were also proposed, extending over several contiguous river valleys. A spatial model for the distribution of individual bands over the South Atlantic Slope, and macrobands over this part of the Southeast, was advanced.

In brief, the hypothesized annual pattern of band-level mobility in the Savannah River basin saw the use of base camps during the winter and short-term foraging camps throughout the remainder of the year. Annual movement was toward the coast during the early spring, back into the Upper Coastal Plain and Piedmont during the later spring, summer, and early fall, with a return to the winter base camp in late fall. The return to the winter base camp may have incorporated side trips to other drainages, for aggregation events by groups from two or more different drainages. Fall Line river terraces are posited aggregation loci, since the dramatic character of this macroecotone, where rocks and shoals first appear proceeding inland from the coast, would facilitate population rendezvous. The occurrence of rich Early Archaic assemblages, characterized by atypical concentrations of formal tools in Fall Line sites across the region, supports an interpretation that these areas saw use in special activities of some kind (Anderson 1979; Michie 1971; Wetmore 1986; Wetmore and Goodyear 1986). Recent testing of this model, by Daniel (1991), working with materials from the Hardaway site, has highlighted the extent to which variability in the occurrence of major lithic raw material sources can influence settlement, particularly the location of residential base camps.

The hypothesized regional distribution of Early Archaic band-level groups reflects, to some extent, regional physiographic conditions, particularly the northwest to southeastward trending flow of most major drainages, from the Appalachian Mountains to the ocean. The maintenance of viable Early Archaic populations, given the inferred population levels within individual drainages, would have required mating networks extending over a large area (Wilmsen and Roberts 1978; Wobst 1974; Wright 1981). Low population densities of between 50 to 150 people per drainage are proposed during the initial

David G. Anderson et al.

Early Archaic occupation of the region; this figure in all probability increased over time, leading to group fission and a concomitant decrease in annual range. To maintain a minimal equilibrium population, at least during the initial Early Archaic, several bands, probably from at least three to five major drainages, would have had to be in regular contact. The fluid movement of individuals, coupled with periodic aggregation of larger social groups at Fall Line locations, are suggested mechanisms by which this interaction was maintained (see also Conkey 1980; Hayden 1982). The need to find and exchange mates in a cultural environment characterized by an extremely low population density thus is thought to have played a major role in shaping Early Archaic, and presumably earlier Paleoindian, settlement systems in the region. As the landscape filled up, over the course of the Paleoindian and subsequent Archaic periods, the strength of this driving force would lessen. Social fluidity may be an entirely appropriate mechanism of intergroup contact during the Middle Archaic, and has been inferred in some local models (Sassaman 1985; Blanton and Sassaman 1989).

Conclusions

Analyses conducted to date at Paleoindian and Early Archaic sites indicate that considerable assemblage variability existed during these periods in the Georgia area. While a general trend toward expedient technologies and foraging adaptive strategies is indicated, the presence of seasonal base camps is also indicated, particularly during winter months. Different types of short-duration camps, representing residential locations, aggregation sites, or areas used by specialized task groups, have also been identified. Unfortunately, specific details about matters such as season and duration of site use, or the size of the resident groups, must await larger excavations, the recovery of preserved floral and faunal remains (or other seasonal indicators), and continued development of analytical strategies used to examine existing data.

Geographically wide-ranging adaptations during both the Paleoindian and Early Archaic periods are indicated by analyses of hafted bifaces from collections along local drainages and across the region (Anderson and Schulden-rein 1983:201; Anderson and Hanson 1988:280–81; Goodyear et al. 1989; Sassaman et al. 1988:85–87). Lithic raw materials used to manufacture hafted bifaces, artifacts readily identified to period, occur at distances of up to 300 kilometers from their source area at some sites. A gradual rather than a dramatic or steplike fall-off in the occurrence of lithic raw materials occurs, suggesting minimal social boundaries. Furthermore, extralocal raw material use appears greatest along rather than across drainages, based on analyses of diagnostic artifacts from riverine and interfluvial contexts, suggesting that most group activities

(except for possible seasonal or annual aggregation events) occurred within individual drainages. Finally, evidence for raw material or finished artifact exchange is completely lacking. The assemblages recovered to date, even at quarry sites, suggest routine tool-kit maintenance, discard and replenishment, or "gearing-up" activity rather than production for exchange.

The high incidence of extralocal raw materials on Early Archaic artifacts that are found on sites over the region might be expected if low numbers of people were moving rapidly over the landscape. The almost exclusive use of local raw materials characteristic of succeeding Middle Archaic populations in the general region (Anderson and Schuldenrein 1985:317; Blanton 1983; Blanton and Sassaman 1989; Sassaman 1983) may reflect increasing regional population densities and a corresponding decrease in annual range (for example, see also Brose 1979; Ford 1974; Smith 1986:18–25; Stoltman 1978). If these raw material distributions are indeed an accurate indicator of regional settlement dynamics, a time-transgressive decrease in the use of extralocal raw materials should be evident over the course of the Early Archaic, as population increased and mobility decreased, something indicated in the archaeological record from the region (Anderson 1991a).

Evidence for a major increase in population, or at least in the use of projectile points, over the interval from the Paleoindian through the Early Archaic periods is indicated by an examination of diagnostic projectile points at four differing localities in the Georgia area. These localities include the upper Oconee River/Wallace Reservoir (O'Steen 1983; O'Steen et al. 1989), the Russell Reservoir (Anderson and Joseph 1988:25), (3) the Savannah River Site (Sassaman et al. 1990), and (4) the Feronia locality (Blanton and Snow 1986, 1989) (Figure 6.5). While this increase is progressive, major increases in the numbers of observed diagnostics are evident between the Middle and Late Paleoindian periods, and again from the Late Paleoindian to the Early Archaic. To some extent, these increases may reflect changing hunting strategies and tool technologies as much as population growth. Dalton and later Early Archaic hafted bifaces, for example, appear to have seen extensive use as multipurpose tools, more so than earlier fluted and unfluted lanceolate forms in the region. If these data do accurately monitor regional popu-lation levels, however, it suggests that major population growth was occurring, and that considerable landscape filling had occurred by the start of the Early Archaic period.

As can be seen from this review, a tremendous amount of information about the early inhabitants of the lower Southeast has been collected since the Macon Plateau fluted point was discovered some 50 years ago. Thousands of early sites, and literally tens of thousands of artifacts,

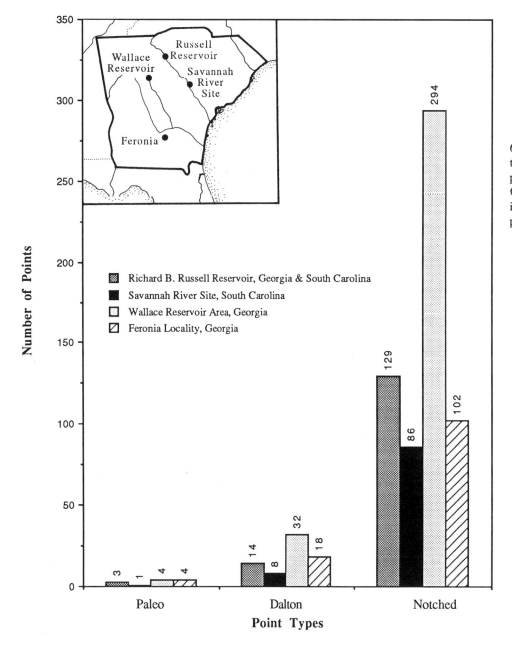

6.5. Evidence for Paleoindian through Early Archaic period population increase in the Georgia area, measured using incidence of diagnostic projectile points.

are now known from across the region, offering considerable potential for synthesis. Effective organization of this data, transcending state boundaries, is the next step. The establishment of regionwide databases, compiling site, paleoenvironmental, and artifactual data, needs to be initiated and used to develop new perspectives on the initial settlement of the region.

Acknowledgments

This document represents a considerably revised and updated version of the paper originally presented at the Ocmulgee National Monument Fiftieth Anniversary Conference, Macon, Georgia, on December 13, 1986. The authors wish to thank all those avocational and professional archaeologists contributing data to the Society for Georgia Archaeology's Paleoindian Artifact Recording Project. Julie Barnes Smith is to be thanked for her help with the artwork.

David G. Anderson et al.

CHAPTER SEVEN

The Swift Creek Site and Woodland Platform Mounds in the Southeastern United States

Richard W. Jefferies

BEGINNING IN 1933 and continuing through the remainder of the decade, archaeological investigations conducted in the Ocmulgee Basin near Macon, Georgia, yielded information that now forms the foundation of much of southeastern archaeology. The archaeological work, carried out under the auspices of the Smithsonian Institution and sponsored by the Works Progress Administration (WPA), focused on four large sites and several smaller ones that yielded an occupational sequence spanning the Paleoindian through the early Historic periods (Kelly and Smith 1975).

Much of the work undertaken as part of the WPA relief effort focused on excavating the large Mississippian flat-topped mounds that were the most prominent cultural features on the Macon Plateau. Excavations conducted there at Macon, and at other Mississippian mound centers, demonstrated that these large earthen structures served as platforms for public buildings and their associated activities. Most Mississippian platform mounds consist of a series of construction stages, with each stage comprising a generally uniform layer of fill deposited on the surface of the preceding stage, often covering the remains of burned buildings. Platform mounds, or temple mounds as they are sometimes called, are considered to be one of the diagnostic traits of Mississippian culture.

Archaeological investigations conducted at a number of sites in the midwestern and southeastern United States have revealed mounds dating to the Woodland period that also apparently served as platforms for a variety of activities. Some of these mound surfaces are covered with postholes that may represent buildings or other kinds of constructions. Other mounds contain prepared surfaces or floors, but lack postholes or other evidence of structures. The nature of these Woodland platform mounds and their relationship to subsequent Mississippian platform mounds remain subjects of great interest to archaeologists today.

Excavations conducted under the supervision of A. R. Kelly at the Swift Creek site near Macon yielded the first stratigraphic evidence for Woodland platform mounds in the Southeast. These investigations revealed what Kelly interpreted to be a habitation accretion or house mound containing primarily Swift Creek ceramics.

This chapter discusses the results of Kelly's work at the Swift Creek site and its subsequent impact on southeastern archaeology. Published information from a number of southeastern sites with Woodland platform mounds is summarized and the stratigraphic nature of a little-known Woodland platform mound in Georgia, the Cold Springs site (9GE10), is described. Comparison of several sites is then undertaken in order to provide further insight into the age, physical nature, and function of Woodland platform mounds in the Southeast.

The Swift Creek Site

The Swift Creek mound and village site (9BI3) is located on the east side of the Ocmulgee River, approximately 6 km southeast of the Macon Plateau (Figure I.1). Initial reconnaissance of the site indicated that several mounds were present. Subsequent excavations, conducted from March 1936 until late 1937, disclosed that all but one, Mound A, were erosional remnants. In a brief report published in 1938 in *Bureau of American Ethnology* (BAE) *Bulletin* 119, Kelly reported that Mound A was originally about 3 m (10 ft.) high and approximately 60 m (200 ft.) in diameter (Kelly 1938c). Investigation of Mound A was accomplished by excavating two intersecting cross

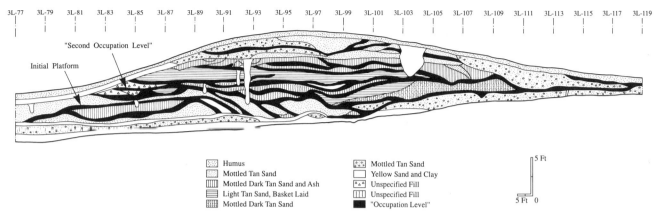

7.1. North-south profile of Mound A, Swift Creek site.

trenches, dividing the mound into quadrants. Additional work was conducted by offsetting excavation trenches and operating in 2.5- or 5.0-foot vertical cuts. Several of these trenches extended to the mound base, exposing profiles that documented the history of mound construction, but most of the mound was only excavated down to what was referred to as the "second occupation level," situated approximately 3.0 ft. below the mound surface. Approximately 40 percent of the mound was excavated following these procedures (Kelly 1938c:26; Kelly and Smith 1975:19–21).

Examination of the resulting mound profiles indicated to Kelly that Mound A began as a number of gradually accumulating midden heaps, or hummocks, with no apparent preconceived plan of mound construction. These efforts created slight elevations that served as "refuge stations" or as "inconsequential building sites." Later, intervening low areas were filled in to provide a broader living area. Through time, what Kelly referred to as the "enveloping heap" acquired the appearance of a mound and construction became more deliberate with the aim of building a formal mound structure (Kelly 1938c:26).

Kelly viewed Mound A as being substantially different from Mounds A, B, and C on the Macon Plateau. He observed that construction of the latter was planned from start to finish. In contrast, he considered Swift Creek Mound A to have grown by the "accretion of soil." Kelly identified seven midden layers in Mound A, representing what he interpreted as habitation surfaces that appeared to run across the mound. Soils between each of the midden or habitation zones consisted of basket-laid sands and other lighter-colored soils (Kelly 1938c:26–27).

Except for the few pages devoted to it in Kelly's 1938 report, nothing was published on the site until 1975, when Kelly and Smith prepared a more comprehensive

report for the National Park Service. Their analysis of the stratigraphy and artifacts revealed new information about the age and function of the mound.

Reexamination of the Mound A profile drawings provided new insights into the history of mound construction. The stratigraphic sequence in the lower left side of several of the north-south profile drawings indicated that mound building started with the construction of a low earthen platform (Figure 7.1). Gradually, the platform was enlarged, extending further to the north (to the right in Figure 7.1) through time. Subsequent additions to the mound were made by piling dirt on and around the original platform. Similar construction techniques have been documented for several other Early Swift Creek platform mounds (Kelly and Smith 1975: 30, 114).

Perhaps the most intriguing aspect of the mound was the occurrence of numerous postholes and features. Although postholes extended down from several Mound A strata, the two most definitive construction stages with summit surfaces are represented by the small platform at the base of the mound and the "second occupation level" exposed during the WPA excavation (Figure 7.1). Most of the documented features and postholes were found immediately above the "second occupation level" (Kelly and Smith 1975: Figure 50). Kelly and Smith's examination of the 1937–38 field diary found references to an alignment on the east side of the mound consisting of approximately 51 postholes spaced about .45 m (1.5 ft.) apart. Based on that description, they suggested that a wall or a square or rectangular structure once stood on the mound summit. Unfortunately, no map showing the posthole distribution existed at the time of the 1975 analysis (1975:92–93). A photograph showing postholes on the second occupation surface indicated that the posts were quite substantial in size (Kelly and Smith

1975: plate 30). Several of the features found just above the occupation surface appear to be circular pits with adjoining trenches that may have been used for erecting large posts in the pits (Kelly and Smith 1975: figure 50). Similar features have been found in other Swift Creek platform mounds (Fish and Jefferies 1986).

Analysis of mound ceramics demonstrated that there was an increasing percentage of plain pottery from the bottom to the top of the mound. This trend was accompanied by an increased complexity of complicated-stamped designs. Kelly and Smith observed that the simple concentric circle motif was the most common element in the lower levels, generally occurring as the only design element on a vessel or interspersed with curving fill lines. Concentric circles tended to occur as fill elements in more complex designs on vessels represented in the upper mound levels (1975:38). A decreased importance of notched and scalloped rims in favor of folded rims and changes in vessel form through time were also noted (Kelly and Smith 1975:63–65).

As a consequence of their analysis, Kelly and Smith concluded that the main component at the site was Swift Creek, and that Mound A was constructed at that time. Construction of Mound A started with the building of a low platform, indicating to them that at least some Swift Creek groups were involved in the deliberate construction of small flat-topped mounds (Kelly and Smith 1975:115).

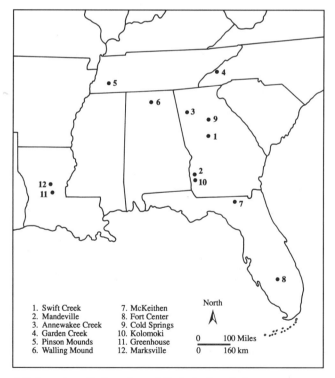

1. Swift Creek
2. Mandeville
3. Annewakee Creek
4. Garden Creek
5. Pinson Mounds
6. Walling Mound
7. McKeithen
8. Fort Center
9. Cold Springs
10. Kolomoki
11. Greenhouse
12. Marksville

North

0   100 Miles
0   160 km

7.2. Location of selected pre-Mississippian platform mound sites.

This interpretation represents a revision of Kelly's 1938 interpretation of the mound as an unplanned occupational structure that grew largely through accretionary expansion.

Unfortunately, no radiocarbon dates are available for the Swift Creek mound. Comparing Mound A ceramics with material from well-dated contexts at Mandeville, Annewakee Creek, and Russell Cave, Kelly and Smith proposed that the site dated to approximately A.D. 500–750 (1975:114).

The Stubbs Mound (9BE12), located approximately 9 km south of the Swift Creek site, was excavated by Gordon R. Willey from August 1936 to February 1937 as part of the WPA investigations at Ocmulgee (Williams 1975). The mound has been identified as a possible Swift Creek platform mound (see Dickens 1975; Williams 1975), but is now generally considered to date to the early Lamar period (Hally and Rudolph 1986; J. Mark Williams, personal communication).

Other Woodland Platform Mounds in the Southeast

Kelly's 1938 description of the Swift Creek site seems to have stimulated little interest in the question of Woodland platform mounds in the Southeast. In fact, the issue was not really raised again until the early 1960s, when excavations were undertaken at the Mandeville site (9CY1) in southwest Georgia (Figure 7.2) (Kellar, Kelly, and McMichael 1962a, 1962b; Smith 1975, 1979). Mandeville Mound A was a large flat-topped structure measuring 73 m by 52 m at the base and more than 4 m high. Excavation revealed that while the upper 1.2 m was attributable to a Fort Walton-Lamar occupation, the underlying levels (Levels I–IV) contained Swift Creek complicated-stamped pottery (Smith 1979:181–82). Examination of the mound profiles showed that mound construction started with a low flat-topped mound (Feature 25) erected directly on the premound midden (Kellar, Kelly, and McMichael 1962a:75). The mound subsequently grew in size as a result of the *in situ* accumulation of occupational debris and the intentional deposition of fill brought in from elsewhere. Ceramic material from the four Middle Woodland levels was quite similar, suggesting continuity in mound construction. Features and fired areas occurred within mound levels, as well as on their surfaces (Smith 1979:181–82). Although no posthole patterns suggesting a structure were observed on any of the occupation surfaces, Kelly referred to Mound A as a domiciliary mound (1973: 37). Radiocarbon dates from Mandeville indicate that construction of Mound A started around A.D. 250; the site appears to have been abandoned by A.D. 500 (Smith 1979:182–83).

Sears's (1956) investigations at Kolomoki, a large

Swift Creek–Weeden Island I site in southwest Georgia (Figure 7.2), revealed several platform mounds. The largest, Mound A, a 17-m-high truncated pyramidal structure, is thought by some to be a Mississippian platform mound built using fill from the earlier Woodland occupations. Pottery found in several other smaller mounds suggests that they were built by the site's Weeden Island I inhabitants between A.D. 100 and 500 (Sears 1956; Milanich et al. 1984:20). Mounds F and H, which Sears assigned to his "Kolomoki period," appear to have served as platform structures during at least part of their "use life." Both mounds measured approximately 20 by 16 m at the base, and 2 m high. The two mounds contained flat-topped mound stages built using white and yellow clay, respectively. While a few postholes and burned areas were located, no definitive evidence of structures was present. Sears proposed that these two mounds were involved in burial ceremonies that took place at the nearby burial mounds (Sears 1956:13).

The Annewakee Creek mound (9DO2), located in northwest Georgia, was initially investigated by Wauchope in the late 1930s (Figure 7.2). His test trench revealed sequential platform stages and abundant Woodland sherds (Wauchope 1966:404–6). Subsequent excavations, conducted by Dickens in 1972, exposed a core mound feature consisting of a 10-by-10-m platform made of bright yellow clay. Its original height was estimated to be about .6 m. The yellow clay was completely exposed, revealing a pattern of postholes suggesting two superimposed structures. One structure was rectangular, measuring approximately 4 m by 6 m. A slightly larger square structure measured about 5 by 5 m. Other postholes intruded the platform surface from above. Charcoal from an intrusive pit feature yielded a radiocarbon determination of 1195 ± 100 years: A.D. 755. A second date of 1345 ± 85 years: A.D. 605 was associated with fill that formed an extension of a possible cap over the yellow clay (Dickens 1975: 35–36). Based on her analysis of the Annewakee Creek ceramic material, Rudolph (1986) has given the mound a Napier cultural affiliation.

Archaeological investigations conducted at the Garden Creek Mound No. 2 in western North Carolina revealed that the surfaces of the two mound stages served as platforms for some kind of Middle Woodland structure (Figure 7.2). The primary mound, measuring ca. 12 m by 18 m and .5 m high, contained numerous postholes on its surface. Several of the postholes were quite large, ranging from .3 to .9 m in diameter and from .3 to 1.5 m deep. Rock-filled hearths and refuse pits, many containing Connestee ceramics, were also associated with the primary mound (Keel 1976:78–85).

The secondary mound, constructed by adding basket loads of clayey loam to the top and sides of the primary mound, measured 25 m by 18 m and was originally about 3 m high. Numerous postholes were also found on the secondary mound surface, but as on the primary mound, no clear alignments were noted. Secondary mound features included a large posthole, refuse pits, and rock-filled hearths. Charcoal from one hearth yielded a radiocarbon determination of 1145 ± 85 years: A.D. 805 (Keel 1976: 85–89). Keel considered this date to be several centuries too recent for some of the material contained in the feature (Keel 1975:14).

Connestee ceramics accounted for the majority of sherds from both mound stages. Swift Creek, Napier, and a variety of Hopewell sherds were also found (Keel 1976: table 16).

Recent work at the Pinson Mounds site, located in western Tennessee (Figure 7.2), has provided important new findings about Woodland platform mounds (Mainfort 1986). The site includes a number of large and small platform mounds, burial mounds, an earthwork, and an associated habitation area. Although the results of limited testing conducted in 1961 indicated that most of the Pinson mounds dated to the Middle Woodland period, the discovery of a wall-trench house led many archaeologists to assume that the large mounds had a Mississippian origin (Mainfort 1986:9).

Testing of Mound 5 (Ozier Mound), the site's second largest platform mound, revealed at least six construction stages. Each stage was marked by a 5-cm-thick capping of sand. Charcoal from two hearths associated with the upper stage yielded radiocarbon determinations of 1970 ± 110 years: 20 B.C. and 1760 ± 160 years: A.D. 190, respectively (Mainfort 1986:15).

Investigation of a smaller, irregularly shaped platform mound, Mound 10, produced examples of nonlocal pottery, including several Swift Creek Complicated Stamped sherds. Charcoal from a large mound feature yielded radiocarbon determinations of 1885 ± 130 years: A.D. 65 and 1680 ± 85 years: A.D. 270 (Mainfort 1986:26).

To date, no indications of structures have been found on any of the excavated platform mounds. Four of the other Pinson platform mounds appear to date to the same period as Mounds 5 and 10, indicating that the site served as a major Middle Woodland ceremonial center (Mainfort 1986:82).

Additional examples of Woodland platform mounds have been documented in several Gulf Coast states. The Walling site, investigated by University of Alabama archaeologists in 1986, is located near the Tennessee River in Madison County, Alabama (Figure 7.2). The site consists of a platform mound, a small village area, and at least one, and possibly two, Copena burial mounds (Knight 1990).

The rectangular platform mound, measuring 38 by 32 m at the base, was approximately 1.4 m high when tested by a WPA crew in 1941. At that time, the mound, comprised of four distinct construction stages, was presumed to date to the Mississippi period. Charcoal samples collected from the premound midden and Stages 1 and 2 during the recent University of Alabama investigations yielded radiocarbon determinations ranging from 1820 ± 80 years: A.D. 130 to 1600 ± 70: A.D. 350, indicating that the first two stages, and probably the third, are attributable to Middle Woodland Copena construction activities (Knight 1990: table 1).

Mound Stages 1 and 2 were characterized by level summits covered by scattered small postholes, large postholes, funnel-shaped postholes, small burned lenses and hearths, small basin-shaped pits, and three very large post features having slide trenches. Some of the small postholes associated with the Stage 2 summit may be aligned, but no obvious structures were observed. Scattered midden deposits containing faunal and botanical remains and lithic and ceramic material were also exposed. No indications of Middle Woodland mortuary activity were noted. As with many other Woodland platform mounds, the Walling mound was reused during the Early Mississippi period, as reflected by two burials, a large shell-filled pit, and several rectangular structures on top of the mound (Knight 1990).

Low platform mounds were constructed by the Grand Lake phase (early Coles Creek) inhabitants of the Greenhouse site in Louisiana (Ford 1951). The mounds had trapezoidal bases and were located at each end of an oval plaza. The top of one mound appeared to have been rounded or D-shaped, with a round structure on the summit. Subsequent stages were built by adding flat caps of clay that did not overlap the sides of the previous stages. Burials were placed in the mound top (Belmont 1967:31). Belmont proposed that these mounds were ancestral to the "temple mound tradition" and a continuation of an earlier platform mound tradition that existed in late Hopewell and Swift Creek, and locally in Marksville-Issaquena (1967:31–32).

Several of the mounds at the Marksville site, Louisiana, are flat-topped structures. Vescelius (1957:419) considered Mound 2, a rectangular mound measuring ca. 88 m by 22 m and 4 m high, to be one of the oldest temple mounds in the eastern United States.

Further to the south, investigations at the McKeithen site, located in Columbia County, Florida, identified three sand mounds arranged in a triangular pattern and dating to about A.D. 375 (Figure 7.2). Although the mounds are thought to have been associated with mortuary activities, they did not contain many burials. The largest of them, Mound A, was originally constructed as a platform measuring 32 m by 42 m and about .5 m high. The presence of multiple empty burial pits, many of which had been reexcavated, suggests that the platform was used to clean the bodies of the deceased. Processing activities appear to have been restricted to a 12-m-by-14-m area at the rear of the platform. This part of Mound A contained large pine posts, some exceeding 60 cm in diameter, that were erected in holes with slide trenches. Most of the posts were apparently removed prior to abandoning the mound. The charnel area, marked by numerous circular features interpreted as burial and maceration pits, was centered over a part of the mound comprised of specially deposited layers of soil consisting of alternating bands of gray and tan sand placed between layers of organic material. Prior to abandonment, the entire platform mound was covered with a 2-m-thick mound cap measuring 45 m by 80 m (Milanich et al. 1984:94–105, Milanich and Fairbanks 1980:132–36).

McKeithen Mound B originally consisted of a small rectangular platform measuring 10.5 m by 14.1 m, averaging less than .5 m high. Posthole alignments indicate that a 6.9-m-by-10.2-m rectangular structure once stood on the mound. A single adult male burial was found below the house floor. As with Mound A, the platform was capped with an additional layer of soil, creating a circular mound measuring 27 m in diameter and 1.5 m high (Milanich et al. 1984:105–12, Milanich and Fairbanks 1980:134–35).

Mound C was a 16-m-diameter circular platform mound that may have supported a charnel structure. At least 36 child and adult burials, reflecting a variety of postmortem treatments, were placed at 1.5 m intervals around the edge and in the southeast quadrant of the circular platform. The entire mound was capped by a 2-m-thick layer of soil (Milanich et al. 1984:112–17; Milanich and Fairbanks 1980:136–37). Milanich et al. (1984:118) have suggested that the three McKeithen platform mounds were constructed, used, and abandoned at the same time, and that they represent components of a relatively complex mortuary program.

Sears's (1982) investigations at the Fort Center site, located in the Lake Okeechobee area of south central Florida, revealed at least two platform structures (Figure 7.2). These mounds were apparently constructed during the Period II occupation, dating to between A.D. 200 and A.D. 600 (1982:186). The mounds were part of a ceremonial center, comprised of the two mounds, an artificial pond, a wooden platform constructed over the pond, and a surrounding earthwork. Although the mounds and associated facilities had a definite ceremonial/mortuary function, the presence of structures and refuse deposits on the two mounds indicated to Sears that they also served as occupation surfaces (Sears 1982:195).

Mound A, located on the east side of the pond, is an irregular earthen platform averaging about 1 m high. Excavations yielded large quantities of cultural remains, including pottery, faunal material, and shell and stone tools. Examination of the submound surface disclosed a number of postholes that intruded from above. Posthole distributions indicate that several 10-m-diameter oval structures were built on the mound.

Mound B, located west of the pond, was a low, flat-topped mound that supported a charnel house (Milanich and Fairbanks 1980:187). Apparently, the dirt excavated from the pond was used to construct the 70-cm-high platform-shaped primary mound, as well as the earthworks encircling the mound and connecting it to Mound A. The recovery of miscellaneous human bones and teeth suggested to Sears that the mound surface was used in the preparation of the deceased for subsequent disposal on the wooden charnel platform that once stood in the pond (Sears 1982:160–62).

Ceramic collections from the surface of Mound B contained a number of nonlocal sherds. The Deptford complex was represented by simple and check stamped sherds. Examples of St. Johns pottery made in the form of Deptford Simple Stamped and Deptford Checked Stamped vessels with tetrapods were also found, as were Pasco ceramics from Florida's west coast (Sears 1982: 27–29).

The Cold Springs Site

The Cold Springs site (9GE10), located in Greene County, Georgia, lies on the east side of the Oconee River, approximately 90 km north of Macon (Figure 7.2). The site, covering some 4.4 ha, is situated on a broad floodplain in what is now the Lake Oconee basin. The site consists of two large circular, gently rounded mounds, and an off-mound activity/habitation area (Figure 7.3). Mound A, the larger of the two mounds, was approximately 50 m in diameter and 2.8 m high; the smaller mound, Mound B, was about 40 m in diameter and 1.6 m high (Fish and Jefferies 1986:61).

The first recorded archaeological investigations at Cold Springs occurred in 1970 as part of a preliminary study for the construction of the Wallace Dam and Lake Oconee (Caldwell 1971). Test excavations placed in mound and off-mound locations indicated that the site had the potential to provide new insights into Swift Creek cultural manifestations in the Georgia Piedmont (Fish 1979).

More systematic testing of Cold Springs was conducted by the University of Georgia in 1974. Several test units were placed in the two mounds; off-mound areas were investigated using a combination of strip plowing and hand and posthole excavations (DePratter 1976b). This work showed that the off-mound area contained artifacts and features dating from the Archaic to the Mississippi period. Stratigraphic information collected from Mound A suggested that it was a flat-topped platform mound consisting of at least five construction stages. Mound A ceramic material indicated that much of the

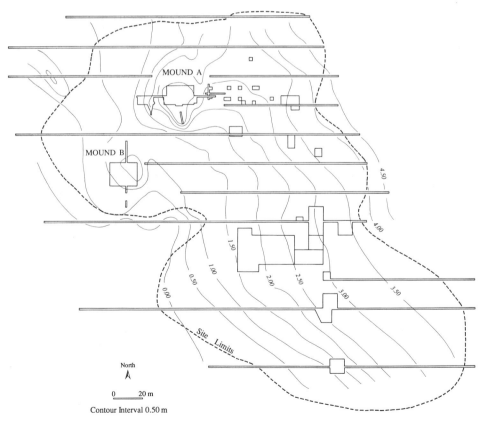

7.3. Site plan and excavation units for Cold Springs site.

Richard W. Jefferies

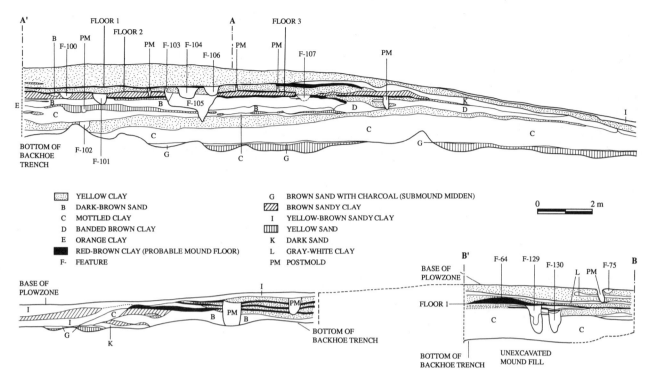

7.4. Generalized profile of south wall of east-west trench through Mound A, Cold Springs site. (See Figure 7.7 for trench location.)

Legend:

YELLOW CLAY
B — DARK-BROWN SAND
C — MOTTLED CLAY
D — BANDED BROWN CLAY
E — ORANGE CLAY
RED-BROWN CLAY (PROBABLE MOUND FLOOR)
F- — FEATURE

G — BROWN SAND WITH CHARCOAL (SUBMOUND MIDDEN)
BROWN SANDY CLAY
I — YELLOW-BROWN SANDY CLAY
YELLOW SAND
K — DARK SAND
L — GRAY-WHITE CLAY
PM — POSTMOLD

0   2 m

mound construction was attributable to the Swift Creek occupation (DePratter 1976b).

Large-scale excavations at Cold Springs were initiated by the University of Georgia in the summer of 1977, and continued, with frequent weather-related interruptions, for one year. Although other sites with Woodland platform mounds had been excavated in the Southeast, relatively little was known about off-mound activities or about the organization of the societies responsible for mound construction. For these reasons, research efforts at Cold Springs focused on determining the site plan and using the resulting data to investigate the nature of the community surrounding the mounds (Fish and Jefferies 1986).

In order to accomplish these goals, major excavation efforts took place in the off-mound area. Approximately 4,700 square meters of off-mound area were excavated using a combination of hand excavation, machine stripping, and systematic backhoe trenching (Figure 7.3). These same techniques were used on a more restricted scale to investigate the two mounds (Fish 1979; Fish and Jefferies 1986).

The most useful information for interpreting mound structure, function, and age came from Mound A. Excavation of the mound was initiated by removing the plowzone, shovel scraping the surface, and recording all features. A backhoe trench oriented east-west was then excavated, bisecting the mound. Later, a backhoe was used to excavate a 15-m-by-11-m area of the mound

summit down to Floor 1, the surface of a late mound stage (Figure 7.3). A premound structure (Structure 5) on the west edge of the mound was also exposed using the backhoe (Fish 1979, Fish and Jefferies 1986).

Inspection of the long east-west trench wall showed that mound stratigraphy generally consisted of continuous layers of sterile yellow, brown, or orange sands and clays (Figure 7.4). The soil in each layer was homogeneous, apparently collected from a single source (Figure 7.5). The first stage extended to the maximum diameter of the mound, with the diameter of each successive stage being slightly smaller. Additional soil layers were placed on top of the mound, but little soil was added to the sides. Features and postholes originated from the surface of at least five levels of the mound, suggesting a variety of mound summit activities (Fish 1979; Fish and Jefferies 1986).

The lowest cultural deposit in the Mound A trench was a thin layer of premound midden containing Swift Creek Complicated Stamped and plain grit tempered pottery (Figure 7.6, A and B). Structure 5, a rectangular structure containing similar pottery, was located below the mound's western edge (Figure 7.6, C–E). A radiocarbon determination of 1660 ± 70 years: A.D. 290 (UGA-2384) was associated with Structure 5.

The lower meter of the mound consisted of sand and clay layers, capped by a thin layer of red-brown clay that extended across most of the mound. Two additional thin layers of red-brown clay occurred above the first, each separated by a layer of clay. Because of the large

7.5. Trench wall profile in Mound A at Cold Springs site.

numbers of postholes and features originating from these layers, they were designated as Floors 1–3 (Fish and Jefferies 1986).

Mound A was capped by several layers of yellow clay. A number of features were delineated at the base of the plowzone on top of the mound, including several burials containing Lamar vessels that intruded into the yellow clay. The burial pits were sealed by the upper clay layer, indicating that it was a late prehistoric (Lamar culture) addition to the mound. Despite the evidence for Late Prehistoric use of the top of Mound A, few post–Swift Creek artifacts were found below the clay cap.

In order to investigate more thoroughly Mound A's internal structure, a large area of the clay cap was removed to expose the surface of Floor 1 (Figures 7.3 and 7.7). Clearing of the floor revealed more than 150 features and postholes. A large, dome-shaped feature (Feature 64), consisting of alternating layers of sand and charcoal, was associated with Floor 1. The few artifacts collected from the feature included simple stamped, curvilinear complicated stamped, burnished, and plain grit tempered sherds (Figure 7.6, F). A charcoal sample from the feature yielded a date of 1505 ± 55 years: A.D. 445 (UGA-2364).

The exposed portion of Floor 1 contained more than 100 postholes of various sizes and configurations (Figure 7.7). Some intruded into Floor 1 from above, but others clearly originated on that surface (Figure 7.4). Many of the postholes were quite large, some being over .5 m in diameter and extending nearly 1.0 m into the mound (Figure 7.8). Many of the larger posts were set off-center in large pits (Figure 7.9). A number of the pits and postholes containing large posts were associated with adjoining trenches that increased in depth as they approached the hole. These "erection" or "slide" trenches were apparently dug to assist in the insertion of a large post into a hole. In many cases, postholes associated with a lower floor were sealed by the subsequent floor, indicating that posts were removed, or that they deteriorated, prior to construction of the next mound stage. Based on the trench-wall profile, similar large posts were associated with Floors 2 and 3. Floor 1 postholes and features contained few artifacts, reflecting the very low frequency of artifacts collected while excavating the floor.

The distribution of the Floor 1 postholes offers little evidence for structures. An alternative possibility is that the large posts associated with slide trenches served as markers rather than structural components. The large diameter and depth of some postholes suggest that posts may have been quite tall. A 50-cm-diameter post could easily be 7 to 8 m long, so the excavation of slide trenches would have greatly facilitated their erection (see Wittry 1977: Figure 27). Similar large posts erected within the charnel area of McKeithen Mound A using the same post insertion technique have been interpreted as grave monuments or markers (Milanich et al. 1984: 101–2). Large marker posts are also known to occur on Mississippian platform mounds, such as Monks Mound at Cahokia (Reed 1977:33).

Another possibility is that the large posts supported some kind of elevated platform or scaffold on top of Cold Springs Mound A. A wooden structure made of tree trunks and unshaped timbers was apparently built during the Period II (A.D. 200–600) occupation at the Fort Center site, serving as a platform to support burials

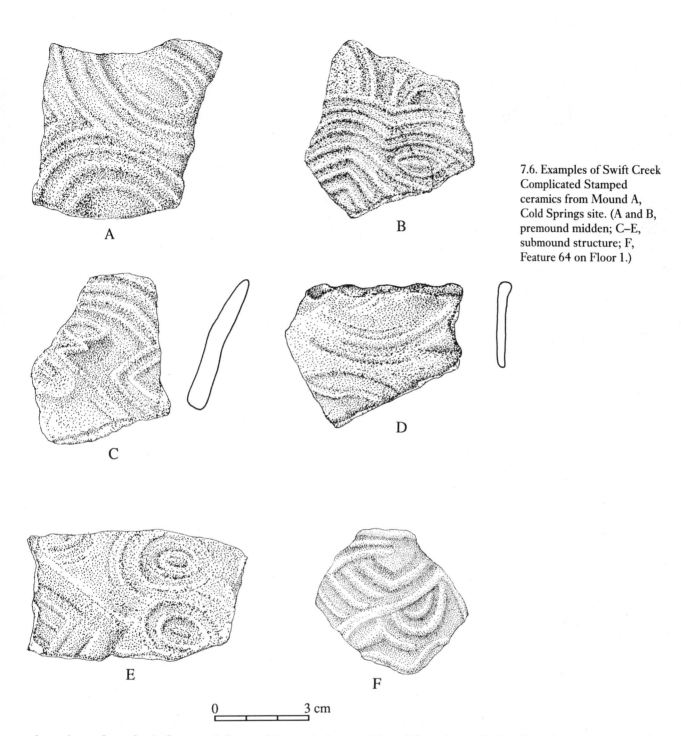

7.6. Examples of Swift Creek Complicated Stamped ceramics from Mound A, Cold Springs site. (A and B, premound midden; C–E, submound structure; F, Feature 64 on Floor 1.)

A

B

C

D

E

F

0   3 cm

above the surface of a shallow pond. Some of the vertical support posts were carved, creating a variety of animal forms (Milanich and Fairbanks 1980:187; Sears 1982: 165–67, figure 9.14).

Both of these explanations for the large Mound A posts involve probable mortuary activities. Although no direct evidence was found associating Cold Springs Mound A with Swift Creek mortuary activities, the presence of calcined bone and an associated copper earspool fragment in nearby Mound B suggests that possibility (see below).

Mound floors located below Floor 1 were not exposed because of time limitations. In view of the number of associated features and postholes visible in the east-west trench, the appearance of Floors 2 and 3 should resemble that of Floor 1.

Although the excavation of Cold Springs Mound A produced a relatively small collection of ceramic material, sherds closely resemble those from other early Swift Creek mounds and habitation sites in the Georgia Piedmont. Swift Creek pottery from Mound A was

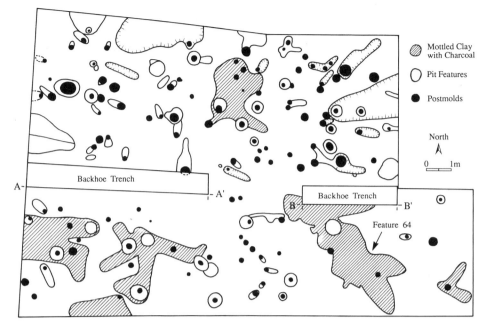

7.7. Features and postholes on Floor 1 of Mound A, Cold Springs site.

Legend:
- Mottled Clay with Charcoal
- Pit Features
- Postmolds

North

0   1m

Backhoe Trench

A — A'

Backhoe Trench

B — B'

Feature 64

decorated with complex designs incorporating a number of decorative elements, including circles, spots, and parallel lines that are characteristic of early Swift Creek (T. Rudolph 1986).

In summary, excavation of Cold Springs Mound A exposed a series of flat-topped construction stages containing homogeneous sterile fill. At least five stages were indicated by the distribution of features and postholes. Ceramic material from below and within the mound suggests that most of the construction occurred during the early Swift Creek occupation. Radiocarbon dates indicate that most of the mound was built between A.D. 290 and A.D. 445. Several intrusive Lamar burials on the mound summit reflect a period of Late Prehistoric mound use, and the final clay cap was added at that time.

The numerous postholes and features on Floor 1 suggest that the surface remained exposed for a considerable period of time and was the scene of much activity. Some postholes may reflect structural alignments, but clear patterns are difficult to discern. Others, particularly the large ones with slide trenches, may represent mound-top markers or monuments. The near absence of artifacts suggests that the mound surfaces were not used for ordinary domestic activities and/or that they were periodically cleaned.

Mound B, located about 50 m southwest of Mound A, was 40 m in diameter and 1.6 m high (Figure 7.3). A burned area located just below the mound summit contained small pieces of bone and a possible copper earspool fragment. The feature, interpreted as cremated human remains, yielded a radiocarbon date of 1550 ± 65 years: A.D. 400. Exposure of the remainder of this mound

stage in 1979 revealed no additional burned areas, but postholes were found on the surfaces of underlying stages. A rectangular alignment was defined on one surface. The mound's internal structure is less clear than that of Mound A, but generally consisted of thin horizontal bands of clay (Fish and Jefferies 1986:71). It appears, based on the radiocarbon determinations, that Mounds A and B were used contemporaneously.

Although the precise nature of on-mound activities at Cold Springs is unclear, some contemporary mounds with similar architectural features (McKeithen, Fort Center) were important components of mortuary programs. The multiple floors observed in Mound A trench-wall profiles, along with the internal banding in Feature 64, suggest that mound-top activities were performed on a recurring basis. The recovery of cremated human remains and a copper earspool fragment from Mound B indicates that at least one of the two mounds functioned in an early Swift Creek mortuary program.

Unlike the excavations undertaken at other sites with Woodland platform mounds, the Cold Springs project provided the opportunity to investigate the off-mound area to determine the nature of occupations associated with mound construction. Excavation of nearly 5,000 square meters around the mounds demonstrated that most of the cultural material is attributable to the Swift Creek occupation and a later Etowah period occupation. Although excavations yielded many Swift Creek artifacts, few structures were identified. Based on site area, area excavated, and number of structures encountered in excavations, an estimated eight off-mound Swift Creek structures were present at Cold Springs (Fish and

Richard W. Jefferies

7.8. Profile of large post originating from Floor 1 of Mound A, Cold Springs site.

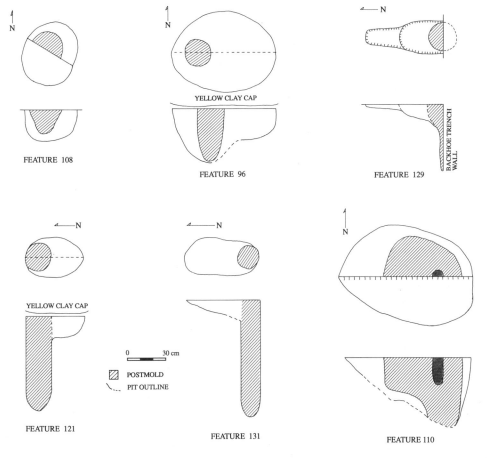

N

FEATURE 108

N

YELLOW CLAY CAP

FEATURE 96

N

BACKHOE TRENCH WALL

FEATURE 129

7.9. Profiles and plan views of postholes associated with Floor 1 of Mound A, Cold Springs site.

N

YELLOW CLAY CAP

FEATURE 121

N

FEATURE 131

0   30 cm

◪ POSTMOLD
⋯ PIT OUTLINE

N

FEATURE 110

Jefferies 1986). It appears that during the Swift Creek occupation, the Cold Springs site was sparsely occupied and contained only a few scattered structures.

Summary and Conclusions

Although Kelly realized in the 1930s that Middle Woodland Swift Creek groups were constructing platform mounds near the Macon Plateau, most archaeologists continued to associate this mound type exclusively with Mississippian society for many more years. Why didn't Kelly's findings have more of an impact on archaeological thought during the ensuing 30 or 40 years? Largely because no comprehensive report on this work existed until 1975. Kelly and Smith's (1975) publication finally made the information available to the archaeological community, joining a then rapidly growing body of literature on Woodland platform mounds.

Considerable progress has been made toward understanding the nature of Woodland platform mounds in the Southeast in the 50 years since the excavation of the Swift Creek mound. The Swift Creek mound seemed unique in the 1930s, but today we see it conforming to a pattern represented at many other Woodland sites. The examples from Georgia, North Carolina, Tennessee, Alabama, Louisiana, and Florida discussed in this chapter are but a few of the many mounds that have provided new insights into the nature of Woodland platform mounds. This list can be expanded to include the Crooks (Ford and Willey 1940) site in Louisiana, the Leake Mound (9BR2) in northwest Georgia (Hally, personal communication), as well as several other Middle Woodland platform mounds in west Tennessee, northeast Mississippi, Louisiana, and Ohio (see Mainfort 1986:82–83).

The mounds discussed in this chapter, generally dating from A.D. 100 to A.D. 600, clearly demonstrate that platform mound construction predates the Mississippi period and was quite widespread in the southeastern United States. However, does this necessarily mean that they were directly ancestral to traditional Mississippian platform mounds? Flat-topped Mississippian mounds generally served as platforms or bases on which buildings and other architectural features were constructed. Mound-summit buildings are generally interpreted as temples or houses used by the elite members of Mississippian society. Most Mississippian platform mounds consisted of several stages. New stages were built by adding layers of soil that covered the sides and top of the preexisting mound. Using this construction technique, a mound increased in basal area as well as height with the addition of each new stage.

The Woodland mounds described in this chapter differ in many respects from this model of Mississippian mound construction and use. While they all have one or more stages with flat surfaces on which activities were carried out, few exhibit good evidence for substantial mound-top buildings. The best evidence for structures comes from the Annewakee Creek, Fort Center, McKeithen (Mound B), and Swift Creek mounds. Other mounds, such as Cold Spring (Mound A), Walling, and McKeithen (Mound A), have surfaces covered with postholes of various sizes and configurations, but they are not arranged in any readily apparent pattern. Some of the small postholes may reflect some kind of mound-top structure. In contrast, the large posts could represent markers or monuments, not structural components of buildings. The excavation of platform mounds at several other sites, including Mandeville and Pinson, revealed prepared mound surfaces, but no postholes or other evidence of structures. Hearths and other kinds of features were noted on these mounds.

Construction techniques used to build some Woodland mounds differed from those used by most Mississippian mound builders. At Cold Springs (Mound A) and Greenhouse, mound stages were constructed by placing a layer of earth on top of the preexisting mound surface; no new fill was added to the sides of the mound. Using this technique, the size of the mound base was established by the plan of the first stage. As subsequent stages were added, the mound top increased in elevation but decreased in surface area (see Belmont 1967; Fish and Jefferies 1986).

The kind of earthen fill used for mound stage construction varies considerably among Woodland mounds. At some sites, such as Cold Springs, the distinctive color and texture of the clay used for each new layer indicates that the builders made a conscious effort to obtain fill from one source to build each new mound stage. Artifacts are rarely found on the surfaces of these mounds, possibly reflecting an intentional effort to keep the mound surface clean. Other mounds, such as Mandeville and Swift Creek, reportedly had thick midden accumulations, apparently reflecting intensive mound-top habitation activities. Some of the midden in these mounds may be attributable to *in situ* refuse accumulation, but much of it could represent mound fill derived from an off-mound habitation area.

Investigation of some Woodland mounds produced evidence that they were involved in some aspect of the mortuary program. In certain cases, these activities appeared to focus on processing the remains of the deceased rather than on their final deposition. Other mounds have yielded less substantial evidence of their associated activities.

Mainfort has pointed out that many major Mississippian mound centers served as foci for large ranked political systems and contained substantial resident populations. In contrast, the large, complex Pinson Mounds site appears to have been built for specific ceremonial purposes and was apparently inhabited by a relatively small number of people (1986:82–82). Similarly, the few Swift Creek structures located during the Cold Springs field investigations suggest that the site maintained a relatively small resident population. Fish (1979) has suggested that mound construction and use involved more than the Cold Springs resident group. The site may have been the focus of a variety of socially integrative activities that incorporated a number of early Swift Creek groups living in the Oconee River valley, but not in the immediate vicinity of the Cold Springs site (Fish and Jefferies 1986:72). In many ways, these Woodland sites appear to represent the early stages of social and political development that reached its height in the Southeast during the Mississippi period.

The characteristics of the Woodland platform mound surfaces suggest not only that activities differed from those proposed for Mississippian platform mounds, but that a great deal of variability existed among the mounds themselves. Differences in construction techniques and mound-top architecture may indicate that Woodland platform mounds were involved in different kinds of activity in various southeastern cultural systems. On the other hand, these differences may simply reflect temporally and/or regionally distinct responses to the same activity. Whatever those relationships, it is clear that the practice of using elevated earthen platforms for "special" activities predates the emergence of Mississippian society. It is obvious that the investigation of Woodland platform

mounds must be continued to determine their roles in Middle and Late Woodland social and political developments, and to clarify further the relationships between these mounds and the classic substructure mounds built during the Mississippi period.

Acknowledgments

I wish to acknowledge all those individuals who were involved in archaeological investigations at the Cold Springs site (9GE10). The first systematic excavation of the site was conducted in 1971 by Archie Smith, under the direction of Joseph Caldwell. Smith's investigations brought the site and its mounds to the attention of the professional community. DePratter's 1974 test excavations yielded information on the site's occupational sequence and provided solid evidence of the mounds' Swift Creek cultural affiliation. Extensive excavations conducted in 1977 and 1978 as part of the Wallace Reservoir Archaeological Project provided much of the data used in this chapter. David J. Hally and Paul R. Fish served as principal investigators for the project. The research design for the Cold Springs investigations was devised by Paul and Suzanne Fish. Suzanne Fish served as project director throughout most of the 1977–78 fieldwork and subsequent artifact analysis. Many of the ideas about the Cold Springs site presented in this chapter are based on the work of these individuals, and their years of dedication and hard work are gratefully acknowledged. Hopefully, I have not misinterpreted the efforts of these professionals and friends.

CHAPTER EIGHT

Macon Plateau Site Community Pattern

David J. Hally and Mark Williams

THE MACON PLATEAU site (9BI1) is a site of extremes. It is the largest Mississippian mound site in Georgia. It is also the earliest securely dated Mississippian mound site in the state. It has been more extensively investigated and has had more written about it than any other site of its kind in the state. Yet it is one of the most poorly understood and controversial Mississippian sites in the southeastern United States: its duration in time and its historical relationship to earlier and later sites in the area are not clearly known; the functional interrelationships among its many architectural features are poorly understood; and several of these features are unique and puzzling.

No synthesis of Macon Plateau site archaeology has ever been written, although one is desperately needed. We do not provide that synthesis here. Instead we attempt to provide a comprehensive review of one element that is critical to an understanding of the site—mound and nonmound construction features. In the following pages we summarize the architectural characteristics of these features, attempt to determine their temporal position within the Macon Plateau phase, investigate their spatial relationships, and speculate about their function. Our goal is to develop an understanding of how the site was organized and used.

The Natural Setting

The Macon Plateau site is located on the east side of the Ocmulgee River at the Fall Line, the point where the river leaves the Piedmont and enters the Coastal Plain (see Figure I.1). Upstream from the site, the river flows through a narrow valley where shoals are common in the river channel and the floodplain seldom exceeds 500 m in width. At the point where the river passes the site, its floodplain expands to a width of 4 km and its channel begins to meander freely.

This kind of location is apparently a preferred one for Mississippian mound centers in the southern Piedmont, as one or more are situated at the Fall Line on almost every major river in Georgia, South Carolina, and North Carolina that flows into the South Atlantic. The reason for this preference seems clear. Immediately below the Fall Line, river floodplains are considerably broader than they are in the Piedmont, and the alluvium that is deposited there in great quantities is richer in mineral nutrients than it is farther downstream in the Coastal Plain. Furthermore, extensive shoals occur at the Fall Line, providing rich fisheries, and the natural resources of both Piedmont and Coastal Plain are readily accessible from this point.

The Macon Plateau site is situated on a relatively flat section of upland hills (usually referred to as the Macon Plateau) bordering the Ocmulgee River on its east side (Figure 8.1). It lies approximately 15 m above the floodplain of the Ocmulgee River and is bounded in places on its river side by a fairly steep escarpment. This type of location is not unique to the Macon Plateau site—Hartley-Posey (9TR2), Tate (9EB86), Roods (9ST1), and Shinholser (9BL1) in Georgia and Moundville in Alabama are similarly situated—but it is not common. Most Mississippian mound sites in the southern Piedmont that are located adjacent to rivers are situated in the floodplain of those rivers.

Two railroad cuts constructed in 1843 and 1871 divide the Macon Plateau into four segments commonly referred to by archaeologists working there in the 1930s as the North, Middle, South, and Southeast Plateaus

(Figure 8.2). Figure 8.1 is a reconstruction of how Macon Plateau probably looked before these railroad cuts were made. It is clear from this map that the site was constructed on a ground surface with considerable topographic relief. Ground surface rises from south to north across the site with the result that the McDougal and Dunlap mounds are elevated approximately 20 m above Mounds A, B, and C. The site area is also divided into three elevated sections by two small, north-south flowing streams. As a result, some parts of the site—for example, Mounds A and C—are separated by low areas as much as 14 m deep. Except for the escarpment bordering the Ocmulgee River floodplain and in the immediate vicinity of the two small streams, however, the surface contours of the site do not seem to be steep enough to have limited how particular areas were utilized.

Description of Site Features

There is no extant map that shows the location and configuration of all archaeological features and excavation units on the Macon Plateau. Figure 8.2 is based on separate maps compiled for different sections of the Plateau (Fairbanks 1956a; Ingmanson 1964a, 1964b, 1965; Williams and Henderson 1974). Unfortunately Figure 8.2 does not show all excavation units and may not be totally accurate with respect to those it does show. It does not show the excavations that were conducted in and around Mound E and the Dunlap Mound and south of Mound C, and it may contain some errors in its depiction of excavation units on the North Plateau. For the most part, these shortcomings are the result of incomplete or missing field records.

Earth Mounds

Mound A (Great Temple Mound), measuring 15 m high and 91 m square at the base, is the largest platform mound on the site (Figure 8.3). From the river, the mound appears to be even larger. It is situated immediately adjacent to the steepest portion of the Macon Plateau escarpment and as a result towers some 27.5 m above

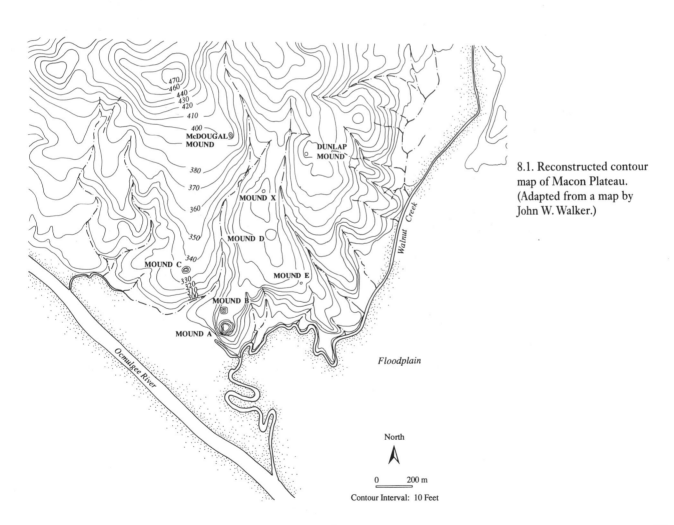

8.1. Reconstructed contour map of Macon Plateau. (Adapted from a map by John W. Walker.)

North

0   200 m

Contour Interval: 10 Feet

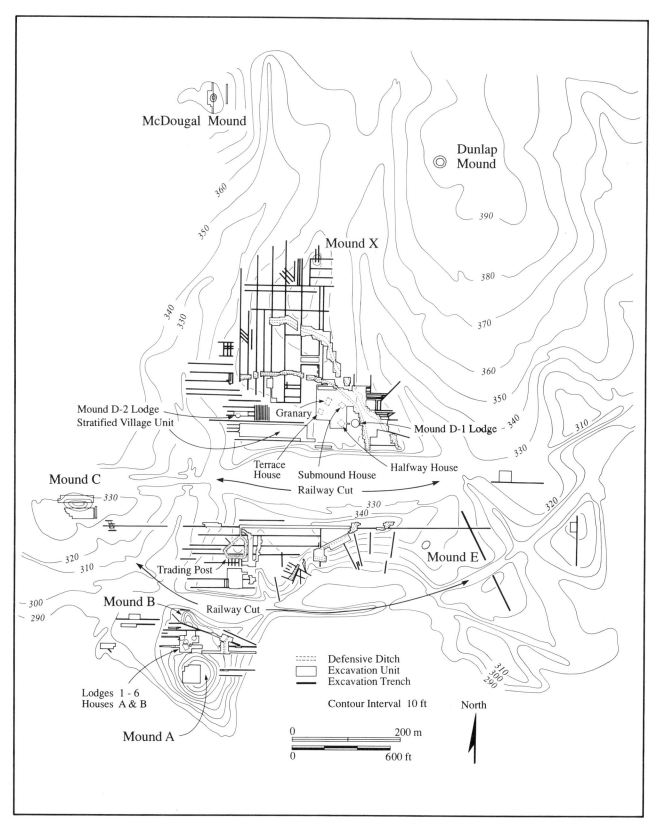

McDougal Mound

Dunlap
Mound

390

Mound X

380

370

360

350

Mound D-2 Lodge
Stratified Village Unit

Granary

Mound D-1 Lodge

340

310

330

Terrace
House

Submound House
Railway Cut

Halfway House

Mound C

330

320

330

340

Mound E

320

320

310

Trading Post

300

290

Mound B

Railway Cut

Lodges 1 - 6
Houses A & B

Mound A

310

300

290

Defensive Ditch
Excavation Unit
Excavation Trench

Contour Interval 10 ft

North

0   200 m

0   600 ft

8.2. Excavation units at the Macon Plateau site. (Compiled from Fairbanks 1956a; Ingmanson 1964a, 1964b, 1965; Williams and Henderson 1974.)

8.3. Aerial view of the Macon Plateau site in 1939 looking southeast. Mounds A and B are in background center. Immediately below them are the Middle Plateau and the Trading Post excavations. From top to bottom, the photograph shows the South Plateau with Mounds A and B and the railway cut through Mound B; the Middle Plateau with the Trading Post excavations; the second railway cut; the North Plateau with the reconstructed Mound D-1 Lodge, Mound D excavations, and fortification ditches; and the visitor center (lower left). (Photograph courtesy of the National Park Service, Southeast Archeological Center.)

the floodplain. Jones (1873) recorded the existence of a terrace on the western side of the mound and ramps on its northern side and northwestern and northeastern corners. Mound orientation is 25 degrees east of north (Stoutamire et al. 1983).

Excavations in the mound in the 1930s encountered evidence for as many as five construction stages, each consisting of sand fill with clay caps (Ingmanson 1964a). These excavations found little evidence of summit architecture and no evidence of the corner ramps. They did reveal, however, that the summit area of the Plateau may have been expanded through time by the addition of artificial fill. Excavations by Walker (1969) in 1967 revealed that the ground surface beneath Mounds A and B had been leveled prior to mound construction and confirmed that the resulting artificial terrace had been enlarged as Mound A underwent additional construction stages. Walker's excavations also found evidence for

stepped ramps on the northern and eastern sides of the mound and a "curb" around the outer edge of the terminal mound summit.

Mound B (Lesser Temple Mound) is located approximately 90 m (measured from the center of each mound) north of Mound A. According to Jones (1873), it was elliptical in shape, 3 m high, and had a maximum summit dimension of approximately 39 m. Most of the mound was removed when the railroad bed was placed across the site in 1843. Excavations in 1934 revealed evidence of four construction stages, at least two of which consisted of sand and clay basket-loaded fill with an overlying clay cap (Ingmanson 1964a). Published reports (Ingmanson 1964a; Stoutamire et al. 1983) make no reference to summit architecture. According to Ingmanson, there is stratigraphic evidence that Mound B was completed prior to the final construction stage of Mound A.

When first described by C. C. Jones in 1873, Mound C

(Funeral Mound) had been recently partially destroyed by the Central of Georgia Railroad cut. He describes the mound as being 12 m high, conical in shape, and having an average summit diameter of 25 m. When excavation began on the mound in 1934, its base measured 70 m along an east-west axis. The mound was erected in seven stages, most of which consisted of clay and sand fill and a clay cap (Fairbanks 1956a). A ramp was present on the western side of the first mound stage and suggests that the mound was oriented with the cardinal directions. Postholes were encountered on most summit surfaces, but no records remain that indicate their arrangement. Burials were placed in a least the first six construction stages.

At the time of its excavation, Mound D (Cornfield Mound) was an oval-shaped mound 2 m high and measuring approximately 67 m by 46 m at its base with its long axis oriented approximately north-south (Nelson, Prokopetz, and Swindell 1974). Only the southern half of the mound was excavated. Difficulty with the interpretation of mound stratigraphy in the field and the loss of field documentation make it difficult to determine the exact size and orientation of the mound. The excavators recorded a 1-m-high platform of red clay measuring 17 m square in the southwestern quadrant of the mound. Elsewhere, there was stratigraphic evidence for only one mound construction stage. This consisted of a 2-m-thick sand fill deposit capped with red clay. It is not clear how this relates stratigraphically with the red-clay platform.

Postholes encountered in the red-clay cap indicate that a circular structure 10 m in diameter was erected on the summit of the mound. A second, rectangular structure (Granary), measuring 12 m square, was delineated by postholes encountered in a blue-clay stratum beneath the red-clay cap. The 1-m-high red-clay platform had a posthole pattern indicative of a rectangular structure (Terrace House) measuring approximately 11.5 m by 10 m and rebuilt one time. Orientation of the Granary and the Terrace House suggest that Mound D itself was oriented approximately 25 degrees east of north.

Mound D was erected over an agricultural field (see Chapter 9) and at least one structure measuring at least 7 m in one dimension. The latter is known as the Sub-Mound House (Nelson, Prokopetz, and Swindell 1974).

Very little is known about Mound E (Southeast Mound). At present, the mound appears as a low rise approximately 1 m in height and 9 m by 15 m in basal extent. Its rounded shape indicates that it has been heavily damaged by plowing and erosion. Virtually no field documentation exists today. Limited evidence indicates that some of the eastern portion of the mound was excavated (Ingmanson 1965), but there is no record of how the mound was constructed, the number of construction stages, or the nature of summit architecture. Artifact collections from the mound excavation published by

Ingmanson (1965: table 12) contain predominantly Macon Plateau phase pottery. In the absence of specific provenience data, however, it is not absolutely certain that these collections actually date the mound.

Mound X is known only from an 1806 map and profiles of several trenches excavated in the area of the feature in the 1930s (Williams and Henderson 1974:38–40). At the time of investigation, the feature was a low rise measuring approximately 21 m in one dimension and 1 m high. Postholes recorded in profiles appeared to originate in the sand fill.

At the time of excavation, the Dunlap Mound was a low circular rise 30 m in diameter and 2 m in height (Ingmanson 1964b). The mound was constructed in at least two stages, each consisting of sand fill and a clay cap. Posthole alignments representing two walls and the corner of a rectangular building of single-post construction were encountered on the summit of the earliest stage. This building was evidently rebuilt at least one time. Its orientation suggests that one axis of the mound was oriented approximately 64 degrees east of north (Ingmanson 1964b: figure 2).

The McDougal Mound was reported to be approximately 9 m tall in 1854 (Ingmanson 1964b). At the time of excavation, much of the mound had been removed for road fill. Excavations showed that the mound measured approximately 30 m across at its base and that it had been erected in at least two construction stages. The only intact construction stage was represented by a platform approximately 1 m high. Posthole patterns indicate that one or more rectangular single-post construction buildings were erected on this platform. Orientation of the building walls suggests that one axis of the mound was oriented approximately 60 degrees east of north (Ingmanson 1964b: figure 11).

Six of the eight mounds excavated provide evidence for the manner in which they were constructed and used. All were erected in multiple stages, with Mound A having at least five stages and Mound C, seven stages. Only Mounds C, D, Dunlap, and McDougal yielded definite evidence for summit buildings, but there is no reason to believe the remaining mounds did not also have them. Mound C is alone in having evidence for the inclusion of burials in construction stages.

The Macon Plateau site mounds differ in no important way from Mississippian platform mounds found elsewhere in the southeastern United States. They were evidently used as substructures for buildings constructed of perishable materials, and they were enlarged at intervals throughout their period of use. Individuals, presumably of high status, were buried in the successive summits of at least one mound.

At the time of its excavation in 1934, the Mound D-1 Lodge (Macon Earth Lodge or Council Chamber) was a low rise 1 m high and 21 m in diameter (Fairbanks 1946b). Beneath this low mound, excavators found a circular structure measuring 13 m in diameter and having a long, narrow entrance passage. Interior furnishings included a centrally located circular fire basin, a low clay bench with molded seats and shallow basins adjacent to the exterior wall, and a low clay platform in the shape of a bird located opposite the entrance passage. The center of the clay platform, the fire basin, and the entrance passage all fall along a single line that is oriented 12 degrees south of east. The exterior wall of the structure consisted of a ridge or buttress of red clay rising to a height of at least 1 m and extending outward as much as 6 m from the floor of the structure. Charred roof timbers and deposits of burned and unburned clay lying on the structure floor have been interpreted to mean that the structure was earth covered and was destroyed by fire (Fairbanks 1946b:97; Kelly 1938c).

Following its destruction, the interior of the structure—the floor area surrounded by the red-clay walls—was apparently filled in. Since the mound showed no "central depression" at the time of excavation (Fairbanks 1946b:95), we may conclude that the interior was filled at least to the level of the standing walls. No profile drawings of the mound have been published, making it impossible to determine how the red-clay ridge relates to the overall mound configuration as it existed in 1934. Nevertheless, Fairbanks's (1946b:95) statement that an exploratory trench "soon intersected a rising shoulder of red clay" does suggest that at least in places the ridge was overlain by a deposit of soil other than plowzone.

A number of Mississippi period platform mounds in Georgia, eastern Tennessee, and the Carolinas are known to have begun as ground level or semisubterranean structures with earth banked against their outer walls to a height of a meter or more (Dickens 1970: figures 20 and 21; Rudolph 1984; Rudolph and Hally 1985). Following their abandonment, the interiors of these structures were filled in and covered with a mantle of earth to form a platform mound. Except that we cannot be certain of the existence of an overlying mantle of fill, the description of the Mound D-1 Lodge stratigraphy sounds surprisingly similar to this pattern. We propose that the Mound D-1 Lodge conforms to this widespread pattern and that after its destruction by fire the structure was covered with a mantle of earth and converted into a platform mound, which was then largely obliterated by plowing and erosion.

Fairbanks's (1956a:24, plate 9) statement that Mound C began with two "nuclear domes [showing] markedly lenticular loads of various colored earths" suggests that this mound also began with an earth-embanked structure. In the east-west profile exposure across the mound, the earth embankment surrounding such a structure would have appeared to excavators as two domes. Unfortunately, whether other Macon Plateau phase mounds began in this fashion cannot be determined with the available stratigraphic evidence.

Fairbanks (1946b) identified seven additional examples of earth lodges at the Macon Plateau site. One of these, the Mound D-2 structure, lies 230 m due west of the Mound D-1 Lodge. The other six are located between Mounds A and B on the southern edge of the site. None of these additional examples has all the architectural characteristics of the Mound D-1 Lodge. None has an interior platform opposite the entrance, only two have peripheral seats, and several have no evidence for the clay buttress and entrance passages. One structure has only two diagnostic architectural features, a circular posthole pattern and a hearth (Ingmanson 1964a). Fairbanks (1946b:101) views this architectural variability as reflecting development of the earth lodge type structure through time. We believe that two other factors are involved. Some variability—for example, the absence of entrance passages for Lodges 4, 4a, and 5—is probably due to incomplete excavation or destruction by later construction activity. In other cases, architecturally and functionally distinct kinds of structures are probably represented. Lodges 2 and 3, which have no diagnostic features beyond their circular shape, central hearth, and roof support posts, should probably be viewed as different kinds of buildings.

It seems likely that the Mound D-1 Lodge is not unique at the Macon Plateau site. If they had been completely excavated, Lodges 4, 4a, and 5 would probably have yielded a similar array of architectural features. A circular structure with nearly all the features of the Mound D-1 Lodge was excavated at Brown's Mount (9BI5), located 9 km southeast of Macon Plateau. It is the only example of this type of structure known to exist outside the Macon Plateau site. The absence of similar structures in earlier and later contexts in central Georgia or in contemporary Mississippian sites elsewhere in the southeastern United States suggests that they may have been unique to the Macon Plateau phase.

Fairbanks (1946b:101) observed that earth lodges at the Macon Plateau (Mound D-1, 4, 4a, and 5 lodges) and Brown's Mount sites were located near platform mounds. In fact, they are located approximately 30 m south or southeast of a platform mound in each case. He further suggests (1946b:106) that this pattern of spatially associated circular structures and rectangular mounds with rectangular summit structures evolved into the "winter house" or "square ground" ceremonial complex of the historic Creek Indians. There are a number of problems with this scheme, but most important is the absence of clear evidence for such a pattern in later Mississippian phases. Nevertheless, the implied interpretation of the earth lodges as structures where group ceremonial activities were held seems reasonable, given the existence of large numbers of seats along their interior walls.

Habitation Features

There is very little evidence for Macon Plateau phase domestic habitation features at the Macon Plateau site. Nonmound structures other than those identified as earth lodges have been reported from four locations: between Mounds A and B, in the vicinity of Mound C, beneath Mound D, southeast of Mound D, and in the vicinity of the Trading Post.

Ingmanson (1964a) summarizes field records for three structures in the area between Mounds A and B. House A is rectangular, measuring approximately 18 m by 12 m, and of single-post construction. House B is represented by a 3-m-diameter ring of individually set posts. Why it is identified as a "House" as opposed to a "Lodge," when Lodges 1a and 2 are also represented by little more than rings of individually set posts and measure 4.5 m and 6 m respectively, is not clear. The third structure is represented by posthole alignments suggestive of two walls and the corner of a rectangular building.

Fairbanks (1956a:34) refers to a "rather extensive area of burned clay" in the vicinity of Mound C and identifies it as a "remnant of a house floor." No posthole pattern or fire basin was found associated with this feature, a fact that weakens its functional identification as a house floor, domestic or otherwise. Posthole alignments suggestive of two walls and the corner of a rectangular structure were also encountered in the Stratified Village excavation unit located southwest of Mound D (Williams and Henderson 1974).

In sterile subsoil beneath Mound D, excavators found two alignments of individually set postholes forming a corner of what they identified as the Sub-Mound House (Nelson, Prokopetz, and Swindell 1974). Because excavation was limited to a 15-foot-wide exploratory trench, the posthole alignments could be traced for only 7 m and 4.5 m respectively. No other evidence indicative of the existence of a four-walled structure was recorded. The lack of corroborative evidence and the fact that the two alignments formed an angle closer to 80 degrees than 90 degrees mean that we cannot be certain that a four-walled and roofed building is represented here.

The term "Halfway House" was applied by the excavators to a group of architectural features located approximately halfway between Mound D and the Mound D-1 Lodge (Williams and Henderson 1974:17). It consists of an "irregular shaped baked clay floor matrix" measuring approximately 10 m across and a number of postholes. Some of the latter form three parallel alignments that extend part way across the baked-clay floor, but there are no postholes or alignments of postholes that can be safely identified as being structurally related to the floor. With presently available evidence, it is not possible to identify these features as representing the remains of a roofed and walled building with any degree of certainty.

Excavation in the vicinity of the Trading Post revealed a number of features that at the time were identified as representing structures. Mason (1963a:81) argued that only four of these features were domestic structures. All of these are located south of the trading house. Houses 1, 2, and 5, are represented only by rectangular patterns of postholes, and these average 14 m by 13 m in size. House 8 was also rectangular but measured only 8 m by 7 m. It had a preserved clay floor and fire basin located in its south-central sector. Prokopetz (1974) identified an additional structure, House 8a, in the same area. This structure underlay House 8 and was represented by a 10-m-diameter circular pattern of postholes.

The component affiliation of these structures is unclear. Mason (1963a:83) argued that all date to the Ocmulgee Fields phase, while Prokopetz (1974:43) dates Houses 1, 2, 5, and 8 to Macon Plateau phase and House 8a to the Woodland period. The difference of opinion is possibly because of the lack of prepared floors or floor features with associated datable ceramics in Houses 1, 2, and 5. Mason based her component identification on the abundance of Ocmulgee Fields pottery and historic artifacts recovered in the vicinity of the structures, the presence of a datable pit and burial in close proximity to the walls of Houses 1 and 2, and the conformity of the architectural evidence to historic descriptions of Creek domestic structures. Mason also states that a kaolin pipe and 18 Ocmulgee Fields sherds were recovered from the clay floor of Structure 8. She does not identify, however, the cultural affiliation of the other 150 sherds found in that same context. Prokopetz bases his component identifications on the fact that postholes for Houses 1, 2, and 5 may have originated from a stratum in which Macon Plateau phase pottery is numerically dominant. The postholes for House 8a likewise reportedly originated in a stratum dominated by Woodland pottery.

The evidence is not compelling for either interpretation. Ocmulgee Fields phase pits and burials do occur in the area south of the Trading Post, suggesting that domestic habitations may have once existed there. There is no stratigraphic evidence to support a historic-period affiliation for the structures, however, and the architectural evidence is weak at best. In fact, one of the clearest pieces of architectural evidence, size of structure, favors a Macon Plateau phase date. The average dimensions of Houses 1, 2, and 5—14 m by 13 m—are twice that of historic-period Creek structures (Mason 1963a:77), but very similar to that for the Terrace House and Granary on Mound D and House A near Mounds A and B. The average dimensions for these three Macon Plateau phase structures are 12.3 m by 11.2 m. On the other hand, it is far from clear that postholes of the structures in question originated in the strata with which Prokopetz identifies them. The fact that as much as 22 percent of the pottery in these strata is Ocmulgee Fields phase (Prokopetz 1974: table 5) could furthermore be interpreted to mean that historic-period houses were erected in an area where there had been an earlier Macon Plateau phase occupation.

Altogether, features representing as many as 12 non-mound, nonearth lodge structures have been reported from the Macon Plateau site. With the exception of Houses 1, 2, 5, 8, and 8a from the Trading Post area, all can be dated to the Macon Plateau component with some certainty. None, however, can be identified as domestic habitations with certainty. Those located on the South Plateau seem unlikely candidates for habitations given their proximity to Mounds A and B. Four of the five complete rectangular posthole patterns seem unlikely candidates for habitation structures because of their large size. Averaging 13 m by 15 m, these four buildings are equal in size to structures erected on the summits of Mound D.

The major portion of the Macon Plateau was covered by an array of trenches and excavation units of various sizes and shapes (Figure 8.2). These excavations should provide an excellent body of information concerning the distribution of residential areas and nonmound public areas (for example, plazas) across the site. Unfortunately, little such information is currently available in published form. Why this is so is not completely clear. Evidently much of the problem stems from the poor condition of the artifact and records collections. A substantial amount of the field documentation is apparently missing. Artifact collections are also missing, and the value of the extant collections is reduced by the lack of uniform-sized recovery units and the loss of much provenience information.

Much fault also lies with the nature of the published reports. These focused on excavation units that yielded large and complex features and largely ignored the vast network of trenches. As a result, information on the distribution of Macon Plateau phase artifacts and pit features and postholes that may belong to that phase is not available.

Outside the immediate vicinity of the mounds, information on Macon Plateau phase artifact density, pit features, and postholes is available for only four locations. Excavations around the Trading Post yielded several burials and pits that are probably Macon Plateau phase and, as discussed earlier, several possible Macon Plateau phase houses (Mason 1963a). Ingmanson (1965) reports a heavy concentration of Macon Plateau phase pottery on the Southeast Plateau southeast of Mound E. The Stratified Village unit, located southwest of Mound D, yielded midden strata and pit features containing abundant Macon Plateau phase pottery, and numerous postholes (Williams and Henderson 1974). Finally, trenching and test pit excavation east and southwest of Mound C yielded evidence of pits and burials that in at least some cases can be identified with Macon Plateau phase (Fairbanks 1956a).

Fortification Ditches

Excavations revealed the existence of long, ditchlike features, termed "dugouts" by Kelly (1938c), in four locations (Figure 8.2) on the Plateau. Two ditches extend for distances of 335 m and 369 m respectively across the eastern half of the North Plateau (Williams and Henderson 1974:32). Segments of two ditches parallel the southern bluff edge of the Middle Plateau (Ingmanson 1965:46–50). A single ditch segment was identified in trenches excavated southeast of Mound C (Ingmanson 1965:51). Segments of a single ditch lie along the eastern and western bluff edge of the South Plateau (Ingmanson 1964a:15–17).

These features are generally considered to represent fortification ditches constructed in order to defend the site from enemy attack (Fairbanks 1956a; Ingmanson 1964a, 1965; Williams and Henderson 1974). Unlike the defensive ditches at the Late Mississippi period Etowah (9BR1) (Larson 1972) and King (9FL5) (Hally 1988) sites in northwestern Georgia, however, these features are quite variable in dimension; ranging between 3 m and 8 m in width and 1 m and 3 m in depth. In fact, they resemble a series of close-spaced and overlapping pits of varying size more than purposefully constructed ditches (Figure 8.4).

Several aspects of these features argue against them being defensive ditches. Most important, they are so shallow in many places that they would seem to present little difficulty to people trying to cross them. This characteristic, however, may be so because excavators were not always able to trace accurately the profile of the ditches. Kelly (1938c:13) alludes to this problem in his description of the basal fill deposit as being "difficult to make out in cross section." Perhaps the irregularity of the ditches is an artifact of the accuracy with which they were excavated and recorded.

A second problem with the fortification hypothesis is that excavators were unable to trace the ditches across the western portion of the North Plateau (Williams and Henderson 1974:32). It may be argued that years of plowing and erosion in this area have cut down the naturally sloping aboriginal ground surface to the point where the ditches simply disappear. This explanation leaves unanswered, however, the question of why ditches

8.4. North Plateau fortification ditch: Dugouts 8 and 9. (Photograph courtesy of the National Park Service, Southeast Archeological Center.)

on the eastern side of the North Plateau and along the steeply sloping bluff edge of the Middle Plateau were not similarly destroyed.

A third problem is the lack of evidence for palisades associated with the ditches. Profiles of several trenches excavated along the southern edge of the Middle Plateau show what might be a line of postholes located less than 6 m from the inner ditch, but in the absence of a plan map for these features, it is not possible to identify them definitely as belonging to a palisade (Ingmanson 1965:50). It is possible that palisades were erected on the crest of earth ridges constructed from ditch fill. If so, destruction of the ridges by plowing and erosion could have destroyed all traces of the palisades.

A fourth problem concerns the location of segments of an outer ditch on the Middle Plateau. Several test trenches supposedly revealed evidence for the ditch some

distance down the steeply sloping side of the Plateau (Ingmanson 1965:49–50). It is difficult to understand why a defensive earthwork would be constructed below the summit of the Plateau on a rather steeply sloping ground surface. It seems likely that the stratigraphic evidence has been misinterpreted in this case.

A final problem concerns the ditch segment located southeast of Mound C. It is unlikely that this ditch connected with those on the North and South Plateau, since such a fortification system would have had to cross a 14-m-deep stream valley. The ditch may have been part of a separate fortification system surrounding Mound C, but this is not supported by the northwest-southeast orientation of the ditch (Ingmanson 1965). Because the ditch was encountered in only one excavation trench, there is also the possibility that it or its orientation was misidentified.

92

David J. Hally and Mark Williams

In spite of these problems, we believe that some dug-outs are the remains of defensive ditches and that these ditches were constructed to enclose a portion of the area occupied by the Macon Plateau phase inhabitants. If only Mounds A, B, and D were enclosed by the fortification system, as seems most likely, given the topography of the Plateau and the distribution of ditch segments, the inner ditch would have been approximately 1700 m long and enclosed an area of approximately 15 ha. These figures are large, but not unreasonable considering that 21 ha were enclosed by the defensive ditch at the Etowah site. Soil from the ditches was probably used as mound fill and may have been used to construct a ridge with a palisade adjacent to the ditches on their interior side.

Internal Site Chronology

Although the Macon Plateau phase is usually considered to be of relatively brief duration, there is stratigraphic and distributional evidence indicating that it persisted long enough for some change to take place in ceramics and in site configuration. Stratified ceramic collections have been described for three locations: the South Plateau (Ingmanson 1964a); Control Trenches 2 and 6 on the Middle Plateau (Smith 1973b); and the Stratified Village on the North Plateau (Williams and Henderson 1974). In none of these instances is there evidence for any significant change in the frequency of Macon Plateau phase pottery types through time. Variability in temper type, however, is another matter. Ingmanson (1964a: table 6) reports that in the approximately 1.5 m of stratified deposits between Mounds A and B on the South Plateau, shell-tempered pottery (including pottery with mixed shell and grit temper) decreases in frequency relative to grit-tempered pottery through time from 80 to 47 percent (Ingmanson 1964a: table 6). No figures are published for temper types from the Stratified Village. In Trench 4 on the Middle Plateau, however, Smith (1973b: tables 14 and 15) reports a similar decrease in shell tempering through time from 72 to 27 percent.

Based on stratigraphy and change in the relative frequency of shell tempering, Ingmanson (1964a: table 1) has proposed that the Macon Plateau phase occupation of the South Plateau can be divided into three subperiods, which he designates Macon Plateau A (early), B, and C (late). The relative frequency of shell-tempered pottery during each subperiod is approximately 80, 60, and 47 percent respectively. Stratigraphic associations allowed Ingmanson (1964a: table 1) to assign the construction of Mound B and Lodges 4–6 to Subperiod A and the construction of Lodges 1–3, Houses A and B, and the final stage of Mound A to Subperiod B. The initial construction of Mound A could not be tied into the

stratigraphic sequence but is probably contemporaneous with Mound B. No construction activities could be identified with Subperiod C.

Given the available evidence, it is not possible to evaluate the validity of Ingmanson's tripartite chronological scheme. There is, however, no reason to doubt that it does reflect change at the site through time. Assuming that temper frequencies were uniform across the inhabited site at any point in time, this scheme can be used as a framework within which to investigate temporal relationships among the different mounds and nonmound features.

Relative frequencies of temper types have been published for pottery collections from Mounds C and E, the Dunlap Mound, and the two fortification ditches on the North Plateau. None of these features have yielded shell temper frequencies approaching 80 percent, suggesting that the earliest Macon Plateau phase ceremonial construction, if not domestic activity, occurred on the South Plateau. Approximately 61 percent of the pottery from the outer ditch on the North Plateau is shell- and shell/grit-tempered, while 51 percent from the inner ditch is similarly tempered (Williams and Henderson 1974: tables 1–6). Assuming that both ditches were filled with midden soil that accumulated while they were in use or shortly after their abandonment, these percentages suggest that the outer ditch was constructed before the inner ditch and that both were constructed during Subperiod B.

Fairbanks (1956a:82) reports that 45 percent of the Macon Plateau phase pottery from the Mound C "general mound collection" is shell- and shell/grit-tempered. Unfortunately, this collection includes sherds from the surrounding village deposits as well as from the mound (Fairbanks 1956a:20) and, as a result, cannot be used to date mound construction accurately. Furthermore, because it contains sherds from a number of different deposits, some of which may have accumulated at different times, it may not accurately reflect the date of human occupancy in this part of the site. Nevertheless, given the very low frequency of shell tempering, it is reasonable to conclude that most of the activity around Mound C occurred in Subperiod C.

A similar problem exists with the pottery collection from Mound E. Because there was no provenience information available to work with, Ingmanson (1964b: 4–5, table 12) was forced to lump all collections together as coming from the Mound E area. As with the Mound C pottery, shell and shell/grit tempering occur with low frequency (32 percent), which suggests that most human activity in the vicinity of Mound E occurred in Subperiod C.

In a collection of 706 sherds from fill of the first construction stage of the Dunlap Mound, shell and shell/grit tempering accounts for 60 percent of the pottery (Ingmanson 1964: table 5). This would place the beginning of the mound no earlier than the latter half of Subperiod B. Since mound construction could have begun anytime after the accumulation of the midden that was used as fill, the mound could have been constructed entirely in Subperiod C.

The available stratigraphic and ceramic evidence indicates that the various mounds and ditches were constructed at different times during the Macon Plateau phase. A reasonable argument can be made that the site initially consisted only of Mounds A and B. Stratigraphy and the spatial proximity of these mounds suggest that they could have been under construction at the same time during Subperiod A. Construction of Mound B apparently ceased before the final stage(s) were added to Mound A, but this does not rule out the possibility that it continued to be used during Subperiod B.

The site may have been expanded during Subperiod B to include Mound D and the Mound D-1 Lodge. While there is currently no ceramic evidence for when these features were constructed, their location within the defensive perimeter formed by the outer ditch on the North Plateau suggests that they were contemporary with at least the later stages of Mounds A and B. The fact that Mounds A and D are similar in compass orientation also argues for their contemporaneity. The Mound D-1 Lodge was evidently abandoned prior to the excavation of the inner ditch, since the ditch cuts through the edge of the red clay stratum that supposedly covers the Mound D-1 Lodge and passes immediately in front of the structure's long entrance passage (Fairbanks 1946b).

Since Mounds A and D have similar compass orientations, it can be argued that they were situated so as to face each other across a plaza, a site plan that is common in Mississippian times. Two things would seem to argue against this interpretation, however. For one, the two mounds are separated by approximately 580 m, a distance several times greater than is usual at Mississippian sites. Second, the presence of Macon Plateau phase burials, pit features, and possibly rectangular structures on the Middle Plateau in the vicinity of the Trading Post indicates that the two mounds may have been separated by a contemporary residential zone. This evidence suggests that Mounds A and B and Mound D were each associated with a different plaza and in a sense formed two separate ceremonial precincts.

There is no direct evidence for when construction of Mound D ceased. The inner ditch was evidently not used for very long, because the incidence of shell-tempered pottery in its fill is not much less than it is in the outer ditch. Presumably Mounds A, B, and D continued to be used as substructures at least until the inner ditch was abandoned.

Although far from definitive, the available ceramic evidence indicates that the Dunlap Mound and Mounds C and E, which are located outside the area enclosed by the defensive ditches, were constructed in Subperiod C after the ditches were abandoned. The location of the McDougal Mound and Mound X outside of the area enclosed by the ditches suggests that they also date late in the occupation of the site. Compass orientations suggest that Mounds C, Dunlap, and McDougal were constructed at a different time than were those located within the outer ditch. Mound C appears to be oriented with the cardinal directions, while the McDougal and Dunlap mounds were oriented 60 degrees and 54 degrees east of north respectively. The similarity in orientation of the latter two mounds could be evidence for their contemporaneity.

Mound stage construction at Mounds A and B evidently had ceased by Subperiod C. This fact strongly suggests that these mounds had ceased serving their original function, which was presumably as substructures for periodically rebuilt elite residences and temples. Whether they subsequently took on a new, perhaps more ideological, role within the site or were completely abandoned unfortunately cannot be determined at present.

Interpretation of Site Configuration

As defined by the distribution of its mounds, the Macon Plateau site measures approximately 1050 m by 660 m and covers an area of approximately 70 ha. As such, it is one of the largest Mississippian sites known, being equaled or exceeded in size only by sites such as Moundville in Alabama (Peebles and Kus 1977: figure 1), Toltec in Arkansas (Sherrod and Rolinson 1987: figure 6), and Cahokia in Illinois (Fowler 1978). Equally distinctive are the great distances that separate its mounds from one another. Excluding the distance separating Mounds A and B, nearest neighbor distances between mounds (measured center to center) range from 250 m to 350 m. By way of comparison, the greatest distance between adjacent mounds at Moundville and Toltec is 205 m and 120 m respectively.

The fact that the mounds at Macon Plateau are separated from their nearest neighbor by 250 m or more and in many cases by small stream valleys indicates that the site was not integrated around a single plaza or group of adjacent plazas as is the case at most Mississippian sites with multiple mounds. Instead, each mound, along with a plaza, may have formed the ceremonial nucleus for a separate residential group much like the "subcommunities" Fowler (1978:466) recognizes at Cahokia. Plazas cannot be identified with the information presently available, but there is evidence for domestic habitation zones between Mounds A/B, C, and D.

Spatial relationships existing between several of the mounds, particularly the outlying ones, suggest that the Macon Plateau site was laid out according to an explicit plan.

1. The McDougal Mound is situated due north of Mound A.
2. The Dunlap Mound is situated due north of Mound E.
3. McDougal and Dunlap mounds are the same distance (1040 m) north of Mound A.
4. Mounds A, D, and Dunlap are located along a straight line.
5. Mounds A, C, E, McDougal, and Dunlap form an elongated pentagon with Mound A at the apex.

The last observation may be spurious, but the others seem unlikely to have come about by chance.

The tendency for Mississippian sites to be oriented with the cardinal directions has been recognized for some time (Phillips et al. 1951). Sherrod and Rolingson (1987) have recently argued that mounds at many Mississippian sites were spaced by means of a standardized unit of measure and were aligned so as to mark the occurrence of celestial events such as the winter and summer solstices. While not arguing that celestial alignments and standardized units of measure are necessarily present at Macon Plateau, we do propose that the arrangement of mounds may have had symbolic significance and that the growth of the site through time may have been guided by cosmological principals of some kind. Even though some mounds may have ceased being used as substructures for elite residences and temples relatively early in the site's development, all could have continued to function as elements in a symbolically structured site plan up to the time of final site abandonment around A.D. 1150.

Summary

We have attempted in this chapter to present an interpretive summary of the published information pertaining to the architectural features and settlement configuration of the Macon Plateau site. The generally poor quality of the available information has made this a difficult undertaking. We have argued in the preceding pages that the Macon Plateau phase occupation at Ocmulgee National Monument was of sufficient duration for a number of major settlement and architectural changes to have taken place. Mounds A and B were probably constructed first. Subsequently, together with Mound D, Mound D-1 Lodge, and some residential areas, they were enclosed by the defensive ditches. Sometime during the latter half of the phase, the later of the two ditches was filled in and Mounds A, B, and D ceased functioning as substructures for elite residences and temples. Mounds C, E, X, Dunlap, and McDougal received most, if not all, of their construction and use in the latter half of the phase.

Mounds A and B were in use at the same time and, together with an as yet undefined plaza, may have constituted the public, ceremonial edifices for a segment of the community that resided immediately to the north on what is today the Middle Plateau. The remaining mounds may have played a similar role in the ceremonial life of other segments of the community. Through time, as new mounds were constructed, their placement was guided by ideological principals designed to give the overall site-configuration symbolic, perhaps cosmological significance. These principals and their overall structure have not been identified.

CHAPTER NINE

Ocmulgee and the Question of Mississippian Agronomic Practices

Thomas J. Riley

DESPITE A LARGE amount of literature on the subject of Mississippian agriculture, very little is known substantively about the agronomic practices of the prehistoric Indians of the southeastern United States. What is known, however, is in large part due to the recognition at Ocmulgee in the mid-1930s of what was tentatively identified as the remains of a prehistoric cornfield. Sealed by Mound D at the Macon Plateau site, these ridges and furrows were the first such North American remains recognized in buried contexts by archaeologists. It has been only since the late 1960s that other potentially buried field systems have been noted by researchers working in Mississippian contexts; and only in the 1980s have some of these fields been subjected to excavation and analysis in the same way that the fields under Mound D were in the 1930s. Ocmulgee, then, is a landmark in the history of the study of Indian agronomy, that is, field agricultural practices in the eastern United States from ca. A.D. 1000–1500.

In this chapter I would like to review some of the evidence for the evolution of our notions of field agriculture among people participating in the Mississippian economic pattern, place Ocmulgee in perspective as a benchmark from which we have begun to recognize these features as important for archaeologists to record and analyze, and underscore the potential importance of these features for any prehistoric socioeconomic reconstruction of Mississippian societies.

Historic Overview

Aboriginal features that were identified as garden beds were noted in Wisconsin and Michigan in the late nineteenth century (Lapham 1855; Schoolcraft 1860), and an interest in these features continued, at least in terms of recording them, into the twentieth (Brown 1906, 1908, 1909; Hinsdale 1925). These were surface-ridged fields, sharing some of the features of the field excavated at Ocmulgee by Kelly (1938c) in the 1930s (Figure 9.1). At the same time, another field practice, that of mounding in traditional cornhills, was reported for sites in northeastern North America, specifically in New England (Delabarre and Wilder 1920) at Taunton and Northampton, Massachusetts. The ridged fields were not investigated by excavation during these early years, although they were regarded as fairly ancient by Schoolcraft (1860) who noted that trees of at least 300 years growth were found on some of them. The eastern cornhills, on the other hand, were subjected to excavation by Delabarre and Wilder, who recorded that stones of all sizes were found in the hills. They write:

Evidently the Indians did not habitually throw these out, as one might naturally expect that they would have done. Very likely a moderate number of them was regarded as desirable, perhaps to keep the soil looser, perhaps even to facilitate digging. Many thin stones were found of such shape that they might well have been employed as hoes, but it was impossible to be sure whether they had actually served as such. Two well shaped oval hoes or spades of slate or similar material, one of them with notches at the sides, two broken arrowheads, and a small mortar such as might have been used for grinding mineral paint, were the only indubitable Indian artifacts discovered. (Delabarre and Wilder 1920:214)

As far as I can tell, this was the first serious excavation of agricultural features in the eastern United States and was not duplicated until the excavations at Ocmulgee in the 1930s.

Shortly after Delabarre and Wilder reported on their excavations, Ralph Linton inferred that the prehistoric agriculture of eastern North American derived from a different tradition than that of Mexico and the Southwest (Linton 1924a). He argued that the presence of the hoe, the lack of the true metate, and the extreme importance of boiling in the preparation of maize and other Meso-american cultigens were distinctive features of the eastern North American food complex, and that they suggested a tradition of agricultural practice that preceded these tropical introductions. Linton wrote:

The Eastern complex [as opposed to the Mexican or southwestern complexes that he posits in his paper] differs so much from the other two that we must either suppose maize culture to have there undergone a local development along lines quite outside those of the original pattern, or consider it the result of the superposition of maize upon some older food complex which was itself rather elaborate. The latter hypothesis seems much more probable, and I believe that the Indians of the eastern United States were already in possession of the hoe and mortar at the time that they acquired maize. (Linton 1924a:349)

Linton concludes that in the east "maize probably arrived as a result of gradual diffusion, lost much of its cultural context in route, and was adopted into a preexisting cultural pattern which had grown up around some other food or foods" (Linton 1924a:349). Linton's initial observations have proven insightful over time, and the recognition by researchers of an eastern domesticated plant complex consisting of squash, gourd, and starch and oil seeds as a precursor to maize agriculture during Late

Woodland and Mississippian times in the southeastern United States validates these observations with archaeological evidence (Yarnell 1978; Cowan 1978; Asch and Asch 1978).

Despite the fact that research had been conducted on preserved fields and that Linton postulated a distinct set of agronomic and food preparation customs for the eastern United States, little attention was paid to agricultural features by archaeologists working in this region of the continent. Presumably this was because archaeologists believed that the evidence of agricultural fields was ephemeral at best and because the problems of agricultural technology and the importance of agricultural intensification were not a primary emphasis in the study of prehistory at the time.

Ocmulgee Excavations

The excavations on the Macon Plateau during the 1930s resulted in the first discovery of subsurface archaeological features that could be recognized and identified as agricultural fields in eastern North America. Their discovery was incidental to excavations at Mound D, commonly called the Cornfield Mound (Kelly 1935b:186, 1938c). The excavations at Mound D were conducted intermittently from 1933 through 1935, with the apparent agricultural field recognized in profile fairly early in the excavations of the mound and labeled Structural Layer 7 (Figure 9.2). Mound D itself was a complex structure exhibiting three house constructions as well as the mound fill. One of these houses, called the Terrace

9.1. Surface ridge and furrow fields located in a county park, Milwaukee, Wisconsin, 1960. (Photo by Moffat and Riley.)

9.2. The ridge and furrow field at Ocmulgee. The Terrace House is in the foreground; the unexcavated portion of Mound D is at the left; and the Halfway House and Mound D-1 Lodge are in the right background. (Photograph courtesy of the National Park Service, Southeast Archeological Center.)

House (Nelson, Prokopetz, and Swindell 1974:21–24), lay right above the apparent field on a low platform, while a second, submound rectangular structural feature was apparently inferior to the field. The Terrace House, because its northwest-southeast alignment paralleled the ridges and furrows of the field, has been felt by some to be contemporaneous with the cornfield. Absolute dating of the field is still open to question, but the predominant ceramics with the submound structure and with the Terrace House were Bibb Plain, with other Macon Plateau ceramics such as McDougal and Halstead Plain notable as well. A radiocarbon date from the Macon Earth Lodge located to the east of Mound D confirmed a date of ca. A.D. 1015 for the feature (Wilson 1964).

An area of the field measuring approximately 18 m by 16 m was opened at the southern edge of the mound during the excavation. Descriptions of the apparent agricultural field are scanty, but a compilation of the fieldnotes by Nelson, Prokopetz, and Swindell (1974) suggests the following features:

1. The feature consisted of regular ridges and furrows aligned in a northwest-southeast direction.
2. The distances between the peaks of ridges ranged from 30 to 50 cm.
3. The tops of the ridges were approximately 13 cm above the bottoms of the furrows.
4. Some indications of individual hillocks up to 13 cm in height above the ridges were noted but were not at all distinct.
5. Paths were noted running perpendicular to the northwest-southeast alignment of the ridges and furrows.
6. At least one intrusive pit was noted in the field.
7. One path apparently intersected a wall of the Terrace House.

Thomas J. Riley

The color of the soil of the ridges and furrows was said to be a dark, humus-stained sand, but no mention was made in the fieldnotes of corncobs, ash, or other material being found in the excavation (Nelson, Prokopetz, and Swindell 1974:22). The full extent of the agricultural field is not known. Besides the 18-m-by-16-m area opened by Kelly, excavations 39 m away at the north edge of the mound revealed signs of what may have been the same feature.

An interesting and important feature of the Ocmulgee ridge and furrow field is its location in the uplands rather than in the river bottoms, as would be expected by most archaeologists working on prehistoric agriculture in the Southeast. This was the case with many of the ridged-field systems in Wisconsin and Michigan, and we may ask whether the association of these particular systems with upland locations has any agronomic significance.

The question of whether the feature that constituted Structural Layer 7 at Mound D represented agricultural fields was never satisfactorily addressed in Kelly's work, and other writers, most notably Nelson, Prokopetz, and Swindell (1974), have considered the point moot. There is, however, considerable recent evidence from Wisconsin, which I will address below, that confirms Kelly's initial identification.

Ridged Fields Elsewhere in Eastern North America

As mentioned above, surface indications of ridged fields are notable from Wisconsin and Michigan. Traces of an apparent field system have been recently reported from eastern Iowa as well (Billeck 1986). Such surface-ridged fields were not subjected to excavation until 1966, when Peske (1966) excavated agricultural areas at the Lasley's Point and Eulrich sites near Oshkosh, Wisconsin. Here heaps of stone are interspersed among the ridges and furrows. Excavations across the garden beds produced a single potsherd, but the rockpiles produced chert flakes, animal bone fragments, potsherds, broken bison and elk scapulae hoes, and corncob fragments. On the basis of the pottery and the proximity to habitation areas, Peske dated the fields to the Lake Winnebago phase of the Oneota Tradition, a period from ca. A.D. 1000–1300. Unfortunately, no measurements are available on the ridges and furrows noted from these two sites.

Melvin Fowler, in an important article on ridged-field features, suggested on the basis of aerial photographs of linear patterns in plowed ground that ridged-field systems existed at the Lunsford Pulcher and the Texas sites on the Kaskaskia River in Illinois (Fowler 1969). Both of these sites are located near Cahokia and have significant Mississippian components that date to the eleventh century A.D. The Texas site also has a Late

Woodland component that may date to ca. A.D. 600–900. The absolute antiquity of the garden beds at these sites is unknown, although it is likely that they are associated with the Mississippian occupation at the Texas site, since Lunsford Pulcher does not have a Late Woodland component. Two other examples of possible garden beds in Illinois are known from indications in the soil after plowing. The first of these is at Cahokia, where the survey for a new museum and interpretive center in 1979 yielded photographic evidence of what might be a ridged-field system. This field system may date as early as Jarrot-Fairmont phase (in the new sequence suggested by Bareis et al. 1984), within the Emergent Mississippian phase cluster dating to ca. A.D. 900–1050 (Fowler and Benchley 1980).

A second set of possible fields, once again noted in aerial photography, has been reported for the Kincaid site on the Ohio River drainage in southern Illinois (Muller 1986). Neither the Cahokia nor the Kincaid patterns have been subjected to either indirect analysis using remote sensing technologies other than white-light photography or to excavation, and so they remain questionable. However, recent excavations at sites near LaCrosse in southwestern Wisconsin tie the Illinois field marks into a distributional pattern that connects ridged-field agricultural practices across the Midwest and the Southeast.

The identification of these apparent field systems from "cropmarks" invites some comment. The term "cropmarks," although used by Fowler (1969; Fowler and Benchley 1980), is somewhat misleading, since the agricultural features in question actually appear under different conditions. The surface features from Wisconsin are recognizable in relief, while the apparent buried features from the Texas site, Cahokia, and Kincaid are detectable as soil discolorations on ground surfaces after plowing. True cropmarks are recognized through differential growth of vegetation that marks the presence of an archaeological site. None of the occurrences of ridged fields in the eastern United States has been recognized in this fashion, and thus are not strictly indicated by cropmarks (Wilson 1982). The surface relief features are direct indications of fields, but the ground patterns noted from aerial photography are only indirect indicators of archaeological features that must be checked by other means. At the present time, only Fowler (1969) has reported on tests that would support an agricultural function for these marks.

The fields reported by Brown (1906, 1908, 1909) from Wisconsin and by Hinsdale (1925, 1931) from Michigan were situated in various locations, but many of them, like those at Ocmulgee, were in uplands. The fields that have been noted at Cahokia and Kincaid, however, are located in bottomlands, so upland situations are not a unique feature of these field systems.

Excavations in the Area of the Sand Lake Site, Wisconsin

Since the summer of 1982, excavations at and near the Sand Lake site by a research team from the Mississippi Valley Archaeology Center and the University of Wisconsin-LaCrosse have revealed buried ridge and furrow agricultural fields (Figure 9.3) that are definitively dated to the fifteenth century A.D. (Gallagher et al. 1985; Gallagher and Sasso 1986; Boszhardt 1983). The fields are situated at the mouth of a small valley that empties into the Mississippi Valley bottomlands near LaCrosse, Wisconsin. They appear to be associated with Orr phase Oneota ceramics that have been recovered from sites in Iowa and at the Valley View site in western Wisconsin some 10.5 km to the north of the Sand Lake agricultural fields (Gallagher et al. 1985:608). The Sand Lake excavations, still ongoing, have been extensively reported elsewhere, and so I will merely enumerate some of the descriptive characteristics of the agricultural features in this section.

By the summer of 1986, Gallagher and his colleagues had excavated at least 300 square meters of the agricultural fields, but I can report only on the excavations through 1985. The immediate environment of the fields was a coulee, which was blocked by Pleistocene outwash sands (Gallagher and Sasso 1986), creating in the distant past a marshy backwater area of about 75 hectares. Sand Lake, as it was called, has since been drained, but was apparently a low prairie with restricted drainage that was subjected to periodic flooding at the time it was in agricultural use in the fifteenth century.

The earliest fields at Sand Lake were constructed on floodplain loams that had been formed from alluvial silts (Gallagher and Sasso 1986). Rebuilding was noted across the field system, however, with as many as ten phases being noted at the eastern edge of the fields where the alluvium from the coulee had buried and separated successive ridge constructions. At different times the ridges and furrows were oriented in different directions. The ridges varied in both height and width, but exhibited a range in height from furrow of 5–26 cm, a ridge width of 23–120 cm and, a furrow width of 47–97 cm. They appear to have been more variable in this respect than those at Ocmulgee, but this may be a circumstance of the greater amount of attention paid to the excavation of these features. An interesting and perhaps important note about the agricultural fields at Sand Lake was the fact that a series of small rounded heaps were noted on some of the ridges (Gallagher and Sasso 1986). These were suggested by the investigators to be the remains of individual planting mounds and are reminiscent of the description of possible planting mounds on the fields at Ocmulgee National Monument.

The Sand Lake fields differed from the Mound D field at Ocmulgee in one important respect. According to Gallagher and Sasso (1986), some evidence of what might have been field preparation was noted in concentrations of charcoal on the ridges and within the ridge matrix. This suggested to the researchers that burning had taken place in the fields. Broken large mammal scapulae, elk antler tools showing polish, and what have been interpreted as scapula hoe chips showing polish were also recovered. Artifacts were sometimes accompanied by midden debris

9.3. Excavated ridge and furrow fields at Sand Lake site, Wisconsin. (Photograph courtesy of James P. Gallagher.)

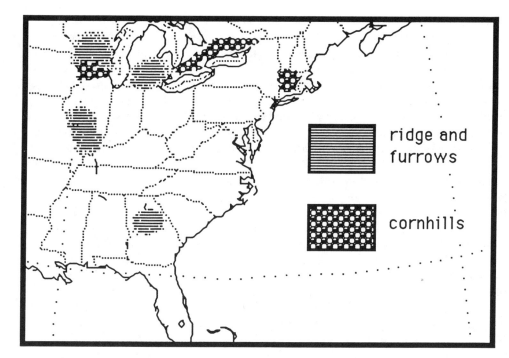

9.4. Distribution of reported ridge and furrow and cornhill agricultural fields in eastern North America.

in the form of fish bone, shell, and ash. Charred remains of corn, squash, and beans were also recovered from the ridges. This was suggested by the researchers to represent composting to enhance tilth and further confirms their use as agricultural fields (Gallagher et al. 1985:608).

Significance of the Ridged Fields

Gallagher and his coworkers at the Sand Lake locality have convincingly dealt with the functions of ridged fields in western Wisconsin, suggesting that the agronomic system there consisted of land preparation in the form of burning and the construction of ridges, the latter occurring before as well as during the process of planting. Ridge construction served a multiple set of functions, including aeration, manipulation of ground temperature (albedo control), and fertilization through the addition of ash and midden on the fields. The fields in Wisconsin and at Ocmulgee are significant as signs of what has to be a complex of agricultural techniques shared by Mississippian societies separated from one another in space by as much as 1500 km and in time by as much as 500 years. The crops grown at Sand Lake included the triumvirate of maize, beans, and squash; at Ocmulgee, only maize and probably squash were represented.

It is interesting and perhaps important to note that there is a major difference in the planting techniques of these ridged-field farmers of the southeastern and the north central states and the "cornhill" farmers who planted in late prehistoric and early historic times in the northeastern United States and eastern Canada

(Figure 9.4). This difference is either in response to differing environmental demands on farmers in the two areas, or it is one of culture and tradition. That it may be the latter is suggested by the fact that Lapham found both ridged fields and cornhills together at one of the sites he recorded in Wisconsin, with the cornhills obviously later in time since they overlay ridge and furrow fields.

More significant, however, than the contrast in agronomic practices of these groups is what these fields potentially can tell us about the sociology of the prehistoric economies that are represented in them. The size and layout of agricultural plots, hinted at by the path at Ocmulgee and by the differing orientation of fields at Sand Lake, have the potential for telling us, among other things: whether family or communal groups planted and harvested; the type of fallow system used and whether it differed from south to north or changed over time; the labor invested in agronomic practices; the potential yields of a single harvest; and the nature of the social surplus that might have been available from a single harvest. These are important questions, and theoretically they can be answered by the excavation and analysis of preserved agricultural fields.

Origins and Spread of the Ridged-field Complexes

Another question plagues the psyche of the archaeologist, however: Where did the ideas for such agronomic practices arise? In earlier papers, my coworkers and I argued that the Wisconsin and Michigan ridged fields were invented independently of those in the south and that they served different functions (Riley and Freimuth 1979; Riley et al. 1980, 1981). The buried features at Sand Lake share so much in form with those under Mound D at Ocmulgee, however, that this hypothesis is clearly untenable, and the question of origins of the complex remains to be answered.

At present two hypotheses—one emphasizing coevolution of existing agricultural tool kits in particular societies and the introduction of maize, and the other the diffusion of both tool kits and maize—must be entertained.

The Coevolution Hypothesis

The variety of hoeing implements in the Southeast and the Midwest suggests that the fact of the intensification of maize cultivation lead to a convergence of techniques for its culture across societies. It may also be that the introduction of maize itself led to a "coevolution" of techniques for its culture across eastern North America, although the contrast of the cornhill regime in the Northeast and the ridging regime in the Southeast and Midwest would suggest that this was not the case. What I mean to imply by coevolution is that the physiological constitution of maize demands a set of agronomic conditions that permit it to come to maturity and be successfully harvested. These demands put human societies in the position of being "domesticated" by maize in the sense that they are forced to create the conditions that the physiology of the crop demands. The outcomes in material culture end up being similar from one human society to another. Thus, the ridge and furrow field systems, in this model, can be seen as an outgrowth of different societies attempting to create the conditions needed for the successful growth and harvesting of maize.

A coevolution of maize and the techniques for its cultivation with a resultant similarity of field remains across the eastern United States is an appealing model for the distribution of the patterns that are notable from Early Mississippian in Georgia to later Upper Mississippian in the north-central United States. The model helps to explain the distribution of such features and their apparent identity across regions and cultures over at least five centuries. It remains to be seen, however, how well such a model will hold together as more information is gleaned about the agronomic practices in question.

The Diffusion Hypothesis

At the present time, a competing model can be offered, one that would suggest a diffusion of the techniques for maize cultivation that created the ridge and furrow patterns. If this is the case, the ridge and furrow patterns

must be seen as part of a complex including agricultural techniques, maize itself, and most probably a set of ceremonies surrounding maize. The diffusion of the complex would either have been from south to north, from Georgia to the Great Lakes and prairie, or it would have spread from a postulated center of Mississippian development if one is so inclined as to think of a Mississippian "heartland." If the latter scenario of central heartland origin is postulated, the earliest dates so far for the agricultural complex are in Georgia, in what has been traditionally interpreted as a Mississippian "intrusion" into an area without a clear Emergent Mississippian phase preceding it (see Chapters 12 and 13, this volume). There must then be an earlier ridged-field pattern, either along the Tennessee River in eastern Tennessee or at an intermediate set of sites that were the predecessors of Macon Plateau phase in central Georgia. At present, no signs of such a complex are present.

The Cahokia field, if indeed it is a ridged field, can be dated to either an Emergent Mississippian phase on the basis of its spatial association with a possible Jarrot-Fairmount phase house (Fowler and Benchley 1980: 61) or to an unidentified "developed" Mississippian phase represented by debris found to the east of apparent agricultural features. If the earlier attribution is correct, then the field at Cahokia would be contemporaneous with that at Ocmulgee, and a south-to-north diffusion of the agricultural complex could be replaced by the notion of a swift diffusion from the central Mississippi Valley.

The Texas site on the Kaskaskia River in Illinois (Fowler 1969) had a significant "Late Woodland" (Emergent Mississippian?) component spatially associated with the apparent ridged-field patterns noted there and broadly dated to A.D. 600–900. If the agricultural fields were contemporaneous with this component, which in my opinion is unlikely, then there is a possible antecedent to Mississippian fields that provides more supporting evidence of a central Mississippi Valley heartland for the diffusion of the practices noted at Ocmulgee and in Wisconsin.

The alternative hypothesis of a coevolution of agricultural techniques based on a conjunction of preexisting technological components and the introduction of maize is a much more satisfying hypothesis for me and, I would assume, for a number of my colleagues who have difficulty with the notion of what actually constitutes diffusion. While diffusion involves human contacts of one kind or another, these can include activities as complex as the transportation of slaves from one polity to another, trade in raw materials and manufactured items, the exchange of men and women in marriage alliances, confederation of two or more neighboring polities, or the simple appropriation of a technological set from a neighboring or distant group. There is a second, important aspect of diffusion, however, that is often ignored by archaeologists: the successful transfer of the ideas or technological expertise from the host to the recipient society. For a disease to be successfully transferred from one individual to another, the recipient must satisfy a set of conditions. In some instances, an alkaline or acidic environment in the recipient will lessen the chances of a successful transfer. I would argue that the successful transfer of a diffused agricultural complex is no different in that it demands environmental—in this case, technological, social, political, and ideological—circumstances that enhance the probability of the success of the transfer.

The concept of coevolution of an agricultural complex such as the one found in the excavations described here depends on the transfer of maize from one society to another, but it emphasizes the social environment into which the maize is transferred, and these environments are quite different from one society to another, even on a local scale. The material correlates of these environments are easily traced and include antler tine rakes, hoes of shell, bone, or stone, the digging stick, and other implements designed for breaking earth and clearing ground. In some premaize societies these implements were probably used in the horticulture of squash, gourd, sunflower, tobacco, and other domesticates before the introduction of maize and could be components in the newly developed agricultural complex. Melding these components into a field agriculture complex, however, had less to do with their presence than it had to do with the economic and social situations of the people at the time maize was introduced. Did the seasonal round place people in a favorable physiographic setting for the use of these implements in planting and harvesting maize? Did the division of labor in particular societies favor the use of these implements in maize agriculture, and are we seeing in the field systems that were developed a communal aspect to field labor that was favored in some societies and not in others? These are questions that cannot be answered satisfactorily at the present time. The contrast between the cornhill farming of the Northeast and the continuous ridged-field agricultural systems of the Southeast and north-central North America, however, suggests that there was a different organization of agriculture in the two places, with continuous fields being emphasized in Mississippian societies and discontinuous planting among the later Late Woodland peoples of the northeastern United States.

The fact that control over maize seed plasm and over particular planting techniques was a female prerogative in some Missouri Basin Indian societies during the historic period (Will and Hyde 1917) suggests another parameter to the question of the coevolution of the field systems

connected with maize agriculture, and also suggests that in some instances, at least, the successful transfer of maize agriculture may have been due to the transfer of women from one society to another in any of a number of ways.

Agricultural Implements and Coevolution

As must be obvious, the environmental parameters in the spread of the practice of field agriculture across the eastern United States are not completely clear, but one of the major technological necessities for the success of such a transfer was the hoe. I would argue that tools of the agronomic practices represented in the ridged fields, specifically hoes of shell, flint, and the scapulae of middle-sized and large animals, were in place before the introduction of maize. This is Linton's (1924a) idea, not mine, and it is supported by the presence of stone hoes in pre-Mississippian contexts at the Baumer site in Illinois (Maxwell 1951) and the occurrence of shell digging implements in Middle Woodland sites in both Illinois and Ohio.

With the presence of digging implements in premaize contexts as a given, the variety or uniformity of digging implements in sites of the Mississippian economic pattern demands some attention. Hoes made from several types of material show up in eastern North America during the period in question. The chert hoe is ubiquitous in most Middle Mississippian contexts. In the central Mississippi Valley, an extensive trade from a small number of quarries in Illinois, Missouri, and Tennessee has been documented by Winters (1981). The objects of this trade have been found as far east as Blennehasset Island in northeastern Ohio, as far west as eastern Oklahoma, and as far south as northern Mississippi. While few of these hoes are present in Late Woodland sites in Illinois and Wisconsin, they have been noted from Aztlan, a Mississippian outlier in Wisconsin (Winters 1981:29). Stone hoes of local origin have been found in agricultural sites in the northeastern United States and eastern Canada as well, although they are not common.

In the area to the north and west of the distribution of the chert hoe, but still within the area of ridged fields, hoes made from the scapulae of elk and bison are reported. These are associated with Oneota sites dating from A.D. 1000–1500 from Iowa, Wisconsin, and Minnesota. Bison scapulae were also in use in various Central Plains Tradition sites, including those of Nebraska and Upper Republican phases of Nebraska and northern Kansas, as well as some of the later Coalescent phases of the Middle Missouri Tradition. The use of bison scapulae continued into historic times in these areas.

The use of small deer-scapula hoes is a marker of sites of the Fort Ancient phase in southern Ohio and Kentucky dating from the later part of the time range in question; although a few stone hoes have been recovered from these sites. Late Woodland settlements in the northeastern United States and lower Canada have yielded deer scapula hoes as well, and moose antlers were apparently used as hoes in those areas of the Northeast where moose was a resource (Heidenreich 1974).

This brief description of the complementary distribution of various excavating implements is not meant to be exhaustive, but it does point to the fact that the same functions were performed by tools representing a variety of materials and forms. It is interesting to note that the distribution of apparent ridge and furrow agricultural fields involves areas where two different hoe types—stone hoes and elk and bison scapula hoes—exist, and yet the forms of the agricultural fields are very much the same. This suggests that the ridged fields were a function either of cultural norms or were determined by environmental parameters of which we have very little knowledge or understanding at the present time.

We may tentatively conclude that the convergence of techniques for maize cultivation must have depended very heavily on the requirements of the varieties of maize under cultivation in the southeastern and north-central parts of North America rather than on the particular implements that were in use for land manipulation across these two regions. This can be considered supporting evidence for the coevolution hypothesis rather than the diffusion of a set of techniques along with maize in a simple and direct transfer from one society to another.

Conclusions

The agricultural field systems of southeastern and north-central North America have become the focus of more intensive research in the last fifteen years. The research conducted at Ocmulgee in the 1930s by Kelly and his colleagues opened up an area of archaeological research that had not existed before and that was subsequently ignored by at least two generations of archaeologists. The fact that the fields existed at the site was noted in a number of texts, but the implications of these fields for the study of prehistoric Indian agricultural practices were not pursued and have only recently attracted the attention of researchers interested in village horticultural economies and their agronomic base. Ocmulgee National Monument is thus a landmark in the recognition of a significant body of evidence related to the agricultural subsistence practices of prehistoric southeastern Indians.

The shared set of agronomic practices across southeastern and midwestern North America was somewhat different from those of the northeastern Indians, which apparently had an origin in early Mississippian times. These agronomic practices are apparently related primarily to maize agriculture but are based on technical achievements that were in use before the advent of maize as a substantial contributor to the crop complex of eastern North America. The distribution of this complex of agronomic traits can either be seen in terms of a coevolution of preexisting components into an agricultural system that was predominantly determined by the requirements of maize or in terms of the diffusion of a total agricultural complex surrounding maize. The social correlates of this agricultural complex remain to be worked out, and it is important to note that the agronomic pattern probably was not present everywhere that maize was cultivated.

Much more work remains to be done in regard to the agricultural complex that is described here, including the determination of whether the bare ground patterns noted at Cahokia, Kincaid, and other sites in the Midwest are in fact the remains of such agricultural systems and whether they follow the general patterns suggested by the excavated fields in Wisconsin and Georgia.

One final note must be added here regarding the importance at the present time for the recognition and preservation of existing surface fields through legislative, professional, and community action. One of the few ridge and furrow fields known in Iowa has recently been reported as destroyed (Billeck 1986), and of more than 50 fields in Wisconsin that were visited by Moffat (1979), only 7 remained at the time of his survey. We do not have a good count of the number of fields preserved in Michigan, but I visited the cornhill locations near Northampton, Massachusetts, reported by Delabarre and Wilder in the 1920s only to find them destroyed by agriculture and construction. Preservation of a good sample of these features should be a high priority in policy decisions for cultural resource management.

CHAPTER TEN

The Case for Earth Lodges in the Southeast

Lewis Larson

EARTH LODGES HAVE been an accepted fact of southeastern prehistory for more than 50 years. Writing in 1938, William Webb described what he interpreted as "earth-covered structures" found on sites excavated in the Norris Basin (Webb 1938:48, 72, 193–94). In that same year, Arthur Kelly reported the discovery of a "circular chamber 42 feet in diameter, covered by an earth shell" (Kelly 1938c:11). Found beneath a small mound near Mound D at Macon Plateau, Kelly identified this chamber as a "ceremonial earth lodge." As far as I am aware, this is the first time that the term "earth lodge" was used in reference to an archaeologically defined structure in the Southeast.

An unpublished thesis by Daniel Crouch (1974) entitled "South Appalachian Earth Lodges" provides the most extensive examination and commentary on southeastern earth lodges to date. He has surveyed the literature of the region pertaining to major sites where earth lodges have been identified, and he has carefully reviewed the evidence for each identification. Initially Crouch recognized three building categories: (1) he uses the terminology "earth lodge" in reference to buildings that are "completely covered" with earth;

(2) his term "earth banked" refers to buildings that have only a "partial" covering of earth; while (3) "earthen construction" is a term that he uses to subsume both of the previous categories (Crouch 1974:2). However, he abandons this terminology in his conclusions. His final sentences, therefore, reflect his ultimate perception of the nature of southeastern earth lodges, namely that earth-covered buildings were not characteristic of the prehistory of the area. "It may be best to think of 'earth lodge' as any ceremonial or domestic building of human construction on which earth, loose or sod, has by deliberate human action been placed either on the walls to significant height or over the walls and at least a part of the roof, as a part of its architecture. While the full earth coverage and perhaps semi-subterranean floor may be applicable elsewhere, they are not suitable criteria for South Appalachian ceremonial structures" (Crouch 1974:136).

The most recent discussion of southeastern earth lodges is that of James Rudolph (1984:33). While the thrust of his paper is not a reexamination of the validity of interpretations of southeastern archaeological structures as earth lodges, he does provide a comprehensive survey of structures that he and others have so identified. Rudolph defines "an earthlodge as an above-ground building that had either an earth-covered roof or an earth embankment buttressing the exterior walls" (Rudolph 1984:33). Rudolph argues that the term "earth lodge" is an appropriate one to use in reference to the earth-embanked structures because "the term 'earthlodge' has historical precedence in the archaeological literature of the Southeast and has served us perfectly well for many years; there is no reason to change it now" (Rudolph 1984:33).

To be sure, the term "earth lodge" has been used in the southeastern archaeological literature for a long time, at least since 1938; without exception, though, it has been applied only to buildings that were interpreted as having earth-covered roofs. It seems to me that Crouch and Rudolph contribute little to the understanding of aboriginal southeastern architecture, except confusion, by categorizing two very distinct building types—that is, earth-covered and earth-embanked—within the same class. My perceptions notwithstanding, Crouch and Rudolph can and should define "earth lodge" in any way that serves well the analytical needs of their research. On the other hand, Rudolph should not justify the application of the term to earth-embanked buildings as sanctioned by historical precedent.

At this point, it is necessary for me to define what I mean by "earth lodge" as I will employ it in this paper. My definition of an earth lodge is more restrictive than those definitions employed by Crouch and Rudolph. As I have already indicated, however, I do not want to dispute their definitions. On the contrary, I wish to dispute the interpretation of certain archaeologically known structures in the Southeast as buildings that had earth- or sod-covered roofs. I am convinced that these interpretations are in error and that, as a consequence, they are not earth lodges in terms of both my definition and the definitions that have been historically employed by anthropologists (including southeastern archaeologists).

The earliest use of the term that I have encountered is in *Houses and House-Life of the American Aborigines* by Lewis Henry Morgan, published in 1881. Accompanying a discussion by Morgan of aboriginal earth-covered houses in California is an illustration captioned "Earth Lodges in the Sacramento Valley" (Morgan 1881: Figure 1). Morgan, however, uses the term "dirt lodges" in reference to the Mandan house type (Morgan 1881:126). Historically, the term has been regularly used by American anthropologists in reference to residential structures that were built on the northern and central Plains during the prehistoric and historic periods. The published description of the Hidatsa earth lodge, based on data collected by Gilbert Wilson from native informants between 1906 and 1918, is perhaps the most detailed and complete that we have for earth lodges from the northern Plains area. These circular buildings were large enough (forty or more feet in diameter) to have accommodated an extended kin grouping along with their horses (Wilson 1934:383–94, figure 11). Constructed with a heavy post framing, they had a pole-supported roof and walls covered with sod underlain with a layer of prairie grass and a mat of willow branches (Wilson 1934: figure 16).

For the most part, the ethnographic literature on the North American Indians has, for over a century, applied the term "earth lodge" to the type of structure described by Wilson. For purposes of this chapter, I will therefore limit the definition of the term to large, and often circular, buildings (on the Plains these were usually residences), having a sod-covered roof supported by a wood post and pole framework.

On the other hand, earth-embanked buildings are found on Mississippi period sites over a broad reach of the Southeast. It is almost certainly true that earth embankments, as a feature of both public and residential buildings, were the rule rather than the exception throughout the area during this period. This in turn suggests that an embankment was needed because of

the technical demands of constructing a building with daub-covered walls and a pent roof with eaves. In order to obtain a seal with the wall plate—a wall plate utilizing post construction, wattle work, and a daub covering—the floor was excavated 30 cm to 50 cm below the surrounding ground surface. The embankment—more massive in public buildings because they were large buildings and more modest in smaller domestic structures—functioned as a seal for the base of the outer surface of the walls of the building and the surface of the ground on which it was built. The sloping embankment served not only as a seal but also to divert rain water, which flowed off the eaves and onto the ground, away from the walls. The construction of the embankment thus functioned to keep the interior of the structure from being flooded and to protect the base of the wall from the erosive effect of rain.

In most Mississippi period construction there is no apparent break in the length of the wall line indicating an entry. I believe that this is because the doorway was constructed with a sill that employed a low stub of the wall along with the embankment to span the door opening in order to maintain the integrity of the walls and their seal throughout their entire length. I view these structures as categorically distinct from the earth lodges that were encountered on the Plains and from those that I define as earth lodges.

Ethnohistorical Evidence

Over sixty years ago, Ralph Linton (1924b:249–53) called attention to the similarity between the earth lodges built on the northern Plains and the dwellings described for the eighteenth-century Muskogean-speaking groups in the Southeast. A review of the available ethnohistorical descriptions, however, suggests that the similarity underscored by Linton was deficient in one important respect. The southeastern buildings lacked a sod-covered roof. The description of Chickasaw houses given by Adair is a case in point. Adair called these southeastern structures "hot-houses" or "winter houses."

The clothing of the Indians being very light, they provide themselves for the winter with hot-houses, whose properties are to retain and reflect the heat, after the manner of the Dutch stoves. To raise these, they fix deep in the ground, a sufficient number of strong forked posts, at a proportional distance, in a circular form, all of an equal height, about five or six feet above the surface of the ground: above these, they tie very securely large pieces of the heart of white oak, which are of a tough flexible nature, interweaving this orbit from top to bottom, with pieces of the same, or the like timber. Then, in the middle of the fabric they fix very deep in the ground, four large pine posts in a quadrangular form, notched atop, on which they lay a number of heavy logs, let into each other, and rounding gradually to the top. Above this huge pile, to the very top, they lay a number of long dry poles, all properly notched, to keep strong hold of the under posts and wall-plate. Then they weave them thick with their split saplings, and daub them all over about six or seven inches thick with tough clay, well mixed with withered grass: when this cement is half dried, they thatch the house with the longest sort of dry grass, that their land produces. They first lay on one round tier, placing a split sapling atop, well tied to different parts of the under pieces of timber, about fifteen inches below the eave: and, in this manner, they proceed circularly to the very spire, where commonly a pole is fixed, that displays on the top the figure of a large carved eagle. At a small distance below which, four heavy logs are strongly tied together across, in a quadrangular form, in order to secure the roof from the power of envious blasts. The door of this winter palace, is commonly about four feet high, and so narrow as not to admit two to enter it abreast, with a winding passage for the space of six or seven feet, to secure themselves both from the power of the bleak winds, and of an invading enemy. As they usually build on rising ground, the floor is often a yard lower than the earth, which serves them as a breast work against an enemy. (Adair 1775: 418–19)

However we read the eighteenth-century syntax of Adair, it is not easy to conclude that the roof of the Chickasaw house was sod-covered in the manner of the northern Plains earth lodges along the Missouri River. The roof that Adair describes is one that is covered with grass thatch. He does, however, describe the use of daub to cover the roof decking. The daub is seemingly used in this manner to insulate the structure by preventing heat loss through the grass thatch of the roof covering. In this instance, the daub is protected from the weather by the overlay of grass thatching. To a lesser extent, the use of daub over the roof deck may also have functioned as a fire barrier, preventing sparks from the hearth being carried by draughts through the roof timbers directly into the thatch roof covering.

William Bartram, whose observations of the southeastern Indians were roughly contemporary with those of Adair, tells us that the roofs of the houses in the Alachua (Seminole) town of Cusowilla were covered "with the bark of the Cypress tree" (Bartram 1928:122). In a later reference to the more northerly dwellings of "Uche town" near the Fall Line on the Chattahoochee River, Bartram states that "these houses are neatly covered or roofed with Cypress bark or shingles of that tree" (Bartram 1928:244).

It is well to note that these references by Adair and Bartram are to buildings that were almost certainly used primarily, if not solely, as residences. Thus, these southeastern houses are functionally comparable to those of the northern Plains. On the other hand, these eighteenth-century southeastern buildings did not have sod-covered

roofs and so they differ from the Plains houses in this important structural characteristic. Recently, Craig Sheldon has provided me with preliminary data on a historic "hot house" of the type described by Adair. The house was excavated by Auburn University during investigations at the Lower Creek site of Fusihatchee on the Tallapoosa River in Elmore County, Alabama, twelve miles northeast of Montgomery. The structure has been identified as belonging in a post-Mississippi period context. Specifically, it was built and occupied during the Atasi phase that has been assigned a time range of A.D. 1600 to 1715. Using the excavated data and relevant ethnohistorical sources, Sheldon rejects, out of hand, any interpretation that identifies this structure and others like it as sod-covered (Sheldon, personal communication 1986).

One of the more interesting ethnohistoric descriptions of aboriginal southeastern construction is that provided by Benjamin Hawkins. Hawkins lived and worked as an agent among Creeks only a few years after Adair and Bartram traveled in the Southeast, thus his observations are more or less coincident with theirs. The building that Hawkins describes is a public building, a council house.

Chooc-ofau thluc-co, the *rotunda* or *assembly room*, called by the trader, "hot house." This is near the square, and is constructed after the following manner: Eight posts are fixed in the ground, forming an octagon of thirty feet diameter. They are twelve feet high, and large enough to support the roof. On these, five or six logs are placed, of a side, drawn in as they rise. On these, long poles or rafters, to suit the height of the building, are laid, the upper ends forming a point, and the lower ends projecting out six feet from the octagon, and resting on posts five feet high, placed in a circle round the octagon, with plates on them, to which the rafters are tied with splints. The rafters are near together, and fastened with splits. These are covered with clay, and that with pine bark; the wall, six feet from the octagon, is clayed up; they have a small door into a small portico, curved round for five or six feet, then into the house. (Hawkins 1848:71)

The description by Hawkins indicates that the rafters are closely spaced and coated with clay, and they are then covered with a layer of pine bark. In spite of the obvious use of daub in an apparent attempt to insulate and seal the roof of the structure in the same manner as that described by Adair, there is no sense of a "sod covered building" conveyed in the statement by Hawkins. Instead, Hawkins describes a bark-roofed or, perhaps more accurately, a bark-shingled building.

Archaeological Evidence

Apparently the earliest identification of a southeastern archaeological building as an earth lodge was the Mound

10.1. Excavation of the Mound D-1 Lodge, Ocmulgee National Monument. (Photograph courtesy of the National Park Service, Southeast Archeological Center.)

D-1 Lodge (Macon Earth Lodge), initially reported by Kelly (1938:11–12) and subsequently described in detail by Fairbanks (1946b) (Figure 10.1). This building was one of two similar archaeological features encountered and excavated near Mound D at the Macon Plateau site (Figure 10.2). Further, it was this building that was reconstructed as an earth lodge and that today is a major element in the interpretation of the prehistory of Ocmulgee National Monument.

The earth lodges identified at Macon Plateau are stated to have had a nonresidential function. They were, in fact, specifically called "council chambers" in the records of the excavations (for example, Williams and Henderson 1974:20, figures 3 and 8). Both Kelly (1938c:11) and Fairbanks (1946b:94) describe the first of the earth lodges at Mound D as "ceremonial." Indeed, it would be difficult to characterize the structure in any other way. The clay eagle effigy platform with its forked eye, the clay bank of

seats encircling the wall (Figure 10.3), and the absence of any household refuse on the floor all argue for a use other than as a dwelling. The adjective "ceremonial" certainly appears to be appropriately applied to the Mound D-1 Lodge. No doubt it accommodated a large number of individuals if the forty-seven positions on the wall bench and the three positions on the eagle platform are correctly interpreted as seats. The number, as well as the arrangement, of seats also presents a strong argument that the building was used for ceremonial activity, although the nature of that activity as political or religious ceremony has yet to be determined.

Swanton (1946:386–420) has provided the most detailed and exhaustive survey of the ethnohistorical literature covering the domestic and public architecture of the southeastern Indians. A review of his survey reveals that there are no structures comparable to the Macon Plateau earth lodge as it has been described by Kelly and

Lewis Larson

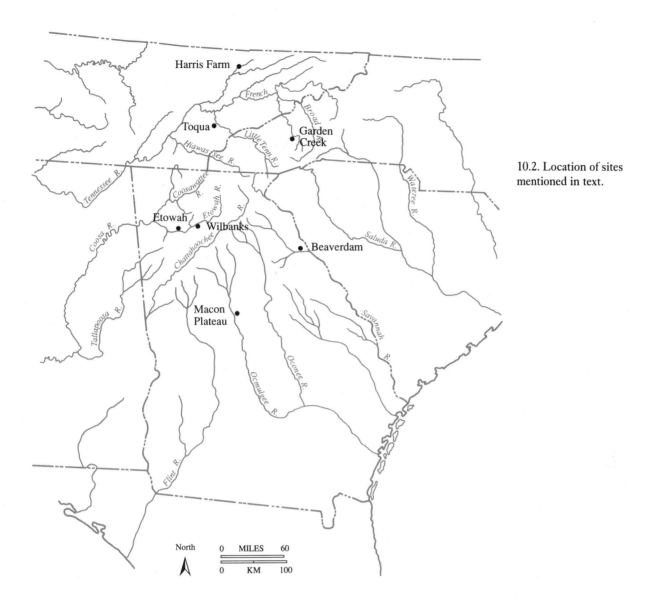

10.2. Location of sites mentioned in text.

Fairbanks. None of the ethnohistorically known buildings had earth- or sod-covered roofs. More important, the roofs of these buildings do not appear to conform to that of the Macon Plateau structure, where we are told that "the roof had been covered by earth" (Fairbanks 1946b: 97). In addition, none of the ethnohistorically known structures had the low, massive, and free-standing clay wall of the Macon Plateau building. On the contrary, the buildings discussed by Swanton had post-supported walls that were usually of a wattle-and-daub construction. These buildings were in marked contrast to the circular wall of the Macon Plateau structure as it is described by Fairbanks: "As the center of the mound was approached, the red clay suddenly dropped away to form a vertical wall. The inner face of the wall was slightly burned. Horizontal stripping exposed a circular structure 42 feet

in diameter surrounded by the remains of a low clay wall or mound. . . . This wall extended 13–21 feet beyond the floor. It remained to a height of 37 inches above the floor at the eastern side but of only 9 inches at the north, where plowing was most severe. This massive buttress surrounded the clay floor so as to give the building the appearance of being semi-subterranean, although it was actually entirely above ground" (Fairbanks 1946b:95).

Interestingly, no postholes outline the wall of the structure, which argues that the wall was not supported by any sort of timbering. In addition, it suggests that the roof beams rested directly on the upper surface of the wall. In this regard it is well to remember that at least some of the tenants of this building were supposedly occupying the seats that encircled the floor immediately against the inner surface of the wall. In order for persons who are between

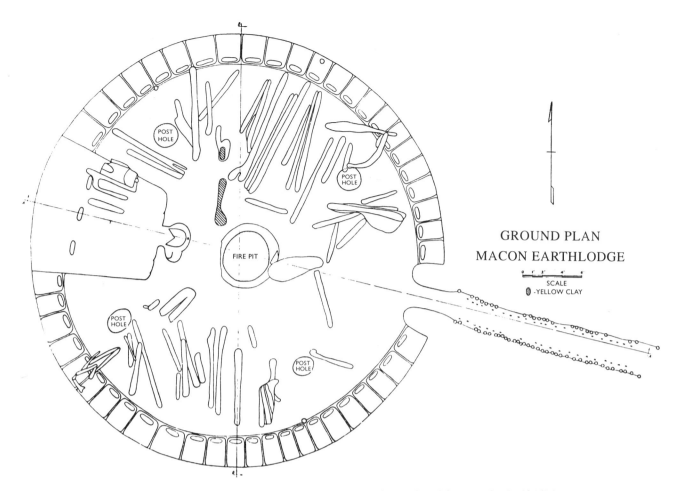

GROUND PLAN
MACON EARTHLODGE

SCALE
◉ -YELLOW CLAY

10.3. Plan view of the Mound D-1 Lodge, Ocmulgee National Monument. (Reproduced from Fairbanks 1946b.)

5 and 6 feet tall to sit up straight in one of these seats, with their backs against the wall and the roof clearing their heads, the wall at the back of the seats would have to have originally extended at least 3.5 feet above the clay surface of the seats themselves. Even this wall height would not have allowed persons to seat themselves without crawling on all fours or backing awkwardly into position.

An examination of the descriptions of buildings from southeastern sites listed by James Rudolph as characterized by earth lodges reveals that in only four instances did those who reported the excavation of the sites interpret any of the archaeological features as the remains of a building that originally had a sod- or earth-covered roof.

These four instances include the Macon Plateau site already noted and the Wilbanks site, both in Georgia, the Harris Farm in Tennessee, and the Garden Creek Mound No. 1 in North Carolina. In the report of the archaeology of each of these sites there is an unequivocal statement that at least one of the structures encountered during excavation was earth-covered (Kelly 1938c:11; Sears 1958:141; Webb 1938:79; Dickens 1976:83). None of the other structures included in the Rudolph survey are

identified as earth lodges by those who originally reported them, with the exception of the structures from the Beaverdam Creek site in Georgia reported by Rudolph and Hally. In the report on that site, we are told by the authors that the term "earth lodge" was used "with some hesitation." This hesitation came in part because, while the Beaverdam Creek Mound structures were earth-embanked buildings, it could not be demonstrated that their roofs were indeed earth-covered (Rudolph and Hally 1985:75).

Discussion

I feel that there are several reasons for questioning the validity of the archaeological identification of earth lodges in the Southeast. First, of the probably hundreds of excavated Mississippi period aboriginal buildings, domestic and public, in the Southeast, there are relatively few instances where such buildings have been identified. Only the four sites noted above—Macon Plateau, Wilbanks, Harris Farm, and Garden Creek—have published descriptions of excavated buildings that have been

Lewis Larson

characterized as having earth-covered roofs. It strikes me as unusual that, of the many excavated examples of prehistoric buildings, those with earth-covered roofs have been found at only these four sites. If an earth-covered roof were a viable construction technique in the region, we might well ask why it was not a more widely used technique. Of course, there is the possibility that, for whatever reasons, such roof construction may have been used only a very few times at a very few sites. Nevertheless, the rarity of the technique does provide a rationale and an argument for a reexamination of those instances where it is said to have been used.

A second reason to question the identification of earth-covered roofs is to be found in a rereading of the published excavation descriptions of the presumed earth lodges. These descriptions are not of an order that precludes an interpretation other than that of an earth lodge. Let me quickly assert, however, that the fault may lie not with reality, but with the description given of it by the several investigators, or in fact, with my reading of these descriptions.

Fairbanks reports that at Macon Plateau the excavation of the floor of the building he identifies as an earth lodge revealed that it "was covered to the plow zone with mixed clay, charcoal, and fragments of burned clay" (Fairbanks 1946b:95).

Upon the floor were numerous pieces of charred timbers resting on from 0.2 foot to nearly one foot of partly burned clay and fragments of charred cane.... These timbers lay close to the floor near the wall and were elevated on fragments of burned clay near the center. Under the smaller poles were larger logs one foot or more in diameter. One of these touched the fire basin. It was evident that all these charred timbers represented debris from a burned roof and that the roof had been covered with earth. In burning the cane had fallen first and allowed much of the covering clay to fall through to the floor before the main timbers burned sufficiently to give way. Thus, when these larger beams fell, they rested on previously fallen roof materials that had originally covered them. (Fairbanks 1946b:97)

At the base of Garden Creek Mound No. 1, Dickens reports two features that he describes as the "collapsed remains of semi-subterranean earth-covered buildings" (Dickens 1976:83). The evidence for the roof lying on the floors of both features was described as follows: "Numerous horizontal molds of fallen roof beams and cane roof covering were present on the floor and benches" (Dickens 1976:86). Dickens further characterized the archaeological situation on the floor of the buildings in a manner that contrasts it sharply with the archaeology of the Macon Plateau collapsed roof. Dickens states that "the collapsed roof material in both of the [Garden Creek Mound No. 1] earth lodges formed a rather thin (about 0.4 to 0.6 foot) layer over the central portion of the floor,

suggesting that there had been only a sparse covering of dirt on the upper portions of the roofs. This layer was much thicker (about 1 to 3 feet) around the walls and the roof margins" (Dickens 1976:86).

What is referred to as the "primary structure" under Mound 2 at the Harris Farm in the Norris Basin is reported by Webb as having an earth-covered roof. The building had burned. He tells us that "the burned structure had collapsed after burning, but in falling had not reached the primary floor. In sections of the collapsed wall every post was shown by its charred remains, the basal end terminating exactly in a post mold at the boundary. But these posts in falling had been held up off the primary floor by as much as a foot or more of red clay. Although the clay was *under* the fallen and burned wall and rested on an unburned floor, yet it was hardened and discolored as a result of the considerable heat action. The clay immediately *over* portions of this structure showed much less effect of burning" (Webb 1938:78–79).

At the Macon Plateau, Harris Farm, and Garden Creek mound sites, the argument for earth-covered roofs on the structures identified as earth lodges depends upon the archaeological interpretation of the clay or earth deposited on the floor and underlying the remains of roof timbers. This clay or earth is identified as that which originally lay on top of these timbers while they supported the roof. The destruction of the buildings by fire caused the earth covering the roof to fall through the roof beams before these beams, in turn, had burned to a point where they too fell to the floor and came to rest on top of that earth.

I would suggest that there are alternative explanations for the charred roof timbers overlying clay or earth deposited on the floors of the buildings. One alternative explanation suggests itself, in this instance as a consequence of reading the descriptions of the archaeology, not only at the Harris Farm but also at the Garden Creek mound and at Macon Plateau. This alternative argues that the buildings were deliberately burned. The burning was preparatory to either the rebuilding of the structure itself or as a prelude to the construction of a platform mound on the site of the structure. After the building had been set on fire, but before the supporting timbers had fallen, loads of clay began to be thrown onto the site of the burning building. If the destruction of the building by fire and its burial under the fill of a mound construction were part of a single event, and this seems to be the case in these situations, it is entirely reasonable to suppose that the addition of the fill may have begun before the heavy roof beams had burned through and fallen to the floor.

Another alternative explanation argues that the earth or clay underlying the charred roof timbers resulted from daub on the walls falling onto the floor as the structure burned and before the heavy roof beams fell. It is also possible that some or all of the charred timbers or log molds on the floor are the remains of wall posts rather than roof beams. Webb, in fact, indicates that this is the situation in that portion of his description of the archaeology of the Harris Farm Mound 2 that is quoted above. Apposite to this point, David Hally reports that "in my own experience, domestic [southeastern Mississippi period] structures often have more daub on the floor near the center of the structure than along the walls. It may be that only the upper walls of structures were sufficiently heated during burning to fire the clay. Walls that collapsed inward would then tend to create piles of daub in the center of the floor" (David Hally, personal communication, May 8, 1987).

It is also possible that the daub in the center of the houses, lying beneath the roof beams, was derived from the destruction of interior partitions within the structure. Such post-supported partitions (as opposed to posts supporting benches or other furniture) are known from several Mississippi period sites. At Hiwassee Island, the floors of six buildings indicated such internal divisions (Lewis and Kneberg 1946:67). The Toqua site, also in Tennessee, had a structure with several interior partitions that produced concentrations of daub on the floor (Polhemus 1985:25–26). At the Irvin Village site (No. 5) in the Norris Basin, Webb encountered a structure (No. 2) with an interior partition (Webb 1938:48–49, figure 14). A second such structure (Feature No. 42) was excavated by Webb at the Ausmus Farm Mounds (No. 10), also within the Norris Basin (Webb 1938:97–99, figure 43).

The most plausible of the alternative explanations, one derived from the ethnohistorical data, suggests itself. The presence of the burned daub on the floors of the burned structures may well be attributable to the use of an insulating layer of daub over the roof timbers and beneath the roof thatch or other covering. In addition to collapsed wall daub, this construction practice, described by both Adair and Hawkins and discussed above, could very likely have been a source of a portion of the burned daub found on the excavated floors of the supposed earth lodges in Tennessee, North Carolina, and Georgia.

While as far as I am aware the following archaeological situation has been found only at two archaeological sites, it would seem incidentally to have pertinence to the subject of earth or daub in or on aboriginal roofs. In 1964, at the Etowah site, I excavated the floor of an aboriginal house that had burned. It was located in the village area of the site, some 125 m east of Mound A. In the process of clearing the floor, an interesting architectural detail was brought to light. A fragment of a large jar was found embedded in the fill of the floor. The body of the jar had been broken away more or less evenly at the shoulder around the entire circumference of the vessel, leaving the entire upper portion, with its short neck and relatively small opening, intact. The jar had a pinched rim and a

plain surface and is of a type generally classified as Lamar. It was approximately 41.9 cm in circumference at the shoulder, while the neck was 6.3 cm high with an orifice 18.4 cm in diameter. It lay upside down with the neck down on the floor. When it was turned over it was found that the vessel had clay, or daub, crudely plastered over much of the exterior surface of the jar. The daub, about 2 cm thick, began immediately below the neck and seemed to extend beyond the broken edge at the shoulder line. I believe that the upper portion of this large jar had been placed on top of the roof, probably at or near the ridge pole, where it served as a chimney or more accurately a fireproof smoke hole. The clay plaster was probably carried down from the surface of the jar over the surface of the thatch or mat roofing material, possibly to keep sparks that might fly out of the smoke hole from igniting the flammable roof.

Richard R. Polhemus (personal communication, May 1990) has recently encountered a similar situation at the Loy site. In this instance, while there was no evidence that a portion of a pottery vessel was used, there were indications that the area surrounding the smoke hole was covered with daub. If this were a feature of other Mississippi period houses, or if such other houses simply had clay or daub placed on the roof around the area of the smoke hole to prevent sparks from igniting the roofing material, then the daub would appear in the center of the floor as the roofing material collapsed onto the floor of a house that burned.

The third site where an earth-covered structure has been reported, the Wilbanks Farm, is for me a genuine *pons asinorum*. It presents an unusual, and apparently more complex, archaeological situation than the others discussed to this point. The Wilbanks structure is markedly different from the premound structures at the Garden Creek site, the "small log" buildings of the Harris Farm, or the circular Macon Plateau Council House with its clay seats and eagle platform. The Wilbanks structure lacks any indication of benches along the walls. Compare this with the Tennessee and North Carolina buildings, where there were post-supported benches along the walls. At Macon Plateau an encircling clay banquette with well-defined seats was an equivalent feature. Two other important differences are seen in the absence of a hearth in the Wilbanks structure or an entry passage.

The explanation, by Sears, of the construction of the Wilbanks feature has not convinced me that there was an earth lodge under the mound. In fact, I am not convinced that there was a building of any kind under the mound. The presumed earth lodge, as it is described by Sears, is not only an architectural anomaly in the Mississippi period of the Southeast, it is structurally implausible. There were, according to the reconstruction by Sears, more than 4,000 square feet of roof supported by poles,

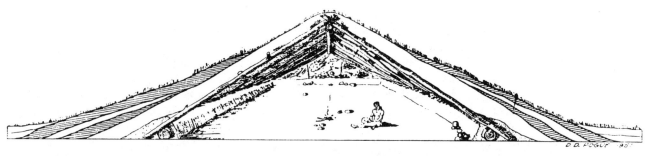

10.4. Artist's reconstruction of the earth lodge at the Wilbanks site. (Reproduced from Sears 1958: Figure 5.)

forty feet long, 4 to 6 inches in diameter, and spaced two feet apart along two opposing walls (Figure 10.4). The roof poles were cantilevered up and out over the floor to form an A-frame-shaped covering. These poles were braced and anchored at their floor ends along each wall line with a large horizontal log and a clay embankment. The pole framing was, in turn, overlain by almost three feet of silt and clay that completed the roof covering. This structure had not burned (Sears 1958:143–44).

My objection to the interpretation of the basal features of the Wilbanks mound by Sears is based in part on the fact that his interpretation results in a roof covered by more than 1,633.5 tons of earth, or a load of 770 pounds per square foot. I am assured by a structural engineer that this weight is well over the load-bearing capacity of a roof of the sort that Sears has reconstructed. Serious engineering questions can also be raised concerning the longitudinal stability of this roof. The latter questions are valid because of the apparent absence of any end-bracing elements for the roof. I must conclude that the data presented by Sears simply does not add up to evidence for any recognizable building. The horizontal logs that served to brace the roof poles and, along with the clay embankment, to define the walls along two sides of the building are not indicated on either the published profiles that show the cross sections of the mound nor on the published floor plan of the feature (Sears 1958: figures 6a, 6b, and 7). Sears reports that the molds of these logs were encountered during the excavation. Interestingly, Wauchope does not report encountering the horizontal log mold, although he too cut a trench across the structure a decade earlier (Wauchope 1966:280–90, 453–55, figure 201). One can only speculate, but it would appear that these large logs could not be traced along the periphery of the presumed floor.

The absence of a fire basin or hearth and any indication of passageway into the structure, regular features not only of Mississippi period houses but also apparently of all public buildings of that period, are additional indications that there is something amiss with the Sears interpretation of the Wilbanks mound.

Finally, I would point out that I also encountered the

pattern formed by what Sears has called "roof poles," during late July and early August of 1958 while I was excavating Mound C at the Etowah site. At that time, many molds of poles approximately 8 cm to 15 cm in diameter were found on the southwest corner of the mound and extending along the southern side of the mound. The molds indicated that most of the poles had been lying in a horizontal position with their long axis parallel to the sides of the mound. Only a few molds were found that suggested that some of the horizontal poles were placed so that they were lying at right angles to the side of the mound. In some instances we were able to trace particular lengths of molds for as much as four meters. The molds indicated that the poles were originally placed in the fill of the second mound construction phase and that they lay over and inside a ridge of sand that was 53 cm in height. The sand ridge was traced for approximately six meters along the western side of the mound. It turned a corner and ran for about six meters more along the southern side of the mound. It ended at a point where the eroding flood waters of the Etowah River and the initial excavations of Warren Moorehead had destroyed the greater portion of the basal section of the southern half of the mound. Numerous rocks lay over and around the sand ridge.

The complete assemblage of features, pole molds, sand ridge, and rocks were interpreted as a phase in the construction of the mound. The sand ridge served to define the basal area that was to be covered by the addition of a new layer or mantle to the mound. Clay was piled inside of the sand ridge and up the sides of the slope of the previous mantle, a technique that allowed the builders to maintain control over the thickness of the mantle. The molds of the timbers or poles were the remains of the palisade that had encircled the base of the earlier mound mantle. The palisade poles were pulled up, and as the new mantle was added, they were incorporated into it, apparently in an attempt to inhibit erosion and to stabilize the addition. Although in all respects the Mound C situation replicates that described by Sears for the Wilbanks mound, I am unable to interpret the Mound C features as those of an earth lodge or any other structure other than that of the mantle addition.

I feel that the third reason to question the interpretations of earth lodges in the Southeast is derived from an examination of the climate of the area. It appears almost certain that the amount of rainfall in the Southeast is too great to have permitted the use of earth-covered roofs on prehistoric buildings. The mean annual precipitation rate for Bibb County, Georgia, the location of the Macon Plateau site, is between 117 and 122 cm, of which very little, if any, falls as snow. The mean annual precipitation rate of Cherokee County, Georgia, the location of the Wilbanks site, is 135 to 137 cm. Again, little of this moisture falls as snow. Similar, if not slightly higher, precipitation rates pertain in the Norris Basin of Tennessee and in the Appalachian Summit area of North Carolina. Curiously, those areas of the Southeast where earth lodges have supposedly occurred prehistorically are the very areas in the eastern United States with the highest annual precipitation rates. Further, little of this precipitation occurs as snow, a form that would allow for relatively slow runoff or little surface penetration. We can contrast this climatic situation with that in the Upper Missouri Basin of North Dakota, where earth lodges are known to have been built in the nineteenth century. At Linton, in the central area of North Dakota, the mean annual precipitation rate is slightly less than 38 cm. Of this amount approximately 28 cm falls during the warm season. Thus the northern Plains earth lodges were characteristic of an area where the precipitation was only one-third to one-quarter of the amount found in the Southeast.

My point here is a simple one. It does not appear reasonable to postulate prehistoric buildings with earth- or sod-covered roofs in areas where there are large amounts of rainfall. Such structures would simply not be tenable because, given the nature of aboriginal construction techniques, any earth-covered roof would promptly dissolve and pour onto the floor during the first heavy rain.

An additional problem exists in that on steeply sloping roofs, roofs that would shed rainwater rapidly, an earth covering would have an irrepressible tendency to slide down the roof and off the eaves onto the ground unless a special method was developed to hold the covering in place. In this regard it can be noted that the drawings and plans for the Hidatsa earth lodges provided by Gilbert Wilson indicate that the slope angle of the roof of these structures was 20 to 25 degrees from the horizontal, while the sloping walls were slightly more than 50 degrees from the horizontal (Wilson 1934). It should also be pointed out that the preferred material for covering the Hidatsa earth lodge was sod (Wilson 1934:366). The roots of the dominant grasses of the northern Plains areas— for example, little bluestem (*Andropogan scoparius*) and buffalo grass (*Buchloe dactyloides*)—formed a tough, almost

impenetrable, mass that made the use of cut blocks of sod in construction feasible. Sod, in the sense that it occurred on the Plains, has never been available in the forest-covered southeastern region.

Although the precipitation rate on the Plains was low enough to make a roof with a relatively slight slope angle practicable and thus capable of employing a sod covering, the southeastern region had a precipitation rate as much as three to five times higher. The slope angle of the roof would have to have been much greater than that characteristic of Plains earth lodges. It was absolutely necessary that rainwater be made to flow rapidly down and off the roof. The slower the rate of flow, the more likely it would be that the rainwater would seep through any but the most impervious of roof coverings. It should thus come as no surprise that the few ethnohistorical references to aboriginal roofs in the Southeast characterize them as steep and high. Garcilaso de la Vega tells us that the roof of the temple in Talomeco "was very lofty and drafty, for since the Indians had not discovered tile, they found it necessary to raise their roofs a great deal in order to keep the houses from leaking. The roof of the temple revealed that it was constructed of reeds and very thin canes split in half" (Vega 1951:315). In reference to a different structure in the same town, Ranjel notes that "the *caney*, or house of the chief, was very large, high and broad" (Ranjel 1922:101). Unfortunately, Ranjel is not at all clear as to whether he is referring to the roof of the house in his use of the adjective "high" or to the location of the house upon a mound. There are several frequently reproduced late seventeenth-century drawings of aboriginal temples and houses located in the lower Mississippi valley. More important, the artists actually saw the buildings that they drew. The Acolapissa temple, drawn by De Batz, has a domed roof that is very steep, while the house of the chief, by the same artist, has a slope angle on its roof that is approximately 55 degrees from the horizontal (Swanton 1946: plate 62). The roof of the Natchez temple shown in the illustration of the mortuary ritual of the Tattooed-Serpent has the same slope angle (Swanton 1946: plate 63). Given the amount of rainfall characteristic of the southeastern region, we must conclude that in order to function effectively, the aboriginal roofs had to have been made of impermeable materials or alternatively they had to be very steep. In either case an earth or clay roof was not a plausible solution.

To summarize my argument against the interpretation of certain archaeological features as earth lodges, I will restate the three reasons that I believe call into question interpretations of aboriginal southeastern constructions as earth lodges. It must be borne in mind that I define the term "earth lodge," in conformity with almost 100 years of American ethnographic usage, as an earth- or sod-covered building. I do not include earth-embanked structures within this definition. First, those buildings presumed to be earth lodges appear as a rare architectural form in the Southeast. Second, there are reasonable and probable alternative interpretations, other than the earth lodge interpretation, for those archaeological features identified as earth lodges. Third and finally, climate, particularly the precipitation rate, in the Southeast appears to preclude the use of earth-covered roofs as a viable construction technique. I should add, in closing, that I do not deny the possibility of earth lodges in the Southeast. I do think, however, that we must be very cautious in developing interpretations that conclude the existence of such structures.

CHAPTER ELEVEN

Human Skeletal Remains from Ocmulgee National Monument

Mary Lucas Powell

ARCHAEOLOGICAL INVESTIGATIONS at Macon Plateau were sponsored from 1933 through 1939 by the Smithsonian Institution, the Civil Works Administration, the Society for Georgia Archaeology, and the Macon Chamber of Commerce (Fairbanks 1956a). Initial excavations under the direction of Arthur R. Kelly at the remnant portion of Mound C, known as the Funeral Mound, uncovered 150 burials in two different locations representing the major prehistoric and historic aboriginal occupations at the site. Field observations on these burials were entered into notebooks, with rough sketches drawn underneath the text. For some burials, more detailed sketches were prepared and photographs taken, but no standardized burial forms were employed for the recording of data. The human skeletal remains were initially curated at Ocmulgee National Monument, along with the other archaeological materials from that site, but in 1964 they were transferred to the National Museum of Natural History (NMNH), Smithsonian Institution. The bioarchaeological analysis of these remains was conducted by the author during her residence at the Smithsonian as a Postdoctoral Fellow in 1985–86.

The extreme acidity of the soil was sufficient even to alter the surface of stone artifacts, and as a result, bone preservation was generally very poor. Numerous burial entries bear the notation, "bones reinterred," because they were considered useless for scientific analysis. Ninety-four burials from Mound C and vicinity are listed in the field records, but the NMNH collections presently include only 46 individuals from 31 specific burials. An additional 23 skeletal individuals from the Mound C vicinity lack documented provenience with specific burials. Several of the unprovenienced isolated skulls most probably represent specimens loaned by Kelly for examination by a local physician named Dr. Childs. Persistent attempts to match these lots with descriptions of burials from which bone had apparently been collected, but is now absent, did not yield satisfactory results.

In the present analysis, a systematic inventory of the skeletal material associated with each accession number in the NMNH series preceded the collection of data on age, sex, and pathology on standardized forms. Demographic assessments were attempted for each individual, based upon criteria outlined in Bass (1979), Ubelaker (1978), Krogman (1973), and Lovejoy et al. (1985). Skeletal pathology was identified by macroscopic evidence and diagnosed with reference to Ortner and Putschar (1981) and Steinbock (1976). These observations represent the first systematic bioarchaeological analysis of the burials from this major Early Mississippian site.

Biological and mortuary data for the burials from Mound C and the adjacent village area are summarized in Table 11.1. Table 11.2 summarizes the human skeletal remains from these locales currently curated at NMNH. The mortuary data are drawn from Table 4 in Fairbanks's 1956 monograph. For some burials, the age and sex estimates in Tables 11.1 and 11.2 do not match the original estimates published by Fairbanks. These discrepancies reflect the problems noted above in the curation of the skeletal materials. For those burials for which no skeletal material is now available, the original field or lab estimates of age and sex are indicated.

Burials from Mound C, Submound, and Mound Construction Stages

Seven construction stages rose above the submound level containing the most elaborate burials, which featured

Table 11.1. Burials from Mound C and the Village Area: Mortuary Data

Burial No.	Age	Sex	Burial Type	Body Form	No. of Individuals	Pit No.	Level	Orientation of Head	Associated Artifacts
1	(A)		P	F	S			H	E	1 red glass bead
2	6–7		P	F	S			H	SE	blue glass trade beads, conch shell cores, sherds
3	30–40	F	P	F	S			H	N	
4	1–2		P	F	S			H	N	white glass bead, conch shell cores
5	40–50	M	P	F	S			H	W	iron knife, red oxide
6	2–3		P		S	58		H		glass beads, olivella shell bead
7	(A)				S					
8	(A)		P	E	S				W	
9	(C)		P	F	S				E	
10	(A)		P	E	S	12			S	
11	(C)		P	E	S	10			N	
12A	A	M	S	B	M	4	IV		
12B	A	F	P		M	4	IV		
13			S	B	M	8			
14	17–19	F	P	E	S	7			S	400 olivella shell beads, 46 tubular conch shell beads, 2 discs, 1 vessel
15			S	B		22	V		
16	12–14		P	E	S				SE	
17	5–6		P	E	S				NE	
18	30–40		S	B		18				skull only in pit
19				B		23	V		
20			P	E	M	19	III		W	with Burial 21
21			S	B	M	19	III			with Burial 20
22			S	B		20	IV		
23			S	B					
24A	A	M	P	E	M	29	V		W	
24B	A	F	S	B	M	29	V		
24C	A		S	B	M	29	V		
25	A		P	E	S	16	III		E	
26	40–50	M	P	E	S	17			
27	40–50	M	P	E	S	3	GpII		S	fragments of wood
28			P	E	S	30			
29			S	B		41	IV		
30	35–45	M	P	E	S		H		E	projectile point at left femur
31	(A)		P	E	S		OS		SW	
32	20–30					39	–V		
33	35–45		P	E	S		H		W	projectile point fragments adjacent to body
34			P	E	S		OS		SW	
35	(A)		P	E	S	31	V		SW	
36			P	E	S	33	OS		
37						28	IV		
38	(A)		P	E		69	IV		SW	conch shell, stone muller
39	A		P	E			OS		NW	
40				C		27	III			mussel shell in pit, small pot in center of calcined bones, ash
41	30–40		P	E	S		OS		W	
42			P	E		42	–V		W	
43			P	E		35	II		SW	
44A	A	M				44	–V		
44B	A	M				44	–V		
45			S	B		50	–V		

continued

Table 11.1. *Continued*

Burial No.	Age	Sex	Burial Type	Body Form	No. of Individuals	Pit No.	Level	Orientation of Head	Associated Artifacts
46				C		2	NS		bark cover, Bibb Plain bottle and jar, 18 disc shell beads, 2 shell spoons
47	(A)		P	E	S	52	NS		
48A	20–30	M	P	E	M	53	SM	W	log tomb, 387 barrel-shaped shell beads, 17,582 disc shell beads
48B	20–30	F	S	B	M	53	SM	W	
49A	20–30	M	P	E	M	56	SM	E	log tomb
49B	12–14		P	E	M	56	SM	E	
49C	3–4		S	B	M	56	SM		
49D	40–50	M	S	B	M	56	SM		
50A	(A)		P	E	M	55	SM	W	log tomb
50B	(A)		P	E	M	55	SM	W	
51						62	−V		
52			S	B		49	II	S	
53			P	E	S	43	OS	E	flat disc shell beads
54			S	B		76	NS		skull only in pit
55			S	B		65	−V		
56			S	B		67	OS		
57			S	B		66	V		copper-covered puma jaws, copper plates
58	20–30		P	E	S	71	VII	W	
59			P	E	S	63	II	E	Halstead Plain bottle at pelvis
60A	A	M	S	B	M	68	VI		
60B	A	F	S	B	M	68	VI		
60C	A	F	S	B	M	68	VI		
61			S	B			OS		4 Bibb Plain sherds
62	(J)		P	E		75	IV	SW	2 oval stone mullers, 4 pebbles
63			P	F	S	48	−V	N	
64	(C)		S	B		70	III		
65			P	E	S	51	II	S	
66			P	E	S	85	IV	NW	
67	+50	F	P	E	S	80	II	W	olivella shell beads around legs
68	A		S	E	S		SM		log tomb, 14 disc shell beads at right side
69A	A	M	P	E	M	54	SM		log tomb, shell gorget, 2 discoidals
69B	A		S	B	M	54	SM		26,000 olivella shell beads, 3 bone pins, 1 conch shell dipper
69C	A		S	B	M	54	SM		
69D	A		S	B	M	54	SM		
69E	A		S	B	M	54	SM		
69F	A	F	P	E	M	54	SM		
69G	10–12		S	B	M	54	SM		
69H	10–12		S	B	M	54	SM		
69I	5–6		S	B	M	54	SM		
70						37	IV		
71	40–50	M	P	E	S	86	SM	W	
72			P	E	S	77	NS	W	celt at head
73			S	B					
74	(A)		P	F	S	90		E	
75	(A)		P	E	S	92	II	W	
76						93			Halstead Plain effigy bottle
77						91			beads, shell near bones, also decayed wood (?)

Table 11.1. *Continued*

Burial No.	Age	Sex	Burial Type	Body Form	No. of Individuals	Pit No.	Level	Orientation of Head	Associated Artifacts
78									
79									
80	20–30		P	E	S	106	GpI	SE	
81			S	B					Conch shell core bead near head
82			S	B					possible cremation
83			P	E	S			B	
84			P	E	S			SW	
85									1 shell bead
86A	(A)		P	E	M	96	GpII	W	
86B	(A)		P	E	M	96	II	E	
87			P	E	S	101	GpII	E	
88	20–30	M	P	E	S	103	GpII	NE	
89	20–30		P	E	S				celt, projectile point
38-1	(A)		P	E	S	38-1	Vi	E	
38-2	(A)		P	E	S	38-2	Vi	SW	
38-3	(A)		P	E	S	38-3	Vi	W	Bibb Plain pot, shell gorget, adz, clay pipe, 5 mussel shell items, 1 oval shell gorget, 2 pieces cut shell
41-1	(A)		P	F	S	41-1	Vi		
41-2			S	B		41-2	Vi		

KEY

Burial No.: field number.

Age: in years or A, adult; C, child; J, juvenile. Parentheses ()
  indicate field estimate, no bones now present.

Sex: F female, M male.

Burial Type: P primary, S secondary, C cremation.

Body Form: E extended, F flexed, B bundle.

No. of Individuals: S single, M multiple.

Level: SM Submound, II–VII Mound levels, OS Old Sod layer,
  NS New Sod layer, GpI Group I, GpII Group II, H Historic,
  Vi Village Area.

multiple primary and secondary interments. Of the six large burial pits, two contained log tombs and three others bore traces of wooden or bark covers. Burial 68 (Figure 11.1), the central tomb of the submound group, included the bones of an adult laid out in an extended position but abnormally compacted, as if the flesh had decomposed within the body's wrappings before burial. Seven shell disc beads lay near the right side. The field-notes indicate that the bones were stained, as if painted with red oxide. Unfortunately, no skeletal material in the collection is associated with this burial number, except for a few fragments excavated from beneath the log tomb.

Burial 49, the other log tomb, contained the extended skeleton of an articulated, young adult male, and the disarticulated remains of a young adolescent and a young child, along with very fragmentary parts from another adult. No grave goods were noted.

Burial 48 (Figure 11.2) contained two adults, male and female, one partially disarticulated and the other arranged as a compact bundle, surrounded by hundreds of shell beads. The legs of the more complete individual were disarticulated from the pelvis, with the femur heads displaced upward at the level of the lumbar vertebrae.

In the photographs, the bones appear to be in excellent condition, and it is unfortunate that only approximately half of the remains are now represented in the collection.

Burial 69 was by far the most complex interment in the submound level (Figure 11.3), containing the incomplete, disarticulated bones of six adults, two adolescents, and a child. Among the adults, three females and three males are represented. The bones of the subadults had been placed in bundles over the legs of the more complete adults. A huge quantity of olivella shell beads, calculated at more than 26,000, had apparently been sewn to the fabric or other material that covered the bones.

Of the four remaining burials from the submound level, Burial 71, an older adult male, is represented by long bone shaft fragments. Burial 32, a young adult, is represented only by an incomplete set of hollow tooth crowns. Burial 50 contained the extended skeletons of two adults, and tiny bone fragments in Pit 9 suggested the extremely decayed remains of an additional burial.

The burials placed in the seven mound construction stages are much simpler in form than are the submound interments. The portion of stage I that was excavated yielded no burials. Stage II included eight burials, of

Table 11.2. Burials from Mound C and the Village Area: Skeletal Remains at the National Museum of Natural History

Burial No.	Age	Sex	Remains Present					
			Skull	Teeth	Spine	Pelvis	Long Bones	Hands/Feet
1	(A)							
2	6–7		P	8	P	P	P	
3	30–40	F	P	15	C	P	C	P
4	1–2		P	12		C	P	
5	40–50	M	C		C	P	C	P
6	2–3		F	10				
7	(A)		C	30				
8	(A)							
9	(C)							
10	(A)							
11	(C)							
12A	A	M	P	11		F	P	
12B	A	F	P	10				
13						P	P	
14	17–19	F	P	2				
15								
16	12–14		F	9		F	P	F
17	5–6		F		P	P	P	
18	30–40		F	1				
19								
20								
21								
22								
23								
24A	A	M	F			P	P	F
24B	A	F	F				P	
24C	A		F				P	
25	A							
26	40–50	M	P				F	
27	40–50	M	P		F		P	
28								
29								
30	35–45	M	P	2	P			
31	(A)							
32	20–30			13				
33	35–45		P	1	F			
34								
35	(A)							
36								
37								
38	(A)							
39	A		P	4	F			
40								
41	30–40		P	4	F			
42								
43								
44A	A	M	P	2			P	
44B	A	M	F				F	
45								
46								
47	(A)							
48A	20–30	M	P	9	P	P	C	C
48B	20–30	F					P	
49A	20–30	M	P		F	P	C	P
49B	12–14		C		P		P	
49C	3–4		F			P	P	

Burial No.	Age	Sex	Remains Present					
			Skull	Teeth	Spine	Pelvis	Long Bones	Hands/Feet
49D	40–50	M				C		
50A	(A)							
50B	(A)							
51								
52								
53								
54								
55								
56								
57								
58	20–30			24				
59								
60A	A	M					P	
60B	A	F					P	
60C	A	F					P	
61								
62	(J)							
63								
64	(C)							
65								
66								
67	+50	F	P				P	
68								
69A	A	M	F				P	F
69B	A						F	
69C	A						F	
69D	A						F	
69E	A						F	
69F	A	F	P		F	F	F	F
69G	10–12		F		P	C	P	P
69H	10–12				P		P	P
69I	5–6		F		F	P	P	F
70								
71	40–50	M	P					
72								
73								
74	(A)							
75	(A)							
76								
77								
78								
79								
80	20–30			6			F	
81								
82								
83								
84								
85								
86A	(A)							
86B	(A)							
87								
88	20–30	M			F	P	P	P
89	20–30			19				
38-1	(A)							
38-2	(A)							
38-3	(A)							
41-1	(A)							
41-2								

KEY
Burial No.: field number.
Age: in years or A, adult; C, child; J, juvenile. Parentheses () indicate field estimate, no bones now present.
Sex: F female, M male.
Remains Present:
Teeth = number present;
Other categories =
C complete (>90 percent),
P partial (25–90 percent),
F fragmentary
(<25 percent).

11.1. Burial 68, Mound C,
Macon Plateau site.
(Smithsonian Institution
photo no. 85-6989.)

11.2. Burial 48, Mound C,
Macon Plateau site.
(Smithsonian Institution
photo no. 85-6991.)

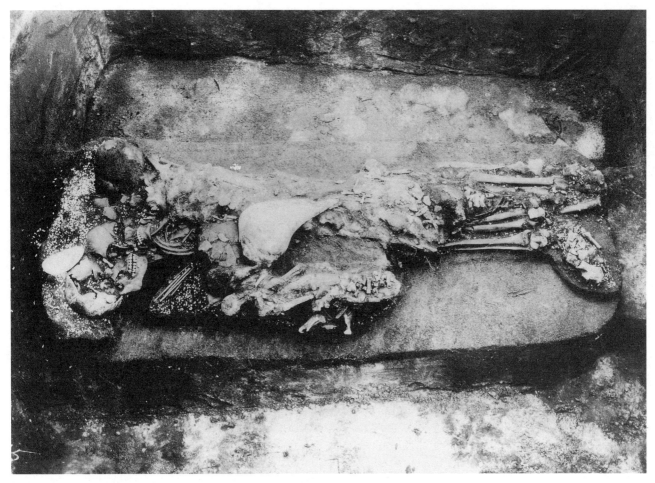

11.3. Burial 69, Mound C, Macon Plateau site. (Smithsonian Institution photo no. 85-6990.)

which one (Burial 65) was a log tomb. Only one of these burials (Burial 67) is represented in the Smithsonian collection, by the incomplete skeleton of an elderly female interred with leg ornaments of olivella shells. Stage III contained six burials, none of which now have associated bone. Of the seven burials placed in mound stage IV, skeletal material is present only from Burial 12, which contained the bundled, commingled skeletons of two young adults.

Mound stage V included the most burials reported for any construction level, 14 interments containing a minimum of 17 individuals. Only Burials 24 and 44— one triple and one double interment of adults—are represented by skeletal material in the collection. The only burial listed for stage VI is Burial 60—the bundled, incomplete remains of three adults, one male and two females. Burial 58 from mound stage VII yielded only a set of teeth representing a young adult.

Eleven burials were identified archaeologically as inclusive within the mound but were not clearly associated with a particular level of construction. Of these, eight (Burials 14, 16, 17, 18, 26, 27, 88, and 89) are represented

by skeletal material in the collection. An additional six burials (Burials 36, 39, 41, 53, 56, and an unnumbered burial) were intrusive to the lower layer of humus that conformed with the original contours of the mound, and probably represent the same population as the inclusive burials. Four other burials (Burials 46, 47, 54, and 72) had been placed through the more recently formed layer of humus, and thus may postdate the earlier mound-building occupation to some extent.

Of the 34 skeletal individuals from identified prehistoric burials, the majority consisted of fragmentary crania and/or long bone shafts with badly eroded cortex. Eight subadults were present in the sample: two children aged 2 to 6 years (Burials 17 and 49C); one juvenile aged 5 to 10 years (Burial 69I); and five adolescents aged 10 to 19 years (Burials 14, 16, 49B, 69G, and 69H). Skeletal representation was adequate only for estimation of age simply as "adult" for 14 of the 26 skeletally mature individuals— four males, three females, and seven of indeterminate sex. Three males and one unsexed adult were aged 20 to 30 years; one male and three unsexed adults were aged 30 to 40 years; three males were aged 40 to 50 years; and one female aged +50 years at death. Sex estimates were not attempted for the subadults but were possible for four female and ten male adults.

This age profile does not match demographic curves calculated from complete population samples (Ubelaker 1974). Infants and young children are disproportionately scarce, and subadult mortality peaks in early adolescence rather than during the weaning years—a complete reversal of "normal" mortality profiles (Weiss 1973). Young adults are somewhat underrepresented, but the peak in adult mortality during the fourth decade of life is a familiar pattern in prehistoric aboriginal agricultural populations in the Southeast (Powell 1983, 1988, 1989, 1990; Milner 1982).

Analysis of skeletal and dental pathology was hampered by fragmentation, cortical erosion, and the adherence of dirt to bone surfaces. No evidence of nutritional deficiencies was observed. Four individuals displayed evidence of healed fractures—three adult males and a young adolescent. Five adults display lesions on tibia and fibula shafts indicative of inflammatory response, in all cases well healed before the time of death. None of the eight subadults exhibited pathological lesions. No skeletal lesions diagnostic of specific infectious diseases were observed, although inflammation of lower leg bones is a characteristic symptom of endemic nonveneral treponematosis identified in contemporary populations elsewhere in the Southeast (Powell 1988, 1989, 1990). The only dental pathology observed was occlusal caries in several adult molars. Occlusal wear was moderately light, indicative of a diet relatively free of grit and rough-textured foods.

Historic Burials from the Vicinity of Mound C

Nine burials (Burials 1, 2, 3, 4, 5, 6, 30, 33, and 39) from the area to the south of the Mound C remnant and one burial from the extreme western edge of the mound (Burial 36) are attributed to the historic aboriginal occupation at Macon Plateau. All are single primary interments. Skeletal material is present from eight of these burials (Table 11.1).

Three subadults appear in the sample: Burial 2, a child aged 6 to 7 years; Burial 4, an infant; and Burial 6, another child aged 2 to 3 years. Five adult burials are also represented, including one female, two males, and two adults of indeterminate sex—all aged 30 to 50 years at death. Thus the very young subadult and older adult segments of the demographic profile are represented, but young adults and adolescents are lacking. Burial 3 is clearly represented in the fieldnotes, photos, and drawings as the interment of one adult, identified as female by the associated skeletal material. The left leg and foot of an adult male bearing the same catalog number, however, also appears in the same box. Such confusion of remains is unfortunately typical of the collection.

No skeletal pathology was observed in the subadults. Three of the adults displayed initial stages of osteophytosis and minor evidence of inflammation of lower leg bone shafts, well healed at death. The remaining two adults were too fragmentary for observation. No dental pathology was noted.

All of the historic burials included items of personal adornment or utilitarian function. Three subadults were buried with glass trade beads, two also had conch shell cores, and one had olivella shell beads. A single red glass bead was recovered from Burial 1. The adult male in Burial 5 was interred with an iron knife, and some of his bones bore traces of red oxide pigment. Projectile points were associated with the adult Burials 30 and 33.

Burials from the Trading Post

During excavations in the portion of the site to the east of Mound C, known as the Middle Plateau, 67 burials were uncovered in the vicinity of a stockaded structure (Mason 1963a). This structure was subsequently identified as a trading post founded by Carolina traders around 1690 to serve the community of Lower Creeks at Ocmulgee Town (Mason 1963a; Chapter 17, this volume). The demographic and mortuary patterns in this area differ markedly from those observed at Mound C (Table 11.3), but the degree of bone preservation was unfortunately equally poor. At the present time, only 26 of the burials are securely associated by skeletal material in the NMNH collection (Table 11.4). An additional 12 lots of skeletal material, representing a minimum of 14 individuals, are associated with this portion of the site, though not with specific burials. Their catalog numbers do not fall within the range of numbers assigned to identified burials, and no information on their provenience was located in the available field and laboratory records. Attempts were unsuccessful to identify them with particular burials for which skeletal material was originally noted as present, but is now lacking.

The Trading Post burials were documented during excavation by fieldnotes entered in a notebook labeled "Burial Book, Middle Plateau" and in many cases also by photographs and additional sketches. No standardized burial recovery forms were utilized. In the records available to the authors, only 61 burials (not the 67 mentioned by Mason) were described. A typical notebook entry, dated "12-19-35," reads "Single Burial 7 in Burial Pit 7. Earth work survey west of Middle Plateau in a 2½ foot cut north of north face profile of control trench 3. This burial was found 31 inches below surface, 5 inches in red sandy loam, in east edge of north and south stockade fill.

Table 11.3. Burials from the Trading Post, Middle Plateau: Mortuary Data

Burial No.	Age	Sex	Burial Type	Body Form	No. of Individuals	Associated Artifacts
1A	A	F	P		M	glass beads
1B			P		M	beads, axe, sword, 6 bullets, 4 gunflints, 2 flint chips, knife, 2 pieces of glass, 1 scabbard fragment
1C	3–4		P		M	5 bullets
2					S	6 lead balls, sherds, gunflints
3	(A)				M	glass beads, musket ball, conch shell core
4					S	glass beads, shell beads, molded bullet
5			P	F	S	glass beads, stone knife
6	30–40	F	P	F	S	glass beads
7	35–45	M	P	F	S	1 gunflint, glass beads, plate glass, 2 scrapers, nail
8	A	M	P	E	S	sherds, "fishtail" projectile point
9	6–8				S	
10	A	M?	P	F	S	15 bells, 11 lead bullets, 100 glass beads, copper fragment sherds
11	A	F	P	E	S	sherds, quartz points, glass bead
12	2–4		P	E	S	sherds, quartz knife
13				B	S	lead ball, sherds, charred corncobs
14					S	
15	A		P	E	S	
16	A		P	F	S	glass bead, green glass fragment
17	A		P		S	flint knife
18	(I)		C		S	gorget, conch shell, gun breach and barrel, brass bell, iron coil bracelet, iron bottle fragment, string of shell beads around neck, hundreds of glass seed beads
19	(C)		P		M	3 conch shell core beads, glass beads, iron knife blade
20	A		P		M	iron axe, rivet and fragments, 3 gunflints, lead bullet, coiled tin wire
21			C		S	
22			P	E	S	
23	A	F	P	F	S	
24	1–2			F	S	4 conch shell cores, 2 brass buttons, glass seed beads, mussel shells
25	3–5		P	E	S	
26			C			
27			P		S	
28			P	F	S	
29	A	(M)	P	F	S	2 metal wire arm bands, glass beads of 4 colors, glass scraper, iron belt buckle, 4 gunflints
30	10–12				S	
31	C				S	bone awl
32	4–6		P	F	S	4 small glass beads, 41 large glass beads, 4 small metal bells
33	A		P	E	S	
34	A		P	F	S	historic sherds
35	A	F	P	E	S	
36			P	F	S	historic sherds
37	A		P	E	S	
38	7–8		P	F	S	18 shell core beads, 4 coils of brass wire, glass beads, 2 small buttons, 1 brass bell
39	4–5		P	F	S	8 large glass beads, small glass beads, 11 conch shell beads, mussel shells
40	C		P	F	S	
41	A			F	S	glass beads, 2 brass arm bands

continued

Table 11.3. *Continued*

Burial No.	Age	Sex	Burial Type	Body Form	No. of Individuals	Associated Artifacts
42	(A)				S	3 brass bells, 2 brass buttons, 4 lead bullets, glass beads
43	A		P	F	S	large glass beads, small piece of rusty iron, flint knife, scrap of copper
44			S	F	S	Notes indicate possible prehistoric origin: head oriented south instead of east or west, no grave goods.
45	A	(F)	P	F	S	beads around neck and waist, lead balls near waist
46	25–35	F	P	F	S	kaolin trade pipe, large knife, gunflints, gun parts, brass object, glass beads
47	A		F	F	S	several glass beads
48			P	E	S	
49			S	B	S	
50			P	E	S	
51	A		P		S	pistol, 4 large brass buttons, 2 brass buckles, 2 small brass buttons, small cloth and metal fragments, glass seed beads
52	A		P	F	S	
53			P	F	S	
54						
55						
56						
57						
58			P	F	S	
59	A				S	
60			P	F	S	
61	(A)		P	F	S	glass beads of assorted sizes
62	(A)		P	E	S	mussel shell spoon, iron wire bracelet, glass beads, 4 small wire coils
64						

KEY

Burial No.: field number.

Age: in years or A, adult; C, child; I, infant. Parentheses () indicate field estimate, no bones now present.

Sex: F female, M male.

Burial Type: P primary, S secondary, C cremation.

Body Form: E extended, F flexed, B bundle.

No. of Individuals: S single, M multiple.

Burial furniture consist[s] of snub nose quartz scraper #1498, another snub nose scraper #1499, smoothing stone #1500, three pieces of glass #1501 a, b, c, small piece of old rusty nail #1502. Between these stations [2-69R17 and 2-71R17]." At the bottom of the page appear two sketches, one showing a plan view of the flexed skeleton with grid coordinates and distances from the north face profile and the other showing a profile of the adjacent section of trench 2, with the distinction between the dark stockade fill and the lighter sandy loam clearly marked. No estimation of age or sex of the individual was noted, nor which bones were present.

Of the 26 skeletal individuals from identified burials, more than half consisted only of fragmentary long bone shafts with badly eroded cortex. Seven subadults were present in the sample: one infant (Burial 24); three children aged 2 to 5 years (Burials 1, individual C; 25;

and 39); two juveniles aged 5 to 10 years (Burials 9 and 32); and one young adolescent aged about 13 years (Burial 30). Skeletal representation was not adequate for more specific estimation of age than simply "adult" for 14 of the 19 adults. Of the remaining five adults, two females were aged 20 to 30 years, and two males and one female were aged 30 to 40 years at death. Sex estimates were not attempted for the subadults, and were possible for only 9 of the adults, seven females and two males.

The 12 lots of skeletal material unassigned to specific burials included the remains of six subadults: an infant (38-10897); two young children aged 2 to 5 years (38-10916 and 38-10529); two juveniles (38-5634 and 38-3835/43); and an older adolescent (38-5634). Two adults could be placed in 10-year age categories—a female (38-10896) who died during her fourth decade and a male (39-12992) aged more than 45 years at death.

Table 11.4. Burials from the Trading Post, Middle Plateau: Skeletal Remains Present at the National Museum of Natural History

| Burial No. | Age | Sex | Remains Present | | | | | |
			Skull	Teeth	Spine	Pelvis	Long Bones	Hands/Feet
1A	A	F					P	
1B	A						F	
1C	3–4			21				
2								
3	(A)							
4								
5								
6	30–40	F				F	P	F
7	35–45	M	F	21	F	F	P	
8	A	M	F			F	P	
9	6–8		P	24				
10	A	M?						
11	A	F				P	P	P
12	2–4			4			F	
13			F	15			F	
14							F	
15	A						F	
16	A						F	
17	A		F	3			F	F
18	(I)							
19	(I)							
20	A							
21								
22								
23	A	F				P	P	
24	1–2		F			P	P	
25	3–5						P	
26								
27								
28								
29	A	(M)						
30	10–12		F	4			F	
31	C							
32	4–6		F	12			F	
33	A							
34	A			2	F		F	
35	A	F	F			F	F	
36								
37	A						F	F
38	7–8							
39	4–5							
40	C							
41	A		F				F	
42	(A)							
43	A			4		F	F	
44								
45	A	(F)						
46	25–35	F	F	10	F	P	P	
47	A							
48								
49								

continued

Table 11.4. *Continued*

Burial No.	Age	Sex	Remains Present					
			Skull	Teeth	Spine	Pelvis	Long Bones	Hands/Feet
50								
51	A							
52	A							
53								
54								
55								
56								
57								
58								
59	A		F				P	
60								
61	(A)							
62	(A)							
64								

KEY
Burial No.: field number.
Age: in years or A, adult; I, infant.
Parentheses () indicate field estimate, no bones now present.
Sex: F female, M male.
Remains Present:
Teeth = number present;
Other categories =
C complete (>90 percent),
P partial (25–90 percent),
F fragmentary (<25 percent).

The remaining 6 individuals were classified simply as "adults." Two additional adults (Burials 10 and 51) were provisionally identified *in situ* as males on the basis of skeletal robusticity, but no bones are present for them in the series.

The total skeletal sample from the Trading Post region of the Middle Plateau thus comprises 40 skeletal individuals—13 subadults and 27 adults representing both sexes and all ages except neonates and very old adults. This pattern matches that of the historic burials recovered near Mound C, but is more demographically complete. Despite the obvious problems of uncertain provenience and poor preservation, the demographic profile assumes a roughly "normal" curve: proportionately higher subadult mortality (5 out of 13 individuals) during the period of weaning (2 to 5 years), followed by a decline during the juvenile, adolescent, and early adult years and a second peak during the fourth decade. This curve parallels those calculated for mature and late Mississippian populations in Alabama (Powell 1985) and coastal Georgia (Powell 1990) as well as modern nonindustrial agricultural populations (Weiss 1973).

Examination of bones and teeth for pathological conditions was greatly hampered by fragmentation, cortical erosion, and the adherence of dirt glued onto bone surfaces with chemical preservatives. No evidence of nutritional deficiencies was observed. Six adults display pathological lesions on tibia and fibula shafts suggestive of endemic treponematosis, all cases being well healed at the time of death. None of the 13 subadults exhibited pathological lesions.

Two adults were apparently the victims of gunshot wounds, but unfortunately neither are represented by skeletal material in the NMNH collection. The laboratory file card listing the bones and grave goods associated with Burial 10 indicates that one of the two hollow musket balls found was "shattered" in the vertebral column. The fieldnotes for Burial 29 (identified as an adult) read: "A flattened lead bullet was troweled out in place inside the thoracic cavity resting against the right collar bone. It would have been an unusual coincidence if this bullet should have been accidentally included or should have fallen in place as a result of postmortem changes in posture." None of the other bullets or lead balls recovered from burial contexts are described as being "shattered" or "flattened," as would result from traumatic impact against bone.

Nineteen of the 26 individuals had been buried with various artifacts, predominantly items of personal adornment. Both the prevalence and types of artifacts in burials mirror the pattern for the historic burials recorded near Mound C. Glass trade beads appeared with all ages and both sexes. Usually only a few beads had been deposited. However, the adult male in Burial 10 had been interred with a cache of 100 glass beads, as well as 13 brass sheep bells, a bagful of lead bullets, a piece of copper, and several ceramic sherds. Metal weapons such as pistols, swords, axes, and muskets never appeared with subadults or adult females, but were restricted to adult males. The young children in Burials 24 and 32 possessed, respectively, 2 brass buttons and 4 brass bells, but all other items of this type were placed with adults, and possibly limited to males. No subadults possessed nails or musket balls, nor did adults identified as female. Of the adults, only one female possessed gunflints, but it seems likely that at least several of the unsexed adults with these items were males. Ceramic sherds appeared in the graves of all ages and both sexes, though whether as deliberate

Mary Lucas Powell

or accidental inclusions was not always clear from the fieldnotes. Marine shell core beads and fragments appeared only with children, and stone implements such as knives appeared only with adults. Other items recovered from burials in the vicinity of the Trading Post included charred corncobs (the adult in Burial 13), mussel shells (the children in Burials 24 and 39), pipes (the adult female in Burial 46), brass wire coils (Burial 38), and a bone awl (Burial 31).

Summary

The prehistoric and historic burials from Mound C and the Trading Post at Macon Plateau present clearly different patterns of demographic inclusion and formal mortuary attributes. The earlier sample is characterized in its earliest, submound, segment by a high proportion of multiple burials including individuals of all ages in various stages of mortuary curation and abundant artifacts, primarily shell items. The burials within mound stages are predominantly primary interments of adults, with very few associated grave goods. By contrast, the two series of historic burials from different locations at the site representing the historic occupation resemble each other very closely with respect to demographic and mortuary characteristics—all ages and both sexes more equitably represented, and less diversity in burial form and association of artifacts (see also Mason 1963a).

It is indeed disappointing that the osteological and paleopathological observations made on the human skeletal remains from Ocmulgee National Monument were able to provide only tantalizing glimpses of the lives of the aboriginal inhabitants. The acidity of the soil is the primary culprit, returning dust to dust with extreme efficiency. Human error further compounded Nature's destruction by separating portions of the remains from their archaeological provenience without preserving the keys to their original identity.

Fortunately, however, recent advances in analytical technology make possible the extraction of certain important types of biological information from fragmentary specimens of human bone. For example, quantitative studies of levels of trace elements and radioactive carbon isotope ratios in the bones of the prehistoric and historic builders of Macon Plateau would contribute significantly to our understanding of the scope and composition of their dietary regimens. Although such studies necessitate destruction of the samples, they represent a valid scientific use of these specimens, and should be undertaken at some future time. Interpretation of the results within appropriate demographic and mortuary contexts may reveal patterns of intrasite dietary differentiation that parallel or crosscut key biological and social dimensions. Such analyses can enlarge our understanding of the biological implications of membership in these two communities, representing the emergent and terminal Mississippian lifeways at Macon Plateau.

Acknowledgments

The research reported here was generously supported by a Smithsonian Institution Postdoctoral Fellowship at the National Museum of Natural History. I would like to thank Dr. Bruce D. Smith for bringing this hitherto neglected skeletal collection to my attention, and for his unstinting advice and encouragement toward completion of the project. Dr. Donald J. Ortner, my Fellowship advisor, and the late Dr. Larry Angel provided valuable technical expertise in the identification and sorting of the commingled and fragmentary skeletal remains, and I am grateful for their kind assistance.

CHAPTER TWELVE

The Origins of the Macon Plateau Site

Mark Williams

THE MACON PLATEAU site is one of the largest, most beautiful, and least understood of all the Mississippian mound centers in the United States. The major feature of the site is Mound A, a 15-m-high truncated pyramid. There is also a reconstructed circular earth lodge—an artifact of incredible interest and beauty. Additionally, there are seven other mounds of varying degrees of preservation scattered over an area greater than 93 ha (230 acres). Finally, there are two separate ditch or moat features within this area that partially surround some of the mounds.

These mounds were built during the Macon Plateau period, probably sometime between A.D. 950 and 1100. The prevailing belief among archaeologists for many years has been that this huge site was settled by people who migrated into central Georgia from outside the area. This belief has been seriously questioned by Bruce Smith (1984). My remarks here are primarily designed to address his concerns.

The stated goals of Smith's paper are to outline the historical development of "the concept of an original 'Mississippian' heartland," and "the hypothesized radiation through migration of the Mississippian cultural tradition" (Smith 1984:13). He effectively shows that there remains much difficulty in defining a Mississippian heartland and concludes that the Creek migration legends have created much confusion in the study of the origins and development of Mississippian. Smith is correct, I believe, in rejecting "the site unit intrusion as a primary general mechanism of Mississippian expansion" (1984:30).

Smith correctly recognizes that the excavations at Macon in the 1930s were critical to the crystallization of the general theory of Mississippian expansion via migration. In rejecting this general theory, however, he strongly questions the theory of migration for the founding of the Macon Plateau site itself. He concludes, "I am not convinced that Macon Plateau should be viewed confidently as a colony of outside invaders arriving from an undetermined starting point, rather than as a result of a local developmental sequence which reflects the acceptance of outside ideas" (1984:27).

Smith's rejection of migration as a valid general explanation for the growth of Mississippian societies in the Southeast leads him to predict what the result of future research into Macon Plateau's origins would be. First, he predicts that "when a fine grained regional chronological sequence is established for the Georgia Piedmont, a clear, if perhaps short, local developmental sequence leading up to Macon Plateau-like material assemblages will be identified" (Smith 1984:27).

Second, he predicts that "early Mississippian assemblages similar to that described for Macon Plateau and on the same time level, will be found to occur over a fairly large area of the Southeast Piedmont" (Smith 1984:27). He reminds us that most of the river floodplains in the southern Piedmont, and the archaeological sites on them, have been buried under thick blankets of silt deposited during 150 years of poor soil management, and he implies that the data on the origins of Macon Plateau may lie buried there.

Origins of the Migration Theory

No one was much concerned with the origins of the people who settled the Macon Plateau site before A. R. Kelly first came to the site in December 1933, as part of a major federal Depression-relief archaeology program. He led huge excavation crews and was able to publish his first summary of the work by March 1935 in *Scientific American*

(Kelly 1935b). In a series of three articles he showed his awareness of a possible connection between the Creek migration myths and the development of Mississippian in general, but was noncommittal about the origins of the Macon Plateau site itself.

One year later, in March 1936, James B. Griffin visited the site for the first time (personal communication). He had recently finished the analysis of the ceramics from the Norris Basin in eastern Tennessee for William Webb (Webb 1938) and was very familiar with that material. When Griffin saw the Macon Plateau ceramics, he immediately noted a high degree of similarity between them and the Norris Basin material. Griffin related this information to Kelly. Kelly reportedly was not immediately impressed with this similarity, at least as far as any potential migration theory was concerned.

By the time of Kelly's 1938 summary report in *Bulletin 119* of the Bureau of American Ethnology, however, he was beginning to accept the possibility of migration. He says: "The Mississippi Basin has also been recognized as the focal point of departure of many trait complexes which found ultimate expression in the Georgia peripheral area" (Kelly 1938c:66). In other places in the same paper, he seems less convinced, however, and states that "whether or not the mound-building activities [at Macon] represent a natural cultural evolution as a continuous process or whether we have to do with an influx of new ideas coming from the Mississippi without marked cultural changes otherwise remains an unsolved problem" (1938c:62).

If Kelly for a time was less than convinced that the origins of the Macon Plateau site were to be found in a migration of peoples, his students and peers working at the site were not. Gordon Willey speaks of "intrusive Mississippian influences" into central Georgia in his 1939 paper on the Cowart's Landing site (Willey 1939). Charles Fairbanks's ideas about the Macon Plateau site were developed in concert with conversations with Griffin, Willey, and others during the late 1930s. He wrote his classic paper "Creek and Pre-Creek" in 1947, although it was not published until 1952 in the Cole Memorial volume (Griffin 1952b). In it, Fairbanks makes the most explicit declaration of the migratory origins of the Macon Plateau site to that point when he states: "I am assuming that there is little argument that Middle Mississippi came into central Georgia from the west as it certainly did not develop out of Swift Creek" (Fairbanks 1952b:293). He further adds that "the whole appearance of the period suggests that it is the remains of a migrant people just arrived in central Georgia" (1952b:294).

Fairbanks had great difficulty specifying the original location for the people he felt migrated to central Georgia, although he was somewhat persuaded by Griffin's argument for the upper eastern Tennessee area. In any event, he maintained this position in his dissertation on the

Funeral Mound (Fairbanks 1956a) and was perhaps the most instrumental archaeologist in defining the nonlocal origin hypothesis for Macon Plateau. Fairbanks stuck firmly to this belief to the end of his career, as shown by his introduction to the republication of the Funeral Mound report in 1980. Fairbanks was probably more familiar with the data from central Georgia than anyone else when these ideas were being formulated. Gordon Willey, who was also very familiar with the data from his 1936 to 1938 excavations there, also felt, in 1953, that the Macon Plateau site was a good case for Mississippian migration and used it as a key example in his influential work "A Pattern of Diffusion-Acculturation" (Willey 1953). Indeed, every archaeologist who has ever worked "hands-on" with the Macon data has come away with the strong impression that, ceramically at least, it owes nothing to the earlier cultures of central Georgia.

New Data

But impressions are not a particularly scientific way to resolve a problem of this sort. It seems to me, as Smith has suggested, that we need to examine the Macon Plateau site in its own regional and chronological context in order to make an objective assessment of its origins. Much new archaeological information has been gathered in Georgia during the past 30 years that bears directly on this issue. A review of that work with reference to the problem of Macon Plateau origins is in order here.

The only traits that are apt to be useful in this task are the ceramics. All other traits associated with Macon Plateau, such as mounds and rectangular houses, are pretty much universal to Mississippi period sites in the South. The key point to be elaborated on here is that, despite extensive new data, there are still no known antecedents in Georgia for the Macon Plateau ceramic series.

The nature of Macon Plateau ceramics must be briefly reviewed. As Fairbanks (1952b:292) says, "The dominant characteristic of Macon Plateau pottery is that it is drab." We are not hampered by small samples of this drab pottery, however, since well over a million sherds of it were recovered in the 1930s. There is neither paddle stamped nor incised nor punctated pottery in this vast collection except on a handful of Macon Thick sherds. Macon Thick itself is but a rare part of the overall assemblage (less than .1 percent). The bulk of the Macon Plateau pottery comes from domestic contexts and is not a specialized ware.

The vast majority of the pottery, over 98 percent, is plain (Williams and Henderson 1974). Most of this plain pottery is classified as Bibb Plain and is represented primarily by poorly made, small to medium size, restricted-rim jars with distinct shoulders and small loop handles. About 35 percent of this pottery is shell tempered. Bibb Plain also occurs in the form of gourd-shaped water bottles. It very rarely is covered with a thin red film. Another type of plain pottery is the better made, but much rarer, Halstead Plain, usually in the form of water bottles. This may occur as effigy vessels also.

The final plain type is McDougal Plain, a coarse shell-tempered ware universally in the form of thick, shallow, round platters, often called "salt pans." Since there are no known local salt springs, this functional classification may not apply at the Macon Plateau site. Fairbanks suggested that they might be food serving plates (Fairbanks 1956a: 43). A companion type, Hawkins Fabric Marked, also occurs only as shallow pans and is the only "decorated" type in the entire assemblage. The rims of all vessel forms are simple and unmodified by notches or folds.

Bibb Plain pottery is very typically fired to a light orange-red oxidized color. The thick McDougal and Hawkins types are typically fired to a darker shade of red. Macon Thick is also usually fired to a reddish color. This reddish color stands in sharp distinction to most Georgia Woodland ceramics, which are dark brown to black in color.

While individual sherds of each of the Macon Plateau types are often difficult to sort from one another, because of form, color, surface finish, and temper they make an unmistakable ceramic assemblage taken as a whole. The question then becomes this: what have we learned in the last 30 years about the distribution of this assemblage through space and time in central Georgia?

Distribution in Space

In the time of Fairbanks's work on Macon Plateau, there were only two sites known to contain the representative ceramic assemblage: the Macon Plateau site itself (9Bi1) and the Brown's Mount site (9Bi5) some 8 km to the southeast. In the 1960s Jack Walker, working with the WPA collections stored at Ocmulgee National Monument, as well as with data from his own surveys in the Macon area, recognized six additional sites (Figure 12.1) in the immediate vicinity of the Macon Plateau site that contained sherds of the Macon Plateau pottery assemblage (Walker 1971b). All these sites are within an 8-km stretch of the river and most are within 3 km of the Macon Plateau site itself.

The most extensive recent surveys in the central Georgia area have taken place in the Oconee Valley, primarily to the northeast of the Macon area (Figure 12.2). Seventy kilometers to the northeast, almost 2,500 archaeological sites were recorded by the University of Georgia between 1974 and 1979 in 7,300-ha Lake Oconee (Fish and Hally 1986). Not a single identifiable sherd recovered from these sites, particularly the Mississippi period Dyar site (9GE5) (Smith 1981), can be assigned to the Macon

Plateau assemblage. This is even more significant when it is realized that the University of Georgia reservoir mitigation project included an extensive program of deep testing in the actual floodplain area of the Oconee River (Fish and Gresham 1990). In addition, informal examination of the University of Georgia ceramic collections from the few sites found in Lake Sinclair before it was impounded in 1949 yielded no Macon Plateau pottery.

More recent excavations by the Lamar Institute and the University of Georgia at the other Mississippi period mound centers in the Oconee Valley have also failed to recover any Macon Plateau pottery. These include excavations at Scull Shoals (9Ge4), Shoulderbone (9Hk1), Shinholser (9Bl1), and Little River (9Mg46) (Williams 1984, 1988, 1990a, 1990b; Williams and Shapiro 1990a). In concert with Marvin Smith's work at the Dyar site (Smith 1981), these excavations have not only documented the nature of these mound centers, but have also greatly refined the Mississippian chronology of the Georgia Piedmont. Additionally, extensive surveys have been conducted on a number of upland tracts near the Oconee in the last ten years (Kowalewski and Hatch 1988). Totaling more than 8,500 acres, these surveys have found over 700 sites, but no Macon Plateau material.

Not much work has been conducted in the Flint River valley to the west to date, but this is changing. Older surveys by Frank Schnell in the Lake Blackshear basin and by Don Gordy in the Sprewell Bluff basin both failed to yield any Macon Plateau material (Schnell, personal communication). More recently, John Worth located 110 sites in a 30-mile stretch of the Flint River just below the Fall Line, but none of these yielded Macon Plateau pottery (Worth 1988) (Figure 12.2).

In the area south of Macon, the only person who has suggested that there might be a site which contained Macon Plateau pottery has been Frankie Snow, who believed that a single duck effigy rim sherd from Telfair County (9Tf49) might be related (Snow 1977). I believe that a better association for this meager evidence would be with the apparently later Rood phase material as defined for the lower Chattahoochee River (Schnell et al. 1981). As for the Rood phase ceramic material itself, despite some similarities in handle form and the high percentage of plain pottery, it is significantly different from the Macon Plateau material. Rood phase lacks the salt-pan forms entirely and has incised pottery in significant quantities. The relevant carbon dates place it a bit later than Macon Plateau anyway, probably after A.D. 1200 (Schnell et al. 1981:233).

Another new source of potential information about the distribution of Macon Plateau pottery is the ever-growing body of data derived from cultural resource management surveys in the central Georgia area. For this article, I have reviewed all 21 cultural resource management reports on

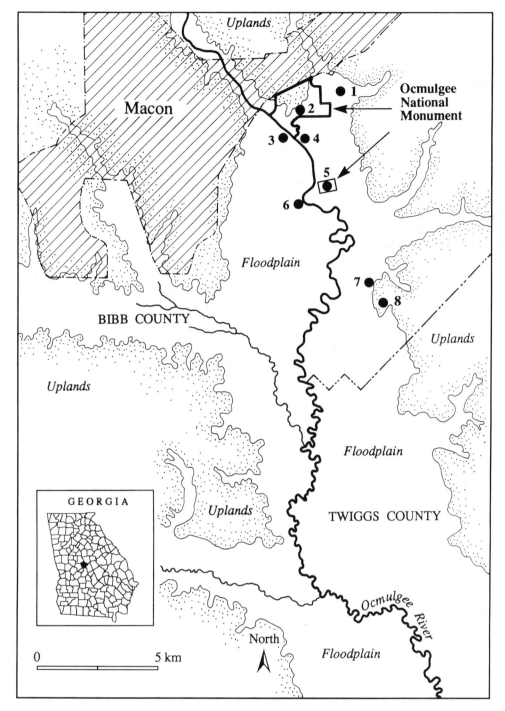

12.1. Location of known Macon Plateau phase sites.

1. Scott (9BI16)
2. Macon Plateau (9BI1)
3. Mile Track (9BI7)
4. New Pond (9BI32)
5. Lamar (9BI2)
6. Horseshoe Bend (9BI10)
7. Willis Farm (9BI49)
8. Brown's Mount (9BI5)

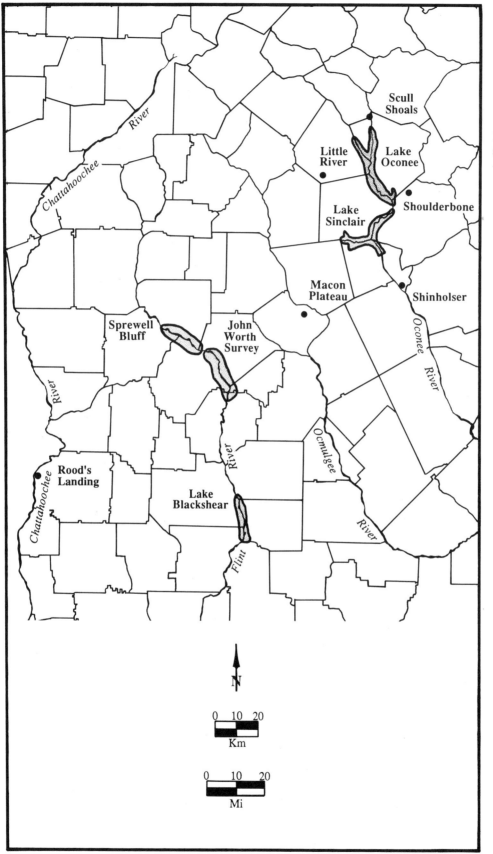

12.2. Location of sites and survey areas discussed in text.

file at the Georgia Archaeological Site Files in Athens that involved work in Bibb County and the six counties that border it (Figure 12.3). These include Monroe, Jones, Twiggs, Houston, Peach, and Crawford counties and, in concert with older site file information, account for more than 500 sites. In none of these reports or site data is there any indication of Macon Plateau components other than the ones already mentioned.

The result of this brief review is clear—there simply are no Macon Plateau sites outside the very small core area around the Macon Plateau site itself. Certainly we need more surveys in the Bibb County area, but the pattern is clear enough. I see no reason why the recent sediment deposits in the Ocmulgee River floodplain should have buried more Macon Plateau period sites than other Mississippi period sites. We can easily trace the distribution of Lamar period sites in the Ocmulgee and Oconee valleys, for example. It defies my usually vivid imagination to believe that a totally separate ceramic sequence could have been developed in a mere 6-km-diameter area of central Georgia and neither have affected nor been affected by a mainstream ceramic sequence that covered an area more than 250 km across.

M.P 950-1100

Distribution in Time

All researchers who have worked with both Macon Plateau ceramics and Central Georgia late Woodland ceramics know that they are completely different from one another. They differ in shape (the Macon Plateau vessels include rounded, in-curving rim jars with handles, gourd-shaped water bottles, and large open plates—the late Woodland vessels are simple straight or flaring-rim jars without handles); decoration (the Macon Plateau ceramics are predominately plain with some fabric marking—the late Woodland ceramics are simple stamped or complicated stamped); paste formula (Macon Plateau ceramics are shell and/or crushed dolomite tempered—the late Woodland ceramics are sand or grit tempered); and firing methods (the Macon Plateau ceramics are always reddish-orange in color—the late Woodland ceramics are black to brown in color). It defies logic that one could have evolved from the other, even assuming there is a gap of a couple of centuries in the known cultural sequence.

There is much disagreement about the latest date for late Swift Creek. Some researchers believe that Swift Creek, as we recognize it, probably ended not much later than A.D. 750 to 800. Some researchers believe it ended even before this date. Others suggest late Woodland ceramic assemblages for central Georgia include the Napier series and the Woodstock series. Teresa Rudolph suggests in a recent paper that late Swift Creek ends by A.D. 600 in the lower Piedmont, and Napier only lasts until A.D. 800 there (1986:46). The one sigma range

for her Napier carbon dates extends as late as A.D. 850–900, however (1986:19). She suggests that the A.D. 800–1000 period is likely filled in northwestern Georgia by the Woodstock series, but states that this series is rare in the lower Piedmont (1986:46–47). She does not suggest what ceramics were used in this area during this critical period, other than possibly simple stamped pottery (1986:37). Whatever the final dates for all these stamped designs eventually turn out to be in different places in Georgia, both Napier and Woodstock clearly followed in the broad tradition of late Swift Creek complicated stamped ceramics. Other than slight design differences, they are very similar to the Swift Creek forms and totally different from the Macon Plateau ceramic assemblage of interest here.

Further, they, like late Swift Creek ceramics before them, but unlike Macon Plateau ceramics, were present over large areas of Georgia (Wauchope 1966). Eventually Woodstock ceramics were supplanted by the very widespread Etowah ceramic series, which includes a wide variety of diamond-shaped complicated stamped designs and red filmed pottery (Hally and Rudolph 1986). Etowah ceramics, which may be contemporary with part of the Macon Plateau occupation (Williams and Henderson 1974:13), are distributed over all northern Georgia and adjacent Tennessee and well into the Georgia Coastal Plain.

Implicit in this discussion is the fact that complicated stamping as a ceramic decorative technique was an old and conservative tradition in Georgia that continued from the early Woodland period, through the Mississippi period, even to historic times. As Caldwell recognized, this sequence forms what, by any reasonable standards, must be called a ceramic tradition (Caldwell 1958).

The possible important role of simple stamped pottery in the late Woodland ceramic assemblage of central Georgia, particularly Mossy Oak Simple Stamped, must now be reconsidered. The work of Padgett (1973), Rudolph (1986), and recent work on the simple stamped Vining series of Putnam and Jones counties by Elliott and Wynn (1991) all show this idea to be worthy of further study. I have no problem including this decorative style, nor even the much misunderstood cord-marked pottery of the Georgia Coastal Plain, in a general scheme defining the central Georgia late Woodland pottery assemblage, although I think it a mistake to exclude completely complicated stamped pottery from the central Georgia late Woodland ceramic assemblage. All these types, however, can be found in some abundance over most of central Georgia in total contrast to the Macon Plateau assemblage.

Another indirect line of evidence relevant to the problem is the potential impact of the Macon Plateau ceramic series on later ceramics in the central Georgia

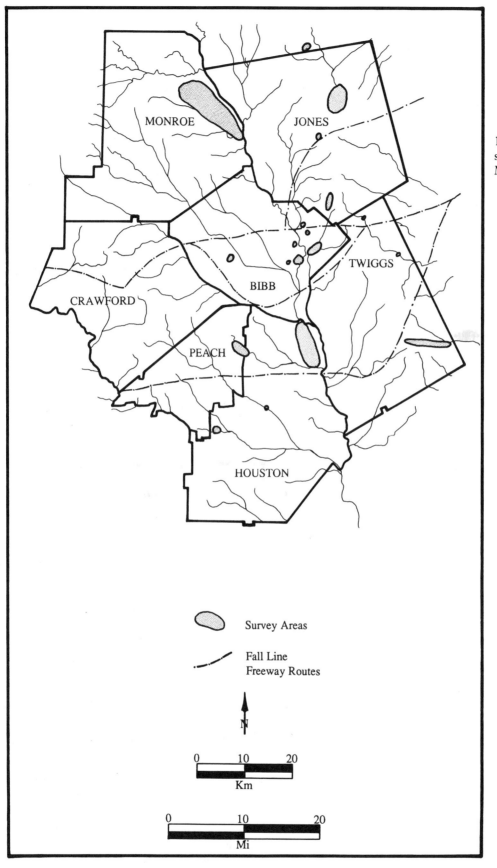

12.3. Location of recent survey areas in the Macon area.

MONROE

JONES

CRAWFORD

BIBB

TWIGGS

PEACH

HOUSTON

Survey Areas

Fall Line
Freeway Routes

N

0   10   20
Km

0   10   20
Mi

area. A number of later Mississippi period mound and village sites have been excavated in the Macon area. These include the Lamar site (9Bi2) (Smith 1973a), the Stubbs site (9Bi12) (Williams 1975), the Bullards site (9Tw1) (Williams et al. 1988), and the Cowart's Landing site (9Bi14) (Hamilton et al. 1975). There is almost no similarity between the ceramics at any of these sites and the Macon Plateau ceramic assemblage. On the other hand, the late Mississippian ceramics of the area show many similarities in vessel shape, decoration techniques, paste formula, and firing methods to those of the late Woodland discussed earlier. These facts thus support the hypothesis of limited to nonexistent historical connections between Macon Plateau ceramics and those of the rest of central Georgia.

On a different note, David Hally has pointed out to me that the Macon Plateau site is different from all the other Mississippian mound sites in Georgia in another interesting and potentially important aspect—it was never reoccupied after its abandonment about A.D. 1100. The majority of mound sites over the rest of Georgia date between A.D. 1250 and 1550. During this period it was the norm for individual sites to be abandoned occasionally, but most were later reoccupied. Often this abandonment and reoccupation of mound centers involved an explicit cycle (Williams and Shapiro 1990b). This pattern seems understandable in light of the accepted sacred nature of mounds and the traditions embodied (figuratively and literally) in them. In this light, the lack of reoccupation of the huge Macon Plateau site until late historic times is quite anomalous. Perhaps this place was not sacred to the later Mississippian people because its occupants had not been their ancestors.

Conclusions

From all this recent data the only reasonable conclusion for the present is that the Macon Plateau site was settled by people who were not natives of central Georgia and who, perhaps, came from northwestern Georgia or eastern Tennessee. I am not particularly worried by the nagging question of the location of the beginning of their migration, however. Unlike Smith and others, I do not consider it essential to answer this question before a reasonable example of prehistoric migration has been effectively demonstrated (Smith 1984:26).

I believe Smith was correct in his rejection of the notion that migration was a fundamental process in the development of Mississippian as we know it. I believe he is correct that there was never any heartland from which Mississippian people spread. I am confident that his description of the critical role the Creek migration legends played in the development of the early simplistic migration theories is accurate. I simply believe that the Macon Plateau site *is* an example of migration in the archaeological record.

What we have here is the Macon Plateau site twice misunderstood. It was first misunderstood in the 1940s to be a model for the growth of Mississippian society and, second, later misunderstood as not a true example of migration. Migration is a real process that must be integrated into models of Mississippian growth and decline. It is just as shortsighted for us to pretend that Mississippian people never moved about as it is for us to assume that all changes documented in the archaeological record result from migrations (Williams and Smith 1989). A balanced approach is essential.

In truth, however, the number of clear examples of migration based on archaeological data we will ever be able to show will continue to be vanishingly small, and thus the effort required to include these few examples into larger theories of culture change may exceed the need. One thing is certain, however. When that final grand unification theory on human cultural evolution is written, it must include migration as a process or it will be incomplete.

CHAPTER THIRTEEN

A Comparison of the Origins of Macon Plateau and Hiwassee Island Cultures

Gerald F. Schroedl

In 1934, A. R. Kelly began archaeological excavations at what was to become the Ocmulgee National Monument (Kelly 1938c). The same year in eastern Tennessee, the Norris Basin fieldwork was completed under the direction of William Webb (Webb 1938; Lewis and Kneberg 1941a). Two years later, Tom Lewis and Madeline Kneberg initiated fieldwork in the Chickamauga Basin of eastern Tennessee, where they conducted particularly extensive work at Hiwassee Island (Lewis and Kneberg 1941a, 1946). Charles Fairbanks (1946b, 1952b, 1956a) is well known for his contributions to the analysis, interpretation, and publication of the Ocmulgee data. Perhaps less well known is his association with the Chickamauga Basin excavations, where he supervised fieldwork at least at five sites, including the Hiwassee Island and Dallas sites (Boyd 1986). There is a clear historical connection between archaeological work in eastern Tennessee and the work done at Macon Plateau.

Archaeological problems in the two areas have also paralleled one another, and until recently their proposed solutions were reached in the same manner. The general problem was describing successive culture replacements using the archaeological record. Change was measured by comparing the occurrence or frequency of culture traits. Confining comparisons to formal similarity was clearly inadequate for this task, and so traits were identified with sociocultural categories as defined by contemporary ethnographers (see Lewis and Kneberg 1941a, 1941b, 1946). The formal similarities became the means for assessing historical and ethnic relationships. It was assumed that distinctive ethnic groups would possess an equally distinctive core of traits. In other words, mutually exclusive groups of traits were the archaeological equivalent of various culture entities, some of which could be linked with historically and ethnographically documented tribes. For their abundance, ubiquity, and distinctiveness, archaeologists concentrated on ceramic sherds to define the traits they needed to describe successive culture replacement.

This culture-historic methodology was used at Ocmulgee and in the eastern Tennessee region. Ocmulgee and eastern Tennessee are further related by the application of this methodology to solve a common specific problem, the origins of Mississippian cultures (Fairbanks 1952b, 1956a; Lewis and Kneberg 1946). Because of formal similarities between traits from Ocmulgee and eastern Tennessee, particularly in ceramic sherds, the archaeological record of eastern Tennessee became part of the solution to Mississippian origins at Ocmulgee (Fairbanks 1952b, 1956a). The reverse of this, so far as I can determine, was not proposed.

Virtually identical methods produced similar but not identical descriptions of Mississippian origins at Ocmulgee and in eastern Tennessee. Skepticism about the efficacy of these descriptions was first noted in eastern Tennessee in the 1960s (Salo 1969), and in the 1980s alternative descriptions of Mississippian origins have become well established (Schroedl et al. 1990). Ocmulgee archaeology has not followed a similar path. Archaeologists trying to understand Mississippian origins and the place of the Macon Plateau site in this development may want to consider the methodological approaches used to address these problems in eastern Tennessee. Regardless of methodological issues, these researchers will surely want to review their current interpretations because the hypothesized cultural connections between the early Mississippian Hiwassee Island and Macon

Plateau cultures are necessarily altered by the eastern Tennessee research.

Culture Replacements

Population migration and cultural replacement were used to account for the Macon Plateau culture at Ocmulgee and the Hiwassee Island culture in eastern Tennessee. Charles Fairbanks repeatedly offered this interpretation and defended it as recently as 1981 (Fairbanks 1981). Lewis and Kneberg (1941a, 1941b, 1946) provide virtually identical views for eastern Tennessee. The correlation of these interpretations with Swanton's (1932) model of the migration of Muskogean-speaking peoples in the Southeast is well documented by Bruce Smith (1984), and Kneberg (1952:194) provides an especially enthusiastic commitment to this view saying: "as seen from Tennessee, there is no question about Middle Mississippi peoples having migrated into this region. It is clear in many other places that this culture superseded earlier ones on the same sites. That the people who brought it were Muskogeans is scarcely debatable. Muskogean tradition contains detailed migration legends that fulfill some of the surmises of the southeastern archaeologists." Concerning Macon Plateau, Fairbanks (1946b, 1952b) and other researchers agreed with Kneberg.

Where had the Macon Plateau and Hiwassee Island cultures come from? Initially, Fairbanks was reluctant to name a place of origin, although he eventually agreed with eastern Tennessee researchers that the Mississippians had arrived via a southeasterly migration through west and middle Tennessee. In some instances, the migrating Mississippians seem to have been a coherent culture group that split apart and respectively traveled into eastern Tennessee and Georgia. In other cases, they were apparently chronologically and culturally slightly different and thus represent separate migrations following the same general route. (In this scenario, of course, it is easier to accommodate the differences in archaeological traits between Hiwassee Island and Macon Plateau cultures.) Wauchope (1966:17) suggested that people from eastern Tennessee migrated to the Macon Plateau. Mark Williams (Chapter 12, this volume) and James B. Griffin (personal communication, 1986) also favor migration from eastern Tennessee as a source of Macon Plateau culture. Diffusion from Hiwassee Island, however, has been regarded by other researchers as the source of Macon Plateau earth lodges and shell-tempered ceramics (Nelson, Prokopetz, and Swindell 1974:38).

In eastern Tennessee and central Georgia, according to these interpretations, early Mississippians encountered indigenous Woodland peoples, but their subsequent interactions with one another eventually produced dif- ferent results. In eastern Tennessee the late Woodland period Hamilton peoples either were conquered and killed, driven into peripheral river valleys, or assimilated into Hiwassee Island culture. Diagnostic ceramic traits of both cultures were found beneath the Mississippian platform mound at Hiwassee Island (Unit 37). This was telling evidence, according to Lewis and Kneberg (1946), for culture replacement. The identical interpretation is made for premound levels at Ocmulgee (see Fairbanks 1946b, 1952b). Here, the early Mississippian Macon Plateau groups established a large village, constructed large platform mounds, and, in distinct contrast to eastern Tennessee, produced an elaborate mortuary pattern. Remarkably, they failed to conquer, kill, drive-out, or assimilate their Woodland neighbors in whose midst they had established themselves. The evidence cited for this interpretation is the uninterrupted sequence of stamping on ceramics and the absence of comparably large and complex sites at an early date in the region. Shell tempering, plain ceramic surface treatments, loop handles, hooded and straight-neck bottles, and salt pan vessels found in the Macon Plateau did not become the ceramic tradition of the Georgia Piedmont as they did in eastern Tennessee. Ocmulgee, as a result, has become the virtual type site of the site-intrusive concept in American archaeology (Willey et al. 1956). Given a common approach to solving archaeological problems with comparable evidence, Hiwassee Island and numerous other early Mississippian sites also are site intrusions (see Krause 1985).

To explain subsequent changes in the archaeological record and to replace Hiwassee Island with Dallas culture in eastern Tennessee, a second migration of Muskogean people was called for (Kneberg 1952). By being Musko- gean, however, the numerous trait similarities between the two cultures were easily accommodated, and Lewis and Kneberg saw a fairly smooth transition from one culture to another (1946). Accounting for later Mississippian cultures in Georgia presented a serious interpretive dilemma. A second migration was called for, but no one produced a very clear description of how Mississippian culture was eventually established yet retained the in- digenous ceramic tradition (Fairbanks 1952b:295). Even Lewis and Kneberg offered their version of Mississippian development in Georgia (1946:98–99).

Alternatives to Replacement

An axiom of archaeological interpretation is that culture trait distributions and replacements interpreted in terms of population migration suffer as chronological and culture resolution are refined (Adams et al. 1978). Put simply, the accumulation of data leads to the demise of culture replacement interpretations because the changes in culture traits appear less abrupt and less dramatic. Because culture differences are less pronounced, researchers are more willing to entertain alternative interpretations that favor gradual adaptive changes to explain the archaeological record. They may, however, ignore culture change problems altogether in favor of synchronic pattern recognition problems such as settlement or mortuary pattern studies. Methods and techniques used to define and compare archaeological entities also may change and contribute to creating new perspectives.

In eastern Tennessee, the use of alternative research strategies and the accumulation of new data have produced a model of *in situ* Mississippian cultural development. The initial data that was difficult to accommodate with the culture replacement model were the ceramics excavated at the Martin Farm site on the lower Little Tennessee River in 1967 (Salo 1969; Schroedl et al. 1985). Limestone-tempered sherds and loop handles representing known Mississippian vessel forms were associated with similar shell-tempered vessels in a single closed context. Ceramic sherds having both shell and limestone temper also came from this context. The initial interpretation offered for these materials was referred to as Mississippianization (Faulkner 1975). This view, however, was perfectly acceptable within the more general model of culture replacement, because Martin Farm was considered a Woodland occupation in a peripheral river valley in the process of assimilating a Mississippian lifeway (Faulkner 1975). This is virtually identical to Kneberg's interpretation of similar ceramic collection from sites excavated in the main Tennessee River valley in the 1930s and 1940s that she called the Roane-Rhea complex (Kneberg 1961). Even so, the Martin Farm ceramics were new data; Woodland ceramics were not just found with Mississippian sherds, Mississippian attributes occurred on otherwise Woodland ceramics. This was novel enough that the label "emergent Mississippian" was applied to the Martin Farm materials.

The second source of new data was generated to solve a problem not initially considered relevant to Mississippian origins in eastern Tennessee. The problem was the chronology of late Woodland Hamilton burial mounds. Virtually all such sites had been excavated prior to the development of radiocarbon dating. Before the 1970s there was only one date on a Hamilton burial mound (Faulkner 1967); then in 1973 11 dates were run on three mounds at the McDonald site (Schroedl 1973). The dates suggested burial mound use preceding as well as contemporary with early Mississippian culture (Schroedl 1973, 1978a). No mortuary data were known for the Hiwassee Island culture until it was suggested that burial mounds had served both late Woodland and early Mississippian

cultures. This interpretation better served a model of *in situ* culture development than one of culture replacement.

Accompanying the growing radiocarbon chronology and the Martin Farm ceramic data was an important change in archaeological methodology. This was the attempt to define culture-historic entities as associated groups of contemporary constituent sherds or sherd assemblages rather than as occurrences of individual types or traits (Schroedl 1978b; Kimball 1980, 1985; Davis et al. 1982). Instead of identifying archaeological cultures by sorting the historic types according to their respective cultures, the materials from contexts with stratigraphic and cultural integrity were regarded as contemporary products of the same culture entity. An additional change in ceramic analysis was to use attribute clusters and not types to characterize assemblage composition. By taking this approach, the notion of cultural and natural mixing to account for ceramic type co-occurrence was largely replaced by a view of culture material variability that was a more sensitive measure of ceramic change over time. As analyses guided by this perspective were undertaken, it became clear that many culture diagnostic traits occurred among a variety of culture-historic entities. The assemblage profiles thus tended to produce a picture of long culture continuity rather than a series of culture replacements.

When the Martin Farm artifacts and materials from other sites were analyzed, assemblages transitional from Woodland to early Mississippian were identified at many sites (Kimball 1980; Schroedl et al. 1985). Among the sites where Martin Farm–like assemblages occurred was the level beneath the Hiwassee Island mound. The very context that Lewis and Kneberg had used to argue for site intrusion and culture replacement was now regarded as evidence for *in situ* culture development. In eastern Tennessee the migration model and the migration-assimilation or Mississippianization interpretation for Mississippian origins have not withstood alternative archaeological methods and the accumulation of data. Mississippian origins are now regarded largely as an *in situ* process with Martin Farm representing a culture-historic unit intermediate with late Woodland and early Mississippian, Hiwassee Island cultures. The elements of this process and their relationships, however, are far from fully understood.

Lessons for Macon Plateau

In eastern Tennessee, culture replacement first questioned in the late 1960s has found few defenders in the 1980s as *in situ* development has received greater support. Skepticism about culture replacement to explain Macon Plateau has been expressed (Nelson, Prokopetz, and

Swindell 1974:36; Stoutamire et al. 1983:19; Williams and Henderson 1974). Researchers examining ceramic type frequencies and contexts have raised the possibility of contemporary manufacture and use of ceramic types previously considered mutually exclusive culture occurrences. Late Woodland ceramic types (Swift Creek and others), for example, are now considered associated rather than mixed with Macon Plateau types in some contexts (for example, Williams and Henderson 1974: 43). As in eastern Tennessee, ceramic temper is also difficult to defend as a culture diagnostic attribute, since Bibb Plain, the predominant Macon Plateau ceramic type, is tempered with grit, shell, or mixed shell and grit, and sherds with each of these tempers are well represented in many contexts. These kinds of ceramic data and radiocarbon dates placing Macon Plateau culture circa A.D. 1000 (see Wilson 1964) have prompted the suggestion that Macon Plateau is emergent Mississippian in the same sense as Martin Farm (Steponaitis 1986). An interpretation that derives Macon Plateau culture from Hiwassee Island culture, furthermore, is difficult to pursue within the radiocarbon chronologies now available. Although comparative counts of vessels are unavailable, Mississippian straight-necked and hooded or effigy bottles and salt pans are poorly represented in the eastern Tennessee archaeological record by the time they are well established at Macon Plateau circa A.D. 900–1100. More difficult to account for is the elaborate mortuary patterning recorded at Macon Plateau, since comparable patterning is not found in eastern Tennessee until A.D. 1200 or later, even though richly endowed individual burials have been recorded for the Hamilton burial mound complex (for example, Burial 12 at the McDonald site [40RE7] [see Schroedl 1978b:105–8]). Overall, much of the culture complexity described for Macon Plateau appears to predate its occurrence in eastern Tennessee, and therefore it is difficult to see how Macon Plateau culture could have originated in eastern Tennessee.

Georgia archaeologists also have had to respond to the general assault on migration as an explanation of culture change (Adams et al. 1978) and the more specific questions about culture replacement as an explanation of Mississippian origins in the Southeast. Bruce Smith (1984) has clearly brought these arguments out in the open, and specific regional studies, such as those in eastern Tennessee, have contributed to the debate (see Smith 1990). So far, the response from Georgia researchers appears ambivalent, with some indicating doubt about culture replacement or showing greater inclination toward diffusion and Mississippianization models, but still not having an alternative for explaining Macon Plateau culture or Mississippian origins. Hally and Rudolph express this quite well saying: "we find ourselves, on the one hand

agreeing with the detractors of the site unit intrusion model that sufficient evidence supporting the model has not been presented. On the other hand, we disagree with the detractor's position that local development is the most suitable explanation" (1986:34). Resolution of these difficulties will surely improve with the acquisition of additional radiocarbon dates. Available dates help identify culture manifestations elsewhere in Georgia apparently contemporary with Macon Plateau (Hally and Rudolph 1986). However, comparative dating currently relies on just two dates for Macon Plateau culture (Wilson 1964). Recent assessments of ceramics from Ocmulgee suggest greater chronological variability than previously recognized, and alternative ceramic assemblage analyses may help resolve some of these issues. Considering the current data, however, it may be necessary to conduct new excavations at Ocmulgee or elsewhere (Smith 1973b).

No one has yet attempted to rescue Macon Plateau culture from the severe methodological criticisms that the culture migration, site-unit intrusion and trait diffusion, culture assimilation, and Mississippianization interpretations have received. Nor has consideration been given to the accumulation of data in eastern Tennessee and elsewhere that fail to support such interpretations. Simply repeating past interpretations of Macon Plateau culture using the same methods and archaeological assumptions can produce no solution to these problems.

Conclusions

Nearly 30 years ago Rouse (1958) outlined criteria for identifying site-unit intrusion. Bruce Smith repeated these for southeastern archaeologists in 1984, and Richard Krause has eloquently restated them in 1985, adding an additional perspective on trait-unit diffusion. Krause states:

Arguing the immigration view requires (1) identifying a parent population from which most, if not all, immigrant groups were derived, (2) adducing reasons for reasonably large-scale migrations, (3) demonstrating that most, if not all, Southeastern Mississippian communities were what Rouse called "site unit intrusions," and (4) showing that resident Woodland populations were expelled. Advancing the second position (that the Mississippian lifestyle constituted a diffusion-induced transformation) requires (1) identifying compatible Woodland predecessors, (2) demonstrating trajectories in Woodland manufacturing and economic practices which, under suitable conditions, could produce elements of succeeding lifestyles, and (3) isolating what Rouse called "trait unit intrusions," which could stimulate "Mississippianization." Defending the third position (limited immigration and immigrant-resident fusion) requires demonstrating that (1) suitable newcomers were in some portions of the Southeast and that (2) a fusion of Woodland resident with Mississippian migrant could explain those transformations in subsistence, settlement, and manufacturing practices which occurred throughout the Southeast. (1985:29)

Site-unit intrusion and trait-unit diffusion, furthermore, often are identified solely as differences in ceramic types and their frequencies. Such identifications should not be made without exercising great caution in assuming first that "pottery styles are inherently more important and more demanding of explanation" than are numerous less diagnostic traits, and second that "changes in pottery" or any other culture traits "are a priori evidence of ethnic change" (Adams et al. 1978:499, 501).

Avoiding these potential hazards requires distinguishing ceramic style or form from function or use in a traditional sense as well as in an evolutionary sense in which "style denotes those forms that do not have detectable selective values and [F]unction is manifest as those forms that directly effect the Darwinian fitness of the populations in which they occur" (Dunnell 1978:199). Furthermore, it is necessary to consider both social interaction and information exchange views of ceramic change and stability (Hill 1985; Wobst 1977). In the former, the degree of stylistic similarity or form is determined by the nature of interaction among artisans and is nonadaptive or nonfunctional "in the maintenance of societal interpersonal or intergroup relations, or anything else" (Hill 1985: 364). Just the opposite is suggested by the information exchange perspective that "views style as both functional and adaptive, especially in the sense of conveying information that helps foster group identity, integration, and boundary maintenance" (Hill 1985:366). The study of style differences resulting from social interaction rather than functional (that is, adaptive) changes resulting from information exchange have guided studies of Macon Plateau culture. Explaining the origins of this and other Mississippian cultures surely would benefit from the use of an explicitly evolutionary framework (Dunnell 1980, 1989).

This is not to say that interests in migration and diffusion are without merit. Comparatively new methods and techniques developed by sociologists, geographers, and economists over the past 30 years and recently discovered by anthropologists, for example, might prove an effective basis for a middle-range theory of archaeological diffusion and migration (Davis 1983; Duke et al. 1978). Regardless of how much these efforts might improve the understanding of the Ocmulgee and eastern Tennessee archaeological records, "Diffusion [and migration] are not *causes* [emphasis added] of the spread or adoption of cultural traits but only a way of referring to class[es] of processes that are engendered by a diverse range of cultural factors. . . . A statement that attributes culture

similarity to diffusion [or migration] 'is only a statement of results not a definition of process. It is descriptive, not explanatory' (Barnett 1953:10–11)" (Davis 1983:57).

There is no escaping the fundamental stylistic similarities, especially in the ceramics, between the Macon Plateau and Hiwassee Island cultures. These similarities are treated as cultural if not ethnic homologues in interpretations based on migration and diffusion. The *in situ* culture development model for eastern Tennessee considers such resemblances as regional analogs with no necessary ethnic or historical connections (Dunnell 1986). In this respect, Macon Plateau and Martin Farm exhibit analogous patterning, especially in ceramics. Both share contemporary use of late Woodland and early Mississippian types as well as the co-occurrence of Woodland attributes (grit or limestone tempering) on Mississippian vessel forms and handles (Fairbanks 1956a: appendix A). Woodland (limestone or grit) and Mississippian (shell) tempers are even found in the same sherds. Georgia researchers have considered the possibility of *in situ* development of Macon Plateau culture, although some wish to keep the interpretation of culture migration and others are undecided. As more radiocarbon dates become available and as the number of ceramic analyses increase and their sophistication improves, the model of *in situ* culture development surely will find greater acceptance just as has occurred in eastern Tennessee.

This, however, leaves unresolved an important issue relevant to the larger question of Mississippian origins in the Southeast: Why in eastern Tennessee was shell-tempered pottery adopted in favor of limestone-tempered pottery, while at Ocmulgee (and presumably elsewhere in central Georgia and adjacent areas) shell tempering (and perhaps other traits too) was tried briefly but rejected in favor of grit tempering, which persisted among the late prehistoric cultures of the region. Interpretations such as the one developed by Osborn (1988) that consider shell tempering as a techno-functional adaptation to the development of corn agriculture appear inadequate to the Georgia data. Corn agriculture and a fully Mississippian lifeway developed in central Georgia despite the absence of shell-tempered pottery. Whatever selective advantage shell tempering might have provided developing Mississippian cultures elsewhere in the Southeast, it was insufficient to supplant grit tempering in Macon Plateau culture and in the cultures that followed it. Here, selection may have been for social rather than techno-functional reasons.

Culture evolutionary models for Mississippian origins in the Southeast must eventually attempt to unify the diversity of regional data, including Macon Plateau, Martin Farm, and Hiwassee Island materials. Confidence in distinguishing archaeological analogs from homologues will surely measure the success of explaining Mississippian cultural evolution. What now seem distinct regional problems may once again prove useful to the solution of a common problem. Surely Charles Fairbanks, A. R. Kelly, Tom Lewis, and Madeline Kneberg would encourage our efforts.

Acknowledgments

I thank David Hally for inviting me to participate in the Macon Plateau Fiftieth Anniversary Conference and for his encouragement in preparing this chapter. Sibbald Smith and Sylvia Flowers graciously assisted me during a brief visit to Ocmulgee National Monument to examine the ceramic collections and records. I had stimulating discussions with Mark Williams about Macon Plateau and many other issues that I continue to thoroughly enjoy. C. Clifford Boyd, Jr., and Michael H. Logan provided critical review and comment on the chapter, which was of considerable help to me. I thank Mary Jane Hinton and Laurie Baradat for typing the manuscript.

CHAPTER FOURTEEN

An Overview of Lamar Culture

David J. Hally

WITH THE PASSAGE of time, the recognition and definition of Lamar culture has proven to be one of the most fruitful achievements of the federal relief archaeological program at Ocmulgee. Over the past 50 years, Lamar has been the subject of more research activity than any other archaeological culture in the region and has come to be one of the best understood. Furthermore, because of its temporal span and spatial distribution, sites with Lamar components have recently come to play a central role in the reconstruction of the routes of the De Soto and Luna expeditions and the Mississippian polities they encountered.

Lamar means different things to different people. It is frequently referred to in the literature as a phase, a culture, a period, a horizon, and a tradition; but it has also been termed an entity, a phenomenon, and even an explosion (Rudolph 1986). In this chapter, Lamar will be treated as a culture in the Willey and Phillips sense; that is, as a taxonomic unit encompassing a number of phases and "possessing traits sufficiently characteristic to distinguish it from all other units similarly conceived" (Willey and Phillips 1958:22, 47–48).

As a culture, Lamar incorporates over two dozen phases that span more than 400 years and an area covering most of Georgia and adjacent portions of Alabama, Florida, South Carolina, North Carolina, and Tennessee. The primary material diagnostic for the culture and its phases is pottery; specifically, a limited array of pottery types—Lamar Incised, Lamar Complicated Stamped, and Lamar Plain—and vessel forms—jars with outflaring, thickened rims and carinated bowls. A number of other material culture traits have geographical and temporal distributions that are to varying degrees coextensive with that of the Lamar ceramic complex. Nevertheless, it is clear that Lamar culture is a polythetic taxonomic unit (Clarke 1968), and that as such its distribution in space and time is arbitrary to some extent.

This chapter is intended as a review of the current state of knowledge concerning Lamar culture. It begins with a brief review of the history of Lamar research. This is followed by a review of various aspects of Lamar culture as they are presently known. In the final section, we will return to the question alluded to above, what is Lamar?

History of Lamar Research

Many characteristics of what we now recognize as Lamar culture were documented in the early decades of the twentieth century by Holmes (1903), Heye, Hodge, and Pepper (1918), and Claflin (1931). The first formal published definition of the culture, however, is provided by A. R. Kelly in his *Preliminary Report on Archeological Explorations at Macon, Georgia*, published in 1938. In this report, Kelly described the excavations that had recently been completed at the Lamar site (9BI2) by Ford and Willey and provided a succinct summary of what was then known about Lamar culture-history. According to Kelly:

1. Lamar was pre–De Soto.
2. The ceramic complex changed through time, with Lamar Incised increasing in frequency and the quality of execution of complicated stamping decreasing.
3. The culture was known from sites located throughout the state of Georgia.
4. Lamar originated from the hybridization of intrusive Mississippian cultural elements and indigenous Southeastern cultural elements. The former were carried into the region by tribes from the Lower Mississippi Valley that were ancestral to the historic Muskogean speaking people of the region.
5. Regional variants of Lamar culture, represented at sites such as Irene, Bull Creek, and Lamar, were the result of

differences in the way the intrusive and indigenous cultures fused together in each locale.

6. Finally, Lamar was ancestral to the historic Ocmulgee Fields culture represented at the Macon Trading Post.

Fieldwork conducted in 1938 by Jennings (1939) at Lamar and by Willey (1939) at Cowarts Landing demonstrated that Lamar culture was later than Swift Creek and Macon Plateau cultures. By 1939 fieldwork had been conducted at the type site on four separate occasions (Kelly 1938c; Jennings 1939; Fairbanks 1940b) and had yielded information on Lamar burial form, house form, and community plan. Unfortunately, little of this research has been published, and the site remains one of the most poorly known of the major Lamar sites in Georgia.

Archaeological survey and excavations by Caldwell (1950, 1957) and Fairbanks (1950) in Allatoona Reservoir and by Wauchope (1950, 1966) in various locations across the northern half of the state in the 1940s resulted in the development of a detailed Mississippi period cultural sequence for northwestern Georgia. Lamar culture was placed at the end of this sequence and was seen as the end result of an unbroken ceramic tradition extending back to Swift Creek culture (Fairbanks 1952b; Wauchope 1948).

The culture-historical significance of Lamar was considered in a number of papers published during the 1940s (Ford and Willey 1941; Griffin 1946) and 1950s (Caldwell 1952, 1958; Fairbanks 1952b, 1956a; Sears 1955, 1956). The distribution of Lamar culture was expanded to include most of Georgia and South Carolina and adjacent portions of Alabama, North Carolina, and Tennessee (Ford and Willey 1941; Fairbanks 1952b; Caldwell 1952). A number of local variants were recognized within this area, including those represented at Lamar, Etowah, Irene, Bull Creek, Neisler, Tugalo, Hollywood, and Nacoochee (Fairbanks 1952b). Lamar was still considered to represent a blend of an indigenous complicated stamped ceramic tradition and Mississippian culture intrusive from the west (Caldwell 1958), although Fairbanks (1952b) now identified the earliest arrival of these Muskogean speakers with Macon Plateau culture. There was less agreement on the chronological position of Lamar; Fairbanks (1952b) and Caldwell (1958) proposed that it covered the period A.D. 1350 to A.D. 1650, while Ford and Willey (1941) opted for a post–De Soto date. There was also disagreement on the ethnic identity of Lamar; Fairbanks (1952b) and Caldwell (1952) argued that Lamar pottery was manufactured by Muskogean, Cherokee, and Siouan speakers, while Sears (1955) argued that Lamar was synonymous with Cherokee. Finally, Ford and Willey suggested that Lamar and other late "Temple Mound II" cultures in the Southeast represented a pan-regional cultural decline that was triggered by European introduced disease.

Lamar culture has been the focus of a number of research projects during the past 15 years (Anderson and Schuldenrein 1985; Braley et al. 1986; DePratter and Judge 1986; Hally 1970, 1975, 1979, 1980; Knight 1980, 1985b; Shapiro 1983; M. Smith 1981; Williams 1983, 1984, 1988). This work has increased our understanding of the temporal and spatial variability in Lamar pottery and has greatly expanded the range of Lamar cultural characteristics for which we have some information.

The Lamar Pottery Complex

Two pottery types, Lamar Complicated Stamped and Lamar Incised, have probably received more attention in the archaeological literature than any other feature of Lamar culture. Kelly devoted almost his entire 1938 discussion of the Lamar site investigation to them, indicating the prominent role they played in the initial recognition of the culture. Jennings and Fairbanks (1939) published detailed type descriptions for them in 1939. In virtually all subsequent research focusing on Lamar, they have served as the defining criteria for the culture and its constituent phases.

Figure 14.1 depicts the approximate area within which these types are known to occur as numerically dominant decorated types. Lamar Complicated Stamped, with its distinctive thickened and pinched/punctated rim, appears in the archaeological record during the latter half of the fourteenth century. Lamar Incised does not appear for another 100 years, but with relatively few exceptions the two types co-occur throughout the area depicted in Figure 14.1 into the seventeenth century.

Plain-surfaced pottery is also common throughout the area depicted in Figure 14.1, and along with Lamar Complicated Stamped and Lamar Incised is one of the three basic types constituting the Lamar pottery complex. Irene Incised, Irene Filfot Stamped, Qualla Complicated Stamped, Altamaha Line Block, Irene Plain, and Qualla Plain are best viewed as regional and temporal variants of these types.

A number of other pottery types may be found in association with the three basic Lamar types, but their occurrence is usually restricted to brief periods of time or limited areas. These include: Dallas Plain, Dallas Incised, Dallas Filleted, Dallas Negative Painted (Lewis and Kneberg 1946; Hally 1979), McKee Island Cord Marked, Rudder Comb Incised (Heimlich 1952), Lamar Coarse Plain, salt pans (Hally 1979), Qualla Check Stamped (Egloff 1967), Kasihta Red Filmed (Jennings and Fairbanks 1940), Chattahoochee Roughened/Brushed, Walnut Roughened (Knight 1985b), Savannah Check Stamped (Pearson 1986), and McIntosh Incised (Larson 1955). In some phases, one or more of these types may predominate numerically—for example, Dallas Plain in Little Egypt

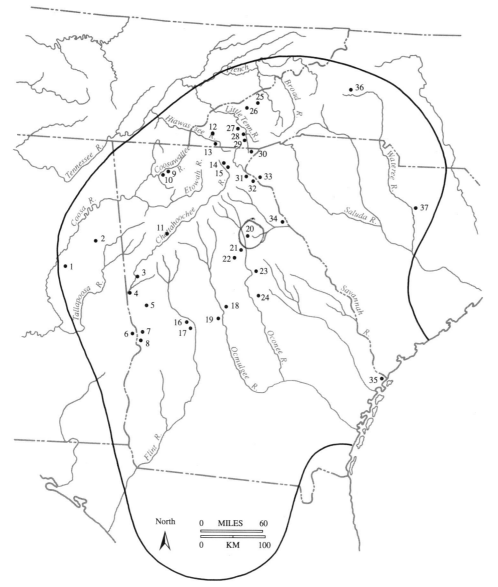

14.1. Distribution of Lamar pottery types and Lamar sites with platform mounds.

1. Hightower (1TA238)
2. Davis Farm (1CA196)
3. Park Mound (9TP41)
4. Avery (9TP64)
5. Winfree (9HS2)
6. Abercrombie (1RU61)
7. Cooper (9ME3)
8. Engineer's Landing (9CE5)
9. Little Egypt (9MU102)
10. Thompson (9GO4)
11. Vandiver (9DO1)
12. Peachtree (31CE1)
13. Spikebuck Town (31CY1)

14. Nacoochee (9WH3)
15. Eastwood (9WH2)
16. Neisler (9TR1)
17. Hartley-Posey (9TR12)
18. Lamar (9BI2)
19. Stubbs (9BI12)
20. Scull Shoals (9GE4)
21. Dyar (9GE5)
22. Little River (9MG46)
23. Shoulderbone (9HK1)
24. Shinholser (9BL1)
25. Nununyi (31SW3)
26. Kituhwa (31SW1)

27. Cowee (31MA5)
28. Nuquassee (31MA1)
29. Coweta Creek (31MA24)
30. Dillard (9RA3)
31. Estatoe (9ST3)
32. Tugalo (9ST1)
33. Chauga (38OC47)
34. Rembert (9EB1)
35. Irene (9CH1)
36. Berry (31BK22)
37. Mulberry (38KE12)

phase (Hally 1979) and Chattahoochee Roughened in Atasi and Tallapoosa phases (Knight 1985b).

Lamar Chronology

Although Caldwell (1957) found evidence in the Allatoona Reservoir to support Willey's stratigraphic findings at the Lamar site, no real progress was made in working out the internal chronology of Lamar until the 1970s. Today we can distinguish two to three sequential phases in most localities where Lamar occurs (Table 14.1), and we can anticipate further sequence refinements in the future. These phase distinctions are proving especially useful in ongoing investigations of the De Soto route (Hudson et al. 1984; Hudson, Smith, Hally, Polhemus, and DePratter 1985), culture change in the post–De Soto era (Smith 1987), and the spatial configuration and settlement composition of late Mississippian polities (Anderson 1986, 1987; Hally 1993, 1992; Hally et al. 1990; Smith and Kowalewski 1981; Williams and Shapiro 1986, 1987).

Phase distinctions are based on a number of chronologically sensitive ceramic features—including the presence/absence of Lamar Incised, changes in the motifs characteristic of Lamar Incised, stylistic changes in the way these motifs are portrayed, changes in the motifs characteristic of Lamar Complicated Stamped, and changes in the form of thickened jar rims. These changes have been documented in almost all areas where Lamar occurs (Anderson et al. 1986; DePratter and Judge 1986; Hally 1979; Hally and Rudolph 1986; Rudolph 1986; Smith 1981; Williams 1984). They occur in the same relative order and are roughly contemporaneous throughout the Lamar area.

Most Lamar ceramic features change slowly through time and in a nonsynchronous fashion. These changes can be best summarized by subsuming them within three largely arbitrary time periods: Early Lamar, A.D. 1350–1450; Middle Lamar, A.D. 1450–1550; and Late Lamar, A.D. 1550–1800 (Table 14.1). Early Lamar pottery is best known from the Rembert, Duvall, Little Egypt, and Irene phases. Lamar Incised is absent or very uncommon and is characterized by a limited number of simple designs executed in two or three broad lines. Complicated stamping is fairly well executed although motifs may be difficult to identify. Filfot cross, figure-9, and figure-8 are common motifs. Temper is fine and uniform in size. Jar rims are decorated with either large individually molded nodes or narrow thickened strips that are notched, punctated, or pinched.

Middle Lamar pottery is best known from the Barnett, Dyar, Tugalo, and Cowarts phases. Lamar Incised is common and characterized by a greater variety of more complex designs that are carried out with narrower lines and a greater number of lines. Temper particles are large

and often protrude through the vessel surface. Complicated stamping is generally poorly executed. Motifs are large, overstamped, and frequently lightly impressed. Jar rims are usually thickened by the addition of a strip or by folding. The width of the thickened rim is greater and modification is predominately pinching along the lower edge of the rim.

Late Lamar pottery is best known from the Bell, Ocmulgee Fields, Estatoe, and Atasi phases. Incising is present in most phases with lines continuing to decrease in width and increase in number. Incising disappears, however, in the Appalachian portion of North and South Carolina, Piedmont South Carolina, and northern Georgia. Complicated stamping continues in most phases, but is replaced by brushing in the Lower Chattahoochee, Coosa, and Tallapoosa drainages. Check stamping becomes common in the Appalachian portion of North and South Carolina and northern Georgia. Thickened jar rims continue to increase in width, and new forms— rolled, "L"-shaped, and filleted strip—appear in the Appalachian area (Hally 1986).

The chronology of the Lamar period is not well delineated in the Appalachian area of North Carolina and Tennessee and the Coastal Plain and coast of Georgia and South Carolina. The Qualla ceramic series, as defined by Egloff (1967) for the Appalachian area, almost certainly spans three to four centuries, although most of the pottery Egloff illustrates in his thesis dates to the Late Lamar period. Very little late prehistoric period research has been conducted in the Coastal Plain (Anderson et al. 1982; Ferguson 1975; Snow 1977), and in only one case has a ceramic complex been defined. In Georgia, Snow (1977, 1990) has defined a Middle Lamar Square Ground phase and has ceramic evidence for earlier and later Lamar occupations.

Unlike the Coastal Plain, the Georgia coast has received a considerable amount of attention from archaeologists since the 1930s. Archaeologists are in general agreement concerning the existence of an Irene phase and an Altamaha/San Marcos phase, the latter dating to the later part of the sixteenth century through the eighteenth century. The chronological position of Irene, however, is subject to considerable debate. One view (Crook 1986) holds that the phase dates after A.D. 1550; the other (DePratter 1979; Cook 1980; Pearson 1986) holds that Irene is entirely prehistoric and begins by approximately A.D. 1350.

Irene phase pottery from the type site manifests a number of typological similarities to Late Savannah (Hollywood, Town Creek, and Adamson phases) and Early Lamar (Rembert and McDowell phases) period ceramic complexes in northern Georgia. Assuming that there is no appreciable time difference in the appearance of these features in both areas, the Irene type site ceramic

Table 14.1. Lamar Phases

Time	Periods	Upper Apalachicola[1]	Lower Chattahoochee[2]	Lower Tallapoosa[2]	Upper Tallapoosa[2]	Middle Coosa[2]	Coosawatee[3]	Etowah[4]
A.D. 1800							Galt	Galt
			Lawson Field	Tallapoosa	Tallapoosa	Childersburg		
A.D. 1700	Late Lamar					Woods Island		
			Blackmon					
				Atasi	Atasi			
A.D. 1600		Leon-Jefferson	Abercrombie Bull Creek	Shine II	Avery	Kymulga	Barnett	Brewster
A.D. 1500	Middle Lamar							
		Yon					Little Egypt	Stamp Creek
A.D. 1400	Early Lamar							
A.D. 1300		Sneads						Wilbanks
	Savannah							
A.D. 1200			Rood					

1. Brose 1984;   2. Knight 1985b.   4. Caldwell 1957.   6. M. Smith 1981; Williams 1984.
   Scarry 1985.   3. Hally 1979.   5. Worth 1988.   7. Hally and Rudolph 1986.

complex has to date to the late fourteenth century (Early Lamar period). Recent work by Braley et al. (1986) and Cook (1980) has revealed the existence of pottery on the central Georgia coast that resembles Middle Lamar period pottery in northern Georgia. The absence of such pottery from the mouth of the Savannah River and adjacent portions of the coast suggests that the area was abandoned after approximately A.D. 1400 until well into the eighteenth century (Anderson et al. 1986; Hally et al. 1985).

One fortunate by-product of our increasing refinement of ceramic change is that we are now able to pin some absolute dates on the Lamar period. Mississippi period radiocarbon dates with good contextual associations from Georgia have been compiled in two recent reports (Hally and Rudolph 1986; Hally and Langford 1988). These strongly suggest that the Savannah period dates to the early fourteenth century and that Early Lamar phases date to the late fourteenth century. Radiocarbon dates as well as early Spanish artifacts (Smith 1976, 1987) place Barnett and other Middle Lamar phases in the sixteenth century. European artifact associations allow us to date the latest Lamar phases in the seventeenth and early eighteenth centuries (Caldwell 1955a, 1957; Huscher 1972; Knight 1985b; Mason 1963b; Smith and Williams 1983). According to this chronology, Lamar culture spans more than 400 years.

Where does the Lamar site fit in this chronological sequence? Willey's test excavations in the village zone yielded stratigraphic evidence for an increase in the frequency of Lamar Incised and a decrease in the quantity of Lamar Complicated Stamped through time (Kelly 1938c). Penman's (1973) reanalysis of the ceramic collections failed to provide any additional insight into the site's chronology. In a one-day study of the collections, working without provenience data, I found typological evidence for Early, Middle, and Late Lamar period components at the site. Interestingly, the Late Lamar ceramic features I saw suggest that site occupation may have continued into the late seventeenth century, in which case it would have been contemporaneous with the ceramically distinct Ocmulgee Fields occupation on the Macon Plateau (Chapter 16, this volume).

Lamar Origins

From the time that the term "Lamar" first appears in print (Kelly 1938c), archaeologists have speculated about the "hybrid" origin of the ceramic complex. The commonly expressed view (Fairbanks 1950, 1952b; Caldwell 1957; Ford and Willey 1941) is that Lamar Complicated Stamped was the end product of a lengthy complicated stamping tradition indigenous to the southern Piedmont and Appalachians; while Lamar Incised, surface burnishing, and the carinated bowl form were introduced from the west by immigrating Mississippian peoples. While there is a certain amount of truth to this view, the development of the ceramic complex as we know it today is much more complicated.

Stratigraphic work in the Allatoona Reservoir in the 1940s demonstrated that Savannah culture immediately preceded Lamar. There was disagreement, however, over

Middle Flint[5]	Middle Oconee[6]	Middle Ocmulgee[7]	Lower Ocmulgee[8]	Upper Savannah[9]	Middle Savannah[10]	Lower Savannah[10]	Wateree[11]	Appalachian Summit[12]	North Carolina Piedmont[13]
		Ocmulgee Fields		Estatoe				Qualla	
	Bell					Altamaha	Daniels		Burke
Lockett	Dyar	Cowarts	Square Ground	Tugalo			Mulberry	Qualla	
	Iron Horse								
Thorton	Duvall	Stubbs		Rembert	Rembert Hollywood	Irene	McDowell Town Creek		
	Scull Shoals							Pisgah	
						Savannah II	Adamson		
Bronson					Beaverdam		Belmont Neck		

8. Snow 1990.
9. Anderson et al. 1986.
10. Caldwell and McCann 1941.
11. DePratter and Judge 1986.
12. Diekens 1978.
13. Moore, personal communication.

whether Lamar Complicated Stamped developed out of Etowah Complicated Stamped (Wauchope 1948) or out of Savannah Complicated Stamped (Fairbanks 1950); the latter usually being seen as intrusive into northern Georgia from the south. Recent research (Rudolph and Hally 1985; Williams 1988) has documented that Savannah Complicated Stamped is well represented across northern Georgia and that it developed *in situ* out of Etowah Complicated Stamped. A number of Savannah period phases are now recognized (Table 14.1). Although regional differences exist—use of shell tempering in northwestern Georgia, occurrence of check stamping in northeastern Georgia—the ceramic complex is relatively uniform wherever it occurs.

Most of the Lamar ceramic complex develops out of Savannah. Complicated Stamped motifs characteristic of Savannah culture—concentric circles, filfot cross, figure-9, and figure-8—all persist into Early Lamar phases such as Rembert (Rudolph and Hally 1985) and Little Egypt (Hally 1979). Jar rim modifications in the form of cane punctations, punctated nodes, and plain and notched thickened rims occur in Savannah phases such as Beaverdam and Hollywood and clearly represent the developmental antecedents for the Lamar thickened jar rim. Carinated bowls with burnished upper walls and stamped lower walls have been recognized in at least one Savannah phase, Beaverdam (Rudolph and Hally 1985), and are almost certainly the antecedent of the standard Lamar Incised vessel form.

The one ceramic element that cannot be derived from the Savannah ceramic complex is Lamar Incised. Incising is either absent or very infrequent in Early Lamar. When it does appear around A.D. 1400, it is characterized by simple designs—horizontal lines interrupted by pendant loops and festoons—that are carried out in two or three broad lines below the rims of bowls. This form of decoration has its closest parallels in the type Point Washington Incised, which occurs in the lower Chattahoochee River Rood phase of A.D. 1000–1300 vintage (Schnell et al. 1981). Archaeologists generally consider Rood phase and Point Washington Incised to be Mississippian in affiliation. In this sense, Lamar Incised can be considered to be an introduced Mississippian type. In the context of what we now know about Mississippi period cultural development in the southern Piedmont, however, it is difficult to see the addition of Lamar Incised to the Lamar ceramic complex as representing any significant new Mississippian influence. Most markers of Mississippian culture—platform mounds, intensive maize agriculture, palisaded towns, wall-trench structures, even shell-tempered pottery—have been present in the area since at least Etowah times (A.D. 1200).

Regional Variation in the Lamar Pottery Complex

Regional variation in the Lamar ceramic complex has been recognized since 1939 when Jennings and Fairbanks (1939) defined the type Lamar Complicated Stamped. Today, we are able to distinguish as many as 12 contemporary regional variants or phases. Figures 14.2–4 show the distribution of Early, Middle, and Late Lamar phases.

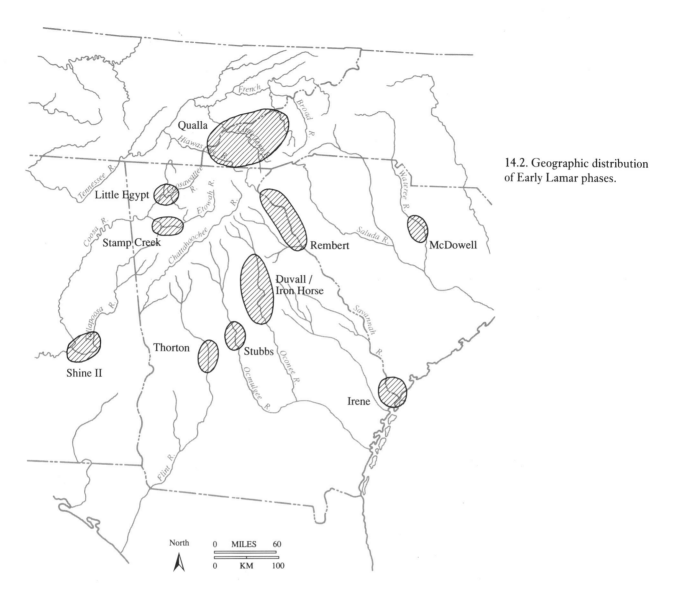

14.2. Geographic distribution of Early Lamar phases.

It is probable that additional phases will be distinguished as detailed ceramic analyses are performed on collections from the Chattahoochee, Coosa, and Tallapoosa river drainages in Georgia and Alabama and the Piedmont and Appalachian areas of western North and South Carolina.

Figures 14.2–4 show phases as being rather limited in geographical extent and separated from one another by fairly large "unoccupied areas." While I believe that this is a fairly accurate picture of the cultural landscape of the region during the Lamar period, there is little evidence to support it. With few exceptions (see "Lamar Settlement Pattern" section), phases are represented by only one or a few components, and the vast areas separating components of neighboring phases are virtually unknown archaeologically.

This situation has two important implications for our understanding of the nature of Lamar phases. First of all, it is not possible to determine whether the ceramic complexes characteristic of each phase are stylistically discrete or whether they represent essentially arbitrary divisions of a spatial stylistic continuum. Secondly, it is not possible to determine the geographical extent of individual phases. The spatial extent of phases depicted in Figures 14.2–4 is intended to reflect what I believe is the general manner in which Lamar period populations were distributed over the landscape: human settlement was concentrated in the valleys and adjacent uplands of the major rivers; the interfluvial uplands separating these rivers, while probably exploited for various resources, were sparsely inhabited. Recent work in the Oconee River drainage of central Georgia, however, demonstrates that small, permanent settlements were common in the interfluvial uplands in at least some regions and during some periods (Hatch 1987; Elliott 1984; Kowalewski and Hatch 1991).

Regional ceramic variability is best documented at

David J. Hally

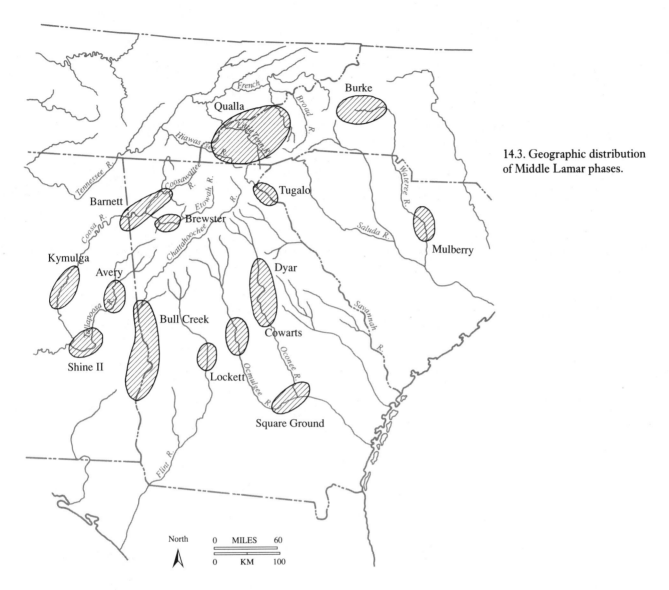

14.3. Geographic distribution of Middle Lamar phases.

North

0	MILES	60
0	KM	100

present for the Middle Lamar period. Table 14.2 lists the relative frequencies of pottery types for several of the better known Middle Lamar phases. Some of the more striking differences are the high frequency of complicated stamping in the Tugalo phase and its low frequency in Dyar and Barnett phases; the high frequency of Lamar Incised in Dyar and Cowarts phases and its low frequency in Bull Creek; and the high frequency of shell tempering in Barnett phase. Middle Lamar phases are also distinguishable by the designs portrayed on the type Lamar Incised. Figure 14.5 illustrates the most common designs in the Barnett, Tugalo, and Bull Creek phase ceramic complexes. The relative frequencies of 16 designs in five Middle Lamar phases is illustrated in Figure 14.6. Some of these designs are fairly evenly distributed among the different phases, but most are rare or absent in two or three phases. In each phase, there is one design that is exceedingly common.

Lamar Subsistence

Lamar subsistence can be outlined in general terms, but there is insufficient evidence to allow detailed reconstruction of specific subsistence systems. Botanical and faunal samples have been collected and analyzed at a number of sites in the Piedmont (Anderson and Schuldenrein 1985; Hally 1980, 1981; Knight 1985b; Manning 1982; J. L. Rudolph 1986; Rudolph and Hally 1985; Shapiro 1981, 1983; M. Smith 1981; M. Smith et al. 1981; M. Williams 1983) and on the Georgia coast (Braley et al. 1986; Cook 1978; Crook 1978; Pearson 1986).

Piedmont faunal samples typically include a number of terrestrial species: white-tailed deer, black bear, raccoon, opossum, rabbit, squirrel, box turtle, and turkey. White-tailed deer, box turtle, and aquatic turtle are the only species that occur with any frequency in most site samples, and of these, white-tailed deer is overwhelmingly

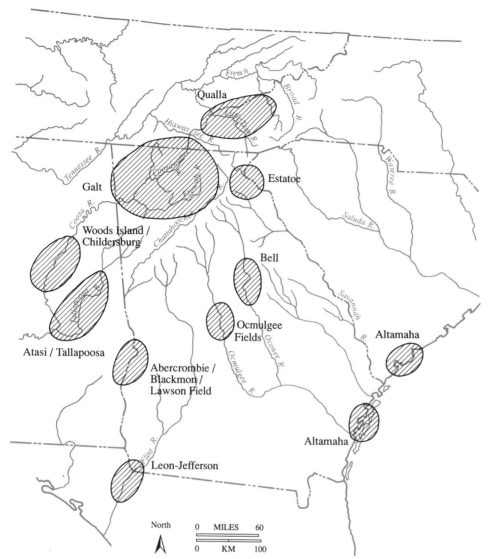

14.4. Geographic distribution of Late Lamar phases.

Table 14.2. Relative Frequency of Pottery Types in Middle Lamar Phases

Pottery Type	Middle Lamar Phases				
	Tugalo	Dyar	Cowarts	Barnett	Bull Creek
Lamar Incised	8	18	15	9	2
Dallas Incised	—	—	—	2	—
Lamar Complicated Stamped	63	8	35	10	26
Check Stamped	1	—	—	—	1
Brushed	—	1	—	—	1
Lamar Plain	29	73	50	55	71
Dallas Plain	—	—	—	24	—
Sample Size	699	3,100	10,700	1,600	7,200

BARNETT PHASE

TUGALO PHASE

BULL CREEK PHASE

14.5. Common Lamar Incised designs in Barnett, Tugalo, and Bull Creek phases.

predominant. Aquatic turtles and fish are numerically important at many sites, although their total meat yield is generally below that of deer. Presumably, white-tailed deer was the single most important animal species in the diet.

Faunal samples from two sites, 9GE175 (Shapiro 1983) and 9PM220 (Rudolph and Hally 1982), that are located adjacent to shoals on the Oconee River in central Georgia differ significantly from this pattern. Site 9GE175 yielded almost exclusively fish, aquatic turtles, and box turtle. The site was apparently occupied for only brief periods of time during the summer for the purpose of exploiting aquatic resources. Site 9PM220 consisted of a thin shell midden containing abundant riverine bivalve and gastropod shells. Vertebrates were present in only small quantities. Presumably mollusc gathering and/or processing was one of the main subsistence activities carried on at this site.

With the exception of turkey, coastal faunal samples generally yield the same range of terrestrial species as is found in the Piedmont. Of these, white-tailed deer is again the most common species. Aquatic species such as oyster, quahog clam, diamond-back terrapin, drum, mullet, sea trout, and catfish are also important and indicate a heavy and perhaps predominant reliance on tidal marsh and estuarine resources.

To judge by the ubiquity and frequency of maize fragments in botanical samples from the Piedmont, Valley and Ridge, and coastal regions of Georgia, maize agriculture was practiced throughout the Lamar area and from earliest to latest times. Squash and beans are less commonly reported, but along with maize probably constituted the major plant foods in the diet. European-introduced cultigens in the form of peach pits are represented in botanical samples from three Late Lamar sites, Joe Bell (M. Williams 1983), Shinholser (M. Williams 1990a), and Tukabatchee (Knight 1985b).

Numerous wild plant species were also consumed. Hickory nut, walnut, and acorn are represented, sometimes in large quantities, in botanical samples from throughout the Lamar area and were probably important dietary elements. Fruits such as grape, plum, persimmon, and maypop are well represented in Piedmont site samples and probably constituted fairly important seasonal additions to the diet. Edible seeds of herbaceous plants such as knotweed (polygonum), however, are not well represented.

Lamar Settlement Pattern

Structures that probably functioned as domestic habitations are known from several Lamar phases: Irene (Caldwell and McCann 1941; Pearson 1986), Rembert (Anderson and Schuldenrein 1985); Duvall (M. Smith 1981); Barnett (Hally 1980, 1988), Cowarts (H. Smith 1973a), Qualla (Dickens 1978), Bell (Hatch 1987), and

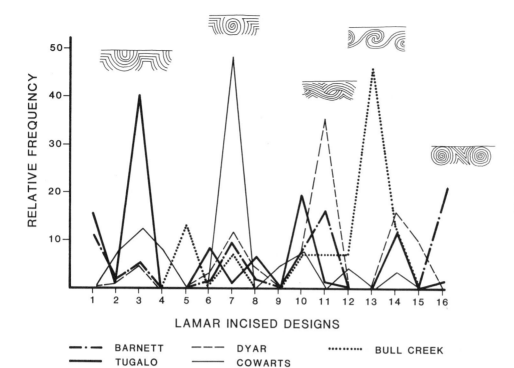

14.6. Relative frequency of Lamar Incised designs in Barnett, Tugalo, Dyar, Cowarts, and Bull Creek phases.

Atasi (Knight 1985b). While excavation has not been sufficient in all cases for complete characterization, most excavated examples conform to a single architectural pattern: rectangular floor plan measuring approximately 6–7 m across, depressed floors, individual-post exterior wall construction, wall-trench entrance passage, four interior roof support posts, interior wattle-and-daub partition walls, and central hearth (Figure 14.7). Exterior walls may have been thatched or daubed. The majority of known structures have been dismantled and rebuilt at least one time.

Similar structures are found in mound and village contexts in Dallas culture sites on the Little Tennessee River (Polhemus 1987) and in village contexts in Mouse Creek phase sites on the Hiwassee River (Sullivan 1986) in eastern Tennessee. Those occurring on mound summits typically have earth banked against their exterior walls to a height of approximately 1 m. Entrance passages may have served to keep this banked earth from washing into the structure. Given that entrance passages are a common feature of village area structures in Dallas as well as Lamar and Mouse Creek cultures, it seems likely that these structures also had earth banked against their exterior walls. Without the protection offered by overlying mound construction stages, these embankments would have been destroyed by plowing in most village contexts.

Smaller, rectangular structures, measuring five meters or less across and possibly lacking depressed floors and wall-trench entrances have been reported at Rucker's Bottom (Anderson and Schuldenrein 1985)

and Tukabatchee (Knight 1985b). In both cases, erosion and cultivation have probably destroyed much of the architectural details of these structures. As a result, it is not possible to determine whether they represent merely smaller versions of the habitation structures described above or whether they differed in a number of architectural features and had different functions.

Five sites—Tukabatchee in Alabama (Knight 1985b), Rucker's Bottom on the Upper Savannah River (Anderson and Schuldenrein 1985), and Lindsey, Sugar Creek, and Carroll Village in the middle Oconee River drainage of Piedmont Georgia (Hatch 1987; Kowalewski and Williams 1989; Kowalewski and Hatch 1991)—have yielded posthole patterns for circular structures measuring up to 9 m in diameter and having individual-post construction. It is not clear what these circular structures represent. Evidence from the small upland sites, Lindsey, Sugar Creek, and Carroll Village, suggest that they were domestic habitations. However, contemporary structures with rectangular plans, depressed floors, and wall-trench entrances occur at the nearby Dyar site (M. Smith 1981). The question then is whether these structures represent different architectural styles, functionally distinct types of buildings, or functionally similar structures adapted to different environmental conditions?

Square and rectangular posthole patterns, representing more lightly constructed buildings are known from the King site as well as the Dallas culture Toqua site (Polhemus 1987) and the Mouse Creek phase sites (Sullivan 1986) in eastern Tennessee. At King and Toqua,

David J. Hally

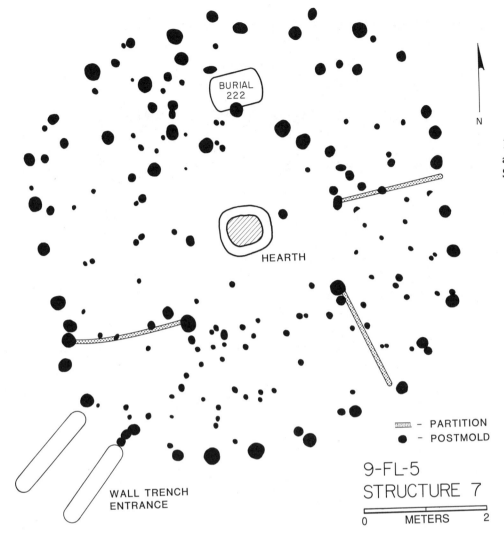

BURIAL
222

N

HEARTH

14.7. Posthole pattern and
associated features of
Structure 7, King site.

▨ – PARTITION
● – POSTMOLD

9-FL-5
STRUCTURE 7

WALL TRENCH
ENTRANCE

0   METERS   2

these patterns measure approximately 3 m by 6 m, often enclose several burials, and are adjacent to structures with depressed floors and wall-trench entrances (Figure 14.8, an especially clean example is located at S285 W700). The Toqua examples typically also enclose areas of fired soil that Polhemus (1987) identifies as hearths. Posthole patterns and burial distributions at the Mouse Creek sites resemble closely those at King and Toqua, suggesting that similar types of structures are present. Sullivan (1986), however, believes that a large rectangular area directly in front of the depressed floor structures was roofed over and that burials were placed around the margins of this area.

Polhemus (1987) and Sullivan (1986) both argue that structures with depressed floors and wall-trench entrances were probably domestic structures occupied during the colder months of the year and that the more lightly constructed buildings adjacent to them were utilized for domestic purposes in the warmer seasons. Polhemus (1987) suggests that this latter kind of structure may have served also as a granary. Artifact content of

structures with depressed floors at Little Egypt support the hypothesized cold season usage (Hally 1981). Among Lamar sites, however, only King has been excavated in such a manner as to demonstrate the coexistence of both structure types. Presumably they occur together in other Lamar phases.

A variety of different site types can be distinguished on the basis of size, physical features, topographic location, and artifact yield. Preeminent among these are sites with earth mounds. With the exception of the Irene site at the mouth of the Savannah River, Lamar period mounds on the coast appear to be exclusively of the burial mound type. These are typically rounded in profile, one meter or less in height, and 15–25 m in diameter (Caldwell and McCann 1941; Larson 1957; Cook 1978; Larsen and Thomas 1986). Stratigraphy typically consists of a shell midden core that is overlain by homogeneous sand or alternating layers of sand and shell. Burial mode is quite variable and includes flexed, extended, bundle, cremation, and urn types. Burial arrangement is typically haphazard

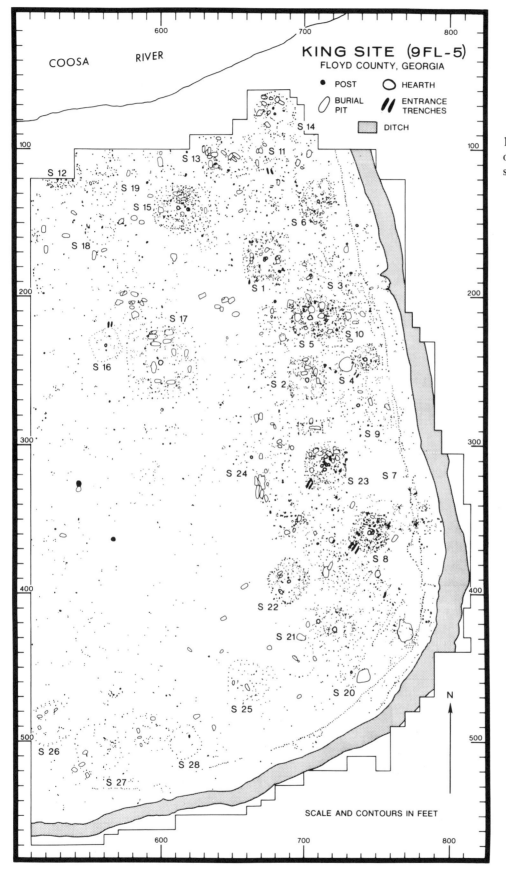

14.8. Posthole patterns and other features at the King site (9FL5).

in appearance, suggesting that mounds grew by accretion over a considerable period of time as interments were added. This type of mound has not been documented for the interior.

A total of 37 sites are known to have multistage platform mounds constructed during the Lamar period in the Piedmont, Valley and Ridge, and Blue Ridge physiographic provinces (Figure 14.1). Only one mound of this type, located at the Irene site, is known for the coast. Platform mounds range in height from 1 m to 13 m. One site (Rembert) had five mounds, one (Little Egypt) may have had three mounds, and five sites (Mulberry, Scull Shoals, Shinholser, Shoulderbone, and Lamar) had two mounds. In only four cases, however—Scull Shoals (Williams 1984), Shinholser (Williams 1990a), Mulberry (Chester DePratter, personal communication), and Little Egypt (Hally 1979)—can it be demonstrated that more than one mound was in use at any time during the Lamar period.

In a majority of cases, the construction and use of Lamar platform mounds spanned several centuries and phases (Hally 1992). Mounds at Dyar (M. Smith 1981), Shinholser (Williams and Shapiro 1987), Shoulderbone (Williams and Shapiro 1986), Tugalo (Williams and Branch 1983), and Chauga (Kelly and Neitzel 1961), for example, were begun in the Etowah or Savannah period, abandoned for a century or more, and underwent further stage construction during the Lamar period. Apparently the great size of most Lamar mounds is due in large part to the fact that they had been in use for so long and rebuilt so many times.

Architectural details are available for a number of excavated mounds. Stream boulders (Kelly and de Baillou 1960; Dickens 1978; Setzler and Jennings 1941) and horizontally laid poles (Setzler and Jennings 1941) were placed on the flanks of some mounds. Refuse, presumably resulting from activities taking place on mound summits, was discarded on the flanks of several mounds (Setzler and Jennings 1941; Williams and Branch 1983; Kelly and Neitzel 1961; M. Smith 1981; M. Williams 1988), usually the northeast flank.

Summit architecture varies considerably, but buildings tend to share a number of features including: 8–12 m square floor plans, individual-post wall construction, interior roof-support posts (4 or 8 in number), central hearth (Dickens 1978; Hally 1980; Kelly and de Baillou 1960; M. Smith 1981; Williams 1975), multiple rebuilding stages with floors separated by only a few centimeters of fill, and reuse of interior roof-support postholes and hearth locations (M. Smith 1981; Kelly and de Baillou 1960). Earth embankments along exterior walls and wall-trench entrances have each been observed at two sites (M. Smith 1981; Williams 1975) but are probably present at others.

The mounds at Estatoe (Kelly and de Baillou 1960) and Coweta Creek (Dickens 1978) had only a single structure on their summits, while more complex arrangements existed at Dyar and Little Egypt. The Late Lamar mound summit at Dyar has the most complex summit configuration known (M. Smith 1981). Two earth-embanked square structures were located on the western half of the summit. The eastern half of the summit was approximately 50 cm lower and had a single lightly constructed building that extended along the entire north/south length of the summit. A nearly identical architectural arrangement has been documented for the roughly contemporaneous Dallas culture Mound A at Toqua (Polhemus 1987).

Mound A at Little Egypt had a central platform large enough to support an arrangement of buildings similar to that recorded at Dyar, although only one structure has been exposed in excavations (Hally 1980). This platform was flanked on two or more sides by buildings erected on lower terraces. One of these buildings is known to have been a domestic structure. Mound A at Toqua was flanked on one side by a terrace bearing a domestic structure. The summits of at least five additional Lamar mounds—Rembert, Shoulderbone, Lamar, Nacoochee, and Neisler—are large enough to have supported multiple buildings.

Nonmound buildings with probable public and cere-monial functions are known from Irene and King sites. A large circular structure, represented by six concentric wall trenches, was located approximately 30 m south of the platform mound at Irene. Measuring 37 m in diameter, the structure bears some resemblance to Creek and Cherokee council houses (Caldwell and McCann 1941). Two structures were located in the plaza at King site (Hally et al. 1975) (Figure 14.8). Structure 17 was 15.5 meters square and had eight interior roof-support posts, a central hearth, and interior partition walls similar to those recorded in several mound structures at Toqua (Polhemus 1987). A structure of similar size and configuration was located on the north edge of the plaza at the Mouse Creek phase Ledford Island site in eastern Tennessee (Sullivan 1986). Given its size and location, Structure 17 at the King site may have been used in a manner similar to that of the eighteenth-century council house. The second structure (Structure 16) at the King site was located adjacent to Structure 17 and resembled a domestic structure in size and architectural features.

Public plazas, large open areas lacking domestic debris and features, can be identified at a number of excavated Lamar sites. At Irene, an area measuring approximately 30 m by 60 m situated between the platform mound and the circular wall-trench structure seems to have been enclosed by walls of wattle-and-daub construction (Caldwell and McCann 1941). At Dyar (M. Smith 1981), a plaza measuring 40 m by 65 m lay east of the mound.

At Little Egypt, Mounds A and B lay on adjacent sides of a probable plaza measuring approximately 60 m by 100 m (Hally 1979). The plaza at the King site measured 50 m by 80 m and contained a large centrally located post pit as well as the structures noted above (Hally et al. 1975) (Figure 14.8). A plaza of considerably smaller size, but containing a large post pit, can also be recognized at Rucker's Bottom (Anderson and Schuldenrein 1985).

Three mound sites—Dyar, Little Egypt, and Coweta Creek—have yielded evidence of domestic structures and, by implication, evidence of a habitation or village zone. Postholes and/or midden deposits at several other sites indicate that most, if not all, Lamar mound sites had an attached village. At Dyar (M. Smith 1981), Little Egypt (Hally 1979), and Coweta Creek (Dickens 1978), this zone borders the plaza on all sides except where there are mounds. Including village zone, plaza, and mound, the Dyar site measures approximately 2.5 ha; Little Egypt covers approximately 5 ha; and Coweta Creek covers approximately 1.2 ha.

Irene site presents a different picture. At the time of excavation, the site covered 2.5 ha. A number of public structures were constructed during the Irene component, including the platform mound, the burial mound, the large circular wall-trench structure, and a square structure containing burials. Only one possible Irene phase domestic structure was identified in excavations, suggesting that the site may not have had a resident domestic population. An undetermined amount of the eastern portion of the site, however, has been destroyed by the meandering Savannah River, and it is possible that domestic habitations were more common there.

Large villages without mounds are known for a number of phases—Barnett, Rembert, Bull Creek, Brewster, Atasi, Tallapoosa—and are usually situated in or immediately adjacent to river floodplains. Only two such sites, King and Rucker's Bottom, have been extensively excavated. Both had fortified perimeters consisting of a ditch and palisade, and both were, at least at one point in their history, square in plan. The King site measured 150 meters square and covered 2 ha. The plaza, measuring 50 m by 80 m, was surrounded by a zone of domestic habitation structures with depressed floors and wall-trench entrances. Twenty-five such structures can be identified in the excavated two-thirds of the site, and it is estimated that the number of structures in the entire village was 47. All excavated structures are similar in architectural configuration and probably served as cold season habitations. At least 10 smaller rectangular, posthole patterns, which probably represent warm season habitations, can also be identified in the domestic zone. The Mouse Creek phase Ledford Island site has many of these characteristics.

It is difficult to get a clear picture of the Rucker's

Bottom site plan. Erosion has destroyed an unknown amount of the village area and obscured posthole patterns. It is possible, furthermore, that some recorded features date to an earlier Savannah period component. The Rembert phase village was apparently initially circular in plan (Anderson and Schuldenrein 1985). In its final form, however, the site was enclosed by a rectangular ditch and palisade, measuring approximately 110 m by at least 60 m. Several different posthole configurations can be identified within the rectangular palisade line (Anderson and Schuldenrein 1985: figure 10.55). One structure (Structure 2), measuring 6 meters square and having a depressed floor and wall-trench entrance passage resembles the structures characteristic of Little Egypt, King, and Dyar sites. Two additional structures of this type may be represented by postholes only.

The most common posthole pattern, with as many as a dozen examples, is that of a square measuring 4–5 m on a side. This configuration may represent the typical domestic structure on the site. If so, it is considerably smaller than the domestic structures characteristic of other Lamar sites. The distribution of these posthole patterns suggests that they surrounded a small plaza located near the center of the site. One large post pit is located in the plaza but is not centered within it or the area enclosed by the rectangular palisade and ditch. As is clear from this discussion, the Rucker's Bottom and King site villages differ in a number of important ways.

Recent investigations in the Oconcc River drainage of central Georgia have revealed the existence of substantial numbers of small Dyar and Bell phase sites situated on ridgetops, often many kilometers from the river (Elliott 1984; Hatch 1987; Kowalewski and Hatch 1991; Kowalewski and Williams 1989). Sites average less than .5 ha and, at least in excavated examples, contain evidence of substantially built round and rectangular structures, burials, and large trash-filled pits. Most sites are probably permanently occupied farmsteads and are apparently the result of an expansion of population into the uplands during the middle decades of the sixteenth century (Kowalewski and Hatch 1988). Upland sites of this type have not been reported elsewhere in the Lamar region.

Limited activity sites have been identified only in the Oconee River drainage in central Georgia and on the Georgia coast. In the former case, small sites located in the Oconee River floodplain adjacent to shoals have yielded faunal remains indicating that they were occupied for the exploitation of various aquatic turtle, fish, and mollusc species (Shapiro 1983; J. L. Rudolph 1986; Rudolph and Hally 1982). The function of other small floodplain sites is less clear (Shapiro 1983; M. Smith et al. 1981), but at least some were probably specialized in nature. Small upland sites were probably used for deer hunting, nut gathering, and other resource procurement

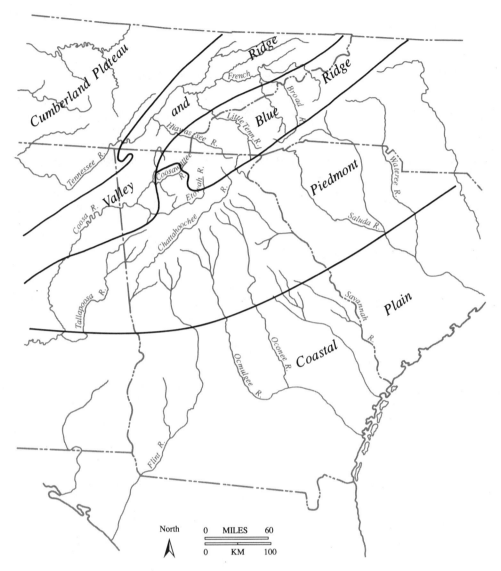

14.9. Physiographic provinces of the Nuclear Southeast.

activities (Manning 1982). Boulder outcrops on ridgetops were used for mortuary purposes with partially burned human skeletal remains and grave goods being placed in crevices between boulders (Braley et al. 1985).

Pearson (1978) has identified limited activity sites on Ossabaw Island on the Georgia coast. These identifications are based on site size and on site location relative to specific environmental variables. Only one such site, 9CH112, has been investigated by means of excavation (Goad 1975).

Regional Variability in Lamar Settlement Pattern

People who made Lamar pottery occupied a variety of habitats, ranging from the salt marshes and estuaries of the coast to the narrow valleys of the Appalachian Mountains (Figure 14.9). Given this habitat variability,

we can expect to find significant differences in the settlement-subsistence systems of some Lamar phases. Bruce Smith's (1978) Mississippian adaptive-niche model provides a useful framework within which to discuss what is currently known about Lamar settlement-subsistence system variability.

Smith argues that Mississippian culture is an adaptation to the floodplain habitat of large river valleys and specifically to the meander-belt habitat zone of the lower valley of the Mississippi River and its major tributaries. The meander-belt habitat is characterized by close juxtaposition of natural levees, cut-off river channels, and backswamps, which together support a variety of biotic communities at high biomass levels. Fertile, well-drained, and easily tilled levee soils were well suited to Mississippian horticultural practices; permanent oxbow lakes and seasonally flooded backswamps supported large annually renewed populations of fish and migratory waterfowl; and

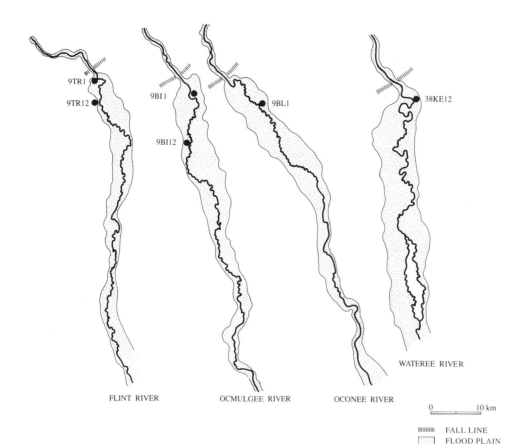

14.10. Location of Lamar sites with platform mounds in the alluvial floodplain of the Flint, Ocmulgee, Oconee, and Wateree rivers below the Fall Line.

the linear interface between levees, swamps, and oxbow lakes provided abundant browse for white-tailed deer and other terrestrial mammals.

Efficient exploitation of this habitat involved maize horticulture and the utilization of a limited number of dependable, seasonally abundant wild plant and animal species, including backwater fish species, migratory fowl, white-tailed deer, raccoon, turkey, nuts, and seeds of pioneer annual plant species. According to Smith, the optimum pattern of settlement for exploitation of these resources would be a dispersed pattern of small settlements located in close proximity to both natural levees and permanent and seasonal lakes. A nucleated settlement pattern, however, is better suited for defense and for promoting internal social cohesion. Smith argues that most Mississippian societies occupying a meander-belt habitat balanced these competing needs with a settlement pattern that included both dispersed settlement in small farmsteads and large, centrally located settlements.

A true meander-belt habitat is found in the Lamar region only along Coastal Plain sections of the Flint, Ocmulgee, Oconee, Savannah, and Wateree rivers (Figure 14.9). Immediately below the "Fall Line," which separates Coastal Plain and Piedmont, floodplain width increases dramatically, stream channels begin to meander

freely, natural levees increase in size, and cut-off channels become common (Figure 14.10). This meander-belt habitat differs from that characteristic of the Lower Mississippi River, however, in one important respect: energy sources are concentrated at the Fall Line rather than being uniformly distributed along the course of the meandering river. Three factors contribute to this situation. To begin with, rivers entering the Coastal Plain carry nutrient-rich sediments derived from freshly weathered metamorphic and igneous Piedmont rocks. These sediments are deposited in great quantities immediately below the Fall Line as a result of the sudden decrease in stream gradient. Further downstream, the amount of deposition decreases while the proportion of less fertile river-borne sediments derived from highly weathered Coastal Plain soils and rocks increases. Second, shoals that undoubtedly served as a major source for fish and other aquatic animal species (Shapiro 1983) occur at the Fall Line, but not downstream. Finally, the juxtaposition of Coastal Plain and Piedmont physiographic provinces meant that a greater variety of natural resources was available immediately below the Fall Line than farther upstream or downstream.

A number of large, Lamar mound sites occur in this Fall Line location: Neisler (9TR1) and Hartley-

160

Posey (9TR2) on the Flint River, Lamar (9BI2) on the Ocmulgee River, Shinholser (9BL1) on the Oconee River, possibly Silver Bluff on the Savannah River (38AK7) (Anderson, Hally, and Rudolph 1986), and Mulberry (38KE12) on the Wateree River. These sites have extensive village areas—Neisler, 9 ha (Worth 1988); Lamar, 8.7 ha (H. Smith 1973a); Shinholser, 18 ha (M. Williams 1990a); Mulberry, at least 3 ha (Ferguson 1974)—indicative of substantial populations. In fact, as a group, they represent the largest villages known to exist during the Lamar period. Smith's model and central place theory (Steponaitis 1978) predict that these mound centers will be located several kilometers downstream from the Fall Line in the middle of the meander-belt zone surrounded by smaller farming communities. In actuality, most are situated at the upriver end of the zone and presumably near the edge of the distribution of local floodplain farming communities (Figure 14.10). This location is probably a response to the greater productivity and diversity of resources that is associated with the Fall Line. What, if any, effect this environmental situation had on the degree of settlement nucleation or dispersion in these regions cannot be determined until systematic site surveys are carried out.

Conditions in the Piedmont contrast strikingly with those existing immediately below the Fall Line. Piedmont rivers such as the Ocmulgee and Oconee are characterized by a pattern of alternating broad, alluvial valleys, and narrow, shoal-filled valleys (Shapiro 1983). Woodruff and Parizek (1956) believe that this pattern is characteristic of most Piedmont streams and refer to it by the term "boudin valley." Active river channels in the broad valley sections are flanked by well-developed levees and low-lying backswamps, but for the most part, valley floors are not sufficiently wide for rivers to meander freely and produce oxbow lakes. Backswamps do flood annually in the late winter and early spring and may have provided opportunities for mass-capture fishing techniques that play an integral role in Smith's Mississippian adaptive niche. The shoals, located at intervals along most Piedmont streams, however, presented an alternative, perhaps equally productive, source of fish and other aquatic resources (Shapiro 1983).

Lake Oconee on the Oconee River encompasses a boudin valley (Shapiro 1983). At the southern end of the basin, the valley is narrow, alluvial bottomland is limited, and the river channel is filled with shoals. Upriver, the valley widens, and alluvial bottomland increases in extent. Small shoals occur at intervals in the upper basin, but generally not in close proximity to areas of extensive floodplain.

Shapiro (1983:263) has observed that the "complimentary distribution of favored horticultural soils and shoals" in the Lake Oconee basin (and presumably on

other Piedmont rivers) meant that settlements could not be located adjacent to both types of resources. The Dyar site, with the largest known Lamar village and the only Lamar platform mound in Lake Oconee, is located in the upper basin on the largest contiguous tract of floodplain soil (Shapiro 1983). Occupation was almost certainly permanent, and horticulture must have been practiced on a large scale in the surrounding bottomland. Fish may have been available in seasonally flooded backswamp areas adjacent to the site. To the extent that shoals were important sources of aquatic resources, however, site inhabitants would have had to travel several kilometers down the Oconee River or up its tributary, the Appalachee River, to reach them (Shapiro 1983: figure 7). Small Lamar sites such as 9GE153 and 9GE175, located adjacent to shoals in the lower lake basin, are identified by Shapiro as specialized aquatic resource procurement sites. He argues that they were used on a temporary basis primarily by people who resided elsewhere, presumably along sections of the Oconee River where there was broad floodplain.

More than 800 Lamar sites have been recorded in the 1,800-acre Lake Oconee basin (Rudolph and Blanton 1981). The great majority are Dyar phase and are quite small (Rudolph, personal communication). Many are probably limited activity sites, but many may be farmsteads. Small Dyar phase sites, some of which can be identified as farmsteads, also occur in the uplands surrounding the Lake Oconee Basin (Kowalewski and Hatch 1991). Dyar, at 2.1 ha, is the largest known middle Lamar site in the region. Large nonmound village sites are unknown. It appears from this evidence that the Dyar phase occupants of the Lake Oconee area were for the most part dispersed in small hamlets or farmsteads. The Dyar site, which does not itself seem to have had an especially large resident population, can be assumed to have served as the ceremonial and administrative center for at least a portion of this dispersed population.

Contiguous tracts of alluvial bottomland are not as extensive along the Oconee River in the Piedmont as they are below the Fall Line. This situation, as well as the complimentary distribution of alluvial bottomland and shoals, may have favored a more dispersed settlement pattern. It is not known whether other Piedmont rivers had a similar dispersed settlement pattern. The existence of the Rucker's Bottom village in Russell Reservoir, however, suggests that at least that portion of the Savannah River valley was characterized by a more nucleated settlement pattern.

The Valley and Ridge province lies immediately west of the Piedmont and is separated from it and the Blue Ridge province by a sharp structural boundary, the Great Smoky Fault (Figure 14.11). Topography within the province consists of a series of parallel valleys and ridges trending

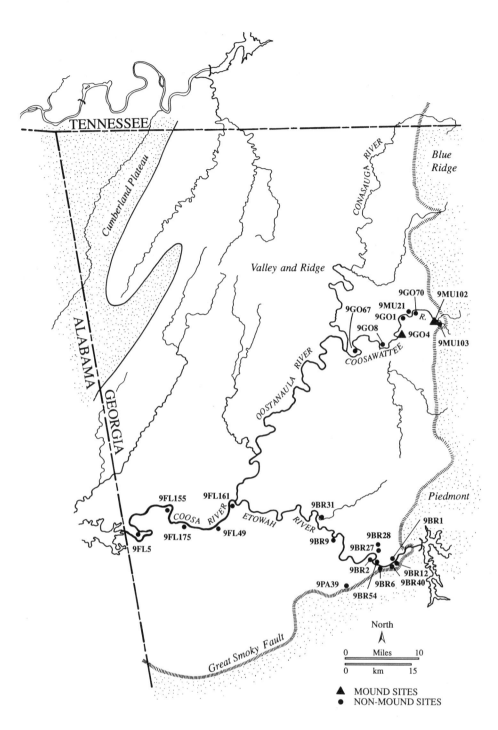

14.11. Middle Lamar period sites in the Georgia Valley and Ridge province.

Map labels:
TENNESSEE
Cumberland Plateau
ALABAMA
GEORGIA
Blue Ridge
CONASAUGA RIVER
Valley and Ridge
9GO67
9GO8
9GO70
9MU21
9GO1
9MU102
R.
9GO4
9MU103
COOSAWATTEE
OOSTANAULA RIVER
Piedmont
9FL155
9FL161
9BR31
9BR1
COOSA RIVER
ETOWAH RIVER
9FL175
9FL49
9BR9
9BR28
9BR27
9BR2
9BR12
9BR40
9FL5
9PA39
9BR6
9BR54
Great Smoky Fault
North
Miles 0 — 10
km 0 — 15
▲ MOUND SITES
● NON-MOUND SITES

in a northeast-southwest direction. The Conasauga, Coosawattee, and Etowah rivers enter the province from the Piedmont and Blue Ridge provinces and join to form the Oostanaula and Coosa rivers. These streams generally flow through broad, alluvium-filled valleys. Shoals are found in only a few locations: along a 15-km stretch of the Etowah River east of Rome and on the Conasauga, Coosawattee, and Etowah rivers where they cross the Great Smoky Fault.

The floodplain of rivers in the Valley and Ridge prov-ince lack most of the topographic and hydrologic features characteristic of Smith's meander-belt habitat. With the exception of a short section of the Conasauga River, valleys are not wide enough to allow streams to meander freely and develop oxbow lakes. Except where rivers leave the Piedmont and Blue Ridge provinces, stream-borne sediments are predominantly fine grained, and as a result, levees and backswamps are poorly developed or nonexistent.

Alluvial soils throughout the Valley and Ridge province

David J. Hally

are structurally well suited to agriculture, but natural fertility is only moderately high because the alluvium is derived from highly weathered limestones and shales. Important exceptions to this situation occur along the Conasauga, Coosawattee, and Etowah rivers where they enter the Valley and Ridge province. At this point and for several kilometers downstream, these streams carry mineral-rich sediments derived from freshly weathered metamorphic and igneous rocks in the Piedmont and Blue Ridge (personal communication, Henry Perkins, Agronomy Department, University of Georgia).

The Middle Lamar period inhabitants of the area appear to have resided in several clusters of large villages (Figure 14.11) (Hally and Langford 1988; Hally et al. 1990). One such cluster consists of seven Barnett phase villages (9MU21, 9MU102, 9GO70, 9GO1, 9GO8, 9GO4, and 9GO67) distributed at fairly regular intervals along an 18.7-km stretch of the Coosawattee River immediately west of the Great Smoky Fault (Langford and Smith 1990). The sites range in size from 1.9 ha to 5.5 ha, and two of them, Little Egypt (9MU102) and Thompson (9GO4), have mounds. A second cluster consists of five Barnett phase villages (9FL5, 9FL49, 9FL155, 9FL161, 9FL175) distributed along a 20.6-km stretch of the Coosa River. These sites are roughly comparable in size to those on the Coosawattee River, but none had mounds. A third group of sites, belonging to the Brewster phase and including at least four large villages (9BR1, 9BR2, 9BR54, and 9PA39), occurs along a 10.8-km stretch of the Etowah River immediately west of the Great Smoky Fault (Wauchope 1966).

There has been heavy occupation and mound-building activity along the Etowah and Coosawattee rivers immediately west of the Great Smoky Fault since at least A.D. 1200, suggesting that these localities were especially attractive to Mississippian societies (Hally and Langford 1988). Proximity to the fault provided ready access to the most extensive shoals in the entire region and to natural resources of both the Valley and Ridge and the Piedmont/Blue Ridge provinces (Larson 1971b). The most fertile soils in the region occurred there as well. The Lamar site clusters on the Coosawattee and Etowah rivers were almost certainly located to take advantage of these conditions. The site cluster on the Coosa River is some 50 km west and southwest of the Etowah and Coosawattee clusters. The location of this site cluster probably reflects a spacing mechanism operating among competing societies.

With one possible exception, the Potts Tract site (9MU103) (Hally 1970), there is no evidence that any portion of these populations resided in small dispersed settlements. Although the absence of such settlements needs to be demonstrated by systematic survey, the presently available evidence indicates that a nucleated

settlement pattern was characteristic of the region. As in the Fall Line case, the casual mechanisms for this kind of settlement pattern are not known at present. It is probably significant, however, that the floodplain habitats below the Great Smoky Fault and below the Fall Line are similar with respect to the co-occurrence of rich alluvial soils, extensive shoals, and increased natural resource availability.

The major streams of the Blue Ridge province are rather small in comparison with those in other regions where Lamar ceramics occur. With the exception of the Ashville, Pigeon, Hendersonville, and Hiwassee basins, bottomlands are narrow and limited in extent (Dickens 1978). Review of USGS 7.5-minute topographic maps for the region suggests that river valleys are similar in many ways to the boudin valleys characteristic of the Piedmont. Broader alluvium-filled valleys alternate with narrow shoal-filled valley sections. In contrast to the Piedmont, narrow degrading valley sections appear to be more extensive and broader, and aggrading sections, more limited in size. Levee and backswamp features may be present along aggrading stream sections, but given the size of most streams, it seems doubtful that they had the ecological significance attributed to them in Smith's model. Cut-off channel segments are absent. Finally, the topographic relief of the province results in marked biotic diversity over short distances and must have inhibited contact between communities in different valleys.

Limited survey and excavation data indicate that Qualla phase settlement patterns included both nucleated villages with mounds and dispersed farmsteads (Dickens 1978). Dickens argues that the former settlement type occurs early in the phase while the latter was characteristic of the post-A.D. 1700 period. He attributes the shift to a more dispersed settlement pattern to "European or European-induced disruption of the precontact cultural-environmental system" (1978:136). Presumably though, the aboriginal Qualla phase settlement system included both nucleated villages and dispersed farmsteads.

Most recorded Qualla sites are located in floodplains or on terraces adjacent to the active floodplain and seem to occur with equal frequency along streams with relatively narrow floodplains and in the larger intermountain basins where bottomland is more extensive (Dickens 1978). Presumably, precontact Qualla villages were situated primarily with respect to availability of arable bottomland. To the extent that such conditions were physically distant from shoals, one can predict that specialized fishing camps were also a common site type in the Blue Ridge province.

Irene and Altamaha/San Marcos phase sites are restricted largely to the narrow coastal zone of barrier islands, tidal marshes, and adjacent mainland (Crook 1978; Larson 1980; Pearson 1977). Natural levees are poorly developed in the estuarine section of the large freshwater rivers. In their absence, the best agricultural soils are found in high-ground areas of the barrier and tidal marsh islands and mainland adjacent to the tidal marsh. Soils in these locations are well drained, but relatively low in natural fertility and are not subject to sedimentation by periodic flooding. The same high-ground areas support mixed hardwood forests that include species of oak and hickory. Fish and molluscs, which were probably among the most important food sources for the late prehistoric and early historic inhabitants of the coast, occur in tidal streams and lagoons and, in the case of some fish species, in freshwater rivers as well. Tidal streams provided access to these resources.

Irene sites range in size from a few hundred square meters to 60 ha (Crook 1980; Pearson 1978). Relatively little excavation has been conducted at large Irene sites. As a result, it is not known whether site size, as measured by the distribution of surface artifacts and discrete shell piles, reflects the actual areal extent of a settlement at a single point in time or rather the shifting location of houses and activity areas through time. Recent settlement pattern studies (Crook 1980, 1986; Pearson 1978) appear to assume that the former situation is true. It seems unlikely, however, that the coastal zone, with its limited agricultural potential (Larson 1980), could have supported even seasonally occupied settlements (Crook 1986) that were larger than the largest Lamar villages in the interior.

The best settlement pattern data available for Irene culture is from Ossabaw Island on the Georgia coast (Pearson 1977). Survey of the 48,000 ha upland portion of the island yielded 47 Irene sites. These were assigned to four size classes. The largest sites, with areas in excess of 10 ha, were found to have burial mounds and to be located on well-drained soils with the highest potential for agriculture and nut production and adjacent to navigable streams. Pearson (1978:74) suggests that these sites were "permanent year round settlements" and that they may have served as social, political, and religious centers. Similar large sites have been investigated by Crook (1986) on Sapelo Island. Crook argues that these "aggregate villages" were occupied by a small elite population throughout the year and that occupation by larger numbers of people occurred only during the summer months.

Small sites, especially those in Pearson's Size Class IV (4,000 square meters), are often located on poorly drained soils at some distance from navigable tidal creeks. Size Class II (26,100–55,740 square meters) and III (7,380–20,800 square meters) sites are identified as permanent or semipermanent habitation sites, while Size Class IV sites are identified as temporary occupation, limited activity sites.

Two small Irene phase sites have been excavated. The Red Bird Creek site (Pearson 1986), covering an area of approximately 6,400 square meters, is located on well-drained soil and has yielded evidence of a substantial wattle-and-daub structure, suggesting permanent year round occupation. Maize was also recovered from the site. Site 9CH112, with an area under 1,000 square meters, is located on low, poorly drained ground, but also yielded evidence of a structure (Goad 1975).

Given the strikingly different environment in which it existed, Irene phase settlement-subsistence system can be expected to differ significantly from those characteristic of interior Lamar phases. A number of fundamental issues—importance of maize agriculture, seasonal duration of settlement occupancy, and the relationship between surface artifact distribution and community size—need to be resolved, however, before we can begin to understand the nature of coastal Lamar settlement-subsistence systems.

It is clear from the preceding discussion that there is considerable regional variability in Lamar settlement pattern. Settlement along the coast may alternate seasonally between a dispersed and a nucleated mode. Settlement in the Valley and Ridge province and along the Fall Line appears to be more nucleated than it is in the Piedmont and Blue Ridge provinces. This latter tendency may be a response to availability of alluvial bottomland. River valley floors are considerably broader in the Valley and Ridge province and Fall Line zone, and the larger tracts of alluvial floodplain would have permitted larger numbers of people to have access to agricultural plots from a single settlement.

Lamar Mortuary Practices

Lamar burials are predominantly flexed, although extended, bundle, urn, and cremation forms also occur (Anderson and Schuldenrein 1985; Ferguson 1974; Caldwell and McCann 1941; Deutschle 1973; Hally 1979; Hamilton et al. 1975; M. Smith 1981). Urn burials usually contain infants and are found in the lower Piedmont and Coastal Plain sections of South Carolina and eastern Georgia during at least the Early and Middle Lamar periods. The best-documented and presumably most common location for burials is in the habitation zone of villages. Burials are commonly placed within or adjacent to cold-season domestic structures (Dickens 1978; Hally 1975, 1980; M. Smith 1981). At the King site, approximately half were placed within these structures while a sizeable number of the remainder were placed within or adjacent to the more lightly constructed summer houses. This same pattern is also characteristic of Dallas (Polhemus 1987) and Mouse Creek (Sullivan 1986) cultures. Sullivan reports that infants and young children were buried almost exclusively within winter houses, while adults were interred around the perimeter of summer houses. No such age/structure type association is evident at the King site.

David J. Hally

The occurrence of burials of all ages and both sexes in winter houses at King suggests that the individuals involved represent household members. The occurrence of Carabelli's cusp, a simply inherited dental trait, in several individuals from one King site structure seems to support this possibility (Talley 1975). Sullivan (1986) has found demographic evidence suggestive of household burial clusters in Mouse Creek culture as well.

Human burials have been found in mounds at several sites: Lamar (9BI2), Nacoochee (9WH3), Little Egypt (9MU102), Hartley-Posey (9TR2), and Park (9TP49). Unfortunately, for a variety of reasons, none of these sites provides useful information on patterns of burial placement or form. No definite Lamar burials were recovered from the extensively excavated platform mounds at Dyar (9GE5), Estatoe (9ST3), Chauga (38OC47), and Irene (9CH1). The absence of burials in the platform mound at Irene is not surprising, given the existence of a burial mound and a mortuary structure at the site. The absence of burials in the other three mound sites cannot be so easily explained.

Burials have been found in nonmound public areas at three Lamar sites. At King, 10 burials were placed in Structure 17 located at the northern end of the plaza, and an additional 43 burials occurred in five clusters along the northern and eastern edges of the plaza. Clusters of burials are also present along the eastern and western edges of the plaza at the Mouse Creek phase Ledford Island site (Sullivan 1986). Anderson and Schuldenrein (1985) report one excavated burial from the plaza at Rucker's Bottom. At Irene, burials were placed in a special mortuary structure and in the rotunda as well as in the burial mound.

Mortuary Evidence for Status Differentiation

Lamar burials are frequently accompanied by nonperishable grave goods. Commonly occurring items include: pottery vessels, ground-stone celts, triangular points, shell beads, shell gorgets, and clay pipes. The only collection of grave goods that has been recovered from a large number of burials using standard archaeological techniques is from the King site in northwestern Georgia. Of the approximately 190 burials recorded at the site, 102 were accompanied by nonperishable grave goods. Grave lot associations among the artifact types represented in the collection have been investigated by Seckinger (1977) using cluster analysis. Five of the six clusters identified by Seckinger tend to crosscut sex and age categories, while one cluster, containing the greatest number of what Seckinger calls socio-technique artifacts, was strongly associated with adult males. Seckinger concludes from this evidence that King site society was ranked but was

less complexly organized than that of the Etowah site during the Wilbanks phase.

Further insight into the nature of King site burial patterning can be gained by looking at the sex, age, and location associations of individual artifact types. Most types of grave goods—pottery vessels, triangular points, conch columella ear pins, shell beads, pipes, bone tools, mussel shell, animal bone—crosscut age and sex categories and accompany burials that are distributed throughout the site. A few artifact types, however, are associated with a single sex or age-sex category. Most of these items were probably highly valued in the community as they are made of nonlocal material, are finely crafted, and in some cases have obvious supralocal symbolic significance. Rattlesnake gorgets occur only with adult females and subadults (females?), while shell masks occur only with adult males and subadults (males?). Large bipointed blades and flint-worker kits, on the other hand, occur exclusively with adult males, most of whom are more than 40 years in age. Iron tools and stone discoidals are also found exclusively with adults, and with one exception these are all males or of indeterminate sex. All of these adult male associated artifacts occur in just 16 burials, and most occur in just six burials. These same six burials also contain the only specimens of spatulate celts and embossed copper cutouts and one of the two conch shell cups in the collection. We can conclude from these observations that status differentiation was characteristic of King site social organization, that sex and age were important factors in determining an individual's social position, and that one or a small number of high status positions were probably dependent on personal achievement as well as sex and age.

With one exception, all 16 of the burials with high status adult male–associated artifacts are located in the plaza and in the northern portion of the village. Structures 1 and 15, fronting the plaza on its northeast corner, contain four of these burials (Figure 14.8). Burials with rattlesnake gorgets and shell masks have essentially the same distribution. We can tentatively conclude from this evidence that the northern section of the village was the preferred residence location for households whose membership included high status adults.

There is insufficient contextual data available from other Lamar sites to demonstrate that the patterns observed at the King site are widespread. Evidence summarized by Sullivan (1986) does, however, suggest that similar patterns are characteristic of the Mouse Creek phase villages in eastern Tennessee. Artifact associations clearly demonstrate that age and sex are important determinants of social status. Large bipointed chert blades and the single example of a spatulate celt are found exclusively with adult males.

A more interesting comparison can be made with

Table 14.3. High Status Artifacts from Savannah and Lamar Period Burials

Artifacts	Savannah Period Sites						Lamar Period Sites						
	Etowah Mound C[1]	Hollywood[2]	Chauga[3]	Shinholser[4]	Beaverdam[5]	Nacoochee[6]	Little Egypt[7]	Neisler[8]	Lamar[9]	King[10]	Park[11]	Dyar[12]	Irene[13]
Embossed copper plates	◇	◇	◇	◇									
Copper-covered wooden ornaments	◇	◇		◇							◇		
Copper cut-outs	◇	◇			◇	◇				◇			
Mica cut-outs	◇												
Sea turtle cut-outs	◇												
Copper celts	◇	◇			◇	◇							
Copper-covered celts	◇												
Monolithic axes	◇												
Spatulate celts	◇					◇							
Pierced stone celts	◇												
Stone paint palettes	◇												
Stone statues	◇									◇			
Stone discoidals	◇	◇				◇	◇		◇	◇			
Large bipointed blades	◇					◇	◇			◇			
Conch shell cups	◇		◇		◇	◇	◇		◇	◇			
Conch columella beads	◇					◇	◇		◇	◇		◇	◇
Conch columella pendants	◇	◇			◇	◇							◇
Rattlesnake gorgets			◇				◇	◇		◇			
Weeping-eye mask gorgets							◇	◇		◇			
Misc. shell gorgets	◇				◇								
Negative painted bottles	◇	◇				◇							
Effigy bottles	◇	◇				◇	◇						

1. Larson 1971a.
2. Anderson 1990–.
3. Kelly and Neitzel 1961.
4. M. Williams 1990a.
5. Rudolph and Hally 1985.
6. Heye et al. 1918.
7. Hally 1979, 1980.
8. Worth 1988.
9. H. Smith 1973a.
10. Seckinger 1977.
11. Huscher 1972.
12. M. Smith 1981.
13. Caldwell and McCann 1941.

slightly earlier Dallas culture sites in Tennessee. Analyzing burials from 18 sites, Hatch (1974) found that large bipointed blades and flint-worker kits were associated exclusively with adult males, while several types of shell gorgets were associated with subadults and adult females. He also found that a small number of items—conch shell cups, painted bottles, copper ear ornaments, and copper head ornaments—were associated exclusively with burials in and adjacent to mounds. Hatch identifies these latter objects as markers of preeminent status in Dallas society because of their relative rareness and superior craftsmanship, and because they required large amounts of exotic nonlocal material to make. Because they occur with individuals of both sexes and all ages, Hatch concludes that the status positions involved were ascribed.

King site has yielded only one of these particular status markers, conch shell cups. There is also no evidence at the site for a preeminent status group that includes both adults and subadults and both males and females. These differences may reflect the fact that the King site was not an important administrative and ceremonial center. The chiefly elite did not reside at King, nor were they buried there.

Table 14.3 lists the exotic artifacts that are known to have been recovered from Lamar mound sites. Most of the more elaborate artifact types found at King have been recovered from mound contexts also. Artifacts comparable to the types identified by Hatch as preeminent status markers include negative painted bottles and copper-covered wooden ear ornaments. The large sheet-copper cutouts in the shape of a human figure and bird claw recovered from a burial at Nacoochee (Heye et al. 1918) are probably comparable in use and symbolic value to the copper headdresses found in Dallas mound burials. Two solid copper celts from Nacoochee, measuring 18 cm and 25 cm in length, may represent additional high status markers. There is then some evidence that the highest ranked individuals in Lamar societies were buried in or adjacent to mounds, as was the case in Dallas culture. Whether they also represent kin-based ascribed status position cannot be determined with available evidence.

Lamar Polities

The size and geographical configuration of Lamar polities (politically integrated societies) have been addressed by several researchers (Smith and Kowalewski 1981; Williams and Shapiro 1987; Hudson, Smith, Hally, Polhemus, and DePratter 1985; Hally 1992, 1993; and Hally et al. 1990). Smith and Kowalewski suggest that a large polity or province existed along the middle Oconee River in Dyar phase times. Six sites with mounds—Scull Shoals (9GE4), Dyar (9GE5), 9GE35, Little River (9MG46), Shoulderbone (9HK1), and Shinholser (9BL1)

are identified as administrative centers for the province. Spacing between these sites and the number of mounds per site suggests that the province was divided into three or four territories and that their integration into the larger system was accomplished by the most centrally located and largest site, Shoulderbone. Recent fieldwork by Williams and Shapiro (1987) has modified this scheme in some details—only five sites actually have Dyar phase mound construction, and the number of mounds at two of the sites is less than originally believed—but it still retains considerable merit.

Working with both documentary and archaeological evidence, Hudson and his colleagues (Hudson et al. 1984) have recently concluded that the Shinholser, Shoulderbone, Dyar, and Scull Shoals sites formed De Soto's province of Ocute. Hudson and his colleagues (Hudson, Smith, Hally, Polhemus, and DePratter 1985) have also proposed that the powerful province of Coosa encountered by both De Soto and Luna extended from about Childersburg, Alabama, to about Newport, Tennessee, and included the Barnett, Kymulga, and Mouse Creek phases and Dallas culture. The capital of this far-flung province is located by the authors at the Little Egypt site (9MU102) on the Coosawattee River in northwestern Georgia.

My own research has focused on the geographical size of Mississippian polities in northern Georgia (Hally 1992, 1993). Starting from the premise that platform mounds served as the architectural focus of political and ceremonial activities in Mississippian societies, I have used the spatial distribution and size of sites with such mounds as evidence for the size, distribution, and hierarchical organization of Mississippian polities. Calculation of the linear distances separating first- and second-order nearest neighbors for 47 Mississippi period mound sites in northern Georgia reveals that contemporaneous mound sites are spaced either less than 18 km apart or more than 32 km apart. Based on this evidence, I have proposed that: (1) contemporaneous mound sites separated by less than 18 km belonged to the same polity; (2) mound sites separated by distances greater than 32 km belonged to different polities; and (3) Mississippian polities seldom exceeded 40 km in spatial extent.

A similar pattern has been noted for prestate complex societies in other parts of the world (Renfrew 1975; Johnson 1982). Many researchers (Renfrew 1975; Johnson 1982; Cherry 1987) believe that this 40-km limit in the size of early complex societies results from the nature of administrative organization of such societies and the increasing costs associated with administering increasingly larger territories. The significance of the 40-km size limit probably lies in the fact that 20 km is close to the maximum intersite distance that can be covered roundtrip on foot in a single day.

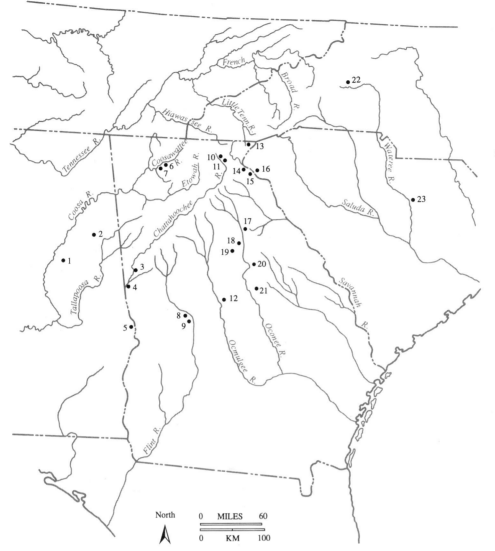

14.12. Middle Lamar period sites with platform mounds.

1. Hightower (1TA150)
2. Davis Farm (1CA196)
3. Park Mound (9TP41)
4. Avery (9TP64)
5. Abercrombie (1RU61)
6. Little Egypt (9MU102)
7. Thompson (9GO4)
8. Neisler (9TR1)

9. Hartley-Posey (9TR12)
10. Nacoochee (9WH3)
11. Eastwood (9WH2)
12. Lamar (9BI2)
13. Dillard (9RA3)
14. Estatoe (9ST3)
15. Tugalo (9ST1)
16. Chauga (38OC47)

17. Scull Shoals (9GE4)
18. Dyar (9GE5)
19. Little River (9MG46)
20. Shoulderbone (9HK1)
21. Shinholser (9BL1)
22. Berry (31BK22)
23. Mulberry (38KE12)

Table 14.4. Middle Lamar Sites with Mounds, Number of Mounds per Site, and Distance to Nearest Neighbor

Number on Figure 14.12 Map	Site	Number of Mounds	Distance to First Nearest Neighbor	Distance to Second Nearest Neighbor
1	Hightower (1TA150)	1	58.0 km	102 km
2	Davis Farm (1CA196)	1	58.0 km	84 km
3	Park (9TP41)	1	15.0 km	76 km
4	Avery (9TP64)	1	15.0 km	64 km
5	Abercrombie (1RU61)	1	64.0 km	76 km
6	Little Egypt (9MU102)	2	8.6 km	90 km
7	Thompson (9GO4)	1	8.6 km	97 km
8	Neisler (9TR1)	1	4.7 km	49 km
9	Hartley-Posey (9TR12)	1	4.7 km	51 km
10	Nacoochee (9WH3)	1	2.7 km	37 km
11	Eastwood (9WH2)	1	2.7 km	34 km
12	Lamar (9BI2)	2	49.0 km	50 km
13	Dillard (9RA3)	1	35.0 km	43 km
14	Estatoe (9ST3)	1	8.2 km	47 km
15	Tugalo (9ST1)	1	6.3 km	39 km
16	Chauga (38OC47)	1	6.3 km	34 km
17	Scull Shoals (9GE4)	2	17.0 km	40 km
18	Dyar (9GE5)	1	17.0 km	29 km
19	Little River (9MG46)	1	28.8 km	40 km
20	Shoulderbone (9HK1)	2	33.0 km	44 km
21	Shinholser (9BL1)	2	44.0 km	50 km
22	Berry (31BK22)	1	225.0 km	
23	Mulberry (38KE12)	3	225.0 km	

With the exception of Shine II, Square Ground, and Brewster, all Early and Middle Lamar phases have at least one site with platform mounds. Information on mound sites is most complete for Middle Lamar, and the following discussion will therefore be limited to that period. Altogether, 23 sites are known to have had mound construction during the Middle Lamar period (Figure 14.12, Table 14.4). Several other sites with mounds (Vandiver [9DO1], Winfree [9HS2], Cooper [9ME3], Engineers Landing [9CE5], and Peachtree [31CE1]) are suspected to date to the period, but have not been adequately investigated or described in print to confirm this belief.

With one exception (the distance between Dyar and Little River—but see below), nearest neighbor distances between Middle Lamar mound sites conform to the general pattern described above. Sites are either less than 18 km or more than 32 km apart (Table 14.4). Those that are less than 18 km apart are less than a day's roundtrip travel from each other and may have belonged to the same polity. This situation is well illustrated by the distribution of Barnett and Brewster phase sites in northwestern Georgia (Figure 14.11). On the Coosawattee River, the Barnett phase Little Egypt site (9MU102) had two, and possible three, platform mounds. Six additional Barnett

phase villages, including Thompson (9GO4) with one platform mound, are distributed downstream from Little Egypt at intervals of approximately 2.5–5 km for a total distance of 18.7 km (Langford and Smith 1990).

Small, limited activity sites probably occur in the Piedmont east of Little Egypt, but the nearest Middle Lamar mound site in that direction is Nacoochee located 90 km away on the Upper Chattahoochee River. Downstream, the nearest contemporary mound site may be at Rome, 49 km from Little Egypt. Jones (1861) reported two mound sites near Rome, but these sites cannot be relocated and consequently their age cannot be determined. Overland to the north and south, the nearest contemporary mound may have been at Etowah (9BR1) on the Etowah River at a distance of 54 km from Little Egypt. Given the proximity of the Coosawattee River sites to one another and the distances separating them from neighboring Middle Lamar mound sites, it seems highly likely that these sites constituted a single politically integrated system with Little Egypt serving as the major administrative center and Thompson serving as a minor center—a two-tier political hierarchy or complex chiefdom in the terminology of Steponaitis (1978).

The seven village sites comprising this polity are located just west of the Great Smoky Fault. On the east side of the

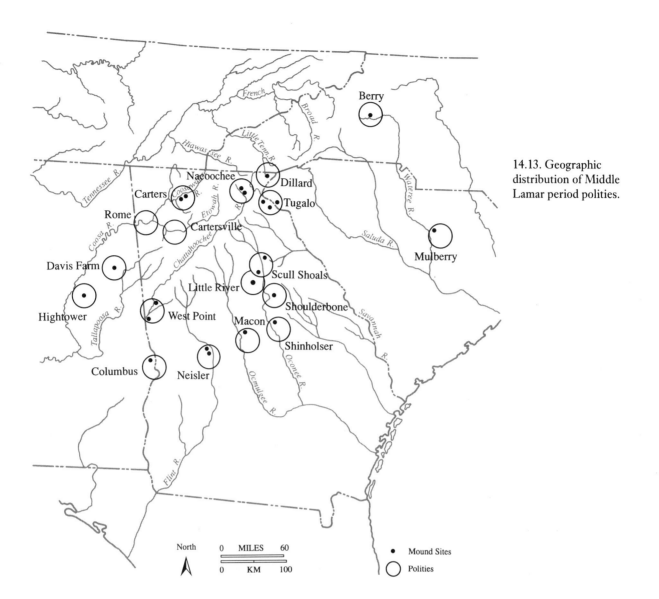

14.13. Geographic distribution of Middle Lamar period polities.

North   0   MILES   60

                0   KM   100

● Mound Sites

◯ Polities

fault, in the Piedmont, upland elevations increase abruptly by 200–300 m, and the Coosawattee flows through a narrow, shoals-filled valley. Little Egypt, located immediately west of the fault, is one of the easternmost sites in the polity. This location does not make sense in terms of administrative efficiency (Steponaitis 1978), and is apparently determined, as in the case of the Fall Line mound sites, by the fact that the most fertile soils along the Coosawattee occur immediately downstream from the Great Smoky Fault. The same situation apparently occurs on most of the rivers—Etowah, Conasauga, Ocoee, Hiwassee, and Little Tennessee—that enter the Valley and Ridge province from the Piedmont or Blue Ridge provinces (Hally et al. 1990). In almost every case, there is a Mississippi period platform mound site adjacent to the fault line at the point where the valley floor widens.

Two other clusters of Middle Lamar sites exist along the Etowah River south of Little Egypt and along the

Coosa River west of Rome, Georgia, and probably represent distinct polities (Figure 14.11). In the former case, four large villages and several smaller sites are distributed along a 10.8-km stretch of the Etowah River that has a broad floodplain. No sites with Middle Lamar mound construction are currently known to exist along this stretch of river, although it is possible that Mound B at Etowah had Brewster phase construction stages. Beyond this cluster of sites, no large contemporary village sites are known either upstream or downstream for a distance of at least 10 km (Ledbetter et al. 1987). The nearest known contemporary mound sites are Little Egypt and Thompson, located 54 km to the north on the Coosawattee River. Unverified mound sites, reported by Jones (1861) on the Coosa and Oostanaula rivers near Rome, are 33 km and 40 km distant respectively.

The Coosa River cluster consists of at least five large village sites distributed at 6–12 km intervals along a 20 km

David J. Hally

Table 14.5. Middle Lamar Period Polities

Polity	Number of Mound Sites	Distance Between Mound Sites	Number of Mounds per Site	Phase	Distance to Nearest Polity[1]
Hightower	1		1	Kymulga	58 km
Davis Farm	1		1	Barnett?	62 km
West Point	2	13.5 km	1, 1	Bull Creek	64 km
Columbus	1		1	Bull Creek	64 km
Carters	2	8.6 km	3, 1	Barnett	90 km
Rome[2]	0		0	Barnett	49 km
Cartersville[2]	0		0	Brewster	54 km
Neisler	2	4.7 km	1, 1	Lockett	49 km
Nacoochee	2	3.8 km	1, 1	none defined	37 km
Macon	1		2	Cowarts	49 km
Dillard	1		1	none defined	35 km
Tugalo	3	7.1 km 7.4 km	1, 1, 1	Tugalo	34 km
Scull Shoals	2	17.0 km	2, 1	Dyar	40 km
Little River	1		1	Dyar	40 km
Shoulderbone	1		2	Dyar	47 km
Shinholser	1		2	Dyar	47 km
Mulberry	1		3	Mulberry	225 km
Berry	1		1	Burke	225 km

1. Straight line distance measured between primary mound centers of neighboring polities.
2. Straight line distance measured from border of site cluster to nearest primary mound center.

stretch of the river. Although there are reports that one of these sites, Mohman (9FL155), had two platform mounds, limited investigation by the author has failed to substantiate this. One of the mound sites reported by Jones (1961) was located where the Oostanaula and Etowah rivers join to form the Coosa River and may have had Middle Lamar construction stages. The nearest known contemporary village (ICE308) (Little and Curren 1981) lies 25 km beyond the site cluster to the west. The nearest known contemporary mound site, Thompson, lies 50 km beyond the site cluster to the northeast.

In 16 cases, Middle Lamar mound sites or mound site clusters are separated from their nearest neighbors by more than 32 km (Figure 14.12, Table 14.4). Following the line of reasoning that has been developed here, these sites were probably the administrative centers for polities that measured 20–30 km in diameter and that were to varying degrees independent of one another. The spatial location and other characteristics of these hypothesized polities and the two located on the Coosa and Etowah rivers for which we do not as yet have evidence for mound construction are mapped and described in Figure 14.13 and Table 14.5. The great distances separating most of these polities probably served as buffer zones. Buffer zones would tend to reduce the frequency and effectiveness of enemy raids and, to the extent that they were unoccupied or only lightly occupied, would have served

as procurement territories and population reservoirs for wild food species such as white-tailed deer (Anderson 1986; Hickerson 1965).

The data presented here tend to support the Smith and Kowalewski (1981) model for a middle Oconee River province. Two of the mound sites, Dyar (9GE5) and Scull Shoals (9GE4), are located close enough to one another that they could have formed a single polity with Scull Shoals, by virtue of its two mounds, as the primary center. The Little River site (9MG46) is only 28.8 km from Dyar, but it is 40.1 km from Scull Shoals, the primary center in that polity. Distances between the remaining mound sites—Little River, Shinholser, and Shoulderbone—are all in excess of 45 km, suggesting that they, along with Scull Shoals and Dyar, represent four distinct polities, comparable to Smith and Kowalewski's "territories." Whether they were in turn integrated into a single, larger polity remains to be demonstrated.

Early Spanish accounts (Hudson et al. 1984; Hudson, Smith, Hally, Polhemus, and DePratter 1985) provide some information on the political relationships that existed between many of the Middle Lamar polities identified in this paper. According to the De Soto route reconstruction of Hudson and his colleagues, the De Soto expedition visited the Neisler, Macon, Shinholser, Shoulderbone, Mulberry, Carters, Cartersville, Rome, Davis Farm, and Hightower polities (Figure 14.13).

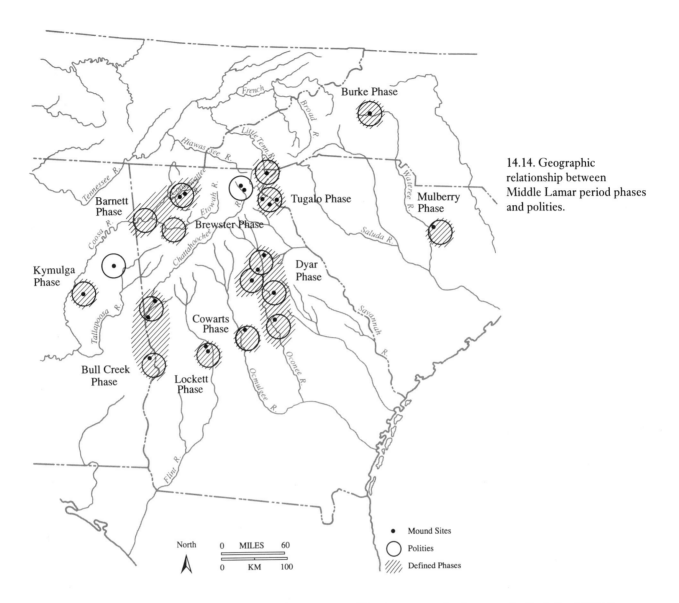

14.14. Geographic relationship between Middle Lamar period phases and polities.

According to expedition chronicles, Toa (the Neisler polity), Ichisi (the Macon polity), and Cofitachequi (the Mulberry polity) were largely independent of neighboring polities (but see Chapter 15, this volume); Altamaha and Cofaqui (the Shinholser and Scull Shoals polities) were subordinate in some fashion to Ocute (the Shoulderbone polity); and Coosa (the Carters polity) had some degree of control over the populations represented by the Cartersville, Rome, Davis Farm, and Hightower polities. Political relationships between the polities in the latter two groups were probably rather tenuous and may have been limited primarily to marriage, military pacts (Hudson, Smith, Hally, Polhemus, and DePratter 1985), symbolic exchange (Helms 1979), and symbolic expressions of subordination and superordination between the leaders of each (Hudson, Smith, Hally, Polhemus, and DePratter 1985). These ethnographic/archaeological equations, of course, require a great deal of further research to verify.

To what extent do the ceramically defined Middle Lamar phases correspond with the polities defined by mound distributions? In at least four instances—Lockett, Cowarts, Mulberry, and Tugalo phases—there is apparently a one-to-one correspondence (Figure 14.14). In three instances—Barnett, Dyar, and Bull Creek—phases include two or more polities. In the remaining cases, ceramic phases and/or polity distributions are not well enough known to allow reliable comparisons to be made. At this point then, the evidence suggests that there is no necessary correspondence between ceramically defined phases and polities defined on the basis of mound and nonmound site distributions.

Linguistic/Ethnic Identity of Lamar

What was the linguistic affiliation of people who made Lamar pottery? Continuities in ceramic development

David J. Hally

from the fifteenth century into the eighteenth century indicate that Lamar pottery was manufactured by Muskogee speakers in the middle Coosa-Tallapoosa area and by Hitchiti speakers along the lower Chattahoochee River (Chapter 16, this volume) and middle Oconee and Ocmulgee rivers (M. Williams 1981). The Hudson, Smith, Hally, Polhemus, and DePratter (1985; Smith 1976) reconstruction of the De Soto route through northwestern Georgia indicates that Lamar ceramics in that area were produced by Muskogee speakers as well. Ongoing research with aboriginal place-names recorded by the Pardo expedition (Booker et al. 1992) indicates that Lamar was the product of Muskogean speakers in the South Carolina coastal plain and the product of Catawban speakers in the Piedmont of North Carolina and eastern South Carolina. Finally, the Qualla variant of Lamar from the Appalachian area of western North and South Carolina, northeastern Georgia, and eastern Tennessee is for the most part clearly associated with Cherokee speakers. We have, then, increasing evidence that one general style of pottery was made by people speaking a variety of languages belonging to three different linguistic families and stocks.

Summary and Conclusions

Since it was first formally recognized in 1938, the identity of Lamar culture has rested almost exclusively on the co-occurrence in time and space of two pottery types, Lamar Incised and Lamar Complicated Stamped and a vessel shape mode, the jar with thickened and pinched/punctated rim. This ceramic complex is distributed over a wide area, including most of Georgia and portions of Alabama, Florida, South and North Carolina, and Tennessee, and over a period of at least 400 years, beginning at approximately A.D. 1350.

Although typically recognized by its ceramic diagnostics, Lamar is homogenous and often distinctive with respect to a wide variety of cultural features, ranging from its mixed horticultural-hunting and gathering subsistence base to the form and placement of human interments and the architectural details of domestic habitation structures. Numerous artifact types not dealt with in this paper are also as widely distributed in time and space as the ceramic complex. Among these are conch columella beads, clay and conch columella ear pins, clay segmented elbow and monolithic-axe effigy pipes, polished stone discoidals, and triangular projectile points.

We have also seen that in many respects Lamar is neither internally homogenous nor distinct from its neighbors. There are regional variations on the ceramic complex sufficiently great to allow us to distinguish phases. Urn burials are restricted primarily to the lower Piedmont and Coastal Plain of South Carolina and

eastern Georgia (Smith 1981). The practice of placing rock mantles over mound construction stages is restricted to northeastern Georgia and adjacent parts of North and South Carolina. And of course, there are major subsistence differences between the coastal, Fall Line, Piedmont, and Valley and Ridge areas.

Features of Lamar domestic architecture and burial furniture known from northwestern Georgia are shared with Dallas and Mouse Creek cultures in eastern Tennessee; so much so that were these our primary cultural diagnostics, we would have to merge the three into a single culture. To the west in east-central Alabama and along the lower Chattahoochee River, the Lamar ceramic complex changes gradually without perceptible break into the complexes characteristic of the Alabama River phase and Fort Walton culture.

It is clear from the foregoing that Lamar culture is polythetic in nature and, therefore, an arbitrary creation of the archaeologist. The definition and spatial/temporal boundaries of Lamar that I have used in this chapter will not be acceptable to all archaeologists concerned. Some will object to the inclusion of Qualla as a phase of Lamar, insisting instead that it is a culture in its own right (Egloff 1967). The inclusion of Fort Walton in Lamar, which can be justified on purely typological grounds, would have met with even greater objection had I been courageous enough to advocate it.

Accepting the polythetic nature of Lamar culture as defined in this chapter, we are confronted with the problem of accounting for the widespread and frequently co-extensive distributions of its many cultural features. Lamar clearly does not represent the physical remains of a single, politically integrated society. The available archaeological evidence indicates that the basic political unit in the nuclear Southeast during the sixteenth century covered an area of approximately 1,500 square kilometers and was integrated around one or two mound centers. Early Spanish accounts indicate that several of these polities might be joined into large, loosely integrated paramount chiefdoms, but there are at least four such polities in the Lamar area during the mid-sixteenth century. Lamar is also not the product of a single ethnic group. Such a group would have to have incorporated several polities and several languages, a situation for which there is no precedent among complex prestate societies that I am aware of.

It seems likely that the cultural homogeneity represented by the typological construct, Lamar culture, is due to a number of factors. Certainly some shared cultural features are the result of common adaptations to similar natural environments. Included here would be such things as the mixed horticultural-hunting and gathering subsistence base characteristic of Lamar and other late prehistoric cultures in the Southeast. The utilization of similar domesticated and wild food species, in turn, encourages development of similar food preparation, storage, and consumption patterns and even similar pottery vessel forms. Likewise, the depressed floor and earth-embanked walls characteristic of Lamar, Dallas, and Mouse Creek domestic and public buildings are probably adaptations to temperature and precipitation conditions common to the South Appalachian region.

By the same token, of course, some cultural variability in Lamar can be attributed to adaptation to different environments. Differences in the availability of wild food species and in the agricultural potential of soils have contributed to the development of different subsistence strategies on the coast and in the Piedmont interior. Likewise, differences in the quantity and distribution of alluvial floodplain soils and riverine animal resources have probably led to major differences in settlement pattern between the Piedmont and Fall Line areas.

Some widespread cultural features undoubtedly follow from the fact that societies throughout the Lamar area have all attained the general level of the same general level of cultural complexity. Similarities in settlement hierarchy, burial programs that emphasize status differences, and the spatial extent of polities probably exist because they reflect characteristics of chiefdoms that are essential to their proper functioning.

Other, more specific kinds of cultural features—decorative motifs on pottery, symbols used to mark status differences, location of burials within domestic structures—have become widespread as a result of interaction among neighboring communities and polities; a mechanism familiar to archaeologists for years, but recently given formal recognition by Renfrew (1986) as "peer polity interaction." Societies seldom develop new cultural features in isolation, nor do they receive the inspiration for them exclusively from distant societies that are more sophisticated than themselves. Societies always have neighbors, and they tend to be roughly comparable to their neighbors in size and political complexity. "Peer polities," to use Renfrew's term, interact with one another in a variety of ways. The result of their interactions over time is the sharing of cultural features.

The concept of peer polity interaction seems to fit very well what we know about Lamar culture. Lamar covers a large area in which there were a number of polities that were largely independent of one another and roughly equivalent in geographical size and level of complexity. Interaction doubtless occurred between neighboring Lamar polities and doubtless occurred at varying levels of intensity throughout the Mississippi period. Archaeological and ethnohistorical evidence documents several types of interaction as occurring among Lamar polities, including warfare, wealth exchange, political alliance, and even political hegemony. We can speculate that other types of interaction also occurred, including wife exchange and competition for prestige among elites.

Similar ecological, evolutionary, and historical processes probably underlie the existence of most other cultures that archaeologists have recognized in the Southeast—Stallings Island, Weeden Island, Coles Creek, Deptford, Dallas—and elsewhere. It is now fashionable among archaeologists to question the validity and scientific significance of such taxonomic units. Indeed, it is increasingly clear that taxonomic units such as Willey and Phillips's "culture" have little value in explaining the past. Their main value is to serve as a framework for communication among archaeologists. Nevertheless, the cultural similarities in time and space that underlie the archaeologist's cultures do exist, and they do need to be explained.

CHAPTER FIFTEEN

The Social Context of the Chiefdom of Ichisi

Charles Hudson

This day they came to a village where some principal Indians appeared as messengers from Ichisi; and one of them addressed Hernando de Soto and said three words, one after the other, in this manner: "Who are you, what do you want, where are you going?" (Ranjel 1922:86)

IN LATE MARCH of 1540 the people of the chiefdom of Ichisi first encountered people who had come to their land from the other side of the world. To these three measured questions asked by the principal men of Ichisi, De Soto replied:

that he was a captain of the great King of Spain; that in his name he had come to make known to them the holy faith of Christ; that they should acknowledge him and be saved and yield obedience to the Apostolic Church of Rome and to the Supreme Pontiff and Vicar of God, who lived there; and that in temporal affairs they should acknowledge for king and lord the Emperor, King of Castile, our Lord, as his vassals; and that they would treat them well in everything and that he would maintain toward them peace and justice just the same as toward all his Christian vassals. (Ranjel 1922:87)

Having no frame of reference in which to interpret "King of Spain," "Christ," "Apostolic Church of Rome," or

"Supreme Pontiff," it is likely that the principal men of Ichisi were baffled by De Soto's reply, and they can have had no real understanding of the true nature of the Europeans they found so abruptly in their midst.

As well, it is unlikely that De Soto or any of his men inquired into the nature of the people of Ichisi. Aside from determining what they could take from the Indians, sixteenth-century Spaniards normally made little inquiry into their cultural and social practices. However, by closely reading the documents of the sixteenth-century Spanish explorers of the Southeast, and by combining this documentary information with archaeological information, it is possible to arrive at a tentative interpretation of the chiefdom of Ichisi.

Since about 1980 a number of colleagues and I have been trying to reconstruct the trails of three parties of Spaniards who explored parts of the Southeast in the sixteenth century. These were the expeditions led by Hernando de Soto in 1539–43, by Tristán de Luna in 1559–61, and by Juan Pardo in 1566–68. In this endeavor I have collaborated with Chester DePratter and Marvin Smith, and I have sought the collaboration and advice of many other archaeologists and historians throughout the Southeast. The reason I have worked so long and seemingly so obsessively in reconstructing the routes of these expeditions is that if they can be firmly tied in with specific archaeological sites, it will become possible to combine information in the documents of these expeditions with a great body of accumulated archaeological information. This will make it possible to reconstruct at least the structural outlines of the more important native societies of the sixteenth-century Southeast. The reconstructions of these societies will necessarily be uneven in terms of fullness or completeness, but together they will constitute a kind of social geography of the entire region.

If these objectives can be achieved, it will provide archaeologists, ethnohistorians, and historians with what they have always lacked in the Southeast—a firmly established social and cultural baseline from which they can press their inquiries back into the prehistoric past and forward into the early historic past (Hudson 1987b). The sixteenth century can appropriately be called the protohistoric era—the time when historical documents were first written, but not in abundance, and the time with reference to which there can be the most fruitful collaboration between historians and archaeologists. I anticipate that we will soon be able to begin addressing questions about the geopolitics of sixteenth-century southeastern chiefdoms, that is, questions about broad interrelations among native polities throughout the entire southeastern region.

It should be understood that the quality and quantity of both historical and archaeological information varies from one part of the Southeast to another. Although the destruction of archaeological sites proceeds apace, in most places the archaeological record can be improved through further field research. With enough time and money, it should be possible, in theory, to compile a qualitatively balanced archaeological picture of the Southeast from the Atlantic Coast to Oklahoma and east Texas.

This is not the case with historical evidence. If the participants in the expeditions did not commit their observations and experiences to paper, they are lost forever. And of the information that was written down, only some of it has survived. And of the information that has survived, only some of it has been dredged out of archives. New documents may be expected to come to light that bear on the sixteenth-century exploration, but I think it can be said that scholars already have available most of the documents that contain information on native polities in the interior of the Southeast in the sixteenth century.

For some of the polities that De Soto encountered, it is possible to reconstruct a structural profile with some confidence. Such has been the case with Coosa, a para-mount chiefdom whose central town was the seat of power of a chief of chiefs (Hudson, Smith, Hally, Polhemus, and DePratter 1985). In this endeavor my colleagues and I were most fortunate in being able to use documents from the Luna and Pardo expeditions as corroborating infor-mation (DePratter et al. 1983; Hudson, Smith, DePratter, and Kelley 1985). The central town of Coosa was at the Little Egypt site, on the Coosawattee River in northwest-ern Georgia (Figure 15.1). The towns over which the chief of Coosa exercised most immediate control extended from the Little Egypt site to a point about 19 km down the Coosawattee River. Another chiefdom closely aligned with Coosa was Ulibahali, situated on the Coosa River in the vicinity of Rome, Georgia. To the north, Coosa had as tributaries the Napochies at present Chattanooga; Chiaha, whose center was on Zimmerman's Island near present Dandridge, Tennessee; and a cluster of towns on the Little Tennessee River, whose capital town may have been Satapo, at the Citico site (Hudson 1987a). To the south, Coosa had influence, if not real power, over the chiefdom of Talisi in the vicinity of present Childersburg, Alabama. The power or influence of the chief of Coosa over his various tributaries must have varied from one to another. His most secure power must have been over the nearby towns on the Coosawattee River. The Napochies paid tribute to Coosa three times a year in the form of deerskins, nuts, and other forest products, and surely it is significant that they do not appear to have been obliged to make payments in corn. Chiaha and Satapo must have paid Coosa tribute of some sort, but it is unlikely that they paid as dearly as did the people of Coosa proper. The people of Talisi may have paid deference to the chief of Coosa, but very little else. In other words, in such a large paramount chiefdom as Coosa, the actual power of a chief may have varied inversely with the distance from the central town. Different kinds of tributary status may have been symbolized by what was paid in tribute: corn, forest products, deference, and so on.

Another paramount chiefdom—Cofitachequi—had its center on the Wateree River near Camden, South Caro-lina (Hudson 1990). Cofitachequi had apparently been struck by an Old World disease before De Soto arrived, and it was in even deeper decline when Pardo arrived 26 years later (Hudson 1990:68–83). But from events that occurred during the two expeditions as revealed in the documents, it is possible to rough out a structural sketch of the size and nature of Cofitachequi. Like the chiefdom of Coosa, Cofitachequi was basically linear in shape, and like Coosa, it exercised control over people living on two river systems. From the testimony of Francisco of Chicora, an Indian who was captured on the South Carolina coast in 1521 by Spanish slavers, it is clear that the Indians of coastal South Carolina were paying tribute to a powerful paramount chief—Datha. From Francisco's account, it is not possible to be certain about where Datha had his seat of power, but Datha may well have been the chief of Cofitachequi. When Pardo visited Cofitachequi, many Indians from the coast and coastal plain congregated there to meet with him, although there was no longer a paramount chief of Cofitachequi. In fact, there was not even a *miko*—only a lower level *orata*. In its heyday the power of Cofitachequi extended east to the chiefdom of Ilasi (or Ilapi), with its center near present Cheraw, South Carolina, on the Pee Dee River. Ilasi controlled the river for an unknown distance upstream and downstream from Cheraw. It is clear from the De Soto documents that in 1540 Ilasi was tributary to Cofitachequi, making payments in corn (Ranjel 1922:100). Cofitachequi dominated towns to the north at least to the vicinity of present Rock Hill, South Carolina. One suspects that Cofitachequi exercised real power over these people, but historical evidence is lacking. Beyond this, when De Soto forced the "Lady of Cofitachequi" to go with him as he traveled northward, Indians all the way to the Blue Ridge Mountains paid deference to her (Gentleman of Elvas 1922:69–70).

The chiefdoms of Coosa and Cofitachequi were both linear in shape. Both were capable of having as tributaries people living on two river systems. Both had their main

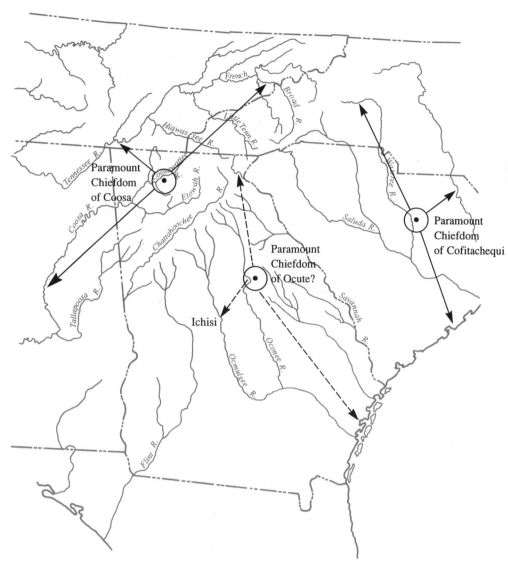

15.1. Proposed territories of paramount chiefdoms of Coosa, Ocute, and Cofitachequi.

towns at mound centers. Both encompassed people of several cultures or archaeological phases. It is known that both encompassed people speaking several different languages, and in the case of Cofitachequi, these languages were from at least two and possibly three or four language families (Booker et al. 1992).

From the De Soto documents it is clear that yet another paramount chiefdom—Ocute—lay to the west of the Savannah River (Hudson et al. 1984). The central towns of Ocute lay on the Oconee River between about present Milledgeville and present Greensboro. A tributary chiefdom—Altamaha—lay downstream. The central town of Altamaha was evidently located at the Shinholser site.

The question is, was the territorial extent of the power and influence of the paramount chiefdom of Ocute limited to the upper Oconee River? If Coosa and Cofitachequi are guides to what we should expect in a paramount chiefdom in what might be called the Lamar Southeast (Chapter 14, this volume), then, given the dimensions just

mentioned, Ocute is decidedly small, a veritable midget of a paramount chiefdom.

I would like to explore the possibility that the territory that was dominated or influenced by Ocute was much larger than this. I hesitate to call this a hypothesis, because the evidence is so scant it may not be possible to disprove this proposition. In many parts of the territory that Ocute may have controlled, much of the necessary archaeological research has not yet been done. Most notably, this includes the floodplain of the Ocmulgee River just below Macon.

Unfortunately the historical evidence is also scanty for the area in question. For Ocute, we lack the corroborating evidence from subsequent explorers that is available for Coosa and Cofitachequi. De Soto was the only major explorer to enter the Ocute area. Governor Mendez Canzo did send a soldier and two priests to Altamaha and Ocute in 1598, but their visit was brief, and they brought back very little social and political information (Worth 1994).

And because De Soto's travel through the area in which Ocute was located was so peaceful and unproblematic, the information in the De Soto documents is less than it would have been had there been more conflict and difficulty. As one might expect, the chroniclers devoted most of their writing to those situations in which the going was rough. Once De Soto entered the upper Coastal Plain and Fall Line area, the greatest obstacle he had to surmount was the several large rivers that had to be crossed. The people offered no resistance whatever.

Let us briefly review the societies De Soto encountered when he marched northward from Apalachee in the spring of 1540. After a difficult crossing to the western side of the Flint River, the first society he came to was Capachequi, whose towns lay southwest of present Albany, in the Chickasawhatchee swamp (Hudson et al. 1984:67). The reaction of the people of Capachequi was similar to that of the people of Apalachee. That is, they fled from their towns and hid in the swamps, and they harassed the Spaniards with guerilla raids. Very little archaeological research has been done in the Chickasawhatchee swamp, but a number of Mississippian sites are known to exist there, including two multiple mound sites whose cultural affiliation appears to be more with Fort Walton culture than with Lamar culture Lockett phase further up the Flint River (Worth 1989).

After resting for a few days at Capachequi, De Soto moved north for an indeterminate number of days to a place where they built a bridge across the Flint River, and here they crossed back to the eastern side of the river. (Why did they cross the Flint River twice when they could have proceeded north without crossing it at all? They did so to seize the food that was stored at Capachequi.) Quite near this second crossing, on the eastern side of the river, they came to a town that they called Toa. Using information in the documents, it is impossible to be certain about where this town was located. Using the location of old trails and roads, the area near present Montezuma seemed a likely location to me and my colleagues in our paper on this segment of the route (Hudson et al. 1984:68). More recently, John Worth has established that a native population (Lockett phase) did exist in the sixteenth century on the Flint River from the Fall Line to about 27 km downriver (1988:169–80). This means that De Soto and his men crossed the Flint several kilometers upstream from present Montezuma.

The chroniclers say very little about the town of Toa. Luys Hernandez de Biedma says it was rather larger than any they had seen up to this time (1922:10), but this may only mean that the settlement pattern of Toa was more compact than they had seen before. Ranjel only says that it was a large village (1922:85). The Gentleman of Elvas has more to say. He points out that they crossed a deserted wilderness between Capachequi and Toa,

and this indicates that they were two separate societies. He also notes that the houses at Toa were constructed differently from the ones they had encountered previously. In his description he makes it plain that beyond Toa they saw similar houses for quite some distance (1922:53).

Unfortunately, none of the chroniclers gives any indication of whether the town of Toa they visited was a part of a larger polity. But given the compact, linear shape of the territories of the next three chiefdoms they encountered—Ichisi, Ocute, and Cofitachequi—it is likely that Toa was the southernmost Lockett phase town.

Even though Toa was the largest town they had seen up to this point, Ranjel makes it clear that some members of the expedition had already concluded that the expedition was unlikely to lead them to the riches they desired, and they were reluctant to go any further. De Soto devised a clever ploy to keep his expedition together. He selected a contingent of 40 cavalry, and in great secrecy he departed from Toa at midnight. He and his cavalry traveled until darkness of the following day, covering the extraordinary distance of 12 leagues—more than twice the distance they ordinarily covered in a day. The next morning they arrived at the first village of Ichisi, on an island in the Ocmulgee River. Those who had been left behind at Toa appear to have fallen for this ploy. They took the secrecy of this maneuver to be an indication that De Soto expected to find great riches at the next town, and they followed, joining up with De Soto a few days later.

Departing from the first village of Ichisi, they traveled up the western bank of the Ocmulgee River to a place where they were ferried in dugout canoes across the river to the main town of Ichisi. My colleagues and I concluded that the most likely location of this was at the Lamar site (9BI2) (Hudson et al. 1984:70). How far did the chiefdom Ichisi extend up and down the Ocmulgee River? The historical evidence gives no answer. Cowarts phase ceramics do not extend very far down the Ocmulgee River from the Bullard site, which is about 19 km below the Lamar site (Williams and Shapiro 1986). Although additional archaeological research is needed on Cowarts phase, it is likely that the territory of Ichisi had a diameter less than the 40 km maximum proposed by Hally (Chapter 14, this volume).

De Soto remained at the main town of Ichisi for only one day. He wanted to press on to Ocute, whose chief was said to be a "great lord." The chief of Ichisi gave them a guide who spoke the language of Ocute, implying that a language difference existed between Ichisi and Ocute. They traveled eastward until they came to the Oconee River. They were ferried to the other side in dugout canoes supplied by the chief of Altamaha, who was subject to the paramount chief of Ocute.

When De Soto went from Altamaha to the main town of Ocute, it took him as much as two days to get there.

This means that it was located at about 25 to 55 km from Altamaha. In our original paper, my colleagues and I placed the center of Ocute at the Shoulderbone site, but recent research at this site by Mark Williams and Gary Shapiro indicates that Shoulderbone was a less impressive site than we had thought, and even more important, it may have had only a small resident population in 1540 (Williams and Shapiro 1986). Williams and Shapiro raise a question about whether the center of Ocute was at the Shoulderbone site, but they do not identify or locate any other site in the vicinity that could have been the central town of the chiefdom. Until such a site is found, the Shoulderbone site is still the best candidate.

To rephrase my initial question: if Ocute exercised real power within this 40-km circle, what was the geographical extent of its influence? One of the most striking things that the De Soto chroniclers report about Ocute and its tributary Altamaha is the unusual degree to which they were opposed to their mutual enemy Cofitachequi, a polity that lay more than 200 km to the east. The chief of Altamaha cautioned De Soto that he would be armed when he came to see him because he had to *habitually* carry arms on account of his enemy Cofitachequi. Perhaps nowhere else in all of De Soto's travels did he encounter such a state of enmity between two native polities.

It is noteworthy that Pedro Menéndez de Avilés encountered a similar enmity on the coast. On his very first visit to the coast to either side of the mouth of the Savannah River, he found that the chiefdom of Guale was at war with Orista and other towns of people who lived around Port Royal Sound. The territory immediately adjacent to the mouth of the Savannah River was as much an unoccupied wilderness as was the land bordering the river to the north (Hudson 1990).

The thread of inference I am following is this: if Cofitachequi and Ocute were so at war with each other, and had been for several generations, then one might expect some kind of parity between them in terms of size and structure. If the influence of Cofitachequi extended from the Fall-Line area north to the mountains and south to the coast, that of Ocute may have also. Then Ocute would have been pressured to place an equivalent team on the playing field. Thus, it is quite possible that the people of Guale were under the influence of Ocute. And although no historical evidence is known to exist, it is conceivable that Ocute had subjects and allies all the way to the mountains, perhaps including the people of Tugalo phase.

Did the power or influence of Ocute extend westward to Ichisi? It is quite conceivable that it did. If Ichisi did not pay tribute to Ocute, then it is at least probable that Ichisi would have lent Ocute military support against Cofitachequi. Both Ichisi and Ocute, it should be noted, were located on rivers that combine to form the Altamaha

River, which in turn empties into the Atlantic just to the northeast of the territory of the chiefdom of Guale.

I would not venture a guess as to what the political alignment of Toa was. Judging from the buffer zone that existed between Toa and Capachequi, they may have been hostile toward each other. But perhaps not: a similar uninhabited zone appears to have existed between the central cluster of Coosa towns on the Coosawattee River and the Dallas phase towns on the French Broad and on the Little Tennessee rivers (DePratter et al. 1985). Moreover, the cultural differences that probably existed between Capachequi and Toa do not in and of themselves mean that they could not have been members of the same polity. As previously indicated, cultural differences existed within both the paramount chiefdoms of Coosa and Cofitachequi.

I have no opinion about whether Toa might have been a tributary or ally of Ocute. So far as is known, neither Coosa nor Cofitachequi are known to have exerted their power or influence beyond a second river system. Toa was two rivers distant from Ocute. Moreover, Toa lay near the Chattahoochee and Tallapoosa rivers, and with the exception of a segment of the Tallapoosa near its junction with the Coosa, the sixteenth-century Spaniards explored neither of these rivers, so that there is absolutely no historical information on the native inhabitants of either of them for this period.

If yet another paramount chiefdom were centered on the Chattahoochee or Tallapoosa rivers, virtually all that we will ever know about it will have to be obtained through archaeological research. Because the more distant social connections of sixteenth-century southeastern paramount chiefdoms appear to have been rather thin, and the chiefdoms themselves unstable, it is at least dubious that archaeological research is capable of supplying the information that is needed. It would not, however, be prudent to altogether rule out this possibility. In any case, it is now up to the archaeological community to see what they can say about this.

It will also have to fall to archaeologists to make sense out of the collapse of the chiefdom that once occupied the Savannah River. When this collapse occurred, is it conceivable that a single vast paramount chiefdom centered on the Savannah River, extending westward to the Ocmulgee-Oconee River and eastward to the Wateree River? If so, this vast chiefdom must have collapsed through internal conflict. Or, as seems more likely, were there three separate chiefdoms on the three rivers? In which case the chiefdom on the Savannah River could have been the victim of aggression from one or both of the other two. And this in no way detracts from David Anderson's recent argument that a severe drought contributed to the decline of this chiefdom (Anderson 1990c).

If enough insight can be had into the causes of Mississippian warfare, then perhaps we may someday have an answer to this intriguing question. I think we would be less than honest if we did not consider the possibility that the chiefdom on the Savannah River may have declined because of an attritional conflict touched off by imponderables. It is possible that the cause of the decline and fall of the Savannah River chiefdom was that somebody said something about somebody else's mother, particularly if the rule of descent in these chiefdoms was matrilineal. I am being facetious to make the point that the cause or causes of the demise of the Savannah River chiefdom may have largely devolved from social causes and may not yield to archaeological analysis.

To me, this question about the relationships among the chiefdoms on the Oconee, Ocmulgee, and Flint rivers is almost as exciting as the answers that will eventually be put forth. It means, as I indicated earlier, that we are now beginning to ask questions about native geopolitics in the sixteenth century. As recently as ten years ago, I would not have thought this question possible.

In deference to the theme of this book, I have attempted to place the chiefdom of Ichisi in its larger social context. I hope that I have made it plain that there are some fundamental problems of evidence here—both historical and archaeological. But despite the tentativeness of this analysis, when Ichisi is situated in the larger social and political context in which it existed, some considerable gains can be realized. In large part, these gains in understanding have been made possible by combining accurate reconstructions of the routes of exploration of Hernando De Soto, Tristán de Luna, and Juan Pardo with great quantities of information that archaeologists have amassed in all parts of the Southeast since the excavations at Ocmulgee fifty years ago.

Charles Hudson

CHAPTER SIXTEEN

Ocmulgee Fields Culture and the Historical Development of Creek Ceramics

Vernon James Knight, Jr.

MACON DURING THE 1930s was the setting of the first important attempt to apply archaeological data to the problem of Creek origins. The topic of Creek origins had been already central to the work of ethnologist John R. Swanton (1911, 1922, 1928b), whose conclusions had rested partly on historical sources and partly on Creek folklore. The archaeological program centered at Macon seemed to hold the further prospect of tracking Creek culture into prehistory, documenting the presumed relevance of Creek ethnology to the large mound sites found in Georgia.

Actually, however, the facts brought to bear on this question proved inconclusive. The picture of proto-Creek archaeological culture has remained, until very recently, indistinct and controversial. There is still no consensus on the ethnic identification of archaeological sites in the Georgia area even as recent as those dated to the sixteenth century. Yet, the problem of Creek origins has not lost its relevance. Creek ethnology and ethnohistory are abundantly documented, and these constitute a profound store of knowledge for which archaeology can supply the developmental context. It still remains to apply the "direct

historical approach" to this question in a vigorous and systematic manner.

The material culture first to be established firmly as historic Creek was that found in the Trading Post context on the Macon Plateau (Kelly 1939) and ultimately referred to as Ocmulgee Fields culture (Fairbanks 1952b). A somewhat older archaeological context was thoroughly explored at the nearby Lamar site; the controversy that ensued centered on whether or not the Trading Post materials were a direct development from Lamar culture. If such a lineal development could be shown, then it could be argued that the earlier Lamar, and by extension also the immediate predecessors of Lamar in central Georgia, were proto-Creek. The problem was that no site in the Macon area, nor any elsewhere, showed this development stratigraphically. Since Margaret Clayton Russell (1976) has already produced a fine analysis of this historical controversy, only a few of the main points need be reviewed here.

Kelly, in the first published summary of the Macon investigations (1938c), discussed the aboriginal ceramic complex from the Trading Post almost entirely in view of its suggested developmental continuity with Lamar. In support of this continuity he cited "the persistence of the site-marking traits of incised pottery decoration, rim treatment, and burial traits to the historic threshold" (1938c:57). In so doing Kelly speculated that Lamar represented the local Creek culture of the precontact period.

It was Fairbanks, however, who fully developed this line of thinking. Fairbanks focused attention on ceramic continuities, not only in specific pottery types but also in aspects of vessel shapes and vessel assemblages, design layouts, motifs, and appendages (1952b, 1955, 1958). He further attempted an explanation of the kinds of changes he observed. Ocmulgee Fields ceramic features appeared in almost all cases as crude or debased versions of Lamar features, which suggested the disruptive effects of European contact as a likely cause. While leaving room for the possibility that the Lamar style in other areas might not be proto-Creek, Fairbanks was firm in his assertion that original "type site" Lamar, because of its continuity with Ocmulgee Fields, must surely have been the product of Muskogean-speaking peoples.

The opposing view was best articulated by Sears (Willey and Sears 1952; Sears 1955, 1969). Sears pointed

181

out that historic Cherokee pottery was closer to Lamar in style than was any known historic Creek complex, including that at the Macon Trading Post. Sears felt that a number of the proposed ceramic continuities from Lamar to Ocmulgee Fields were merely broad horizon styles having little to do specifically with Creek culture. While Fairbanks thought that the dominant brushed surface treatment on Ocmulgee Fields series jars was related to Lamar-style complicated stamping, Sears disagreed, proposing that brushing was an introduced trait of western origin. Further, the aboriginal pottery at the Trading Post was largely shell tempered, in this respect differing not only from the grit tempered Lamar, but also from the grit and sand tempered historic Creek pottery of Kasita on the Chattahoochee. Sears concluded that the Ocmulgee Fields complex was not derived from any kind of Lamar; that it was basically intrusive in central Georgia; and that its ancestry was probably to be found in one of the Alabama-area complexes, perhaps even at Moundville.

At that point, the question of proto-Creek archaeological culture reached an impasse. More recent students of the problem, including Russell (1976), Penman (1976), and Dickens (1979), brought slightly different perspectives, but few new facts. As recently as 1975, Russell (1976:63) could still assert (here following Sears 1955: 148) that no one had yet demonstrated a convincing developmental sequence linking any of the historic Creek complexes to any kind of Lamar. Penman (1976), in the meantime, having been involved in Hale Smith's restudy of the original Lamar site materials (Smith 1973a), arrived at the conclusion that Lamar in central Georgia was Cherokee.

For many years, Fairbanks's position regarding the genesis of Ocmulgee Fields was suspended in a field of doubt, and not only because of the lack of stratigraphic data to support it. It should be understood also that the original arguments in favor of a Lamar-Ocmulgee Fields development were not based on any real ceramic analysis other than trait-by-trait comparisons (Fairbanks 1952b: 295, 298). Certainly no quantitative or even adequately descriptive studies of Trading Post or Lamar site ceramics (other than the type descriptions) were available for three decades following the Macon area excavations. Naturally, this handicapped comparative study.

Further, there were taxonomic problems, both at the level of pottery types and at the level of the archaeological phase or culture called Ocmulgee Fields. Because of the specific nature of the Trading Post pottery assemblage, the types Ocmulgee Fields Incised and Ocmulgee Fields Plain were defined without reference to a shell/nonshell temper dichotomy, and Walnut Roughened was set up to potentially include a range of roughening techniques such as brushing, stippling, and corncob stamping. This was perfectly adequate for the original collections, but

as extended to materials in other regions and of slightly different date, pottery collections could be classed as Ocmulgee Fields that were quite dissimilar from the original. Partly for this reason, the term "Ocmulgee Fields" eventually was extended far beyond its original meaning to encompass a number of surprisingly different things.

In considering the further resolution of this controversy, it has become clear first of all that the problem would have to be attacked from within the core area of Creek development, rather than on the periphery (compare Russell 1976). This has meant that new data would have to be forthcoming from the Coosa, Tallapoosa, and Chattahoochee river valleys. More particularly, the key gap was in the investigation of sites dating to the critical seventeenth-century period—that is, the period dating between that of most Lamar complexes and that of the various documented historic Creek assemblages. It is in these areas that substantial progress can be reported for the past decade.

Before reporting on this progress, it will be helpful to agree upon a firm conception of "Creek." The historic Creeks were a polyethnic confederation of tribes during the Colonial period, and in searching for "Creek origins," one has to be careful to specify exactly whose history and whose culture is being sought. For the present purpose, this usage will refer specifically to the early history and culture connected with the dominant group of Muskogee and Hitchiti-speaking towns that formed the indigenous core of the confederacy. During Colonial times these core towns resided on the Coosa, Tallapoosa, and Chattahoochee rivers. Within the same region, evidence of local continuities in material culture permits the tracing of their prehistoric antecedents. A minimal list of these dominant towns would include Coosa, Abihka, Okfuskee, Tukabatchee, Tallassee, Coweta, Kasita, and Apalachicola, along with their various branch towns and outsettlements.

In the central Coosa River valley of Alabama, the Colonial-era home of the Coosa/Abihka branch of the Creeks, recent surveys and excavations have begun to clarify the local cultural sequence from the sixteenth century through the early nineteenth. The University of Alabama inaugurated the East Alabama Archaeological Survey in 1983 (Knight et al. 1984; Knight 1985a), whose aims were focused primarily on the question of proto-Creek culture in that area. As a result of this preliminary work, three seasons of excavation were devoted to the Hightower Village site (Walling and Wilson 1985), a site of local Lamar (Kymulga phase) affiliation dating to the late sixteenth and early seventeenth century. Hightower Village is located in the Tallasseehatchee Creek drainage of southern Talladega County. Complementing this is the excavation by the University of Alabama at Birmingham of the Rodgers-CETA site, another local Lamar-related village located a short distance from Hightower on Talladega Creek (Nance 1988).

The Tallapoosa River valley has also witnessed a flurry of new work aimed at late prehistoric and early historic occupation. Auburn University at Montgomery has contributed an excavation of the Shine II phase (Lamar) component of the Kulumi site on the lower Tallapoosa River (unpublished data provided by Ned J. Jenkins), which promises to improve the understanding of the Late Mississippian and Early Historic periods in that region. Reanalysis of Fairbanks's stratigraphic testing at the site of Big Tallassee (Knight and Smith 1980), along with excavations by the University of Alabama at Tukabatchee (Knight 1985b), has clarified the definition and chronological position of the Atasi phase, a local post-Lamar manifestation. The University of Alabama has also sponsored work on the upper Tallapoosa River where yet another local Lamar variation, called the Avery complex, is in evidence (Knight 1980). Finally, Auburn University has conducted a comprehensive survey of the lower Tallapoosa (Waselkov 1981), has completed excavations at Fort Toulouse (Waselkov et al. 1982), and is currently involved in extensive excavations at the Creek sites of Huithlewauli and Fushatchi.

For the lower Chattahoochee River valley, the University of Alabama has conducted relevant surveys and excavations during the past several years (Knight and Mistovich 1984), most recently including excavations at the Blackmon site, type site for the seventeenth-century Blackmon phase in that region (Mistovich and Knight 1986). Work by the Columbus Museum of Arts and Sciences has been carried out at such important sites as Abercrombie, Coweta Tallahassee, and Yuchi Town (Schnell 1982, 1984).

All of this recent research, especially the excavation of several early historic aboriginal town sites in the core area of Creek development, cannot fail to have an effect on the questions so long held in dispute. The information is in need of synthesis; in the remaining discussion the terminology currently favored in the various University of Alabama projects will be emphasized. A revision of the overall taxonomic structure, which defines regional sub-traditions segmented into local short-term phases, has served the purpose of integrating and correlating the local sequences. The corresponding project of revising local ceramic classification, so that a degree of intersite comparability is achieved, has not yet been carried as far. This situation is evident in the outline of phase characterizations appended to this chapter, where rosters of pottery types are listed as they presently stand in various stages of refinement. A limited adherence to traditional typological approaches may actually be, in this case, an impediment to explaining variability and change, and one may expect that future comparative approaches oriented to other

ceramic variables would prove rewarding. Nonetheless, a preliminary generalization may be advanced here: All of the various historic Creek material culture assemblages are the products of three indigenous regional sub-traditions within eastern Alabama and western Georgia. In all cases, historic Creek assemblages have seemingly clear predecessors in local Lamar-related manifestations, and the development from Lamar to Creek in these areas can now be shown in some detail. Fairbanks, it seems, is vindicated.

The three regional sub-traditions are at home in the Coosa, Tallapoosa, and Chattahoochee river drainages respectively (Figure 16.1). Change within each of the three sequences is currently handled by means of a series of short-term phases that can be identified with distinctive pottery type assemblages (Figure 16.2). Summary characteristics of these assemblages as they are now understood are given in an appendix to this chapter.

The three sub-traditions are to a certain degree interrelated. While it is convenient to classify the late Mississippian horizon in each case as a regional expression of "Lamar" culture (that is, jars possessing complicated stamped surface treatment, grit-tempered paste and pinched-rims), it should also be appreciated that a central commonality linking together the three sub-traditions is the degree of stylistic borrowing and interaction evident among them with non-Lamar cultures to the west and north. Indeed, some of the phases that lie at the background of Creek culture seem to owe as much to Dallas culture as to Lamar. Several of the changes seen in any one sub-tradition are also seen in the other two, reflecting horizon styles, yet it is interesting that the local flavor of ceramic development persists through the historic period and accounts for the main regional variation in historic Creek ceramics. The features of the case recall the concept of the "area co-tradition" as used by Bennett (1948) and Rouse (1957).

In the middle Coosa drainage, the local late Lamar complex is called the Kymulga phase. This is closely similar to the Barnett phase (Hally 1970) of the upper Coosa drainage, as seen at the Little Egypt and King sites. Excavated Kymulga assemblages at Rodgers-CETA and Hightower Village show the co-occurrence of Lamar-style complicated stamping, brushing, and cob stamping on ceramic jars. Hightower Village, in addition, appears to show a smooth transition to the subsequent Woods Island phase (Morrell 1965), a transition mainly involving a loss and simplification of certain ceramic elements (including loss of complicated stamping, with retention of brushing). A parallel and converging development is seen upstream in the change from Barnett phase to Weiss-type McKee Island (Little and Curren 1981), although in the Weiss Basin this shift appears to occur at a slightly earlier period than downstream. The eighteenth-century product of

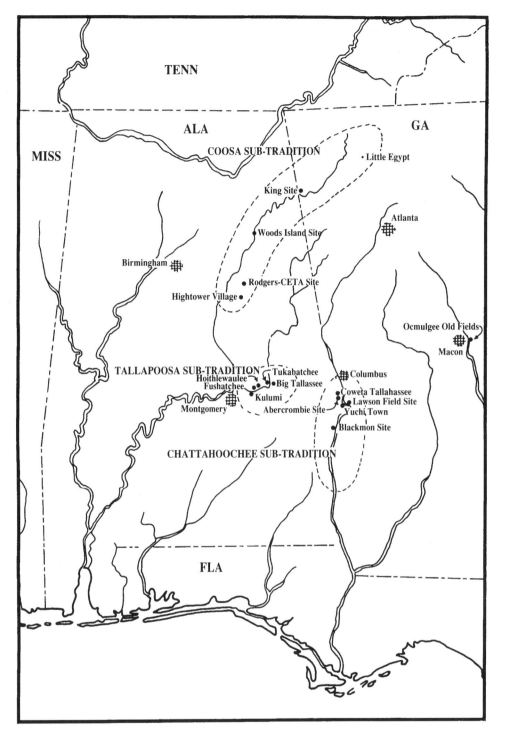

16.1. Map showing location of Creek pottery sub-traditions.

this regional sub-tradition is the shell-tempered pottery of the Childersburg phase (DeJarnette and Hansen 1960). (Post-Childersburg phase pottery of the middle Coosa drainage, known from Fort Leslie of the Creek War period, is primarily sand tempered and is almost indistinguishable from late Tallapoosa phase ceramics to the south and east.)

The regional sub-tradition located in the Tallapoosa

Valley has Shine II as the local Lamar variant, followed by the Atasi phase and terminating with the historic Creek Tallapoosa phase of the eighteenth and early nineteenth centuries. Of importance here is the observation that Atasi phase ceramics are perfectly intermediate in style between Shine II Lamar and the local historic Creek (Knight and Smith 1980; Knight 1985b).

The third regional sub-tradition, that of the Lower

Year	COOSA SUB-TRADITION		TALLAPOOSA SUB-TRADITION		CHATTAHOOCHEE SUB-TRADITION
	Upper Coosa	Middle Coosa	Upper Tallapoosa	Lower Tallapoosa	
1850	Removal	Removal	Removal	Removal	Removal
1800	Cherokee	Fort Leslie	Tallapoosa Phase	Tallapoosa Phase (Late / Early)	Lawson Field Phase (Late / Early)
1750		Childersburg Phase			
1700	"Weiss-Type" McKee Island	Woods Island Phase	Atasi Phase (confined to southern Piedmont)	Atasi Phase (Late / Early)	Blackmon Phase
1650		Kymulga Phase (Lamar) (Late / Early)			Abercrombie Phase (Late / Early)
1600	Barnett Phase (Lamar)		Avery Phase (Lamar)	Data Gap (Late Shine II Phase ?)	
1550					Stewart Phase (Lamar)
1500	Little Egypt Phase (Lamar)	unoccupied	unoccupied	Shine II Phase (Lamar)	
1450					Bull Creek Phase (Lamar)
1400					

16.2. Chronological chart for the three pottery sub-traditions.

Chattahoochee Valley, has the Bull Creek and Stewart phases as the local variants of Lamar. The late Lamar Stewart phase is followed by the Abercrombie and Blackmon phases, then by the Lawson Field phase representing eighteenth- and nineteenth-century Lower Creek culture. Again, a regular progression of ceramic style from Lamar to Creek may be documented. However, such a progression is especially complicated, in this case, by the additional contribution of many non-Lamar ceramic features derived from the north and west, which imparts to the intermediate assemblages a "hybrid" character.

This stylistic contribution is recognized in the following elements: shell-tempered vessel forms; specific rectilinear and curvilinear incised designs; shell-tempered, cord-marked, and noded vessels; and modeled decorative features and appendages, most of which are probably borrowed from Dallas and McKee Island phases in the eastern Tennessee-northeastern Alabama area. Such stylistic borrowing shows continuity through time, being evident in Stewart, Abercrombie, and Blackmon phase assemblages. Abercrombie ceramics also show an emphasis on reduction firing/burnishing, dry-paste fine-line incising, and appliqué work, which are features indicating an additional stylistic connection with non-Lamar central Alabama material. What these external relationships might signify for cultural processes is still unclear, yet they are not so pervasive as to cancel out the essential continuity of the sequence as a local sub-tradition (compare Schnell et al. 1981:245).

While most of the details of ceramic change during this period are different from region to region, there are a few trends that are common to all three. Among these are: (1) the virtually complete loss of complicated stamping by the first quarter of the seventeenth century, (2) replacement on the same vessel forms by brushing (with evident overlap with complicated stamping in Abercrombie and Kymulga), (3) appearance of corncob stamping as a minority mode during the seventeenth century, and (4) progressive reduction in incised line width and line spacing from the sixteenth through the eighteenth century. These trends are more or less as Fairbanks had predicted based on materials having much poorer control.

Returning to Macon, does original Ocmulgee Fields material culture find a place within this taxonomic structure? It does, and its parentage is where the historic documentation says it ought to be—on the Chattahoochee. The movement of a few Creek towns eastward to the Ocmulgee and Oconee rivers took place briefly between about 1690 and the Yamassee War. The towns involved were primarily Lower Creek from the Chattahoochee (Boyd 1958). On a 1690 timeline these would be recognized as Blackmon phase villages with, for example, incised pottery tempered with mixed shell and sand, shell-tempered roughened jars crudely incised above the shoulder, cob-marked ware, handles, and so forth. This is just what is found at the Macon Trading Post: essentially a geographically transplanted Blackmon phase assemblage, minus certain minority types that, on the Chattahoochee River, indicate contact with the Apalachee mission area.

The Trading Post ceramic complex does have an ancestry in Lamar ceramics, not in central Georgia Lamar but in Stewart phase Lamar and Abercrombie of the Chattahoochee sequence (compare Russell 1976, who first suggested this). "Type site" Lamar has nothing to do with it, and in this sense Sears was exactly right: Ocmulgee Fields pottery *is* intrusive in central Georgia (and also on the Savannah, at Palachacolas Town; Caldwell 1948). Ironically, Ocmulgee Fields seems a clearer archaeological example of an intrusive population in central Georgia than is the much-debated example of Macon Plateau culture.

Having outlined these relationships, it is intriguing to consider possible implications for proto-Creek archaeological culture and the ethnic correlation of archaeological phases. Recognizing that this procedure is full of hazards, the following hypotheses are nonetheless suggested, supported on the strength of the identified sub-traditions and their historic correlation with ethnic and linguistic groupings. First, Kymulga phase Lamar of the middle Coosa region is Muskogee, specifically ancestral to the Abihka group of Creek towns. Second, Shine II phase Lamar, and by extension the mature Mississippian Shine I phase, are also Muskogee, specifically ancestral to the Tallapoosa group of Creek towns. Finally, Bull Creek and Stewart phase Lamar, and by extension the earlier Rood phase Mississippian out of which Bull Creek develops, represent Hitchiti-speaking peoples ancestral to the Hitchiti-Apalachicola group of Lower Creek towns.

Where does this leave the Lamar site? By itself, unfortunately, but Hudson and his associates may rescue it from complete historical obscurity by suggesting that De Soto may have come across it by the name of Ichisi. In that case, it is evidently ancestral to Ocheese, which in later Creek history was simply a little-noticed Lower Creek town. That these people were originally distinct from the Hitchiti speakers of the Lower Chattahoochee area is suggested by their name, a Hitchiti-language term for "people of foreign speech" (Swanton 1922:148).

Appendix: Phase Characterizations

KYMULGA PHASE, COOSA SUB-TRADITION

Estimated Dating: ca. A.D. 1500–1650. An acceptable radiocarbon date of 380 ± 90 years: A.D. 1570 has been reported for the Rodgers-CETA site (Nance 1984). European goods at Hightower Village are estimated to date between ca. 1560 and 1650 (Walling and Wilson 1985).

Documented Sites: Hightower Village, 1TA150 (Walling and Wilson 1985); Rodgers-CETA, 1TA171 (Nance 1988).

Basic References: Knight et al. 1984; Knight 1985a.

Roster of Ceramic Types (after Knight et al. 1984):
    grit-tempered plain
    grit/grog-tempered plain
    coarse sand/shell-tempered plain
    fine shell-tempered plain
    coarse shell-tempered plain

shell/grog-tempered plain
clay/grog-tempered plain
Coarse Shell-Tempered Brushed
clay/grog-tempered brushed
shell/grog-tempered brushed
Alabama River Appliqué
grit/grog-tempered incised
coarse shell-tempered incised
clay/grog-tempered incised
coarse sand/shell-tempered complicated stamped
grit tempered-complicated stamped

Discussion: No formal typology has yet been proposed for Kymulga phase ceramics (see Knight 1985a; Nance 1988). The diagnostic pottery assemblage overall bears a strong resemblance to that of the Barnett phase (Hally 1970), one of the chief differences being the significant presence of clay or grog tempering in Kymulga in contrast to its apparent absence in Barnett.

Continuities: No immediate predecessor to the Kymulga phase is currently known in the middle Coosa Valley. See Woods Island phase for continuities with Kymulga.

WOODS ISLAND PHASE, COOSA SUB-TRADITION

Estimated Dating: ca. A.D. 1650–1715. European associations at the type site appear to date largely between 1670 and 1700, with some post-1700 material.

Type Site: Woods Island, 1SC40 (Morrell 1965).

Basic References: Morrell 1965; Knight et al. 1984; Knight 1985a.

Roster of Ceramic Types (after Morrell 1965):
    McKee Island Plain
    McKee Island Incised
    McKee Island Brushed
    McKee Island Cord Marked

Discussion: Woods Island phase ceramics are quite similar to the varieties of McKee Island culture found upriver in the Weiss Basin (DeJarnette et al. 1973) and the Gadsden, Alabama, area. The same roster of types is shared, although brushed and cord-marked shell-tempered pottery are greatly diminished in frequency in the Weiss Basin (Morrell 1965). This seems to be merely a function of chronological difference; the Weiss Basin sites are earlier.

Continuities: Continuities from Kymulga are apparent in the similarity of plain, brushed, and incised pottery, and in associated vessel forms, appendages, and rim decoration. However, many of these same features are also shared with late Dallas/McKee Island shell-tempered pottery of the Tennessee Valley. Since the latter is clearly the source of cord marking in Woods Island, the actual degree of ceramic continuity between Kymulga and Woods Island remains, for the present, an open question. Cord marking appears to be extremely rare in Kymulga. There is no doubt, however, that all of these phenomena, including Barnett, participate in the same ceramic tradition, all indicating late Dallas as an inspiration for the shell-tempered pottery.

CHILDERSBURG PHASE, COOSA SUB-TRADITION

Estimated Dating: ca. A.D. 1715–80. European trade material from the type site has been dated between 1700 and 1775, with the bulk of the material datable to a more restricted range of 1750–75 (DeJarnette and Hansen 1960).

Type Site: Childersburg site, 1TA1 (DeJarnette and Hansen 1960).

Other Documented Sites: Bead Field (Abihkutci), 1TA208; and others reported by Knight et al. (1984).

Basic References: DeJarnette and Hansen 1960; Knight et al. 1984; Knight 1985a.

Roster of Ceramic Types (after DeJarnette and Hansen 1960):
  McKee Island Plain
  McKee Island Incised
  McKee Island Brushed
  Childersburg Plain
  Childersburg Incised

Discussion: This typology is a minimal one because no detailed work with Childersburg phase materials has been performed since the excavation of the type site. Childersburg Plain and Childersburg Incised are sand-tempered types apparently equivalent to Tallapoosa phase types. University of Alabama collections from the Childersburg phase site of Bead Field (Abihkutci) were recently analyzed (Knight et al. 1984), and in them were recognized substantial amounts of fine clay/grog temper in combination with the dominant shell temper. If the attribute of clay/grog temper were incorporated into a Childersburg phase typology, this collection and others would undoubtedly require several additional types.

Continuities: Childersburg phase pottery assemblages are so closely similar to earlier Woods Island phase assemblages that the two are usually impossible to distinguish in small collections. Continuities include incised designs, brushing, rim features, vessel forms, and shell as the dominant temper.

SHINE II PHASE, TALLAPOOSA SUB-TRADITION

Estimated Dating: ca. A.D. 1400–1550. No radiocarbon dates are presently available. Ceramic cross-ties are apparent with Stewart phase Lamar on the Chattahoochee. Earlier Shine I is Mature Mississippian, with some features indicating partial contemporaneity with Dallas.

Type Site: Jere Shine site, 1MT6.

Other Documented Sites: Kulumi, 1MT3 (N. J. Jenkins, personal communication); Tukabatchee, 1EE32 (Knight 1985b).

Basic References: Chase 1979; Knight 1985b.

Roster of Ceramic Types:
  nonshell-tempered plain
  black burnished
  Lamar Complicated Stamped
  Mercier Check Stamped
  Lamar Incised (varieties undefined)
  shell-tempered plain
  shell-tempered burnished plain
  shell/grog-tempered plain

Discussion: No adequate discussion of a Shine II pottery assemblage yet exists in print. Most of the pottery of the Shine II component at Kulumi reportedly is plain (ca. 85 percent). Lamar Complicated Stamped comprises only about 10 percent of the assemblage, the stamping modes being reminiscent of Stewart phase Lamar on the Chattahoochee. The other types occur in small frequency.

Continuities: Much of the curvilinear incising found in the later Atasi phase appears to be prefigured in Shine II. Incising on the interior rim of flaring-rim bowls is a noteworthy point of continuity into Atasi. Apparently there is also considerable ceramic continuity from earlier Shine I, but this must await a detailed examination.

ATASI PHASE, TALLAPOOSA SUB-TRADITION

Estimated Dating: ca. A.D. 1600–1715. At Tukabatchee, associated European goods have an estimated date of ca. 1630–50 (Knight 1985b).

Type Site: Atasi site, 1MC9.

Other Documented Sites: Big Tallassee, 1MC1 (Knight and Smith 1980); Tukabatchee, 1EE32 (Knight 1985b).

Basic References: Knight and Smith 1980; Knight 1985b.

Roster of Ceramic Types (after Knight 1985b):
  nonshell-tempered coarse plain
  nonshell-tempered burnished plain
  Lamar Incised, *var. Ocmulgee Fields*
  Lamar Incised, *var. Atasi*
  Lamar Burnished Incised, *var. Atasi*
  Chattahoochee Roughened, *var. Chattahoochee*
  Chattahoochee Roughened, *var. Wedowee*
  shell-tempered coarse plain
  shell-tempered burnished incised
  Walnut Roughened, *var. McKee Island*

Discussion: The Atasi phase, as recognized ceramically, is arbitrarily carved out of a tight stylistic continuum from Shine II (Lamar) through Tallapoosa phase (Upper Creek). Atasi incising is distinguished from the later material by its broad line and relatively wide spacing in designs made up of parallel lines. The shell-tempered complement is scarce and its relationships so far undetermined.

Continuities: Among the inheritances from Shine II are bold, curvilinear incising on bowl exteriors and the interior rims of flaring-rim bowls. Coarse sand or grit temper remains dominant, with shell as a minority. The bulk of the pottery is undecorated.

TALLAPOOSA PHASE, TALLAPOOSA SUB-TRADITION

Estimated Dating: ca. A.D. 1715–1836. The only point at issue is the arbitrary beginning date. Securely dated contexts at Nuyaka (Dickens 1979) and Tukabatchee (Knight 1985b) belong to the second half of the eighteenth century and later. Contexts dated to ca. 1730 at Huithlewauli are included in the phase construct.

Documented Sites: Nuyaka, 1TP25 (Dickens 1979); Big Tallassee, 1MC1 (Knight and Smith 1980); Tukabatchee, 1EE32 (Knight 1985b).

Basic References: Fairbanks 1962; Dickens 1979; Knight 1985b.

Roster of Ceramic Types (after Knight 1985b):
nonshell-tempered coarse plain
nonshell-tempered burnished plain
Lamar Incised, var. *Ocmulgee Fields*
Lamar Incised, var. *Atasi*
Lamar Burnished Incised, var. *Ocmulgee Fields*
Lamar Burnished Incised, var. *Atasi*
Chattahoochee Roughened, var. *Chattahoochee*
Chattahoochee Roughened, var. *Wedowee*
Kasita Red Filmed
shell-tempered coarse plain
shell-tempered coarse incised
Walnut Roughened, var. *McKee Island*

Discussion: This material has been previously referred to as the "Ocmulgee Fields" horizon on the Tallapoosa. The complex is well known from a number of large eighteenth-century Creek town sites.

Continuities: The Tallapoosa phase roster of pottery types is virtually the same as that for the preceding Tallapoosa phase, the initial differences being largely a matter of relative frequencies (for a comparison see Knight 1985b). During the late portion of the phase, the roster is greatly simplified with many varieties disappearing.

STEWART PHASE, LOWER CHATTAHOOCHEE SUB-TRADITION

Estimated Dating: A.D. 1475–1550. A MASCA-corrected radiocarbon date of A.D. 1530–1610 ± 70 is available for a Stewart phase structure on Mound A at the Rood's Landing site, 9SW1. No European goods have been recovered from Stewart phase contexts to date.

Type Site: Rood's Landing site, 9SW1, final construction stage of Mound A (Caldwell 1955b).

Other Documented Sites: Kolomoki (Sears 1956); site 9CY51 (Kelly et al. 1962).

Basic References: Schnell 1989, 1990.

Roster of Ceramic Types:
Lamar Plain
Lamar Complicated Stamped (local varieties)
Lamar Incised
Pinellas Incised (local varieties)
Fort Walton Incised
Roods Incised
Mercier Check Stamped

Discussion: The Stewart phase results from a recent subdivision of the Bull Creek phase as previously discussed by McMichael and Kellar (1960), Ferguson (1971), and Knight and Mistovich (1984), among other writers. The name "Bull Creek phase" is now restricted to site components ceramically similar to the Bull Creek type site in Muskogee County, Georgia, 9ME1, which

apparently predates the Stewart phase and probably belongs roughly to the period A.D. 1400–1475. Although no standard or widely accepted ceramic typology has been worked out for the Stewart phase, a good assemblage description is available from Broyles's work on site 9CY51 (Kelly et al. 1962). The assemblage is generally characterized as a blend of Lamar and Fort Walton.

Continuities: Pottery of the Stewart phase fits within a formal continuum beginning with the early Mississippian Rood phase and continuing through the Bull Creek phase of Lamar culture. The Lamar pottery that forms part of the post-Stewart Abercrombie phase is little modified from Stewart. Curvilinear incising on Pinellas and Roods Incised of the Stewart phase stylistically prefigures Abercrombie Incised.

ABERCROMBIE PHASE, LOWER CHATTAHOOCHEE SUB-TRADITION

Estimated Dating: ca. A.D. 1550–1650. Late sixteenth-century European goods have been found with burials by Schnell (1983). The European goods previously found in other Abercrombie site burials excavated by Moore (1907) and Hurt (1975) are evidently more recent, dating to the mid-seventeenth century. One radiocarbon date run on charred corncobs is available for the type component: 160 ± 90 years: A.D. 1790.

Type Site: Abercrombie (aka Kendrick) site, 1RU61.

Other Documented Sites: Woolfolks, 9CE3 (Hurt 1975).

Basic References: Hurt 1947, 1975; Fairbanks 1955; Schnell 1970; Kurjack 1975.

Roster of Ceramic Types (after Kurjack 1975; see also Fairbanks 1955, Hurt 1975, Mistovich and Knight 1986):
Lamar Complicated Stamped
Lamar Bold Incised
Fort Walton Incised
Abercrombie Incised
Abercrombie Brushed
Abercrombie Plain
Walnut Roughened
red filmed
coarse shell plain
fine shell plain
residual brushed
residual incised
residual check stamped

Discussion: There is little agreement in the Abercrombie typologies favored by Fairbanks, Hurt, and Kurjack. Basically, Abercrombie ceramics segregate into two series, one grit tempered (Lamar) and the other shell tempered, with little overlap in decoration. The shell-tempered series has an apparent Dallas-like aspect and also exhibits a relationship with Alabama River phase pottery. Fine shell and sand temper are used in combination.

Continuities: Lamar and Fort Walton types of the Abercrombie phase are inherited directly from the preceding Stewart phase of Lamar culture. Abercrombie phase incised motifs bear a relationship to those of the earlier Stewart phase types Roods Incised and Pinellas Incised.

BLACKMON PHASE, LOWER CHATTAHOOCHEE
SUB-TRADITION

Estimated Dating: ca. A.D. 1650–1715. The best firmly dated association is Fort Apalachicola, 1RU101, dating to 1689–91 (Kurjack and Pearson 1975). Contexts at the type site (Mistovich and Knight 1986) appear to predate the establishment of English trade in the area (ca. 1685).

Type Site: Blackmon site, 1BR25 (Mistovich and Knight 1986).

Other Documented Sites: Yuchi Town, 1RU63 (Schnell 1982); Fort Apalachicola, 1RU101 (Kurjack and Pearson 1975); Patterson site, 1RU66 (Kurjack 1975); Abercrombie site, 1RU61 (probably) (Kurjack 1975).

Basic References: Schnell n.d.; Knight and Mistovich 1984; Mistovich and Knight 1986.

Roster of Ceramic Types (after Mistovich and Knight 1986; see also Kurjack 1975; Kurjack and Pearson 1975):
   shell-tempered plain
   shell-tempered burnished plain
   shell-tempered incised
   shell-tempered burnished incised
   Walnut Roughened, *var. McKee Island*
   Fortune Noded, *var. Crow Creek*
   McKee Island Cord Marked
   nonshell-tempered plain
   nonshell-tempered burnished plain
   Chattahoochee Roughened, *var. Chattahoochee*
   Lamar Incised, *var. Ocmulgee Fields*
   Lamar Burnished Incised, *var. Ocmulgee Fields*
   Mission (Kasita) Red Filmed
   Leon Check Stamped
   Lamar Complicated Stamped, *var. Curlee*

Discussion: Before initial recognition of the phase by Schnell, Blackmon phase assemblages were not distinguished either from Abercrombie or from "Ocmulgee Fields." External connections are evident with McKee Island/Woods Island phases in Alabama and with the Apalachee mission area in Florida. As Schnell (1990:69) points out, "This phase is to be identified with the Apalachicola province of the early Spanish documents."

Continuities: Continuities from the Abercrombie phase include shell, often mixed with sand or grit, as the dominant pottery temper; burnishing on incised vessels; brushing, corncob marking, and stipple roughening on jars; and vessel shapes.

LAWSON FIELD PHASE, LOWER CHATTAHOOCHEE
SUB-TRADITION

Estimated Dating: ca. A.D. 1715–1836. The primary basis for dating is the abundant, datable English, French, and Spanish trade goods found in most Lawson Field phase contexts.

Type Site: Lawson Field site (Kasita town), 9CE1 (Willey and Sears 1952).

Other Documented Sites: Jackson site (Tamathli), 1BR35 (Kurjack 1975); Hitchiti Town, 9SW50 (Kelly et al. 1969); Yuchi Town, 1RU63 (Schnell 1982); Sites 1RU20/21 (Holland 1974); Blackmon, 1BR25 (Mistovich and Knight 1986); and others (see Knight and Mistovich 1984).

Basic References: Willey and Sears 1952; Schnell 1970; Kurjack 1975; Knight and Mistovich 1984; Mistovich and Knight 1986.

Roster of Ceramic Types (after Mistovich and Knight 1986; see also Willey and Sears 1952; Kurjack 1975):
   shell-tempered plain
   shell-tempered burnished plain
   Walnut Roughened, *var. McKee Island*
   shell-tempered incised
   nonshell-tempered plain
   nonshell-tempered burnished plain
   Chattahoochee Roughened, *var. Chattahoochee*
   Chattahoochee Roughened, *var. Wedowee*
   Lamar Incised, *var. Ocmulgee Fields*
   Mission (Kasita) Red Filmed
   Lamar Complicated Stamped
   Toulouse Plain
   Toulouse Incised

Discussion: The ceramic assemblage characteristic of the Lawson Field phase has been well known since the publication of Willey's work at the type site (Willey and Sears 1952). The basic inventory has been duplicated many times over in the excavation of historic Lower Creek sites of Muskogee, Hitchiti, and Yuchi linguistic affiliation. The pottery is predominantly sand or grit tempered, with shell temper in diminished frequency or altogether absent. The main textured type is Chattahoochee Roughened, *var. Chattahoochee* (called Chattahoochee Brushed in most of the published literature). Early and late Tallapoosa phase pottery assemblages can be distinguished, but usable criteria for their separation have not been worked out. The assemblage, overall, is strongly similar to that of the contemporaneous Tallapoosa phase. One apparent difference is the much higher frequency of Mission or Kasita Red Filmed in Lawson Field phase contexts.

Continuities: Continuities from the Blackmon phase include specific incised designs on cazuela bowls, brushing on jars, and various other features. A number of types are shared by the Blackmon and Lawson Field phases; gradual changes involve shifts in the relative frequency of types (for a review, see Mistovich and Knight 1986).

CHAPTER SEVENTEEN

The Macon Trading House and Early European-Indian Contact in the Colonial Southeast

Gregory A. Waselkov

At Okmulge, the old waste town . . . [the Creek Indians] strenuously aver, that when necessity forces them to encamp there, they always hear, at the dawn of the morning, the usual noise of Indians singing their joyful religious notes, and dancing, as if going down to the river to purify themselves, and then returning to the old town-house. . . . Whenever I have been there, however, all hath been silent. (Adair 1775:35–36)

I N 1929 Matthew W. Stirling, chief of the Smithsonian Institution's Bureau of American Ethnology, aptly characterized a malady then afflicting North American archaeology: "Many a field investigator has suffered a real sense of disappointment upon finding himself dealing with a post Columbian site. After excavating a number of articles of native origin, and feeling rather triumphant about it, upon encountering a string of glass beads or a silver ornament he is very likely to experience a feeling of depression" (Stirling 1929:25).

The work of A. R. Kelly and his colleagues at Macon in the 1930s and early 1940s did much to dispel the notion that historic Indians were less than legitimate subjects for archaeological study. Instead of viewing historic-period Indians as tainted by their contact with Europeans and European material culture and, consequently, "less Indian" than their prehistoric forebears, the Macon archaeologists attempted to understand the entire continuum of human occupation (Kelly 1939: 329; Harrington 1952:341). In the process, they discovered a structure of considerable historical interest and significance, a fortified trading house that is apparently undocumented in contemporary written sources. No longer could archaeology be considered only a consumer of historical data. The Macon excavations provided one of the first examples of archaeology functioning as an independent window into the American historical past, proving that it need not play a role subsidiary to archival research.

While excavations were still in progress, Kelly published two preliminary reports (Kelly 1938c, 1939), concerned mainly with architectural details of the Trading House and the large surrounding Indian settlements. In the course of digging exploratory trenches across what was called the Middle Plateau at Macon, a footing ditch for a pentagonal stockade was discovered quite by chance (Figure 17.1). Inside this fort, which measured nearly 43 m on the longest side, were two areas of dark soil and clustered postholes, presumably the locations of two cabins or storerooms (Figure 17.2). A broad, shallow moat extended around a little more than one-third of the stockade perimeter (Figure 17.3). Past the front of the fort ran a narrow but well-worn trail that turned sharply at the southwest corner of the stockade and was obviously contemporaneous with it. Excavators traced this trail for more than 1 km across the site and identified it as a branch of the Creek Trading Path, which is known to have crossed the Ocmulgee River here in the eighteenth century. Numerous posthole clusters around the trading house were interpreted as Indian house locations. The presence of historic graves, middens, and other features inside and outside the stockade, some intrusive into the ditches and some intruded by them, provided "conclusive evidence that the same people had lived on the site before, during, and after the building of the Trading Post" (Kelly 1939:332).

The excavators' other major interpretive concern, to determine the date of this fortuitously discovered historic component, reflected a near-obsession with chronology

17.1. The excavations at the Ocmulgee Trading House. (Photograph courtesy of the National Park Service, Southeast Archeological Center.)

shared by most American archaeologists during the 1930s. All of the datable European-made objects pointed consistently to the period between 1680 and 1720, a range that coincided closely with the historical evidence (Kelly 1938c:55, 1939:332; for later confirmation of this conclusion, see Hanson 1970, 1971b; Irwin 1959; Mason 1963a, 1971; South 1977:271). The only documented period of large-scale, historic Indian occupation of the Macon Plateau had occurred between 1690 and 1716. For nearly a century, the Muskogee-speaking people living in the Chattahoochee Valley, known to the Florida Spaniards as the Apalachicolas and to the English shortly thereafter as Lower Creeks, had traded with their Florida neighbors. Beginning in 1685, English competition lured most of this profitable traffic to the newly founded colony of South Carolina. The Spaniards attempted unsuccessfully to regain control of the trade in 1690 by the establishment of a small military post near the town of Coweta on the Chattahoochee River (Bolton 1925:119; Serrano y Sanz 1912:219–21; Kurjack and Pearson 1975). In response, however, most of the Lower Creeks moved to the middle Ocmulgee and Oconee river valleys in 1690 to escape Spanish domination and to maintain contact

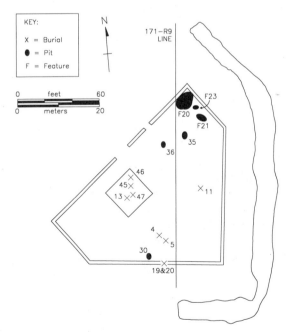

17.2. Plan view of the Trading House excavations. (Adapted from Mason 1963a: Figure 4.)

Macon Trading House and Early European-Indian Contact

191

17.3. Excavations of the unfinished moat along the east side of the Trading House palisade. (Photograph courtesy of the National Park Service, Southeast Archeological Center.)

with English traders. The Lower Creeks remained in what is now central Georgia until 1716, when they returned to their Chattahoochee Valley townsites in the aftermath of the Yamasee War. Thus, the archaeological evidence and historical evidence coincide regarding the date and relatively short duration of the historic Indian village or villages at Macon.

Over twenty years passed before Carol Mason analyzed the excavated material from the historic-period occupation at Macon. She presented the results in her dissertation, written under the direction of James B. Griffin at the University of Michigan, but inspired to a great extent by Charles Fairbanks, who had co-directed the second phase of excavations at the Trading House site in 1939–40 (Mason 1963a:45–46). In a thorough historical review, Mason identified the historic Creek site at Macon as the Hitchiti town of Ocmulgee and, by at least 1710, the residence of the English trader James Lucas (Mason 1963a:224–39; McDowell 1955:6). Based

on town locations shown on the Herbert Map of 1725, Marvin Smith (1992) has recently suggested that the Macon Plateau site was actually Kasihta. Since none of the eighteenth-century maps depict all of the Creek towns known to have existed in the Ocmulgee area, the Macon site may, in fact, have been occupied by several closely spaced towns.

According to Mason's interpretation of the original excavation fieldnotes, the stockade posts evidently had been removed before the site was abandoned. A square cabin (measuring 3.4 m on a side) of native wattle-and-daub construction had existed opposite the main gate inside the stockade, and a similar rectangular building (measuring 4.6 m by 7.6 m) stood adjacent to it (Mason 1963a:56–60). Creek residential structures surrounding the Trading House were large wattle-and-daub buildings, measuring 7.6 to 13.7 m on a side, and were built completely aboveground, perhaps organized in household clusters (Mason 1963a:81–96). Most of the numerous

192

Gregory A. Waselkov

historic-period burials contained European-made trade goods, including glass beads, iron knives and bracelets, gunparts, and brass ornaments. Marine shell beads were frequently associated with infant and child burials (Mason 1963a:96–130). From her study of the types and distributions of trade goods present at Ocmulgee town between 1690 and 1716, Mason concluded that "the new articles brought to the Creeks through trade did not present to them a new technology at all. The new artifacts, manufactured by processes unknown to the Indians and probably unimportant to them, simply substituted for the aboriginal artifacts within the framework of an essentially aboriginal technology and aboriginal economic system. Changes, of course, did occur as a result of the introduction of these new tools but only in so far as the new tools intensified through increased efficiency an already existing means of exploiting the environment" (Mason 1963b:78). In this concise statement, Mason touched on a topic still of considerable interest to archaeologists— the adaptations of native Americans that occurred as they came increasingly into contact and competition with European colonial societies.

Following a reevaluation of the Trading House evidence, the remainder of this chapter focuses on the information and artifacts obtained through archaeological excavations at Macon and elsewhere that contribute to our understanding of Creek Indian culture change during the historic period.

The Macon Trading House Reconsidered

Before proceeding with an analysis of historic Creek culture, it is important to understand the actual function of the structure identified as the source of European-made artifacts, the Macon Trading House. Two elements of its construction, the unfinished surrounding ditch or moat and the dismantled stockade, suggest that efforts to fortify the place were initiated and abandoned within a brief time span. The historical record provides some helpful clues regarding the circumstances of this episode. Although most Lower Creeks fled their homes in the Chattahoochee River valley in 1690 to escape Spanish insistence on a trade monopoly, the Spaniards persevered in their attempts to reestablish trade relations. After repeated rebuffs by the Creeks, a combined Spanish-Apalachee expedition attacked the villages of Coweta, Oconee, Kasita, and Tiquipache in their haven on the Ocmulgee in 1695 (Serrano y Sanz 1912:224–27; Bolton 1925:125; Crane 1956:37). This raid seems to have prompted the Lower Creeks to resume limited trade with Spanish Florida until relations were again disrupted in May 1702, when the English-led Creeks destroyed the Timucuan mission of Santa Fé (Bolton 1925:126).

In anticipation of Spanish reprisals, "two stockades or forts of wood" were reportedly constructed by the Creeks that summer, the one at Coweta town being a typical Indian-style palisade (Boyd 1953:469–70; compare Rowland and Sanders 1927:307–8). The location of the other was not specified, but both seem to have been large enclosures in which an entire village might seek refuge during an attack. The small size and European configuration of the partially completed fort excavated at Macon more nearly resembles the palisaded English warehouses occasionally reported during this era (compare Crane 1956:44). A Spanish retaliatory force was defeated in the summer or fall of 1702, and any threat of further attacks was eliminated in 1704 by the devastation of the Apalachee missions of north-central Florida by Colonel James Moore's army, which originated from Ocmulgee town (Barnwell Map of c. 1722; Salley 1934:20, 103–4; Carroll 1836: vol. 2, p. 574). So the need for defensive structures was short-lived, which probably explains the unfinished and dismantled features found archaeologically.

Both of the houses enclosed by the stockade were constructed in native fashion of wattle and daub, which differs from the usual horizontally laid, notched log construction used in contemporaneous English trading houses in the Carolinas (McDowell 1955:80, 132; Lawson 1967:223–24). However, the dimensions of the rectangular house are identical to those of a warehouse built by South Carolina traders at Santee in 1716, which suggests that Creek labor and methods were employed at Macon under English direction. Trade goods were definitely concentrated in the vicinity of the structure at Macon, so Kelly and Mason seem to have been justified in their conclusion that this was the location of a trading house (Mason 1963a:60, 76).

Creek Culture Change During the Early Historic Period

The effects of English trade with the Creeks cannot be understood in isolation. The Southeast in the late seventeenth and early eighteenth centuries was a complex, multiethnic frontier; a place where both England and Spain actively competed for political influence and trading partners among numerous linguistically diverse Indian tribes. Since the late sixteenth century, Indian intermediaries had carried Spanish trade goods into the interior Southeast to be exchanged for deerskins and other commodities. By the mid-1600s, Spaniards were trading directly with the Apalachicolas (Bolton and Ross 1925: 26–27; Bushnell 1978:417). Other tribes had relocated along the borders of Spanish Florida, partly to escape English-inspired raids by northern Indians, partly to gain direct access to Spanish trade goods, and they, too, acted as middlemen in the widespread trade network, conveying foreign objects far inland (Waselkov 1989).

Indirect trade of European goods to the interior

probably began at the Franciscan missions of Timucua, Guale, and Apalachee. A continuing demand for marine shell (Smith and Smith 1989) among the interior tribes had maintained vestiges of the old Mississippian exchange network throughout the late sixteenth century, despite the disruptive effects of disease and population displacement caused by the De Soto invasion (Smith 1987). As missionized Florida Indians obtained glass beads, brass bells, iron knives, and other European-made items from Spanish friars and soldiers, some of these objects, passing through many hands, filtered deep into the interior Southeast. Because copper had been highly prized for centuries by the inhabitants of this region, the Spaniards soon learned that their own artifacts of brass and copper were eagerly sought by native Americans who attached to them the same symbolic value attributed to their aboriginal counterparts. Eventually large numbers of disc gorgets, armbands, and tubular beads, all of brass, were manufactured specifically for this trade (Smith 1987; Waselkov 1989). Iron axes, hoes, and knives were also traded in quantity, increasingly so by the late seventeenth century. By the same routes, certain Old World domesticates— peaches, black-eyed peas, watermelons—found a place in Creek plant husbandry.

So the Indians of the interior Southeast became quite familiar with European material culture long before English traders began to move westward from Charlestown in the 1680s. This extended period of low volume, indirect trade allowed the Creeks to make two important adaptations before the eighteenth century began. One was the gradual development of the Creek confederacy, a loose organization of towns that maintained cohesiveness by extending consensus decision-making beyond intra-town boundaries to resolve intertown conflicts. This allowed the Creeks to assimilate numerous refugee tribes, a transition that is evident archaeologically in the gradual simplification and homogenization of Creek ceramic traditions (Waselkov and Cottier 1985; Chapter 16, this volume).

The second adaptation of major significance to eighteenth-century Creek society was the gradual and selective adoption of items of European material culture, a process that permitted native cultural reorganization to occur without the stresses imposed by direct colonialism. As Mason cogently stated thirty years ago, while maintaining their traditional value system, the Creeks selectively accepted innovative objects and interpreted them according to their similarity to familiar native items (Waselkov and Paul 1981:316; Miller and Hamell 1986:326). By 1690 the essence of historic Creek culture was evident in the Upper and Lower towns: no longer a pristine aboriginal culture, but a synthetic one incorporating both European and traditional artifacts, values, and activities in a new, distinctive, stable cultural format.

The widespread similarity in Creek culture at this date can be seen in a comparison of the archaeological remains from Macon and contemporaneous sites in the Coosa and Tallapoosa valleys (DeJarnette, Kurjack, and Keel 1973; Morrell 1965; and recent excavations at 1EE191 by Auburn University). A similar variety of native and European-made artifacts is found at all of these sites, perhaps most strikingly exemplified (impressionistically, at least) by the presence of individuals buried with brass bells around their waists at Ocmulgee (Kelly 1939: plate 18, figure 1), at the Law's site in the Guntersville Basin of the Tennessee Valley (Webb and Wilder 1951:141, plate 39B), and at Fusihatchee on the lower Tallapoosa River (Auburn University archaeological collections) (compare Bushnell 1908:573).

Among these disparate groups that gradually coalesced to form the Creek confederacy, a parallel convergence of aboriginal material culture was also underway. A single type of projectile point, an elongated triangular form known as the Guntersville point, was adopted throughout the region. Stone and ceramic smoking pipes continued to be produced, but their forms now incorporated elements of European pipe styles. A few varieties of marine shell ornaments, particularly some small, two-holed pendants (Williams 1980) and knobbed pins, were widely distributed across the Southeast, a faint reflection of the remarkable diversity of Mississippian worked-shell inventories. Ceramics, too, underwent a functional simplification with many vessel forms disappearing, leaving only cooking jars and truncated bowls (both in a range of sizes) by the mid-eighteenth century.

Many factors influenced the course of Creek material culture change during the late seventeenth century, but one of the most significant certainly was the new social and demographic organization of Indian populations. Individuals, families, entire villages, and even larger social groupings moved great distances (voluntarily, in many instances, but also as war captives or slaves). This social rearrangement, which must have exceeded in rapidity and scale anything occurring prehistorically in the region, brought into direct association peoples differing in language, social organization, and material culture. Each of the major native societies of the historic period (that is, the Creeks, Cherokees, Chickasaws, Choctaws, Catawbas, and eventually the Seminoles) was a relatively recent composite comprising groups drawn together by mutual convenience. As new group boundaries and identities were being defined spatially, the adoption of similar forms of material culture could have strengthened feelings of a shared ethnicity, which may account in part for the trend toward homogeneity in artifact forms.

Archaeological evidence also seems to support the contention that Creek society was essentially egalitarian at this time, since mortuary offerings appear to have been distributed on the basis of age and sex differences rather than crosscutting such distinctions, as occurred in the earlier rank stratified Mississippian societies. This essentially concurs with Thomas Nairne's 1708 description of Creek elders (*isti atcagagi*): "Some ar of that order by birth (being the heads of such fameiles as first settled the society) others are such Considerable old officers, as are taken into that designly for their merit. Of these are more or less in every Town. The people themselves know and respect them, but it's imposible for a stranger to Distinguish them by their garb and Fashion, which in nothing Differs from the rest" (Nairne 1988: 32–33).

The Macon artifact assemblage is characterized by a dramatic decrease in Spanish trade goods compared to slightly earlier sites. Apart from a few sherds of Spanish ceramics, a silver coin, one lug-eyed hoe, and a mutilated sheet brass disc gorget (Mason 1963a:150–71), English-imported items dominate the trade goods assemblage, reflecting the effective competition of English traders. English encouragement of slave raids led directly to the destruction of many unconfederated tribes in the region, and for a while, slave-hunting dominated trade activities in the Southeast. But limited sources of Indian slaves meant a short life for the practice, and even before the 1715 Yamasee War, deerskins again provided the basis for the southeastern Indian trade economy.

The sudden increase in demand for deerskins beginning in 1685 was probably indirectly responsible for changes in Creek domestic architecture. Prior to that date, Creek houses were of two forms: a rectangular, aboveground style used mainly in the summer, and an octagonal, semisubterranean style for winter occupancy. With the advent of long winter hunts, villages were virtually abandoned during that season in favor of temporary, mobile hunting camps. In place of the modest number of deerskins formerly obtained for personal clothing, large quantities of easily perishable skins now needed to be stored until they could be sold to itinerant traders. These factors combined to create new architectural needs not met by the traditional semisubterranean houses, which were neither suitable for large-scale deerskin storage nor any longer necessary for winter warmth in villages now occupied by only a fraction of their summer population. So labor-intensive pit construction was soon abandoned for domestic use, surviving only for special purpose structures such as town rotundas. Ground-level houses, with areas for living and storage, were the only form discovered in the historic village excavations at Macon.

Increased deerskin demand in the late seventeenth century also caused a dramatic shift in Creek hunting strategies; from group hunts and drives organized primarily to acquire meat and enough deerskins for their own clothing, the emphasis changed to producing vast surpluses of deerskins, far beyond their own immediate needs. Others have argued that the large-scale depopulation of the Southeast during the sixteenth and seventeenth centuries resulted in decreased deer hunting by the Indians and the abandonment of many fields, thereby removing pressure on the deer population while creating new deer habitat (White 1983:10–11). As the trade for European goods accelerated between 1690 and 1715, deer hunting increased, prompting the Creeks to maintain recently created old field habitat by controlled burning. The end result was a greatly increased deer carrying capacity for the region, largely as a consequence of disease mortality and the trade opportunities introduced by traders. (Pigs, cattle, and horses were introduced into the Creek country early in the eighteenth century, but raising these domesticates did not replace deer hunting until a decline in worldwide demand for deerskins and American settlement of hunting ranges forced a shift in the economic basis of Creek culture in the late eighteenth and early nineteenth centuries.)

In the course of the next century and a half, the adaptability and resilience of Creek culture were sorely tested by the demands of the intruding British and French, and finally the Americans. Colonial officials depended on the allure of exotic ornaments, the physical dependence induced by rum and brandy, and the enticing efficiency of firearms and iron tools to reduce the Creeks to political subservience through economic necessity. "That discre[e]t Preparative Stroak of Trade," as Proprietor John Archdale called it in 1707 (Salley 1911:310), which began in earnest in central Georgia during the 1690s, was only a prelude to economic domination and eventual expulsion of the Creeks from their lands. Indeed, the story of the Creeks in the Southeast can be viewed as a general process of assimilation of the Creek subsistence system into the European trade network and world market. In an economic sense, Creek society was transformed from a state of independence and self-sufficiency to one of subordination and dependency (Meillassoux 1981:97–98; Wolf 1982:193; White 1983:xvii–xix, 319). But as this was occurring, the Creeks were creatively altering their resilient culture by selectively adopting elements of European material culture and behavior that were especially amenable to reinterpretation. Throughout the historic period, the Creeks responded to events "according to their own customary self-conceptions and interests" (Sahlins 1985:138). The structure of Creek culture was transformed repeatedly, but the continuity of tradition was always evident. That this subject is finally attracting serious study by archaeologists is in some measure due to the pioneering work done fifty years ago at Macon by those excavators with the foresight to recognize the research potential of the historic southeastern Indians.

Acknowledgments

I am indebted to David Hally, Carol Mason, Alexander Moore, and Craig Sheldon for their helpful comments on this essay. Many of the ideas and conclusions discussed here were developed with material support for excavation and museum collections research provided by four National Science Foundation grants (BNS-8305437, BNS-8507469, BNS-8718934, and BNS-8907700).

Gregory A. Waselkov

REFERENCES CITED

Adair, James.
1968   *The History of the American Indians.* 1775. Reprint, New York: Johnson Reprint Corp.

Adams, William Y., Dennis P. Van Gerven, and Richard S. Levy.
1978   The Retreat from Migrationism. *Annual Review of Anthropology* 7:483–582.

Anderson, David G.
1979   *Excavation at Four Fall Line Sites: The Southeastern Columbia Beltway Project.* Report no. R-2008. Jackson, Mich.: Commonwealth Associates.

1986   Stability and Change in Chiefdom-level Societies: An Examination of Mississippian Political Evolution on the South Atlantic Slope. Paper presented at the 43d annual meeting of the Southeastern Archaeological Conference, Nashville, Tenn.

1987   Mississippian Political Evolution in the Savannah River Valley. Paper presented at the 44th annual meeting of the Southeastern Archaeological Conference, Charleston, S.C.

1988   The First Occupants: The PaleoIndian and Early Archaeic Periods. In *Prehistory and History Along the Upper Savannah River: Technical Synthesis of Cultural Resource Investigations, Richard B. Russell Multiple Resource Area*, edited by D. G. Anderson and J. W. Joseph. Vol. 1, 97–132. Russell Papers 1988. Atlanta: Interagency Archeological Services Division, National Park Service.

1990a   A North American Paleoindian Projectile Point Database. *Current Research in the Pleistocene* 7:67–69.

1990b   The PaleoIndian Colonization of Eastern North America: A View from the Southeastern United States. In *Early PaleoIndian Economies of Eastern North America*, edited by Kenneth Tankersley and Barry Isaac, 163–216. *Journal of Economic Anthropology* Supplement 5.

1990c   Political Change in Chiefdom Societies: Cycling in the Late Prehistoric Southeastern United States. Ph.D. diss., Department of Anthropology, University of Michigan, Ann Arbor.

1991a   The Bifurcate Tradition in the South Atlantic Region. *Journal of Middle Atlantic Archaeology* 7:91–106.

1991b   Examining Prehistoric Settlement Distribution in Eastern North America. *Archaeology of Eastern North America* 19.

Anderson, David G., Charles E. Cantley, and A. Lee Novick.
1982   *The Mattassee Lake Sites: Archaeological Investigations Along the Lower Santee River in the Coastal Plain of South Carolina.* Special Publication 1982. Atlanta: Interagency Archeological Services, USDI National Park Service.

Anderson, David G., David J. Hally, and James L. Rudolph.
1986   The Mississippian Occupation of the Savannah River Valley. *Southeastern Archaeology* 5:32–51.

Anderson, David G., and Glen T. Hanson.
1988   Early Archaic Settlement in the Southeastern United States: A Case Study from the Savannah River Valley. *American Antiquity* 53:262–86.

Anderson, David G., and J. W. Joseph.
1988   *Prehistory and History Along the Upper Savannah River: Technical Synthesis of Cultural Resource Investigations, Richard B. Russell Multiple Resource Area.* Russell Papers 1988. Atlanta: Interagency Archeological Services Division, National Park Service.

Anderson, David G., R. Jerald Ledbetter, and Lisa D. O'Steen.
1986   Georgia PaleoIndian Recordation Project: Towards a Descriptive Inventory of Georgia PaleoIndian Fluted and Lanceolate Project Points. Society for Georgia Archaeology. *The Profile* 52:6–11.

1990a   *PaleoIndian Period Archaeology of Georgia.* Laboratory of Archaeology Series, Report no. 28. Athens: University of Georgia.

1990b   Update on the Georgia PaleoIndian Survey. *Current Research in the Pleistocene* 7:70–72.

Anderson, David G., R. Jerald Ledbetter, Lisa O'Steen, Daniel T. Elliott, and Dennis Blanton.
1987   Recent PaleoIndian Research in Georgia. *Current Research in the Pleistocene* 4:47–50.

Anderson, David G., Sammy T. Lee, and A. Robert Parler.
1979   *Cal Smoak: Archaeological Investigations Along the Edisto River in the Coastal Plain of South Carolina.* Occasional Papers, no. 1, Archeological Society of South Carolina.

Anderson, David G., and Joseph Schuldenrein.

1983   Early Archaic Settlement on the Southeastern Atlantic Slope: A View from the Rucker's Bottom Site, Elbert County, Georgia. *North American Archaeologist* 4 (3): 177–210.

1985   *Prehistoric Human Ecology Along the Upper Savannah River: Excavations at the Rucker's Bottom, Abbeville, and Bullard Site Groups.* Russell Papers 1985. Atlanta: Interagency Archeological Services Division, National Park Service.

Asch, David L., and Nancy B. Asch.

1978   The Economic Potential of *Iva annua* and Its Prehistoric Importance in the Lower Illinois Valley. In *The Nature and Status of Ethnobotany*, edited by Richard I. Ford, 300–341. Anthropological Papers, no. 67. Ann Arbor: Museum of Anthropology, University of Michigan.

1985   Prehistoric Plant Cultivation in West-Central Illinois. In *Prehistoric Food Production in North America*, edited by Richard Ford, 149–203. Anthropological Papers, no. 75. Ann Arbor: Museum of Anthropology, University of Michigan.

Asch, Nancy B., Richard I. Ford, and David L. Asch.

1972   *Paleoethnobotany of the Koster Site.* Report of Investigations, no. 24. Springfield: Illinois State Museum.

Bareis, Charles J., and James W. Porter.

1984   *American Bottom Archaeology: A Summary of the FAI-270 Project Contribution to the Culture History of the Mississippi River Valley.* Urbana: University of Illinois Press.

Barnett, Homer G.

1953   *Innovation: The Basis of Culture Change.* New York: McGraw Hill.

Barnwell, John.

c. 1722   [Map of Southeastern North America.] Great Britain, Public Record Office, Colonial Office Library, North American Colonies, General 7.

Bartlett, Myron.

1828   Macon Land Sales—Antiquities. *Macon Telegraph* 2 (44): 1.

Bartram, William.

1928   *Travels of William Bartram.* 1791. Edited by Mark Van Doren. Reprint, New York: Dover.

Bass, W.

1979   *Human Osteology: A Laboratory and Field Manual.* 2d ed. Columbia: Missouri Archaeological Society.

Belmont, John S.

1967   The Culture Sequence at the Greenhouse Site, Louisiana. *Southeastern Archaeological Conference Bulletin* 6:27–34.

Belmont, John S., and Stephen Williams.

1965   The Foundations of American Archaeology. Ms on file, Tozzer Library, Harvard University, Cambridge.

Bennett, Wendell C.

1948   The Peruvian Co-Tradition. *Memoirs of the Society for American Archaeology* 4:1–7.

Biedma, Luys Hernandez de.

1922   Relation of the Conquest of Florida. In *Narratives of the Career of Hernando de Soto in the Conquest of Florida.* Vol. 2. Translated by Buckingham Smith. Edited by Gaylord G. Bourne, 3–40. New York: Allerton.

Billeck, William T.

1986   Garden Beds in Blackhawk Country. *Iowa Archaeological Society Newsletter* 36 (4): 5–6.

Binford, Lewis R.

1980   Willow Smoke and Dogs' Tails: Hunter-Gatherer Settlement Systems and Archaeological Site Formation. *American Antiquity* 45:4–20.

1983   Long Term Land Use Patterns: Some Implications for Archaeology. In *Lulu Linear Punctate: Essays in Honor of George Irving Quimby*, edited by Robert C. Dunnell and Donald K. Grayson, 27–53. Anthropological Papers, no. 72. Ann Arbor: Museum of Anthropology, University of Michigan.

Blakely, Robert L., editor.

1988   *The King Site: Continuity and Contact in Sixteenth-Century Georgia.* Athens: University of Georgia Press.

Blanton, Dennis B.

1983   Lithic Raw Material Procurement and Use During the Morrow Mountain Phase in South Carolina. Master's thesis, Department of Anthropology, Brown University, Providence.

Blanton, Dennis B., and Kenneth E. Sassaman.

1989   Pattern and Process in the Middle Archaic Period in South Carolina. In *The Archaeology of South Carolina: Papers in Honor of Dr. Robert L. Stephenson*, edited by Glen T. Hanson and Albert C. Goodyear III, 53–72. South Carolina Institute of Archeology and Anthropology, Anthropological Studies, no. 7. Columbia: University of South Carolina.

Blanton, Dennis B., and Frankie Snow.

1986   PaleoIndian and Early Archaic Lithic Assemblage Composition in South Georgia: Evidence from the Feronia Locality. Paper presented at the 43d annual meeting of the Southeastern Archaeological Conference, Nashville, Tenn.

1989   PaleoIndian and Early Archaic Occupations at the Feronia Locality, South-Central Georgia. Paper presented at the 54th annual meeting of the Society for American Archaeology, Atlanta.

Bolton, Herbert E.

1925   Spanish Resistance to the Carolina Traders in Western Georgia (1680–1704). *Georgia Historical Quarterly* 9 (2): 115–30.

Bolton, Herbert E., and Mary Ross.

1925   *The Debatable Land: A Sketch of the Anglo-Spanish Contest for the Georgia Country.* Berkeley: University of California Press.

Booker, Karen, Charles Hudson, and Robert Rankin.

1992   Place Name Identification and Multilingualism in the Sixteenth Century Southeast. *Ethnohistory* 39:399–451.

Bowen, William Rowe.

1979   Augusta Railroad Relocation Demonstration Project: Intensive Archaeological Survey Identification of

Resources and Assessment of Impacts. Ms. on file, Georgia Department of Transportation, Atlanta.

Boyd, Donna C.
1986   A Survey and Assessment of Extant Data Pertaining to Prehistoric Cultural Resources of the Chickamauga Reservoir. Department of Anthropology, University of Tennessee. Submitted to the Tennessee Valley Authority.

Boyd, Mark F.
1949   Diego Pena's Expedition to Apalachee and Apalachicola in 1716. *Florida Historical Quarterly* 28:1–27.

1958   *Historic Sites in and Adjacent to the Jim Woodruff Reservoir, Florida-Georgia*, 195–314. Smithsonian Institution, Bureau of American Ethnology Bulletin 169. Washington, D.C.

Boyd, Mark F., editor.
1953   Further Consideration of the Apalachee Missions. *Americas* 9 (4): 459–79.

Bozhardt, Robert.
1983   Ridged Fields at the Sand Lake Site near La Crosse, Wisconsin. *Minnesota Archaeological Newsletter* 30:6–8.

Braley, Chad O., Jerald Ledbetter, and Mark Williams.
1985   Newly Recognized Late Mississippian Ceremonial Sites in the Oconee Province. Paper presented at the annual meeting of the Society for Georgia Archaeology, Savannah, Ga.

Braley, Chad O., Lisa D. O'Steen, and Irvy R. Quitmyer.
1986   *Archaeological Investigations at 9MC141, Harris Neck National Wildlife Refuge, McIntosh County*. Southeastern Archaeological Services Inc. Submitted to USDA, Fish and Wildlife Service. Contract no. 14–16–004–84–019.

Brennan, Louis.
1982   A Compilation of Fluted Points of Eastern North America by Count and Distribution: An AENA Project. *Archaeology of Eastern North America* 10:27–46.

Brockington, Paul B.
1971   A Preliminary Investigation of an Early Knapping Site in Southeastern Georgia. *Notebook* 3 (2): 34–46. South Carolina Institute of Archeology and Anthropology. Columbia, University of South Carolina.

Brook, George.
1981   *Geoarchaeology of the Oconee Reservoir*. Wallace Reservoir Project, Contribution no. 15. Department of Anthropology, University of Georgia, Athens.

Brooks, Mark J., Peter A. Stone, Donald J. Colquhoun, Janice G. Brown, and Kathy B. Steele.
1986   Geoarchaeological Research in the Coastal Plain Portion of the Savannah River Valley. *Geoarchaeology* 1:293–307.

Brose, David S.
1979   A Speculative Model of the Role of Exchange in the Prehistory of the Eastern Woodlands. In *Hopewell Archaeology: The Chillicothe Conference*, edited by D. S. Brose and N'omi Greber, 3–8. Kent, Ohio: Kent State University Press.

1984   Mississippian Period Cultures in Northwestern Florida. In *Perspectives on Gulf Coast Prehistory*, edited by Dave D. Davis, 165–97. Gainesville: University Presses of Florida.

Brown, Calvin S.
1926   *Archeology of Mississippi*. University: Mississippi Geological Survey.

Brown, Charles.
1906   A Record of Wisconsin Antiquities. *Wisconsin Archaeologist* 5:289439.

1908   Additions to the Record of Wisconsin Antiquities: II. *Wisconsin Archaeologist* 7:125–31.

1909   Additions to the Record of Wisconsin Antiquities: III. *Wisconsin Archaeologist* 8:113–38.

Broyles, B. J.
1971   *Second Preliminary Report: The St. Albans Site, Kanawha Valley, West Virginia*. Report of Archaeological Investigations, no. 3. Morgantown: West Virginia Geological and Economic Survey.

Bryan, Benjamin L.
1940   Guide Manual, Ocmulgee National Monument. Ms. on file, Ocmulgee National Monument, Macon, Ga.

Bushnell, Amy T.
1978   The Menéndez Marquéz Cattle Barony of La Chua and the Determinants of Economic Expansion in Seventeenth-Century Florida. *Florida Historical Quarterly* 56 (4): 407–31.

Bushnell, David I., Jr.
1908   The Account of Lamhatty. *American Anthropologist* 10:568–74.

1935   *The Manahoac Tribes in Virginia, 1608*. Smithsonian Miscellaneous Collections 94 (8). Smithsonian Institution, Washington, D.C.

Butler, John C.
1960   *Historical Record of Macon and Central Georgia*. Reprint, Macon, Ga.: J. W. Burke. Original edition, Macon, Ga.: J. W. Burke, 1879.

Cable, John S.
1982   Organizational Variability in Piedmont Hunter-Gatherer Assemblages. In *The Haw River Sites: Archaeological Investigations at Two Stratified Sites in the North Carolina Piedmont*, compiled by Stephen R. Claggett and John S. Cable, 637–88. Report no. R-2386. Jackson, Mich.: Commonwealth Associates.

Caldwell, Joseph R.
1948   Palachacolas Town, Hampton County, South Carolina. *Journal of the Washington Academy of Sciences* 38 (10): 321–24.

1950   A Preliminary Report on Excavations in the Allatoona Reservoir. *Early Georgia* 1 (1): 5–21.

1952   The Archaeology of Eastern Georgia and South Carolina. In *Archeology of Eastern United States*, edited by James B. Griffin, 312–21. Chicago: University of Chicago Press.

1953   Appraisal of the Archeological Resources of Hartwell Reservoir, South Carolina. Ms. on file, Southeast Archeological Center, National Park Service, Tallahassee, Fla.

1954   The Old Quartz Industry of Piedmont Georgia and South Carolina. *Southern Indian Studies* 6:37–39.

1955a   Cherokee Pottery from North Georgia. *American Antiquity* 20:277–80.

1955a   Cherokee Pottery from North Georgia. *American Antiquity* 20:277–80.

1955b   Investigations at Rood's Landing, Stewart County, Georgia. *Early Georgia* 2 (1): 22–49.

1957   *Survey and Excavations in the Allatoona Reservoir, Northern Georgia.* Ms. on file, Department of Anthropology, University of Georgia, Athens.

1958   *Trend and Tradition in the Prehistory of the Eastern United States.* American Anthropological Association, Memoir no. 88. Menasha, Wisc.

1971   Historical and Archaeological Investigation in the Wallace Reservoir of the Georgia Power Company. Contract proposal submitted to the Georgia Power Company. Ms. on file, Department of Anthropology, University of Georgia, Athens.

1976   Comments on the Papers. In *Georgia Prehistory: An Overview in Time and Space*, edited by Marilyn Pennington. *Early Georgia* 3 (1): 68–72.

1978   *Report of the Excavations at Fairchild's Landing and Hare's Landing, Seminole County, Georgia.* Edited by Betty A. Smith, Kennesaw College. Submitted to Southeast Archeological Center, National Park Service, Tallahassee, Fla. Contract no. 589070204.

Caldwell, Joseph R., and Catherine McCann.
1941   *Irene Mound Site, Chatham County, Georgia.* Athens: University of Georgia Press.

Caldwell, Joseph R., Charles E. Thompson, Sheila K. Caldwell.
1952   The Booger Bottom Mound: A Forsyth Period Site in Hall County, Georgia. *American Antiquity* 17:319–28.

Caldwell, Joseph R., and Antonio J. Waring, Jr.
1939   Pottery Type Descriptions. *Newsletter of the Southeastern Archaeological Conference* 1 (6): 1–11.

Carroll, B. R.
1836   *Historical Collections of South Carolina.* 2 vols. New York: Harper & Brothers.

Chance, Marsha A.
1974   *The WPA Glynn County Project: A Ceramic Analysis.* Master's thesis, Department of Anthropology, Florida State University, Tallahassee. Submitted to Southeast Archeological Center, National Park Service, Tallahassee, Fla. Contract no. 5049L30024.

Chapman, Jefferson.
1973   *The Icehouse Bottom Site (40MR23).* Reports of Investigations, no. 13. Department of Anthropology, University of Tennessee, Knoxville.

1975   *The Rose Island Site and the Bifurcate Point Tradition.* Reports of Investigations, no. 14. Department of Anthropology, University of Tennessee, Knoxville.

1976   The Archaic Period in the Lower Little Tennessee River Valley: The Radiocarbon Dates. *Tennessee Anthropologist* 1:1–12.

1977   *Archaic Period Research in the Lower Little Tennessee River Valley—1975, Icehouse Bottom, Harrison Branch, Thirty Acre Island, Calloway Island.* Reports of

Investigations, no. 18. Department of Anthropology, University of Tennessee, Knoxville.

1978   *The Bacon Farm Site and a Buried Site Reconnaissance.* Report of Investigations, no. 23. Department of Anthropology, University of Tennessee, Knoxville.

1985   Archaeology and the Archaic Period in the Southern Ridge-and-Valley Province. In *Structure and Process in Southeastern Archaeology*, edited by Roy S. Dickens and H. Trawick Ward, 137–53. Tuscaloosa: University of Alabama Press.

Chapman, J. Jefferson, and Andrea Shea.
1981   The Archaeobotanical Record: Early Archaic to Contact in the Lower Little Tennessee River Valley. *Tennessee Anthropologist* 6:61–84.

Charles, Tommy.
1981   Dwindling Resources: An Overture to the Future of South Carolina's Archaeological Resources. *Notebook* 13:1–85. South Carolina Institute of Archeology and Anthropology. Columbia: University of South Carolina.

1983   Thoughts and Records from the Survey of Private Collections of Prehistoric Artifacts Throughout South Carolina: A Second Report. *Notebook* 15:1–37. South Carolina Institute of Archeology and Anthropology. Columbia: University of South Carolina.

1986   The Fifth Phase of the Collectors Survey. *Notebook* 18:1–27. South Carolina Institute of Archeology and Anthropology. Columbia: University of South Carolina.

Chase, David W.
1979   A Brief Synopsis of Central Alabama. Paper presented at the winter meeting of the Alabama Archaeological Society, Auburn.

Cherry, John F.
1987   Power in Space: Archaeological and Geographical Studies, In *Landscape and Culture: Geographical and Archaeological Perspectives*, edited by J. M. Wagstaff, 146–72. Oxford: Basil Blackwell.

Claflin, William H., Jr.
1931   *The Stalling's Island Mound, Columbia County, Georgia.* Peabody Museum Papers, vol. 14, no. 1. Cambridge: Harvard University.

Claggett, Stephen R., and John S. Cable, compilers.
1982   *The Haw River Sites: Archaeological Investigations at Two Stratified Sites in the North Carolina Piedmont.* Report R-2386. Jackson, Mich.: Commonwealth Associates.

Clarke, David L.
1968   *Analytical Archaeology.* London: Methuen and Co.

Clausen, C. J., A. D. Cohen, Cesaire Emeliani, J. A. Holman, and J. J. Stipp.
1979   Little Salt Spring, Florida: A Unique Underwater Site. *Science* 203:609–14.

Coe, Joffre L.
1964   *The Formative Cultures of the Carolina Piedmont.* Transactions of the American Philosophical Society, vol. 54, pt. 5. Philadelphia.

Conkey, Margaret W.

1980   The Identification of Prehistoric Hunter-Gatherer Aggregation Sites: The Case of Altamira. *Current Anthropology* 21:609–30.

Cook, Fred C.

1978   The Kent Mound: A Study of the Irene Phase on the Lower Georgia Coast. Master's thesis, Department of Anthropology, Florida State University, Tallahassee.

1980   Chronological and Functional Reexamination of the Irene Ceramic Complex. In *Excursions in Southeastern Geology: The Archaeology—Geology of the Georgia Coast*, edited by James D. Howard, Chester B. DePratter, and Robert W. Frey, 160–69. Guidebook no. 20. Atlanta: Geological Society of America.

Cooper, Allen H., and John W. Walker.

1987   Archeological Monitoring of Water and Sewer Systems Improvements, Ocmulgee National Monument, Georgia. Ms. on file, Southeast Archeological Center, National Park Service, Tallahassee, Fla.

Corgan, James X.

1976   *Vertebrate Fossils of Tennessee.* Bulletin 77. Division of Geology, State of Tennessee Department of Conservation, Nashville.

Cornelius, Elias.

1819   Aboriginal Remains on the High Tower River, Georgia. *American Journal of Science* 1:322–24.

Cosner, Oliver J.

1973   *Stratigraphy of an Archeological Site, Ocmulgee Flood Plain, Macon, Georgia.* U.S. Geological Survey Water-Resources Investigations 54–73. Atlanta: U.S. Geological Survey.

Cowan, C. Wesley.

1978   The Prehistoric Use and Distribution of Maygrass in Eastern North America: Cultural and Phytogeographic Implications. In *The Nature and Status of Ethnobotany*, edited by Richard I. Ford, 263–88. Anthropological Papers, no. 67. Ann Arbor: Museum of Anthropology, University of Michigan.

1985   Understanding the Evolution of Plant Husbandry in Eastern North America: Lessons from Botany, Ethnography, and Archaeology. In *Prehistoric Food Production in North America*, edited by Richard I. Ford, 205–43. Anthropological Papers, no. 75. Ann Arbor: Museum of Anthropology, University of Michigan.

Crane, H. R., and James B. Griffin.

1962   University of Michigan Radiocarbon Dates VII. *Radiocarbon* 4:183–203.

Crane, Verner W.

1956   *The Southern Frontier, 1670–1732.* Reprint, Ann Arbor: University of Michigan Press. Original edition, Durham: Duke University Press, 1928.

Crook, Morgan R., Jr.

1978   Mississippian Period Community Organizations on the Georgia Coast. Ph.D. diss., Department of Anthropology, University of Florida, Gainesville.

1980   Spatial Associations and Distribution of Aggregate Village sites in a Southeastern Atlantic Coastal Area.

In *Sapelo Papers: Researches in the history and Prehistory of Sapelo Island, Georgia*, edited by Daniel P. Juengst, 77–88. West Georgia College Studies in the Social Sciences, vol. 19. Carrollton, Ga.

1986   *Mississippi Period Archaeology of the Georgia Coastal Zone.* Laboratory of Archaeology Series, Report no. 23. Athens: University of Georgia.

1987   *Lowe Site Report: A Contribution to the Archaeology of the Georgia Coastal Plain.* Occasional Papers in Cultural Resource Management 3. Georgia Department of Transportation, Atlanta.

1990   *Rae's Creek: A Multicomponent Archaeological Site at the Fall Line Along the Savannah River.* Department of Anthropology, Georgia State University, Atlanta.

Crouch, Daniel.

1974   South Appalachian Earth Lodges. Master's thesis, Department of Anthropology, University of North Carolina, Chapel Hill.

Daniel, I. Randolph.

1991   Hardaway Revisited—Old Tools, New Ideas. Paper presented at the 48th annual meeting of the Southeastern Archaeological Conference, Jackson, Miss.

Daniel, I. Randolph, and Michael Wisenbaker.

1987   *Harney Flats: A Florida PaleoIndian Site.* New York: Baywood Publishing Company.

Davis, Dave D.

1983   Investigating the Diffusion of Stylistic Innovations. In *Advances in Archaeological Method and Theory*, edited by Michael B. Schiffer. Vol. 6, 53–89. New York: Academic Press.

Davis, Hester A.

1962   Current Research in the Southeast. *American Antiquity* 28:263.

Davis, Margaret B.

1983   Holocene Vegetational History of the Eastern United States. In *Late Quaternary Environments of the United States.* Part 2, *The Holocene*, edited by H. E. Wright, Jr., 166–81. Minneapolis: University of Minnesota Press.

Davis, R. P. Stephen, Jr., and I. Randolph Daniel.

1990   *Projectile Point Classification Project: The Classification of Projectile Points in Existing Archaeological Collections from North Carolina.* Research Laboratories of Anthropology. Chapel Hill: University of North Carolina.

Davis, R. P. Stephen, Jr., Larry R. Kimball, and William W. Baden, editors.

1982   An Archaeological Survey and Assessment of Aboriginal Settlement Within the Lower Little Tennessee River Valley. Department of Anthropology, University of Tennessee. Submitted to the Tennessee Valley Authority.

Day, H. Summerfield.

1936   Report on Ocmulgee National Monument. Ms. on file, Southeast Archeological Center, National Park Service, Tallahassee, Fla.

DeJarnette, David L., and Asael T. Hansen.

1960   *The Archaeology of the Childersburg Site, Alabama.*

Notes in Anthropology, no. 4. Department of
Anthropology, Florida State University, Tallahassee.

DeJarnette, David L., Edward Kurjack, and James Cambron.
1962   Stanfield-Worley Bluff Shelter Excavations. *Journal of Alabama Archaeology* 8 (1–2): 1–124.

DeJarnette, David L., Edward B. Kurjack, and Bennie C. Keel.
1973   Archaeological Investigations of the Weiss Reservoir of the Coosa River in Alabama. *Journal of Alabama Archaeology* 19 (1–2): 1–201.

Delabarre, Edmund B., and Harris H. Wilder.
1920   Indian cornhills in Massachusetts. *American Anthropologist* 22:203–25.

Delcourt, Paul A., and Hazel R. Delcourt.
1985   Quaternary Palynology and Vegetational History of the Southeastern United States. In *Pollen Records of Late-Quaternary North American Sediments*, edited by V. M. Bryant and R. G. Holloway, 1–37. Dallas: American Association of Stratigraphic Palynologists Foundation.
1987   *Long Term Forest Dynamics of the Temperate Zone: A Case Study of Late-Quaternary Forests in Eastern North America.* New York: Springer-Verlag.

DePratter, Chester B.
1976a   The Archaic in Georgia. *Early Georgia* 3 (1): 1–16.
1976b   *The 1974–75 Archaeological Survey in the Wallace Reservoir, Greene, Hancock, Morgan, and Putnam Counties, Georgia.* Department of Anthropology, Uiversity of Georgia. Submitted to the Georgia Power Company, Atlanta.
1979   Ceramics. In *The Anthropology of St. Catherine's Island 2. The Refuge—Deptford Mortuary Complex*, edited by David Hurst Thomas and Clark Spencer Larsen, 109–31. American Museum of Natural History, Anthropological Papers, vol. 56, pt. 1. New York.
1991   *W.P.A. Archaeological Excavations in Chatham County Georgia: 1937–1942.* Laboratory of Archaeology Series, Report no. 29. Athens: University of Georgia.

DePratter, Chester B., Charles Hudson, and Marvin T. Smith.
1983   Juan Pardo's Explorations in the Interior Southeast, 1566–1568. *Florida Historical Quarterly* 62:125–58.
1985   The Hernando de Soto Expedition: From Chiaha to Mabilia. In *Alabama and the Borderlands, from Prehistory to Statehood*, edited by R. Reid Badger and Lawrence A. Clayton, 108–26. Tuscaloosa: University of Alabama Press.

DePratter, Chester B., and Chris Judge.
1986   A Provisional Late Prehistoric and Early Historic Ceramic Sequence for the Wateree River Valley, South Carolina. Paper presented at the LAMAR Institute Conference on South Appalachian Mississippian, May 9–10, Macon, Ga.

Deutschle, Stephen A.
1973   The Site and Its Setting with a Description of Excavations. In *Analysis of the Lamar Site (9 Bi 7) Materials at the Southeast Archeological Center*, edited by Hale G. Smith, 1–18. Submitted to the Southeast Archeological Center, National Park Service, Tallahassee, Fla. Contract no. 500031136.

Dickens, Roy S., Jr.
1970   The Pisgah Culture and Its Place in the Prehistory of the Southern Appalachians. Ph.D. diss., Department of Anthropology, University of North Carolina, Chapel Hill.
1975   A Processual Approach to Mississippian Origins on the Georgia Piedmont. *Southeastern Archaeological Conference Bulletin* 18:31–42.
1976   *Cherokee Prehistory: The Pisgah Phase in the Appalachian Summit Region.* Knoxville: University of Tennessee Press.
1978   Mississippian settlement patterns in the Appalachian Summit Area: The Pisgah and Qualla phases. In *Mississippian Settlement Patterns*, edited by Bruce D. Smith, 115–40. New York: Academic Press.
1979   *Archaeological Investigations at Horseshoe Bend National Military Park, Alabama.* Special Publication no. 3. University: Alabama Archaeological Society.

Duke, P. G., J. Ebert, G. Langemann, and A. P. Buchner, editors.
1978   *Diffusion and Migration: Their Roles in Cultural Development.* Proceedings of the Tenth Annual Conference of the Archaeological Association of the University of Calgary.

Dunbar, James S., Michael K. Faught, and S. David Webb.
1988   Page/Ladson (8Je591): An Underwater Paleo-Indian Site in Northwestern Florida. *Florida Anthropologist* 36:18–30.

Dunnell, Robert C.
1978   Style and Function: A Fundamental Dichotomy. *American Antiquity* 43:192–202.
1980   Evolutionary Theory and Archaeology. In *Advances in Archaeological Method and Theory*, edited by Michael B. Schiffer. Vol. 3, 35–99. New York: Academic Press.
1986   Five Decades in American Archaeology. In *American Archaeology Past and Future*, edited by David J. Meltzer, Don D. Fowler, and Jeremy A. Sabloff, 23–49. Washington, D.C.: Smithsonian Institution Press.
1989   Aspects of the Application of Evolutionary Theory in Archaeology. In *Archaeological Thought in America*, edited by C. C. Lamberg-Karlovsky, 35–49. Cambridge: Cambridge University Press.

Egloff, Brian J.
1967   An Analysis of Ceramics from Historic Cherokee Towns. Master's thesis, Department of Anthropology, University of North Carolina, Chapel Hill.

Elliott, Daniel T.
1978   Wallace Reservoir Collector Survey: 1977–1978. Ms. on file, Department of Anthropology, University of Georgia, Athens.
1982   *Flint River Archaeological Survey and Testing, Albany Georgia.* Athens, Ga.: Soil Systems Inc.
1984   Finch's Survey. *Early Georgia* 9 (1–2): 14–24.

Elliott, Daniel T., and Roy Doyon.
1981   *Archaeological and Historical Geography of the Savannah River Floodplain near Augusta, Georgia.* Laboratory of Archaeology Series, Report no. 22. Athens: University of Georgia.

Elliott, Daniel T., and Jack T. Wynn.

1991   The Vining Revival: A Late Simple Stamped Phase in the Central Georgia Piedmont. *Early Georgia* 19 (1): 1–18.

Ewers, John C.

1940a   Exhibit Plan for Ocmulgee National Monument Museum. Ms. on file, Ocmulgee National Monument, Macon, Ga.

1940b   Interpreting Archeology to the Public. *Proceedings of the Society for Georgia Archaeology* 3 (1): unpaginated.

Fagette, Paul H., Jr.

1985   Digging for Dollars: The Impact of the New Deal on the Professionalization of American Archaeology. Ph.D. diss., Department of History, University of California, Riverside.

Fairbanks, Charles H.

1940a   The Macon Earthlodge. *Society for American Archaeology Notebook* (April): unpaginated.

1940b   The Lamar Palisade. *Proceedings of the Society for Georgia Archaeology* 3 (1): unpaginated.

1940c   Mound C, Macon Group. *Newsletter of the Southeastern Archaeological Conference* 2 (3): 4.

1940d   Salt Pans from the Southeast. *American Antiquity* 6:65–67.

1941a   Archaeological Site Report on the Kolomoki Mound Group. Ms. on file, Southeast Archeological Center, National Park Service, Tallahassee, Fla.

1941b   Culture History of the Lamar Aspect. Paper presented at the 6th Southeastern Arhaeological Conference, Lexington, Ky.

1941c   Stallings Island Focus Defined and Compared with Kentucky Archaic and New York Laurentian. Paper presented at the 6th Southeastern Archaeological Conference, Lexington, Ky.

1941d   Palisaded Town. *Regional Review* 6 (5–6): 3–9.

1942   The Taxonomic Position of Stallings Island, Georgia. *American Antiquity* 7:223–31.

1946a   The Kolomoki Mound Group, Early County, Georgia. *American Antiquity* 11:258–60.

1946b   The Macon Earth Lodge. *American Antiquity* 12:94–108.

1950   Preliminary Segregation of Etowah, Savannah, and Lamar. *American Antiquity* 16:142–51.

1952a   Archeological Explorations at Fort Caroline National Historical Park Project, Florida. Ms. on file, Southeast Archeological Center, National Park Service, Tallahassee, Fla.

1952b   Creek and Pre-Creek. *In Archeology of Eastern United States*, edited by James B. Griffin, 285–300. Chicago: University of Chicago Press.

1953a   The Protohistoric Creek of Georgia. *Newsletter of the Southeastern Archaeological Conference* 3 (3): 21–22.

1953b   Report on Excavations at Fort Frederica National Monument, 1953. Ms. on file, Southeast Archeological Center, National Park Service, Tallahassee, Fla.

1954a   The Excavation of Mound C, Ocmulgee National Monument, Macon, Georgia. Ph.D. diss., Department of Anthropology, University of Michigan, Ann Arbor.

1954b   1953 Excavations at Site 9-Hl-64, Buford Reservoir, Georgia. *Florida State University Studies* 16:1–26.

1954c   The Stabilization of the Funeral Mound. Ms. on file, Southeast Archeological Center, National Park Service, Tallahassee, Fla.

1955   The Abercrombie Mound, Russell County, Alabama. *Early Georgia* 2 (1): 13–19.

1956a   *Archeology of the Funeral Mound, Ocmulgee National Monument, Georgia*. Archeological Research Series, no. 3. USDI National Park Service, Washington, D.C.

1956b   The Excavation of the Hawkins-Davidson Houses, Fort Frederica National Monument, St. Simons Island, Georgia. *Georgia Historical Quarterly* 49 (3): 213–29.

1958   Some Problems of the Origin of Creek Pottery. *Florida Anthropologist* 11 (2): 53–64.

1962   Excavations at Horseshoe Bend, Alabama. *Florida Anthropologist* 15 (2): 41–56.

1973   The Cultural Significance of Spanish Ceramics. In *Ceramics in America*, edited by Ian M. G. Quimby, 141–74. Charlottesville: University Press of Virginia.

1979   The Function of Black Drink Among Creeks. In *Black Drink: A Native American Tea*, edited by Charles M. Hudson, 120–49. Athens: University of Georgia Press.

1981   Introduction to the Second Printing. In *Archeology of the Funeral Mound, Ocmulgee National Monument, Georgia*, by Charles H. Fairbanks, unpaginated. Reprint, Ocmulgee National Monument Association, Macon, Ga. Original edition, Washington, D.C.: National Park Service, 1956.

Fairbanks, Charles H., Arthur R. Kelly, Gordon R. Willey, and Pat Wofford, Jr.

1946   The Leake Mounds, Bartow County, Georgia. *American Antiquity* 12:126–27.

Faulkner, Charles H.

1967   Tennessee Radiocarbon Dates. *Tennessee Archaeologist* 23:12–30.

1975   The Mississippian-Woodland Transition in the Eastern Tennessee Valley. *Southeastern Archaeological Conference Bulletin* 18:19–30.

Faust, Richard D.

1971   Archeological Survey of the Proposed Keokee Lake, Jefferson National Forest, Virginia. Ms. on file, Southeast Archeological Center, National Park Service, Tallahassee, Fla.

Faust, Richard D., and Hale G. Smith, compilers.

1973   Lamar Symposium. Ms. on file, Southeast Archeological Center, National Park Service, Tallahassee, Fla.

Ferguson, Leland G.

1971   South Appalachian Mississippian. Ph.D. diss., Department of Anthropology, University of North Carolina, Chapel Hill.

1975   *Archaeology at Scott's Lake: Exploratory Research in 1972, 1973.* Institute of Archaeology and Anthropology, Research Manuscript Series, no. 68. Columbia: University of South Carolina.

Ferguson, Leland, editor.
1974   Archaeological Investigations at the Mulberry Site. *Notebook* 6 (3–4): 57–122. South Carolina Institute of Archaeology and Anthropology. Columbia: University of South Carolina.

Ferguson, Leland G., and Randolph J. Widmer.
1976   *Archaeological Examination of a Transect Through the Middle Savannah River Valley, The Bobby Jones Expressway*. South Carolina Institute of Archeology and Anthropology, Research Manuscript Series, no. 89. Columbia: University of South Carolina.

Figgins, Jesse D.
1927   The Antiquity of Man in America. *Natural History* 27 (3): 240–47.
1933   A Further Contribution to the Antiquity of Man in America. *Proceedings of the Colorado Museum of Natural History* 12 (2).

Fish, Paul R., and Thomas Gresham.
1990   Insights from Full-Coverage Survey in the Georgia Piedmont. In *The Archaeology of Regions: A Case for Full-Coverage Survey*, edited by Suzanne K. Fish and Stephen A. Kowalewski, 147–72. Washington, D.C.: Smithsonian Institution Press.

Fish, Paul, and David J. Hally.
1986   The Wallace Reservoir Archaeological Project: An Overview. *Early Georgia* 11 (1–2): 1–19.

Fish, Suzanne K.
1979   Archaeological Investigations at the Cold Spring Site (9Ge10). Ms. on file, Department of Anthropology, University of Georgia, Athens.

Fish, Suzanne K., and Richard W. Jefferies.
1986   The Site Plan at Cold Springs, 9Ge10. *Early Georgia* 11:61–73.

Ford, James A.
1934   Mound Builders Were Pit Dwellers. *El Palacio* 36 (9–10): 74–75.
1936   *Analysis of Indian Village Site Collections from Louisiana and Mississippi*. Anthropological Study no. 2, Department of Conservation, Louisiana State Geological Survey, New Orleans.
1937   An Archaeological Report on the Elizafield Ruins. In *Georgia's Disputed Ruins*, edited by E. Merton Coulter, 193–225. Chapel Hill: University of North Carolina Press.
1951   *Greenhouse: A Troyville–Coles Creek Period Site in Avoyelles Parish, Louisiana*. Anthropological Papers, vol. 44, pt. 1. New York: American Museum of Natural History.

Ford, James A., and James B. Griffin.
1960a   A Proposal for a Conference on Pottery Nomenclature for the Southeastern United States. Reprint, *Newslettter of the Southeastern Archaeological Conference* 7 (1): 5–9. Originally circulated by the Ceramic Repository for the Eastern United States, Museum of Anthropology, University of Michigan, Ann Arbor.
1960b   Report of the Conference on Southeastern Pottery Typology Held at the Ceramic Repository for the Eastern United States, Museum of Anthropology, University of Michigan, May 16–17, 1938, Ann Arbor. Reprint, *Newsletter of the Southeastern Archaeological Conference* 7 (1): 10–12. Original edition, Ann Arbor: Ceramic Repository for the Eastern United States, Museum of Anthropology, University of Michigan.

Ford, James A., and Gordon R. Willey.
1940   *Crooks Site: A Marksville Period Burial Mound in LaSalle Parish, Louisiana*. Anthropological Study no. 3. Department of Conservation, Louisiana Geological Survey, New Orleans.
1941   An interpretation of the prehistory of the Eastern United States. *American Anthropologist* 43:325–63.

Ford, Richard I.
1974   Northeastern Archaeology: Past and Future Directions. *Annual Review of Anthropology* 3:385–413.

Ford, Richard I., editor.
1978   *The Nature and Status of Ethnobotany*. Anthropological Papers, no. 67. Ann Arbor: Museum of Anthropology, University of Michigan.
1985   *Prehistoric Food Production in North America*. Anthropological Papers, no. 75. Ann Arbor, Museum of Anthropology, University of Michigan.

Fowler, Melvin L.
1969   Middle Mississippian Agricultural Fields. *American Antiquity* 34:365–75.
1978   Cahokia and the American Bottom: Settlement Archaeology. In *Mississippian Settlement Patterns*, edited by Bruce D. Smith, 455–78. New York: Academic Press.

Fowler, Melvin L., and Elizabeth Benchley.
1980   *Final Report of 1979 Archaeological Excavations at the Interpretive Center Tract Cahokia Mounds Historic Site*. Report of Investigations, no. 40. University of Wisconsin-Milwaukee Archaeological Research Laboratory.

Gallagher, James P., Robert Boszhardt, Robert F. Sasso, and Katherine Stevenson.
1985   Oneota Ridged Field Agriculture in Southwestern Wisconsin. *American Antiquity* 50 (3): 605–12.

Gallagher, James P., and Robert F. Sasso.
1986   Further Investigations into the Oneota Ridged Field Agriculture in Southwestern Wisconsin. Paper presented at the 51st annual meeting of the Society for American Archaeology, New Orleans, La.

Gardner, William M.
1977   Flint Run PaleoIndian Complex and its Implications for Eastern North America Prehistory. *Annals of the New York Academy of Sciences* 288:251–63.
1983   Stop Me If You've Heard This One Before: The Flint Run PaleoIndian Complex Revisited. *Archaeology of Eastern North America* 11:49–59.

Gentleman of Elvas.
1922   True Relation of the Vicissitudes That Attended the Governor Don Hernando De Soto and Some Nobles of Portugal in the Discovery of the Province of Florida. In *Narratives of the Career of Hernando de Soto in the Conquest of Florida*. Vol. 1. Translated by Buckingham Smith. Edited by Edward Gaylord Bourne. New York: Allerton.

Goad, Sharon I.
1975   Excavations on Skidaway Island: 9CH112. Ms. on file, Department of Anthropology, University of Georgia, Athens.

Goggin, John M.
1968   *Spanish Majolica in the New World: Types of the Sixteenth to Eighteenth Centuries*, edited by Irving Rouse and Anne F. Wilde. Yale University Publications in Anthropology 7.

Goodyear, Albert C., III.
1974   *The Brand Site: A Techno-functional Study of a Dalton Site in Northeast Arkansas.* Arkansas Archaeological Survey Research Series, no. 7. Fayetteville.
1979   *A Hypothesis for the Use of Cryptocrystalline Raw Materials Among PaleoIndian Groups of North America.* South Carolina Institute of Archeology and Anthropology, Research Manuscript Series, no. 156. Columbia: University of South Carolina.
1982   The Chronological Position of the Dalton Horizon in the Southeastern United States. *American Antiquity* 47:382–95.
1983   A Review and Synthesis of Early Archaic Research in South Carolina. Paper presented at the 40th annual meeting Southeastern Archaeological Conference, Columbia, S.C.
1991   The Early Holocene Occupation of the Southeastern United States: A Geoarchaeological Summary. In Ice Age Peoples of North America, edited by Robson Bonnichsen, George C. Frison, and Karen Turnmire. Orono, Me.: Center for the Study of the First Americans.

Goodyear, Albert C., and Tommy Charles.
1984   *An Archaeological Survey of Chert Quarries in Western Allendale County, South Carolina.* South Carolina Institute of Archaeology and Anthropology, Research Manuscript Series, no. 195. Columbia: University of South Carolina.

Goodyear, Albert C., John H. House, and Neal W. Ackerly.
1979   *Laurens-Anderson: An Archaeological Study of the Inter-riverine Piedmont.* South Carolina Institute of Archeology and Anthropology, Anthropological Studies, no. 4. Columbia: University of South Carolina.

Goodyear, Albert C., James L. Michie, and Tommy Charles.
1989   The Earliest South Carolinians. In *The Archaeology of South Carolina: Papers in Honor of Dr. Robert L. Stephenson*, edited by Glen T. Hanson and Albert C. Goodyear III., 19–52. South Carolina Institute of Archeology and Anthropology, Anthropological Studies, no. 7. Columbia: University of South Carolina.

Gould, Stephen Jay.
1986   Evolution and the Triumph of Homology, or Why History Matters. *American Scientist* 74:60–69.

Gresham, Thomas H., and Teresa P. Rudolph.
1986   *Archeological Survey of Anternative Routes for the Fall Line Freeway, Georgia.* 2 vols. Southeastern Archeological Services, Inc. Submitted to Georgia Department of Transportation, Atlanta.

Griffin, James B.
1938   The Ceramic Remains from Norris Basin, Tennessee. In *An Archaeological Survey of the Norris Basin in Eastern Tennessee*, by William S. Webb, 253–59. Smithsonian Institution, Bureau of American Ethnology Bulletin 118. Washington, D.C.
1946   Cultural Change and Continuity in Eastern United States. In *Man in Northeastern North America*, edited by Frederick Johnson, 37–95. Papers of the Robert S. Peabody Foundation for Archaeology. Vol. 3. Andover, Mass.: Phillips Academy.
1952a   Culture Periods in Eastern United States Archeology. In *Archeology of Eastern United States*, edited by James B. Griffin, 325–64. Chicago: University of Chicago Press.
1976   A Commentary on Some Archaeological Activities in the Mid-Continent 1925–1975. *Midcontinental Journal of Archaeology* 1:5–38.
1985a   Epilogue: Joffre Lanning Coe: The Quiet Giant of Southeastern Archaeology. In *Structure and Process in Southeastern Archaeology*, edited by Roy S. Dickens, Jr., and H. Trawick Ward, 287–307. University: University of Alabama Press.
1985b   An Individual's Participation in American Archaeology, 1928–85. *Annual Reviews in Anthropology* 14:1–23.

Griffin, James B., editor.
1952b   *Archeology of Eastern United States.* Chicago: University of Chicago Press.

Griffin, James B., and Arthur R. Kelly.
1936   Pottery Classification Code for Central Georgia. Ms. on file, Southeast Archeological Center, National Park Service, Tallahassee, Fla.

Griffin, John W.
1964   The Archaic Sequence in the Ocmulgee Bottoms. Paper presented at the 29th annual meeeting of the Society for American Archaeology, Chapel Hill, N.C.
1969a   Excavation of the Osceola Grave at Fort Moultrie, South Carolina. Paper presented at the 21st annual meeting of the Florida Anthropological Society, Gainesville, Fla.
1969b   The Search for Osceola, paper presented at the 21st annual meeting of the Fort Lauderdale Historical Society, Fort Lauderdale, Fla.
1969c   The Intensity and Nature of the Occupation of Russell Cave, Alabama. *Southeastern Archaeological Conference Bulletin* 11:36–41.
1974   *Investigations in Russell Cave.* Publications in Archeology 13. National Park Service, Washington, D.C.

Guthe, Carl E.
1952   Twenty-five Years of Archeology in the Eastern United States. In *Archeology of Eastern United States*, edited by James B. Griffin, 1–12. Chicago: University of Chicago Press.

Haag, William G.
1961   Twenty-five Years of Eastern Archaeology. *American Antiquity* 27:16–23.

1985 Federal Aid to Archaeology in the Southeast, 1933–1942. *American Antiquity* 50:272–80.

Hally, David J.
1970 *Archaeological Investigation of the Potts' Tract Site (9Mu103), Carters Dam, Murray County, Georgia.* Laboratory of Archaeology Series, Report no. 6. Athens: University of Georgia.

1975 *Archaeological Investigation of the King Site, Floyd County, Georgia*, Report submitted to the National Endowment for the Humanities, Grant no. 20561–74–441.

1976 The Mississippi Period. *Early Georgia* 3 (1): 37–52.

1979 *Archaeological Investigation of the Little Egypt Site (9Mu102), Murray County, Georgia, 1969 Season.* Laboratory of Archaeology Series, Report no. 18. Athens: University of Georgia.

1980 *Archaeological Investigation of the Little Egypt Site (9Mu102), Murray County, Georgia, 1970–72 Seasons.* Department of Anthropology, University of Georgia. Submitted to the Heritage Conservation and Recreation Service, United States Department of the Interior, Atlanta. Contract nos. 14–10–9–900–390, 1910P21041, 9911T000411, and C5546.

1981 Plant Preservation and the Content of Paleobotanical Samples: A Case Study. *American Antiquity* 46:723–42.

1986a The Cherokee Archaeology of Georgia. In *The Conference on Cherokee Prehistory*, compiled by David G. Moore, 95–121. Swannanoa, N.C.: Warren Wilson College.

1988 Archaeology and Settlement Plan of the King Site. In *The King Site: Continuity and Contact in Sixteenth-Century Georgia*, edited by R. L. Blakely, 3–16. Athens: University of Georgia Press.

1992 Platform Mound Construction and the Instability of Mississippian Chiefdoms. Ms. on file, Department of Anthropology, University of Georgia, Athens.

1993 The Territorial Size of Mississippian Chiefdoms. In *Archaeology of Eastern North America: Papers in Honor of Stephen Williams*, edited by James B. Stoltman, 143–68. Mississippi Department of Archives and History, Archaeological Report no. 25. Jackson.

Hally, David J., Patrick H. Garrow and Wyman Trotti.
1975 Preliminary Analysis of the King Site Settlement Plan. *Southeastern Archaeological Conference Bulletin* 18:55–62.

Hally, David J., C. M. Hudson, and C. B. DePratter.
1985 The Proto-Historic Along the Savannah River. Paper presented at the 42d annual meeting of the Southeastern Archaeological Conference, Birmingham, Ala.

Hally, David J., and James B. Langford, Jr.
1988 *Mississippi Period Archaeology of the Georgia Valley and Ridge Province.* Laboratory of Archaeology Series, Report no. 25. Athens: University of Georgia.

Hally, David J., and James L. Rudolph.
1986 *Mississippi Period Archaeology of the Georgia Piedmont.* Laboratory of Archaeology Series, Report no. 24. Athens: University of Georgia.

Hally, David J., Marvin T. Smith, and James B. Langford, Jr.
1990 The Archaeological Reality of DeSoto's Coosa. In *Columbian Consequences,* edited by David Hurst Thomas. Vol. 2, *Archaeological and Historical Perspectives on the Spanish Borderlands East,* 121–38. Washington, D.C.: Smithsonian Institution Press.

Hamilton, Christopher E.
1977 Development of Lamar Period Ceramics in Central Georgia. Master's thesis, Department of Anthropology, Florida State University, Tallahassee.

Hamilton, Christopher E., James Lauro, and David E. Swindell III.
1975 *Analysis of Material Culture Remains from the Cowarts Landing Site.* Department of Anthropololgy, Florida State University, Tallahassee. Submitted to Southeast Archeological Center, National Park Service, Tallahassee, Fla. Contract no. CX500050175.

Hanson, Glen T.
n.d. Unpublished research notes on file at the South Carolina Institute of Archeology and Anthropology, Columbia.

Hanson, Lee H., Jr.
1968 *Archeological Excavations in the Water Batteries at Fort Donelson national Military Park, Tennessee.* Office of Archeology and Historic Preservation, National Park Service, Washington, D.C.

1969 Archeological Survey of Town Creek Watershed Dam Number 46A, Natchez Trace Parkway. Ms. on file, Southeast Archeological Center, National Park Service, Tallahassee, Fla.

1970 Gunflints from the Macon Plateau. *Historical Archaeology* 4:51–58.

1971a Kaolin Pipe Stems: Boring in on a Fallacy. *The Conference on Historic Archaeology Papers 1969,* vol. 4, pt. 1: 109–11.

1971b A Reply to Gunflints and Chronology at Ocumlgee National Monument. *Historical Archaeology* 5:109–11.

Harrington, Jean C.
1952 Historic Site Archeology in the United States. In *Archeology of Eastern United States,* edited by James B. Griffin, 335–44. Chicago: University of Chicago Press.

Harris, Walter A.
1935 Old Ocmulgee Fields: The Capital Town of the Creek Confederacy. *Georgia Historical Quarterly* 19 (4): 273–90.

1944 *The Creek.* Macon, Ga.: J. W. Burke.

1958 *Here the Creeks Sat Down.* Macon, Ga.: J. W. Burke.

Harrold, Charles C.
1936 Old Ocmulgee Fields. *Macon Telegraph,* 1 May 1936.

1939 Georgia Archeology with Especial Reference to Recent Investigations in the Interior and on the Coast. *Georgia Historical Quarterly* 23 (1): 55–76.

Hatch, James W.
1974 Social Dimensions of Dallas Mortuary Patterns. Master's thesis, Department of Anthropology, Pennsylvania State University, State College.

1987 Upland Lamar Farmsteads in the Ocute Province: The Pennsylvania State University Archaeological

Program in Piedmont Georgia. Paper presented
at the 44th annual meeting of the Southeastern
Archaeological Conference, Charleston, S.C.

Hawkins, Benjamin.
1848   *Sketch of the Creek Country, in the Years 1798 and 1799.*
        Collections of the Georgia Historical Society, vol. 3,
        pt. 1. Savannah.
1916   *Letters of Benjamin Hawkins, 1796–1806.* Collections
        of the Georgia Historical Society, vol. 9. Savannah.
1966   Independence Letterbook: Col. Benjamin Hawkins,
        Indian Agent. Transcribed by Bernard Berg. Ms. on
        file, Ocmulgee National Monument, Macon, Ga.

Hayden, Brian.
1982   Interaction Parameters and the Demise of Paleo-
        Indian Craftsmanship. *Plains Anthropologist*
        27:109–23.

Haywood, John.
1823   *The Natural and Aboriginal History of Tennessee.*
        Nashville: George Wilson.

Heidenreich, C. H.
1974   A Relict Indian Corn Field Near Creemore, Ontario.
        Canadian Geographer 18 (4): 379–94.

Heimlick, Marion D.
1952   Guntersville Basin pottery. *Museum Paper 32.*
        Geological Survey of Alabama, University.

Helms, Mary W.
1979   *Ancient Panama: Chiefs in Search of Power.* Austin:
        University of Texas Press.

Hester, James J.
1972   *Blackwater No. 1: A Stratified Early Man Site in
        Eastern New Mexico.* Fort Burgwin Research Center,
        Publication no. 8. Ranchos de Taos, New Mexico:
        Southern Methodist University.

Heye, George, F. W. Hodge, and George H. Pepper.
1918   *The Nacoochee Mound in Georgia.* Museum of the
        American Indian, Heye Foundation Contributions,
        vol. 4, no. 3. New York: Museum of the American
        Indian, Heye Foundation.

Hickerson, Harold.
1965   The Virginia Deer and Intertribal Buffer Zones in
        the Upper Mississippi Valley. In *Man, Culture, and
        Animals*, edited by A. Leeds and A. P. Vayda, 43–65.
        AAAS Monograph.

Hill, James N.
1985   Style: A Conceptual Evolutionary Framework.
        In *Decoding Prehistoric Ceramics*, edited by Ben A.
        Nelson, 362–85. Carbondale: Southern Illinois
        University Press.

Hinsdale, Wilfred B.
1925   Indian Corn Culture in Michigan. *Proceedings of
        the Michigan Academy of Sciences, Arts and Letters*
        8:31–49.

Hodge, Frederick W.
1916   The Nacoochee Mound in Georgia. *Smithsonian
        Miscellaneous Collections* 66 (3): 75–82. Smithsonian
        Institution, Washington, D.C.

Holder, Preston.
1938   Excavations on Saint Simons Island and Vicinity,
        Glynn County, Georgia (Winter 1936–1937).

Proceedings of the Society for Georgia Archaeology 1 (1):
8–9.

Holland, C. G.
1974   A Mid-Eighteenth Century Indian Village on the
        Chattahoochee River. *Florida Anthropologist* 27 (1):
        31–46.

Holman, J. Alan
1982   Late Pleistocene Fossils in Georgia Jungle. *Explorer's
        Journal*, 160–63.
1985   Herpetofauna of Ladd's Quarry. *National Geographic
        Research* 1 (3): 423–36.

Holmes, William H.
1903   Aboriginal Pottery of the Eastern U.S. *Twentieth
        Annual Report of the Bureau of American Ethnology,
        1898–99.* Smithsonian Institution, Washington, D.C.

Holstein, Harry O., and Keith Little.
1987   *A Short Term Archaeological Investigation of the Davis
        Farm Archaeological Complex, A Multicomponent Pre-
        historic Site in Calhoun Co., Alabama.* Archaeological
        Resource Lab Research Series 1. Jacksonville, Ala.:
        Jacksonville State University.

Hudson, Charles M.
1987a   Juan Pardo's Excursion Beyond Chiaha. *Tennessee
        Anthropologist* 12:74–87.
1987b   An Unknown South: Spanish Explorers and
        Southeastern Chiefdoms, In *Visions and Revisions:
        Ethnohistoric Perspectives on Southern Cultures*, edited
        by George Sabo and William Schneider, 6–24.
        Proceedings of the Southern Anthropological
        Society, no. 20. Athens: University of Georgia Press.
1990   *The Juan Pardo Expeditions: Explorations of the Carolinas
        and Tennessee, 1566–1568.* Washington, D.C.:
        Smithsonian Institution Press.

Hudson, Charles, Marvin T. Smith, and Chester B. DePratter.
1984   The Hernando de Soto Expedition: From Apalachee
        to Chiaha. *Southeastern Archaeology* 3:65–77.
1990   The Hernando de Soto Expedition: From Mabilia
        to the Mississippi River. In *Towns and Temples Along
        the Mississippi*, edited by David Dye and Cheryl
        Anne Cox, 181–207. Tuscaloosa: University of
        Alabama Press.

Hudson, Charles, Marvin T. Smith, Chester B. DePratter, and
Emilia Kelley
1985   The Tristán de Luna Expedition, 1559–1561.
        Southeastern Archaeology 8:31–45.

Hudson, Charles, Marvin Smith, David Hally, Richard
Polhemus, and
Chester DePratter.
1985   Coosa: A Chiefdom in the Sixteenth-Century
        Southeastern United States. *American Antiquity*
        50:723–37.

Hurt, Wesley R.
1947   An Archaeological Survey, Chattahoochee Valley,
        Alabama. Ms. on file, Division of Archaeology,
        Alabama Museum of Natural History, Moundville.
1975   The Preliminary Archaeological Survey of the
        Chattahoochee Valley Area of Alabama. In *Archaeo-
        logical Salvage in the Walter F. George Basin of the
        Chattahoochee River in Alabama*, edited by D. L.

DeJarnette, 5–24. University: University of Alabama Press.

Huscher, Harold A.
1972   *Archaeological Investigations in the West Point Dam Area: A Preliminary Report*. Department of Anthropology, University of Georgia. Submitted to United States Department of the Interior, National Park Service. Contract nos. 14-10-0131-1616, 14-10-7:911-3, and 14-10-7:911-16.

Ingmanson, J. Earl.
1964a   Archeology of the South Plateau. Ms. on file, Southeast Archeological Center, National Park Service, Tallahassee, Fla.
1964b   Dunlap and McDougal Mounds, Ocmulgee National Monument. Ms. on file, Southeast Archeological Center, National Park Service, Tallahassee, Fla.
1964c   Survey of Archeological Resources of the Tobesofkee Creek Reservoir, Bibb County, Georgia. Ms. on file, Ocmulgee National Monument, Macon, Ga.
1965   Mound E, Southeastern Plateau and Middle Plateau Fortifications, Ocmulgee National Monument. Ms. on file, Southeast Archeological Center, National Park Service, Tallahassee, Fla.

Ingmanson, J. Earl, and George R. Fischer.
1966   An Unusual Archaic Site in Central Georgia: The Alligator Pond Site in Dooly County, Georgia. Ms. on file, Southeast Archeological Center, National Park Service, Tallahassee, Fla.

Irwin, Carol A.
1959   Dating English Pipe Stems. *Florida Anthropologist* 12 (3): 71–72.

Jennings, Jesse D.
1938a   The Archeological Significance of Kolomoki. In *Report on Kolomoki Mounds State Park*, by Charles M. Graves, unpaginated. Ms. on file, Southeast Archeological Center, National Park Service, Tallahassee, Fla.
1938b   Ocmulgee Archeology: Summary Through May 1938. Ms. on file, Ocmulgee National Monument, Macon, Ga.
1938c   *Ocmulgee Archaeology*. Southwestern Monuments Monthly Report for June, National Park Service, Coolidge, Ariz.
1939   Recent Excavations at the Lamar Site, Ocmulgee National Monument, *Proceedings of the Society for Georgia Archaeology* 2 (2): 45–55.
1957   Review of *Archeology of the Funeral Mound, Ocmulgee National Monument, Georgia*, by Charles H. Fairbanks. *American Antiquity* 23:93–94.

Jennings, Jesse D., and Charles H. Fairbanks.
1939   Pottery Type Descriptions. *Newsletter of the Southeastern Archaeological Conference* 1 (2): 1–8.
1940   Pottery Type Descriptions. *Newsletter of the Southeastern Archaeological Conference* 2 (2): 1–10.

Jochim, Michael A.
1976   *Hunter-Gatherer Subsistence and Settlement: A Predictive Model*. New York: Academic Press.

Johnson, Gregory A.
1982   Organizational Structure and Scalar Stess. In *Theory and Explanation in Archaeology*, edited by C. Renfrew, M. J. Rowlands, and B. A. Segraves, 389–421. New York: Academic Press.

Jones, Charles C., Jr.
1861   *Monumental Remains of Georgia*. Savannah: John M. Cooper and Co.
1873   *Antiquities of Southern Indians, Particularly of the Georgia Tribes*. New York: D. Appleton.

Judd, Neil M.
1929   The Present Status of Archaeology in the United States. *American Anthropologist* 31:401–18.
1967   *The Bureau of American Ethnology: A Partial History*. Norman: University of Oklahoma Press.

Kahler, Herbert E.
1935   November 29, 1935, Letter to Arthur R. Kelly. Ms. on file, Southeast Archeological Center, National Park Service, Tallahassee, Fla.

Kappler, Charles J., compiler.
1972   *Indian Treaties, 1778–1883*. New York: Interland Publishing.

Keel, Bennie C.
1975   On South Appalachian Mississippian in the Appalachian Summit Area. *Southeastern Archaeological Conference Bulletin* 18:12–18.
1976   *Cherokee Archaeology: A Study of the Appalachian Summit*. Knoxville: University of Tennessee Press.

Kellar, James H., A. R. Kelly, and Edward V. McMichael.
1962a   *Final Report on Archeological Explorations at the Mandeville Site, 9Cla1, Clay County, Georgia, Seasons 1959, 1960, 1961*. Laboratory of Archaeology Series, Report no. 8. Athens: University of Georgia.
1962b   The Mandeville Site in Southwestern Georgia. *American Antiquity* 27:336–55.

Kelly, Arthur R.
1933   Some Problems of Recent Cahokia Archaeology. *Transactions of the Illinois State Academy of Science* 25 (4): 101–3.
1935a   Discovery of a Prehistoric Pit House Village in Central Georgia. Ms. on file, Southeast Archeological Center, National Park Service, Tallahassee, Fla.
1935b   Exploring Prehistoric Georgia. *Scientific American* 152, nos. 3–5, 117–20, 185–87, 244–46.
1935c   Discovery of an Early Flint Industry with Possible Folsom Implications on an Archaeological Site in Central Georgia. Ms. on file, Southeast Archeological Center, National Park Service, Tallahassee, Fla.
1935d   Georgia. *American Antiquity* 1:61–63.
1936a   January 16, 1936, Letter to Verne E. Chatelain, Acting Assistant Director, National Park Service. Ms. on file, Southeast Archeological Center, National Park Service, Tallahassee, Fla.
1936b   March 4, 1936, Letter to John R. Swanton. Ms. on file, Southeast Archeological Center, National Park Service, Tallahassee, Fla.
1937a   Glimpses of a Macon Chronology: A Statement of Progress at the End of Three Years of Field Work. Ms. on file, Southeast Archeological Center, National Park Service, Tallahassee, Fla.
1937b   Lamar and Related Site Exploration in Georgia.

Ms. on file, Southeast Archeological Center, National Park Service, Tallahassee, Fla.

1938a   January 18, 1938, Letter to James A. Ford. Ms. on file, Southeast Archeological Center, National Park Service, Tallahassee, Fla.

1938b   The Need of a Museum of Southeastern Archaeology. Paper presented at the spring meeting of the Society for Georgia Archaeology, Savannah.

1938c   *A Preliminary Report on Archeological Explorations at Macon, Georgia.* Smithsonian Institution, Bureau of American Ethnology Bulletin 119. Washington, D.C.

1938d   The Southeast as an Archaeological Area. Paper presented at a regional meeting of the Society for American Archaeology, Milwaukee, Wisc.

1939   The Macon Trading Post: An Historical Foundling. *American Antiquity* 4:328–33.

1940   Archaeology in the National Park Service. *American Antiquity* 5:274–82.

1945   Jessups Bluff: A New Early Stamped Pottery Site at Ocmulgee National Monument. *American Antiquity* 11:134–35.

1965   Notes on a Prehistoric Cultivated Field in Macon, Georgia. *Southeastern Archaeological Conference Bulletin* 3:49–51.

1973   Early Villages on the Chattahoochee River, Georgia. *Archaeology* 26:26–33.

Kelly, Arthur R., and Fay-Cooper Cole.

1931   Rediscovering Illinois. *Blue Book of the State of Illinois, 1931–1932*, 328–33. Springfield.

Kelly, Arthur R., and Clemens de Baillou.

1960   Excavation of the Presumptive Site of Estatoe. *Southern Indian Studies* 12:3–30.

Kelly, Arthur R., Clemens de Baillou, Frank T. Schnell, Margaret V. Clayton, Francis J. Clune, Jr., and Ann L. Schlosser.

1969   *Excavations in Stewart County, Georgia, Summer and Fall, 1961.* Department of Anthropology, University of Georgia. Submitted to the USDI National Park Service. Contract nos. 14 10 0131–803 and 14 10 0131–823.

Kelly, Arthur R., and Robert S. Neitzel.

1961   *The Chauga Site in Oconee County, South Carolina.* Laboratory of Archaeology Series, Report no. 3. Athens: University of Georgia.

Kelly, Arthur R., Richard Nonas, Bettye Broyles, Clemens de Baillou, David W. Chase, and Frank T. Schnell, Jr.

1962   *Survey of Archaeological Sites in Clay County Georgia, Other than Mandeville, 9Cla1: 9Cla2, Cla7, Cla15, Cla28, Cla38, Cla51, and Qu25.* Laboratory of Archaeology Series, Report no. 5. Athens: University of Georgia.

Kelly, Arthur R., and Betty A. Smith.

1975   *The Swift Creek Site, 9-Bi-3, Macon, Georgia.* Department of Anthropology, University of Georgia. Submittted to Southeast Archeological Center, National Park Service, Tallahassee, Fla. Contract no. 500041720.

Kelly, Robert L.

1983   Hunter-Gatherer Mobility Strategies. *Journal of Anthropological Research* 39:277–306.

Kidder, Alfred V.

1931   *Pottery of Pecos.* Vol. 1, *The Dull-Paint Wares.* Papers of the Phillips Academy Southwestern Expedition, no. 5. New Haven: Yale University Press.

Kidder, Alfred V., and Anna O. Shepard.

1936   *Pottery of Pecos.* Vol. 2, *The Glaze-Paint, Culinary and Other Wares.* Papers of the Phillips Academy Southwestern Expedition, no. 7. New Haven: Yale University Press.

Kimball, Larry R.

1980   The 1977 Archaeological Reconnaissance and an Overall Assessment of the Archaeological Resources of Tellico Reservoir. Department of Anthropology, University of Georgia. Submitted to the National Park Service and Tennessee Valley Authority. Contract nos. CX5000–7-5544, CX5000–9-5944, and TV53015A.

1985   *The 1977 Archaeological Survey: An Overall Assessment of the Archaeological Resources of Tellico Reservoir.* Report of Investigations, no. 40. Department of Anthropology, University of Tennessee, Knoxville.

King, Blanche Busey (Mrs. Fain King).

1971   *Under Your Feet.* Reprint, Freeport, N.Y.: Books for Libraries Press. Original edition, New York: Dodd, Mead, 1939.

Kneberg, Madeline.

1952   The Tennessee Area. In *Archeology of Eastern United States*, edited by James B. Griffin, 190–98. Chicago: University of Chicago Press.

1961   Four Southeastern Limestone Tempered Pottery Complexes. *Newsletter of the Southeastern Archaeological Conference* 7 (2): 3–14.

Knight, Vernon J., Jr.

1980   Culture Complexes of the Alabama Piedmont: An Initial Statement. *Journal of Alabama Archaeology* 26 (1): 1–27.

1985a   *East Alabama Archaeological Survey: 1984 Season.* Office of Archaeological Research, Report of Investigations, no. 44. Tuscaloosa: Alabama State Museum of Natural History, University of Alabama.

1985b   *Tukabatchee: Archaeological Investigations at an Historic Creek Town, Elmore County, Alabama, 1984.* Office of Archaeological Research, Report of Investigations, no. 45. Tuscaloosa: Alabama State Museum of Natural History, University of Alabama.

1990   *Excavation of the Truncated Mound at the Walling Site: Middle Woodland Culture and Copena in the Tennessee Valley.* Division of Archaeology, Report of Investigations, no. 56. Tuscaloosa: Alabama State Museum of Natural History, University of Alabama.

Knight, Vernon J., Jr., Gloria G. Cole, and Richard Walling.

1984   *An Archaeological Reconnaissance of the Coosa and Tallapoosa River Valleys, East Alabama: 1983.* Office of Archaeological Research, Report of Investigations, no. 34. Tuscaloosa: Alabama State Museum of Natural History, University of Alabama.

Knight, Vernon J., Jr., and Tim S. Mistovich.

1984   *Walter F. George Lake: Archaeological Survey of Fee Owned Lands, Alabama and Georgia.* Office of

Archaeological Research, Report of Investigations, no. 42. Tuscaloosa: Alabama State Museum of Natural History, University of Alabama.

Knight, Vernon J., Jr., and Marvin T. Smith.
1980   Big Tallassee; A Contribution to Upper Creek Site Archaeology. *Early Georgia* 8 (1–2): 59–74.

Kowalewski, Stephen A., and James W. Hatch.
1991   The Sixteenth-Century Expansion of Settlement in the Upper Oconee Watershed, Georgia. *Southeastern Archaeology* 10:1–17.

Kowalewski, Stephen A., and Mark Williams.
1989   The Carroll Site: Analysis of 1936 Excavations at a Mississippian Farmstead in Georgia. *Southeastern Archaeology* 8:46–67.

Krause, Richard A.
1985   Trends and Trajectories in American Archaeology: Some Questions about the Mississippian Period in Southeastern Prehistory. In *Alabama and the Borderlands: From Prehistory to Statehood*, edited by R. Reid Badger and Lawrence A. Clayton, 17–39. University: University of Alabama Press.

Krogman, Wilton M.
1973   *The Human Skeleton in Forensic Medicine.* Springfield, Ill.: C. C. Thomas.

Kurjack, Edward B.
1975   Archaeological Investigations in the Walter F. George Basin. In *Archaeological Salvage in the Walter F. George Basin of the Chattahoochee River in Alabama*, edited by D. L. DeJarnette, 87–198. University: University of Alabama Press.

Kurjack, Edward B., and Fred Lamar Pearson, Jr.
1975   Special Investigations of 1Ru101, The Spanish Fort Site. In *Archaeological Salvage of the Walter F. George Basin of the Chattahoochee River in Alabama*, edited by D. L. DeJarnette, 200–222. University: University of Alabama Press.

Langford, James B., Jr., and Marvin T. Smith.
1990   Recent Investigations in the Core of the Coosa Province. In *Lamar Archaeology: Mississippian Chiefdoms in the Deep South*, edited by Mark Williams and Gary Shapiro, 104–16. Tuscaloosa: University of Alabama Press.

Lapham, Increase A.
1885   Antiquities of Wisconsin. *Smithsonian Contributions to Knowledge*, vol. 7, art. 4. Washington D.C.

Larsen, Clark Spencer, and David Hurst Thomas.
1986   *The Archaeology of St. Catherine's Island: 5. The South End Mound Complex.* Anthropological Papers, vol. 63, pt. 1, New York: American Museum of Natural History.

Larsen, Curtis E.
1982   Geo-archaeology of the Haw River. In *The Haw River Sites: Archaeological Investigations at Two Stratified Sites in the North Carolina Piedmont*, compiled by Stephen R. Claggett and John S. Cable, 145–222. Report no. R-2386. Jackson, Mich.: Commonwealth Associates.

Larson, Lewis H., Jr.
1955   Unusual Figurine From the Georgia Coast. *Florida Anthropologist* 8 (3): 75–81.
1957   The Norman Mound, McIntosh County Georgia. *Florida Anthropologist* 10 (1–2): 37–52.
1971a   Archaeological Implications of Social Stratification of the Etowah Site, Georgia. In *Approaches to the Social Dimensions of Mortuary Practices*, edited by James A. Brown, 58–67. Society for American Archaeology, Memoir 25.
1971b   Settlement Distribution During the Mississippian Period. *Southeastern Archaeological Conference Bulletin* 13:19–25.
1972   Functional Considerations of Aboriginal Warfare in the Southeast During the Mississippi Period. *American Antiquity* 37:383–92.
1976   Introduction. *Early Georgia* 3 (1): vii.
1980   *Aboriginal Subsistence Technology on the Southeastern Coastal Plain During the Late Prehistoric Period*, Gainesville: University Presses of Florida.

Lawson, John.
1967   *A New Voyage to Carolina by John Lawson.* Edited by Hugh T. Lefler. Chapel Hill: University of North Carolina Press.

Ledbetter, R. Jerald.
1978   Subsurface Backhoe Testing Program, Wallace Reservoir Project. Ms. on file, Department of Anthropology, University of Georgia, Athens.
1988   The Pig Pen Site: Archeological Investigations at 9Ri158, Richmond County, Georgia. Ms. on file, Southeastern Archeological Services, Athens, Ga.

Ledbetter, R. Jerald, Stephen A. Kowalewski, and Lisa D. O'Steen.
1984   Chert of Southern Oconee County, Georgia. *Early Georgia* 9:1–13.

Ledbetter, R. Jerald, W. Dean Wood, Karen G. Wood, Robbie F. Ethridge, and Chad O. Braley.
1987   *Cultural Resources Survey of Allatoona Lake Area.* Southeastern Archaeological Services, Athens, Ga. Submitted to U.S. Army Engineer District, Mobile, Ala. Contract no. DACWO1–85–R-0061.

Lewis, Thomas M. N., and Madeline Kneberg.
1941a   The Prehistory of the Chickamauga Basin. Ms. on file, Frank H. McClung Museum, University of Tennessee, Knoxville.
1941b   *The Prehistory of the Chickamauga Basin in Tennessee: A Preview.* Anthropological Papers, no. 1. Department of Anthropology, University of Tennessee, Knoxville.
1946   *Hiwassee Island: An Archaeological Account of Four Indian Peoples.* Knoxville: University of Tennessee Press.

Linton, Ralph.
1924a   The Significance of Certain Traits in North American Maize Culture. *American Anthropologist* 26:345–49.
1924b   The Origin of the Plains Earthlodge. *American Anthropologist* 26:247–57.

Little, Keith, and Caleb Curren, Jr.
1981   Site 1CE308: A Protohistoric Site on the Upper

Coosa River in Alabama. *Journal of Alabama Archaeology* 27:117–24.

Lovejoy, C. Owen, Richard S. Meindl, Thomas R. Pryzbeck, and Robert P. Mensforth.

1985　Chronological Metamorphosis of the Aricular Surface of the Ilium: A New Method for the Determination of Adult Skeletal Age at Death. *American Journal of Physical Anthropology* 68 (1): 15–28.

Lyon, Edwin A., II.

1982　*New Deal Archaeology in the Southeast: WPA, TVA, NPS, 1934–1942*. Department of History, Louisiana State University. Ann Arbor: University Microfilms.

McDowell, William L., editor.

1955　*Journals of the Commisssioners of the Indian Trade, September 20, 1710–August 29, 1718*. Columbia: South Carolina Archives Department.

McIntyre, Lucy B.

1939　The Use of Negro Women in W.P.A. Work at Irene Mound, Savannah. *Proceedings of the Society for Georgia Archaeology* 2 (1): 23–25.

McKusic, Marshal.

1971　*The Grant Oneota Village*. Iowa City: University of Iowa.

McMichael, Edward V., and James A. Kellar.

1960　*Archaeological Salvage in the Oliver Basin*. Laboratory of Archaeology Series, Report no. 2. Athens: University of Georgia.

McMurray, Carl D.

1974　Swift Creek Site Fieldnotes. Ms. on file, Department of Anthropology, West Georgia College, Carrollton.

Mainfort, Robert C., Jr.

1986　*Pinson Mounds: A Middle Woodland Ceremonial Center*. Research Series, no. 7. Division of Archaeology, Tennessee Department of Conservation, Nashville.

Manning, Mary Kathleen.

1982　*Archaeological Investigations at 9PM260*. Wallace Reservoir Project, Contribution no. 16. Department of Anthropology, University of Georgia, Athens.

Marsh, Alan.

1986　Ocmulgee National Monument: An Administrative History. Ms. on file, Ocmulgee National Monument, Macon, Ga.

Marshall, Richard A.

1971　An Unusual House at the Browns Mountain Site. *Newsletter of the Southeastern Archaeological Conference* 10 (2): 24–25.

Martin, Paul S.

1984　Prehistoric Overkill: The Global Model. In *Quaternary Extinctions: A Prehistoric Revolution*, edited by Paul S. Martin and Richard G. Klein, 354–403. Tucson: University of Arizona Press.

Martin, Paul S., and Richard G. Klein, editors.

1984　*Quaternary Extinctions: A Prehistoric Revolution*. Tucson: University of Arizona Press.

Mason, Carol Irwin.

1963a　*The Archaeology of Ocmulgee Old Fields, Macon, Georgia*. University of Michigan. Ann Arbor: University Microfilms.

1963b　Eighteenth Century Culture Change Among the Lower Creeks. *Florida Anthropologist* 16:65–80.

1971　Gunflints and Chronology at Ocmulgee National Monument. *Historical Archaeology* 5:106–9.

1973　Historic Archaeology on the Middle Plateau. In *Middle Plateau Accession Analysis*, edited by Hale G. Smith, Appendix A, unpaginated. Florida State University, Tallahassee. Submitted to Southeast Archeological Center, National Park Service, Tallahassee, Fla. Contract no. 500031293.

Mattison, Ray H.

1946　The Creek Trading House: From Colerain to Fort Hawkins. *Georgia Historical Quarterly* 30:176–83.

Maxwell, Moreau S.

1951　*The Woodland Cultures of Southern Illinois: Archaeological Excavations in the Carbondale Area*. Logan Museum Publications in Anthropology, no. 7. Beloit, Wisc.

Mead, Jim I., and David J. Meltzer.

1984　North American Late Quaternary Extinctions and the Radiocarbon Record. In *Quaternary Extinctions: A Prehistoric Revolution*, edited by Paul S. Martin and Richard G. Klein, 440–50. Tucson: University of Arizona Press.

Meillassoux, Claude.

1981　*Maidens, Meals and Money: Capitalism and the Domestic Community*. Cambridge: Cambridge University Press.

Meltzer, David J.

1984　*Late Pleistocene Human Adaptations in Eastern North America*. Department of Anthropology, University of Washington, Seattle. Ann Arbor: University Microfilms.

1988　Late Pleistocene Human Adaptations in Eastern North America. *Journal of World Prehistory* 2:1–53.

Meltzer, David J., and Bruce D. Smith.

1986　Paleoindian and Early Archaic Subsistence Strategies in Eastern North America. In *Foraging, Collecting, and Harvesting: Archaic Period Subsistence and Settlement in the Eastern Woodlands*, edited by Sarah W. Neusius, 3–31. Occasional Paper no. 6. Center for Archaeological Investigations. Carbondale: Southern Illinois University.

Michie, James L.

1968　The Edgefield Scraper. *Chesopiean* 6:30–31.

1969　Excavations at Tom's (Thom's) Creek. *Notebook* 1 (10): 2–16. South Carolin Institute of Archeology and Anthropology. Columbia: University of South Carolina.

1971　Excavations at the Taylor Site. *Southeastern Archaeological Conference Bulletin* 13:47–48.

1972　The Edgefield Scraper: A Tool of Inferred Antiquity and Use. *South Carolina Antiquities* 4:1–10.

1977　Early Man in South Carolina. Ms. on file, South Carolina Institute of Archeology and Anthropology, University of South Carolina, Columbia.

Milanich, Jerald T., Ann S. Cordell, Vernon James Knight, Jr., Timothy A. Kohler, and Brenda J. Sigler-Lavelle.

1984　*McKeithen Weeden Island: The Culture of Northern Florida, A.D. 200–900*. Orlando: Academic Press.

Milanich, Jerald T., and Charles H. Fairbanks.

1980　*Florida Archaeology*. Orlando: Academic Press.

Miller, Christopher L., and George R. Hamell.
1986   A New Perspective on Indian-White Contact: Cultural Symbols and Colonial Trade. *Journal of American History* 73 (2): 311–28.

Milner, George R.
1982   *Measuring Prehistoric Levels of Health: A Study of Mississippian Period Skeletal Remains from the American Bottom, Illinois*. Department of Anthropology, Northwestern University. Ann Arbor: University Microfilms.

Milner, George R., and Virginia G. Smith.
1986   *New Deal Archaeology in Kentucky: Excavations, Collections and Research*. Program for Cultural Resource Assessment, Occasional Papers in Anthropology, no. 5. Lexington: University of Kentucky.

Mistovich, Tim S., and Vernon James Knight, Jr.
1986   *Excavations at Four Sites on Walter F. George Lake, Alabama and Georgia*. Office of Archaeological Research, Report of Investigations, no. 51. Tuscaloosa: Alabama State Museum of Natural History, University of Alabama.

Moffat, Charles R.
1979   Some Observations on the Distribution and Significance of the Garden Beds of Wisconsin. *Wisconsin Archaeologist* 60:222–48.

Moore, Clarence B.
1897   Certain Aboriginal Mounds of the Georgia Coast. *Journal of the Academy of Natural Sciences of Philadelphia* 11, pt. 1, 5–138.
1907   Mounds of the Lower Chattahoochee and Lower Flint Rivers. *Journal of the Academy of Natural Sciences of Philadelphia* 13, pt. 3: 426–56.

Moore, Jackson W., Jr.
n.d.   Excavations at the Purported Davis Tavern Site, Cumberland Gap National Historical Park, Kentucky-Tennessee-Virginia. Ms. on file, Southeast Archeological Center, National Park Service, Tallahassee, Fla.

Moorehead, Warren K, editor.
1932   *The Etowah Papers*. Department of Archaeology, Phillips Andover Academy Publications. Vol. 3. New Haven: Yale University Press.

Morgan, Lewis H.
1881   *Houses and House-Life of the American Aborigines*. U.S. Geographical and Geological Survey of the Rocky Mountain Region: Contributions to North American Ethnology. Vol. 4. Government Printing Office. Washington.

Morrell, L. Ross.
1965   *The Woods Island Site in Southeastern Acculturation, 1625–1800*. Notes in Anthropology 11. Department of Anthropology, Florida State University, Tallahassee.

Morse, Dan F.
1971   Recent Indications of Dalton Settlement Pattern in Northeast Arkansas. *Southeastern Archaeological Conference Bulletin* 13:5–10.
1973   Dalton Culture in Northeast Arkansas. *Florida Anthropologist* 26 (1): 23–38.

Muller, Jon.
1986   *Archaeology of the Lower Ohio River Valley*. New York: Academic Press.

Nairne, Thomas.
1988   *Nairne's Muskhogean Journals: The 1708 Expedition to the Mississippi River*. Edited by Alexander Moore. Jackson: University Press of Mississippi.

Nance, C. Roger.
1984   The Rodgers-CETA Site, Talladega County, Alabama. *LAMAR Briefs* 3:6. Watkinsville, Ga.
1988   Archaeology of the Rodgers-CETA Site, a Lamar Village on Talladega Creek, Central Alabama. *Journal of Alabama Archaeology* 34 (1–2): 1–240.

National Research Council.
1929   *Conference on Midwestern Archaeology, St. Louis, Missouri*. National Research Council, Division of Anthropology and Psychology, Committee on State Archaeological Surveys, Washington, D.C.
1932   *Conference on Southern Pre-History, Birmingham, Alabama*. National Research Council, Division of Anthropology and Psychology, Committee on State Archaeological Surveys, Washington, D.C.
1935   *Indianapolis Archaeological Conference, Indianapolis, Indiana*. National Research Council, Division of Anthropology and Psychology, Committee on State Archaeological Surveys, Washington, D.C.

Nelson, Ben A., A. Wayne Prokopetz, and David Swindell III.
1974   *Analysis of Mound D and Macon Earthlodge (1-Bi-3) Materials at the Southeast Archeological Center*. Department of Anthropology, Florida State University, Tallahassee. Submitted to Southeast Archeological Center, National Park Service, Tallahassee, Fla. Contract no. 500041078.

Nelson, Ben A., David Swindell III, and J. Mark Williams.
1974   *Analysis of the Ocmulgee Bottoms Materials at the Southeast Archeological Center*. Department of Anthropology, Florida State University, Tallahassee. Submitted to Southeast Archeological Center, National Park Service, Tallahassee, Fla. Contract no. 500041296.

Neusius, Sarah W., editor.
1986   *Foraging, Collecting, and Harvesting: Archaic Period Subsistence and Settlement in the Eastern Woodlands*. Center for Archaeological Investigations, Occasional Paper no. 6. Carbondale: Southern Illinois University.

Nielsen, Jerry.
1967   *Anthropology Study*. Department of Anthropology, Georgia State University. Submitted to Heart of Georgia Planning and Development Commission, Eastman, Ga.

Oliver, Billy A.
1985   Tradition and Typology: Basic Elements of the Carolina Projectile Point Sequence. In *Structure and Process in Southeastern Archaeology*, edited by Roy S. Dickens, Jr., and H. Trawick Ward, 195–211. Tuscaloosa: University of Alabama Press.

Ortner, Donald J., and Walter G. J. Putschar.
1981   Identification of Pathological Conditions in Human

Skeletal Remains. *Smithsonian Contributions to Anthropology*, no. 28. Washington, D.C.: Smithsonian Institution.

Osborn, Alan J.
1988   Limitations of the Diffusionist Approach: Evolutionary Ecology and Shell-Tempered Ceramics. In *The Transfer and Transformation of Ideas and Material Culture*, edited by Peter J. Hugill and D. Bruce Dickson, 23–43. College Station: Texas A&M Press.

O'Steen, Lisa D.
1983   Early Archaic Settlement Patterns in the Wallace Reservoir: An Inner Piedmont Perspective. Master's thesis, Department of Anthropology, University of Georgia, Athens.
1986   *CRM: Barnett Shoals Survey*. Garrow & Associates, Atlanta, Georgia. Submitted to Georgia Power Company, Atlanta.

O'Steen, Lisa D., R. Jerald Ledbetter, Daniel T. Elliott, and William W. Barker.
1989   PaleoIndian Sites of the Inner Piedmont of Georgia: Observations of Settlement in the Oconee Watershed. *Early Georgia* 14 (1–2): 1–63.

Padgett, Thomas.
1973   Some Observations on Mossy Oak. Paper presented at the 30th annual meeting of the Southeastern Archaeological Conference, Memphis.

Patterson, Isabel Garrard (Mrs. Wayne Patterson).
1936   Archaeological Survey of the Chattahoochee Valley in Georgia. Paper presented at the 2d annual meeting of the Society for American Archaeology, Washington, D.C.
1950   Notes on the Exploration of the Bull Creek Site, Columbus, Georgia. *Early Georgia* 1 (1): 35–40.
n.d.   Archaeology of Georgia. Ms. of file, Department of Anthropology, University of Georgia, Athens.

Pearson, Charles E.
1977   *Analysis of Late Prehistoric Settlement on Ossabaw Island, Georgia*. Laboratory of Archaeology Series, Report no. 12. Athens: University of Georgia.
1978   Analysis of Late Mississippian Settlements on Ossabaw Island, Georgia. In *Mississippian Settlement Patterns*, edited by Bruce D. Smith, 53–80. New York: Academic Press.
1986   Red Bird Creek: Late Prehsitoric Material Culture and Subsistence in Coastal Georgia. *Early Georgia* 12 (1–2): 1–40.

Peck, Rodney M.
1988   Clovis Points of Early Man in North Carolina. *Piedmont Journal of Archaeology* 6:1–22.

Peck, Rodney M., and Floyd Painter.
1984   The Baucom Hardaway Site: A Stratified Deposit in Union County, North Carolina. *Chesopiean* 22:2–41.

Peebles, Christopher S.
1979   *Excavations at Moundville, 1905–1951*. Ann Arbor: University of Michigan Press.

Peebles, Christopher S., and Susan M. Kus.
1977   Some Archaeological Correlates of Ranked Societies. *American Antiquity* 42:421–48.

Penman, John T.
1973   Ceramic Analysis. In *Analysis of the Lamar Site (9 Bi 7) Materials at the Southeast Archeological Center*, edited by Hale G. Smith, 19–39. Department of Anthropology, Florida State University, Tallahassee. Submitted to the Southeast Archeological Center, National Park Service. Contract no. CX 500031136.
1976   The Lamar Phase in Central Georgia. *Southeastern Archaeological Conference Bulletin* 19:18–21.

Percy, George W., James Ditty, and Jerry Jones.
1973   Preliminary Report on Analysis of Ground Stone Celts from the Macon Plateau Site. In *Middle Plateau Accession Analysis*, edited by Hale G. Smith, Appendix B, unpaginated. Florida State University, Tallahassee. Submitted to Southeast Archeological Center, National Park Service, Tallahassee, Fla. Contract no. 500031293.

Peske, G. R.
1966   Oneota Settlement Patterns and Agricultural Patterns in Winnebago County. *Wisconsin Archaeologist* 47:188–95.

Petrullo, Vincenzo.
1954   The 4-H Foundation Archaeological Project: Investigations at Rock Eagle and Other Putnam County, Georgia Archaeological Sites. Ms. On file, Rock Eagle 4-H Center, Eatonton, Ga.

Phillips, Philip, James A. Ford, and James B. Griffin.
1951   *Archaeological Survey in the Lower Mississippi Alluvial Valley, 1940–1947*. Peabody Museum Papers, no. 25. Cambridge: Harvard University.

Polhemus, Richard R.
1985   Mississippian Architecture: Temporal, Technological, and Spatial Patterning of Structures at the Toqua Site (40MR6). Master's thesis, Department of Anthropology, University of Tennessee, Knoxville.

Polhemus, Richard R., editor.
1987   *The Toqua Site: A Late Mississippian, Dallas Phase Town*. Report of Investigations, no. 41. Department of Anthropology, University of Tennessee, Knoxville.

Pope, Gustavus D., Jr.
1953   Ocmulgee Old Fields Creeks. *Newsletter of the Southeastern Archaeological Conference* 3 (3): 20–21.
1956   *Ocmulgee National Monument, Georgia*. National Park Service, Historical Series 24. Washington, D.C.

Powell, Mary L.
1983   Biocultural Analysis of Human Skeletal Remains from the Lubbub Creek Archaeological Locality. In *Prehistoric Agricultural Communities in West Central Alabama*, edited by Christopher S. Peebles. Vol. 2 (AD-A155 048/2/GAR), 430–77. National Technical Information Service, Washington, D.C.
1988   *Status and Health in Prehistory, a Case Study of the Moundville Chiefdom*. Washington, D.C.: Smithsonian Institution Press.
1989   The Nodena People. In *Nodena, An Account of 90 Years of Archeological Investigation in Southeast Mississippi County, Arkansas*. Edited by Dan F. Morse, 65–95, 127–50. Arkansas Archeological Survey Research Series, no. 30. Fayetteville.

1990   On the Eve of the Conquest: Life and Death at Irene Mound, Georgia. In *The Archaeology of Mission Santa Catalina de Guale: 2. Biocultural Interpretations of a Population in Transition*, edited by Clark S. Larsen, 26–35. Anthropological Papers, vol. 68. New York: American Museum of Natural History.

Prokopetz, A. Wayne.
1974   An Analysis of Post Houses: Site 1-Bi-4, Macon, Georgia. Master's thesis, Department of Anthropology, Florida State University, Tallahassee. Submitted to Southeast Archeological Center, National Park Service, Tallahassee, Fla. Contract no. 5049L30025.

Purdy, Barbara A.
1981   *Florida's Prehistoric Stone Technology*. Gainesville: University of Florida Presses.

Quimby, George I.
1979   A Brief History of WPA Archaeology. In *Uses of Anthropology*, edited by Walter Goldschmidt, 110–23. Special Publication of the American Anthropological Association, no. 11. Washington, D.C.

Ranger's Report of Travels with General Oglethorpe, 1739–1742.
1916   In *Travels in the American Colonies*, edited by Newton D. Mereness, 215–36. New York: Macmillan.

Ranjel, Rodrigo.
1922   A Narrative of De Soto's Expedition. In *Narratives of the Career of Hernando de Soto in the Conquest of Florida*. Vol. 2. Translated and edited by Edward G. Bourne, 41–150. Allerton, N.Y.

Rayl, Sandra L.
1974   A PaleoIndian Mammoth Kill Site Near Silver Springs, Florida. Master's thesis, Department of Anthropology, Northern Arizona University, Flagstaff.

Reed, Nelson A.
1977   Monks and Other Mississippian Mounds. In *Explorations into Cahokia Archaeology*, 2d rev. ed., edited by Melvin L. Fowler, 31–42. Illinois Archaeological Survey, Bulletin no. 7. Urbana: University of Illinois.

Renfrew, Colin.
1975   Trade as Action at a Distance: Questions of Integration and Communication. In *Ancient Civilization and Trade*, edited by Jeremy A. Sabloff and C. C. Lamberg-Karlousky, 3–59. Albuquerque: University of New Mexico Press.
1986   Introduction: Peer Polity Interaction and Socio-Political Change. In *Peer Polity Interaction and Socio-Political Change*, edited by Colin Renfrew and John F. Cherry, 1–18. Cambridge: Cambridge University Press.

Riley, Thomas J., and Glen Freimuth.
1979   Field Systems and Frost Drainage in the Prehistoric Agriculture of the Midwest. *American Antiquity* 44:271–85.

Riley, Thomas J., Charles Moffat, and Glen Freimuth.
1980   Campos Elevados Prehistoricos en el Medioeste Superior De Los Estados Unidos, *America Indigena* 60 (4): 797–85.
1981   Prehistoric Raised Fields in the Upper Midwestern United States: An Innovation in Response to Marginal Growing Conditions. *North American Archaeologist* 2:101–16.

Rouse, Irving B.
1957   Culture Area and Co-Tradition. *Southwestern Journal of Anthropology* 13:123–33.
1958   The Inference of Migrations from Anthropological Evidence. In *Migrations in New World Culture History*, edited by Raymond A. Thompson, 63–68. Tucson: University of Arizona Press.

Rowland, Dunbar, and Albert G. Sanders, editors.
1927   *Mississippi Provincial Archives, French Dominion, Volume I (1729–1740)*. Jackson: Mississippi Department of Archives and History.

Rudolph, James L.
1984   Earthlodges and Platform Mounds: Changing Public Architecture in the Southeastern United States. *Southeastern Archaeology* 3:33–45.
1986   Lamar Period Exploitation of Aquatic Resources in the Middle Oconee River Valley. *Early Georgia* 11 (1–2): 86–103.

Rudolph, James L., and Dennis B. Blanton.
1981   A Discussion of Mississippian Settlement in the Georgia Piedmont. *Early Georgia* 8 (1–2): 14–36.

Rudolph, James L., and David J. Hally.
1982   *Archaeological Investigations at Site 9PM220*. Wallace Reservoir Project, Contribution no. 19. Department of Anthropology, University of Georgia, Athens.
1985   *Archaeological Investigations of the Beaverdam Creek Site (9Eb85), Elbert County, Georgia*. Russell Papers 1985. Atlanta: Interagency Archeological Services Division, National Park Service.

Rudolph, Teresa P.
1986   Swift Creek and Napier in North Georgia. Paper presented at the Ocmulgee National Monument 50th Anniversary Conference, Macon, Ga.

Russell, Margaret Clayton.
1976   Lamar and the Creeks: An Old Controversy Revisited. *Early Georgia* 3 (1): 53–67.

Sahlins, Marshall.
1985   *Islands of History*. Chicago: University of Chicago Press.

Salley, Alexander S., editor.
1911   *Narratives of Early Carolina, 1650–1708*. New York: Charles Scribner's Sons.
1934   *Journals of the Commons House of Assembly of South Carolina for 1703*. Columbia: Historical Commission of South Carolina.

Salo, Lawr V., editor.
1969   *Archaeological Investigations in the Tellico Reservoir, Tennessee, 1967–1968: An Interim Report*. Report of Investigations, no. 7. Department of Anthropology, University of Tennessee, Knoxville.

Sassaman, Kenneth E.
1983   Middle and Late Archaic Settlement in the South

Carolina Piedmont. Master's thesis, Department of Anthropology, University of South Carolina, Columbia.

1985 The Middle Archaic Period in the Savannah River Valley: Patterns of Adaptive Flexibility. Paper presented at the 42d annual meeting of the Southeastern Archaeological Conference, Birmingham, Ala.

Sassaman, Kenneth E., Mark J. Brooks, Glen T. Hanson, and David G. Anderson.

1990 *Native American Prehistory of the Middle Savannah River Valley: A Synthesis of Archaeological Investigations on the Savannah River Site, Aiken and Barnwell Counties, South Carolina.* South Carolina Institute of Archeology and Anthropology, Savannah River Archaeological Research Papers 1. Columbia: University of South Carolina.

Sassaman, Kenneth E., Glen T. Hanson, and Tommy Charles.

1988 Raw Material Procurement and the Reduction of Hunter-Gatherer Range in the Savannah River Valley. *Southeastern Archaeology* 7:79–94.

Scarry, John F.

1985 A Proposed Revision of the Fort Walton Ceramic Typology: A Type-Variety System. *Florida Anthropologist* 38:199–233.

Schmitt, Karl.

1943 A Dated Silt Deposit in the Ocmulgee River Valley, Georgia. *American Antiquity* 8:296–97.

Schnell, Frank T.

1970 A Comparative Study of Some Lower Creek Sites. *Southeastern Archaeological Conference Bulletin* 13:133–36.

1976 The Woodland Period South of the Fall Line. *Early Georgia* 3 (1): 27–36.

1982 *A Cultural Resource Investigation of Sites 1Ru63 and 9Ce66, Fort Benning, Alabama and Georgia.* Columbus Museum of Arts and Sciences, Columbus, Georgia. Submitted to the U.S. Army Corps of Engineers, Savannah District.

1983 Activities of the Columbus (Ga.) Museum of Arts and Sciences. *LAMAR Briefs* 2:13–14. Watkinsville, Ga.

1984 Late 17th and Early 18th Century Sites on the Lower Chattahoochee. *LAMAR Briefs* 3:8–9. Watkinsville, Ga.

1989 A Preliminary Culture History of the Lower Chattahoochee Valley in the 16th Century. Ms. in possession of the author.

1990 Middle Chattahoochee River [Phase Characteristics]. In *Lamar Archaeology: Mississippian Chiefdoms in the Deep South*, edited by Mark Williams and Gary Shapiro, 67–69. Tuscaloosa: University of Alabama Press.

n.d. Ceramics in the Southern Half of the Chattahoochee Valley. Ms. in possession of the author.

Schnell, Frank T., Vernon J. Knight, and Gail S. Schnell.

1981 *Cemochechobee, Archaeology of a Mississippian Ceremonial Center on the Chattahoochee River.* Gainesville: University Presses of Florida.

Schoolcraft, Henry R.

1860 *Archives of Aboriginal Knowledge.* Vol 1. Philadelphia: Lippincott.

Schroedl, Gerald F.

1973 Radiocarbon Dates from Three Burial Mounds at the McDonald Site in East Tennessee. *Tennessee Archaeologist* 29:3–11.

1978a *The Patrick Site (40MR40), Tellico Reservoir, Tennessee.* Report of Investigations, no. 25. Department of Anthropology, University of Tennessee, Knoxville.

1978b *Excavations of the Leuty and McDonald Site Mounds in the Watts Bar Nuclear Plant Area.* Report of Investigations, no. 22. Department of Anthropology, University of Tennessee, Knoxville.

Schroedl, Gerald F., C. Clifford Boyd, Jr., and R. P. Stephen Davis, Jr.

1990 Explaining Mississippian Origins in East Tennessee. In *The Mississippian Emergence*, edited by Bruce D. Smith, 175–96. Washington, D.C.: Smithsonian Institution Press.

Schroedl, Gerald F., R. P. Stephen Davis, Jr., and Clifford C. Boyd, Jr.

1985 *Archaeological Contexts and Assemblages at Martin Farm.* Report of Investigations, no. 39. Department of Anthropology, University of Tennessee, Knoxville.

Schwartz, Douglas W.

1967 *Conceptions of Kentucky Prehistory.* Studies in Anthropology, no. 6. Lexington: University of Kentucky Press.

Sears, William H.

1948 *Excavations at Kolomoki, Season I-1948.* University of Georgia Series in Anthropology, no. 2. Athens: University of Georgia Press.

1955 Creek and Cherokee Culture in the 18th Century. *American Antiquity* 21:143–149.

1956 *Excavations at Kolomoki: Final Report.* University of Georgia Series in Anthropology, no. 5. Athens: University of Georgia Press.

1958 *The Wilbanks Site (9CK5), Georgia*, 129–94. Smithsonian Institution, Bureau of American Ethnology Bulletin 169. Washington, D.C.

1969 Review of *The Waring Papers: The Collected Works of Antonio J. Waring, Jr.*, edited by S. Williams. *American Antiquity* 34:187–90.

1982 *Fort Center: An Archaeological Site in the Lake Okeechobee Basin.* Gainesville: University Presses of Florida.

Seckinger, Ernest W., Jr.

1977 Social Complexity During the Mississippian Period in Northwest Georgia. Master's thesis, Department of Anthropology, University of Georgia, Athens.

Serrano y Sanz, Manuel, editor.

1912 *Documentos Históricos de la Florida y la Luisiana, Siglos XVI al XVIII.* Librería General de Victoriano Suárez, Madrid.

Setzler, Frank M.

1956 Introduction. In *Archeology of the Funeral Mound, Ocmulgee National Monument, Georgia*, by Charles H.

Fairbanks, 1–2. Archeological Research Series, no. 3. USDI National Park Service, Washington, D.C.

Setzler, Frank M., and Jesse D. Jennings.

1941   *Peachtree Mound and Village Site, Cherokee County, North Carolina.* Smithsonian Institution, Bureau of American Ethnology Bulletin 131. Washington, D.C.

Setzler, Frank M., and William Duncan Strong.

1936   Archaeology and Relief. *American Antiquity* 1:301–9.

Shapiro, Gary.

1981   *Archaeological Investigations at Site 9GE75.* Department on Anthropology, Wallace Reservoir Project, Contribution no. 13. Athens: University of Georgia.

1983   Site Variability in the Oconee Province: A Late Mississippian Society of the Georgia Piedmont. Ph.D. diss., Department of Anthropology, University of Florida, Gainesville.

Sherrod, P. Clay, and Martha Ann Rolingson.

1987   *Surveyors of the Ancient Mississippi Valley: Modules and Alignments in Prehistoric Mound Sites.* Arkansas Archaeological Survey Research Series, no. 28. Fayetteville.

Smith, Betty A.

1975   Re-Analysis of the Mandeville Site, 9Cla1, Focusing on Its Internal History and External Relations. Ph.D. diss., Department of Anthropology, University of Georgia, Athens.

1979   The Hopewell Connection in Southwest Georgia. In *Hopewell Archaeology: The Chillicothe Conference*, edited by D. S. Brose and N'omi Greber, 181–87. Kent, Ohio: Kent State University Press.

Smith, Bruce D.

1978   Variation in Mississippian Settlement Patterns. In *Mississippian Settlement Patterns*, edited by Bruce D. Smith, 479–503. New York: Academic Press.

1984   Mississippian Expansion: Tracing the Historical Development of an Explanatory Model. *Southeastern Archaeology* 3:13–22.

1986   The Archaeology of the Southeastern United States: From Dalton to deSoto, 10,500–500 B.P. *Advances in World Archaeology* 5:1–88.

Smith, Bruce D., editor.

1990   *The Mississippian Emergence.* Washington, D.C.: Smithsonian Institution Press.

Smith, Hale G., editor.

1973a   *Analysis of the Lamar Site (9-Bi-7) Materials at the Southeast Archeological Center.* Department of Anthropology, Florida State University, Tallahassee. Submitted to Southeast Archeological Center, National Park Service, Tallahassee, Fla. Contract no. 500031136.

1973b   *Middle Plateau Accession Analysis.* Department of Anthropology, Florida State University, Tallahassee. Submitted to Southeast Archeological Center, National Park Service, Tallahassee, Fla. Contract no. 500031293.

Smith, Marvin T.

1976   The Route of De Soto Through Tennessee, Georgia, and Alabama: The Evidence from Material Culture. *Early Georgia* 4:27–48.

1981   *Archaeological Investigations at the Dyar Site, 9GE5.* Wallace Reservoir Project, Contribution no. 11. Department of Anthropology, University of Georgia, Athens.

1987   *Archaeology of Aboriginal Culture Change in the Interior Southeast: Depopulation During the Early Historic Period.* Gainesville: University Presses of Florida.

1992   *Historic Period Indian Archaeology of Northern Georgia.* Laboratory of Archaeology Series, Report no. 30. Athens: University of Georgia.

Smith, Marvin T., David J. Hally, and Gary Shapiro.

1981   *Archaeological Investigations at the Ogeltree Site, 9GE153.* Wallace Reservoir Project, Contribution no. 10. Department of Anthropology, University of Georgia, Athens.

Smith, Marvin T., and Stephen A. Kowalewski.

1981   Tentative Identification of a Prehistoric "Province" in Piedmont Georgia. *Early Georgia* 8:1–13.

Smith, Marvin T., and Julie Barnes Smith.

1989   Engraved Shell Masks in North America. *Southeastern Archaeology* 8 (1): 9–18.

Smith, Marvin T., and J. Mark Williams.

1983   European Trade Material from Tugalo, 9ST1. *Early Georgia* 6:38–53.

Smith, Richard W.

1938   Resolutions Adopted at the Spring Meeting of the Society for Georgia Archaeology, Savannah, Georgia, May 6–7, 1938. *Proceedings of the Society for Georgia Archaeology* 1 (1): 11–14.

1939   A History of the Society for Georgia Archaeology. *Proceedings of the Society for Georgia Archaeology* 2 (2): 13–17.

Snow, Frankie.

1975   *Archaeology of the Big Bend Region.* Douglas: South Georgia College.

1977   *An Archaeological Survey of the Ocmulgee Big Bend Region.* Occasional Papers from South Georgia, no. 3. Douglas: South Georgia College.

1980   The Nipple Point. Society for Georgia Archaeology. *The Profile* 28:3–4.

1990   Pine Barrens Lamar. In *Lamar Archaeology: Mississippian Chiefdoms in the Deep South*, edited by Mark Williams and Gary Shapiro, 82–93. Tuscaloosa: University of Alabama Press.

South, Stanley.

1977   *Method and Theory in Historical Archeology.* New York: Academic Press.

Squier, Ephraim G., and Edwin H. Davis.

1848   Ancient Monuments of the Mississippi Valley. *Smithsonian Contributions to Knowledge*, vol. 1. Washington, D.C.

Steinbock, R. T.

1976   *Paleopathological Diagnosis and Interpretation.* Springfield, Ill.: C. C. Thomas.

Steponaitis, Vincas P.

1978   Location Theory and Complex Chiefdoms: a Mississippian Example. In *Mississippian Settlement Patterns*, edited by Bruce D. Smith, 417–53. New York: Academic Press.

1983   *Ceramics, Chronology, and Community: An Archaeological Study at Moundville.* New York: Academic Press.

1986   Prehistoric Archaeology in the Southeastern United States, 1970–1985. *Annual Review of Anthropology* 15:363–404.

Stirling, Matthew W.

1929   Discussion of Mr. Hodge's Paper. In *Report of the Conference on Midwestern Archaeology, Held in St. Louis, Missouri,* 24–28. National Research Council Division of Anthropology and Psychology, Committee on State Archaeological Surveys, Washington, D.C.

1930   Report of the Chief. *Forty-sixth Annual Report of the Bureau of American Ethnology, 1928–1929,* 1–16. Smithsonian Institution, Washington, D.C.

1932   The Pre-Historic Southern Indians. In *Conference on Southern Pre-History, Birmingham, Alabama,* 20–31. National Research Council, Washington, D.C.

1934   Smithsonian Archaeological Projects Conducted Under the Federal Emergency Relief Administration, 1933–1934. *Annual Report of the Smithsonian Institution for 1934,* 371–400. Washington, D.C.

Stoltman, James B.

1973   The Southeastern United States. In *The Development of North American Archaeology,* edited by James E. Fitting, 117–50. University Park: Pennsylvania State University Press.

1978   Temporal Models in Prehistory: An Example from Eastern North America. *Current Anthropology* 19:703–46.

Stoutamire, James W., L. Christine Beditz, Gary D. Knudson, and Jill S. Palmer.

1978   *The Mossy Oak Site (11-Bi-17), Bibb County, Georgia.* Department of Anthropology, Florida State University, Tallahassee. Submitted to Southeast Archeological Center, National Park Service, Tallahassee, Fla. Contract no. 5000061184.

Stoutamire, James W., Chad O. Braley, Thomas R. Gest, and Patricia A. Logan.

1977   *The Tuft Springs # 1 (11-Bi-25) and # 2 (11-Bi-19) Sites in Central Georgia Prehistory.* Department of Anthropology, Florida State University, Tallahassee. Submitted to Southeast Archeological Center, National Park Service, Tallahassee, Fla. Contract no. 5000071206.

Stoutamire, James W., Pamela Fesperman, Robert A. Karwedsky, and Patricia D. O'Grady.

1983   *The Archeology of Mounds A and B and the South Plateau (11-Bi-2), Ocmulgee National Monument, Georgia.* Florida State University, Tallahassee. Submitted to Southeast Archeological Center, National Park Service, Tallahassee, Fla. Contract no. 5000071206.

Sullivan, Lynne Anne Peters.

1986   The Late Mississippian Village: Community and Society of the Mouse Creek Phase in Southeastern Tennessee. Ph.D. diss., Department of Anthropology, University of Wisconsin-Milwaukee.

Swanson, James T., Jr.

n.d.   A Report Including Discovery, Excavation, and Restoration of a Prehistoric Indian Ceremonial Earth Lodge, Ocmulgee National Monument, Bibb County, Georgia. Ms. on file, Southeast Archeological Center, National Park Service, Tallahassee, Fla.

Swanton, John R.

1911   *Indian Tribes of the Lower Mississippi Valley and the Adjacent Coast of the Gulf of Mexico.* Smithsonian Institution, Bureau of American Ethnology Bulletin 43. Washington, D.C.

1922   *Early History of the Creek Indians and their Neighbors.* Smithsonian Institution, Bureau of American Ethnology Bulletin 73. Washington, D.C.

1928a   *The Identification of Aboriginal Mounds by Means of Creek Customs. Annual Report of the Smithsonian Institution for 1927,* 495–506. Washington, D.C.

1928b   Social Organization and Social Usages of the Indians of the Creek Confederacy. *Forty-second Annual Report of the Bureau of American Ethnology, 1924–1925,* 23–472. Smithsonian Institution, Washington, D.C.

1932   The Relation of the Southeast to General Culture Problems of American Prehistory. In *Conference on Southern Pre-History, Birmingham, Alabama,* 60–74. National Research Council, Washington, D.C.

1936   March 14, 1936, Letter to Arthur R. Kelly. Ms. on file, Southeast Archeological Center, National Park Service, Tallahassee, Fla.

1939   *Final Report of the United States De Soto Expedition Commission.* United States Congress, House of Representatives, 76th Congress, 1st Session, H. Doc. 71.

1946   *The Indians of the Southeastern United States.* Smithsonian Institution, Bureau of American Ethnology Bulletin 137. Washington, D.C.

Tally, Lucy.

1975   Preliminary Demographic Analysis of the King Site Burial Population. *Southeastern Archaeological Conference Bulletin* 18: 74–75.

Taylor, Walter W., Jr.

1936   September 20, 1936, Telegram to Arthur R. Kelly. Ms. on file, Southeast Archeological Center, National Park Service, Tallahassee, Fla.

Thomas, Cyrus.

1891   *Catalogue of Prehistoric Works East of the Rocky Mountains.* Smithsonian Institution, Bureau of American Ethnology Bulletin 12. Washington, D.C.

1894   Report on the Mound Exploration of the Bureau of American Ethnology. *Twelfth Annual Report of the Bureau of Ethnology, 1890–1891.* Smithsonian Institution, Washington, D.C.

Tippitt, V. Ann, and William H. Marquardt.

1984   *The Gregg Shoals and Clyde Gulley Sites: Archaeological and Geological Investigations at Two Piedmont Sites on the Savannah River.* Russell Papers 1984. Atlanta: Interagency Archeological Services Division, National Park Service.

Trimble, Stanley Wayne.

1974   *Man-Induced Soil Erosion on the Southern Piedmont*

1700–1970. Ankeny, Iowa: Soil Conservation Society of America.

Ubelaker, Douglas H.

1974   *Reconstruction of Demographic Profiles from Ossuary Skeletal Samples: A Case Study from the Tidewater Potomac*. Smithsonian Contributions to Anthropology, no. 18. Washington, D.C.

1978   *Human Skeletal Remains, Excavation, Analysis, Interpretation*. Chicago: Aldine Press.

Vega, Garcilaso de la.

1951   *The Florida of the Inca*. Translated and edited by John G. Varner and Jeanette J. Varner. Austin: University of Texas Press.

Vescelius, Gary S.

1957   Mound 2 at Marksville. *American Antiquity* 22:416–20.

Walker, John W.

1961   A Preliminary Report on the History and Archeology of the Ocmulgee River Flood Plain, Ocmulgee National Monument. Ms. on file, Southeast Archeological Center, National Park Service, Tallahassee, Fla.

1963   Excavations at Appomattox Court House, 1962 Season. Ms. on file, Southeast Archeological Center, National Park Service, Tallahassee, Fla.

1967   A Preliminary Report on the Natural History and Archeology of the Proposed Upper Saluda Reservoir, Santee River Basin, South Carolina. Ms. on file, Southeast Archeological Center, National Park Service, Tallahassee, Fla.

1969   Comments on the Construction of Mound A, Ocmulgee National Monument. *Southeastern Archaeological Conference Bulletin* 11:30.

1971a   *Excavation of the Arkansas Post Branch of the Bank of the State of Arkansas*. Office of Archeology and Historic Preservation, National Park Service, Washington, D.C.

1971b   Known Archeological Sites in the Vicinity of Macon, Georgia. Ms. on file, Southeast Archeological Center, National Park Service, Tallahassee, Fla.

1974   Distribution and Significance of Weeden Island Sites in Georgia and Alabama. Paper presented at the 39th annual meeting of the Society for American Archaeology, Washington, D.C.

1989   *Ocmulgee Archeology: A Chronology*. Southeast Archeological Center, National Park Service, Tallahassee, Fla.

Walker, John W., and Joseph A. Murciak.

1971   A Preliminary Report on the Andrew Site, Houston County, Georgia. Paper presented at the 28th Southeastern Archaeological Conference, Macon, Ga.

Walling, Richard, and Robert C. Wilson.

1985   Archaeological Test Excavations: The Hightower Village Site, 1Ta150. Paper presented at the annual meeting of the Southern Anthropological Society, Memphis.

Waring, Antonio J.

1968a   Paleo-Indian Remains in South Carolina and Georgia. In *The Waring Papers, The Collected Works of Antonio J. Waring, Jr.*, edited by Stephen Williams, 236–40. Peabody Museum Papers, vol. 58. Cambridge: Harvard University.

1968b   A History of Georgia Archaeology. In *The Waring Papers, The Collected Works of Antonio J. Waring, Jr.*, edited by Stephen Williams, 288–99. Peabody Museum papers, vol. 58. Cambridge: Harvard University.

1968c   *The Waring Papers: The Collected Works of Antonio J. Waring, Jr.* Edited by Stephen Williams. Peabody Museum Papers, vol. 58. Cambridge: Harvard University.

Waring, Antonio J., Jr., and Preston Holder.

1945   A Prehistoric Ceremonial Complex in the Southeastern United States. *American Anthropologist* 47:1–34.

Waselkov, Gregory A.

1981   *Lower Tallapoosa Cultural Resources Survey, Phase I Report*. Department of Sociology and Anthropology, Auburn University, Auburn, Ala.

1989   Seventeenth-Century Trade in the Colonial Southeast. *Southeastern Archaeology* 8:117–33.

Waselkov, Gregory A., and John W. Cottier.

1985   European Perceptions of Eastern Muskogean Ethnicity. In *Proceedings of the Tenth Meeting of the French Colonial Historical Society*, edited by Philip P. Boucher, 23–45. Lanham, Md.: University Press of America.

Waselkov, Gregory A., and R. Eli Paul.

1981   Frontiers and Archaeology. *North American Archaeologist* 2:309–29.

Waselkov, Gregory A., B. M. Wood, and J. M. Herbert.

1982   *Colonization and Conquest: The 1980 Archaeological Investigations at Fort Toulouse and Fort Jackson, Alabama*. Archaeological Monograph no. 4. Auburn: Auburn University.

Watts, W. A.

1971   Postglacial and Interglacial Vegetation History of Southern Georgia and Central Florida. *Ecology* 52 (4): 676–90.

1980   Late Quaternary Vegetation History at White Pond on the Inner Coastal Plain of South Carolina. *Quaternary Research* 13: 187–99.

Wauchope, Robert W.

1948   The Ceramic Sequence in the Etowah Drainage, Northwest Georgia. *American Antiquity* 13:1–34.

1950   The Evolution and Persistence of Ceramic Motifs in Northern Georgia. *American Antiquity* 16:16–22.

1966   *Archaeological Survey of Northern Georgia with a Test of Some Cultural Hypotheses*. Memoir 21. Society for American Archaeology, Salt Lake City.

Webb, S. David, Jerald T. Milanich, Roger Alexon, and James S. Dunbar.

1984   A *Bison antiquus* Kill Site, Wacissa River, Jefferson County, Florida. *American Antiquity* 49:384–92.

Webb, William S.

1935   November 18, 1935, Letter to Arthur R. Kelly. Ms. on file, Ocmulgee National Monument, Macon, Ga.

1938   *An Archaeological Survey of the Norris Basin in Eastern Tennessee.* Smithsonian Institution, Bureau of American Ethnology Bulletin 118. Washington, D.C.

Webb, William S., and Charles G. Wilder.

1951   *An Archaeological Survey of Guntersville Basin on the Tennessee River in North Alabama.* Lexington: University of Kentucky Press.

Weiss, Kenneth M.

1973   On the systematic bias in skeletal sexing. *American Journal of Physical Anthropology* 37:239–49.

Wenhold, Lucy L., transcriber and translator.

1936   A Seventeenth Century Letter of Gabriel Diaz Vara Calderon, Bishop of Cuba, Describing the Indians and Indian Missions of Florida. *Smithsonian Miscellaneous Collections* 95 (16): 1–14. Smithsonian Institution, Washington, D.C.

Wetmore, Ruth.

1986   The Nipper Creek Site (38RD18): A Study in Archaic Period Change. Master's thesis, Department of Anthropology, University of South Carolina, Columbia.

Wetmore, Ruth, and Albert C. Goodyear III.

1986   *Archaeological Investigations at Nipper Creek (38RD18): An Archaic Fall Line Site.* South Carolina Institute of Archeology and Anthropology, Research Manuscript Series, no. 201. Columbia: University of South Carolina.

Whatley, John R., Jr.

1986   Egg Stones: A General Discussion. Society for Georgia Archaeology. *The Profile* 53:6–8.

White, George.

1849   *Statistics of the State of Georgia.* Savannah: W. Thorne Williams.

1854   *Historical Collections of Georgia: Containing the Most Interesting Facts, Traditions, Biographical Sketches, Anecdotes, etc. Relating to the History and Antiquities from Its First Settlement to the Present Time.* New York: Pudney and Russell.

White, Richard.

1983   *The Roots of Dependency: Subsistence, Environment, and Social Change Among the Choctaws, Pawnees, and Navajos.* Lincoln: University of Nebraska Press.

Will, George Francis, and George E. Hyde.

1917   *Corn Among the American Indians of the Upper Missouri.* St. Louis, Mo.: William Minor.

Willey, Gordon R.

1936   Report on Fort Hawkins Excavations. Ms. on file, Southeast Archeological Center, National Park Service, Tallahassee, Fla.

1937a   Notes on Central Georgia Dendrochronology. *Tree-Ring Bulletin* 4 (2): 6–8.

1937b   Preliminary Dendrochronological Studies in Central Georgia. Paper presented at a regional meeting of the Society for American Archaeology, New Haven, Conn.

1938a   Excavations at the Lawson Field Site, Fort Benning Reservation, Columbus, Georgia. Ms. on file, Southeast Archeological Center, Natioknal Park Service, Tallahassee, Fla.

1938b   Time Studies: Pottery and Trees in Georgia. *Proceedings of the Society for Georgia Archaeology* 1 (2): 15–22.

1939   Ceramic Stratigraphy in a Georgia Village Site. *American Antiquity* 5:140–47.

1945   The Weeden Island Culture: A Preliminary Definition. *American Antiquity* 10:225–54.

1949   *Archeology of the Florida Gulf Coast.* Smithsonian Miscellaneous Collections, vol. 113. Smithsonian Institution, Washington, D.C.

1953   A Pattern of Diffusion-Acculturation. *Southwestern Journal of Anthropology* 9:369–83.

Willey, Gordon R., Charles C. Di Peso, William A. Ritchie, Irving Rouse, John H. Rowe, and Donald W. Lathrap.

1956   An Archaeological Classification of Culture Contact Situations. In *Seminars in Archaeology: 1955,* edited by Robert Wauchope, 1–30. Memoir no. 11. Society for American Archaeology, Salt Lake City.

Willey, Gordon R., and Philip Phillips.

1958   *Method and Theory in American Archaeolgy.* Chicago: University of Chicago Press.

Willey, Gordon R., and Jeremy Sabloff.

1980   *A History of American Archaeology.* 2d ed. San Francisco: W. H. Freeman.

Willey, Gordon R., and William H. Sears.

1952   The Kasita Site. *Southern Indian Studies* 4:2–18.

Willey, Gordon R., and Richard B. Woodbury.

1942   A Chronological Outline for the Northwest Florida Coast. *American Antiquity* 7:232–54.

Williams, J. Mark.

1975   Stubbs Mound in Central Georgia Prehistory. Master's thesis, Department of Anthropology, Florida State University, Tallahassee. Submitted to Southeast Archeological Center, National Park Service, Tallahassee, Fla. Contract no. 589050053.

1983   The Joe Bell Site: Seventeenth Century Lifeways on the Oconee River. Ph.D. diss., Department of Anthropology, University of Georgia, Athens.

1984   *Archaeological Excavations, Scull Shoals Mounds, Georgia.* Cultural Resources Report no. 6. United States Department of Agriculture, Forest Service, Southern Region.

1988   *Scull Shoals Revisited: 1985 Archaeological Excavations at 9GE4.* Cultural Resources Report No. 1, United States Department of Agriculture, Forest Service, Southern Region.

1990a   *Archaeological Excavations at Shinholser (9BL1), 1985 and 1987.* Lamar Institute, Watkinsville, Ga.

1990b   *Archaeological Excavations at Shoulderbone Mounds and Village, 9HK1.* Lamar Institute, Watkinsville, Ga.

Williams, Mark, Don Evans, and Bruce Dod.

1988   The Bullard Site: Twenty-four Mounds in the Georgia Swamp. Paper presented at the 45th annual meeting of the Southeastern Archaeological Conference, New Orleans, La.

Williams, J. Mark, and Joseph N. Henderson.

1974   *The Archeology of the Macon North Plateau: 1974.* Florida State University, Tallahassee. Submitted

to Southeast Archeological Center, National Park
Service, Tallahassee, Fla. Contract no. 500041597.

Williams, Mark, and Gary Shapiro.

1986 Shoulderbone Was a Fourteenth Century Frontier
Town. Paper presented at the 43d annual meeting
of the Southeastern Archaeological Conference,
Nashville, Tenn.

1987 The Changing Contexts of Political Power in
the Oconee Valley. Paper presented at the 44th
annual meeting of the Southeastern Archaeological
Conference, Charleston, S.C.

1990a *Archaeological Excavations at Little River (9Mg46): 1984
and 1987.* Lamar Institute, Watkinsville, Ga.

1990b Paired Towns. In *Lamar Archaeology: Mississippian
Chiefdoms in the Deep South*, edited by Mark Williams
and Gary Shapiro, 163–74. Tuscaloosa: University of
Alabama Press.

Williams, Mark, and Marvin T. Smith.

1989 Power and Migration. Paper presented at the 46th
annual meeting of the Southeastern Archaeological
Conference, Tampa, Fla.

Williams, Marshall, and Carolyn Branch.

1983 The Tugalo Site. *Early Georgia* 6:32–37.

Williams, Stephen.

1958 Review of *Archeology of the Funeral Mound*, by
Charles H. Fairbanks. *American Journal of Archaeology*
62:252–54.

1960 A Brief History of the Southeastern Archaeological Conference. *Newsletter of the Southeastern
Archaeological Conference* 7 (1): 2–4.

1973 Introduction. In *Antiquities of the Southern Indians,
Particularly of the Georgia Tribes*, by Charles C.
Jones, Jr., 7–12. Reprint, New York: AMS Press.
Original edition, New York: D. Appleton, 1873.

1980 Armorel: A Very Late Phase in the Lower Mississippi
Valley. *Southeastern Archaeological Conference Bulletin*
22:105–10.

1986 Pioneers in the Archaeology of Middle Tennessee. Paper presented at the 43d Southeastern
Archaeological Conference, Nashville, Tenn.

Williams, Stephen, editor.

1968 *The Waring Papers: The Collected Works of Antonio J.
Waring, Jr.* Peabody Museum Papers, vol. 58.
Cambridge: Harvard University.

Williams, Stephen, and Jeffrey P. Brain.

1983 *Excavations at the Lake George Site, Yazoo County,
Mississippi, 1958–1960.* Peabody Museum Papers,
vol. 74. Cambridge: Harvard University.

Williams, Stephen, and James B. Stoltman.

1965 An Outline of Southeastern United States Prehistory
with Particular Emphasis on the PaleoIndian Era.
In *The Quaternary of the United States*, edited by
H. E. Wright and D. G. Frey, 669–83. Princeton:
Princeton University Press.

Wilmsen, Edwin N., and Frank H. H. Roberts, Jr.

1978 *Lindenmeier, 1934–1974: Concluding Report on Investigations.* Smithsonian Contributions to Anthropology,
no. 24. Washington, D.C.: Smithsonian Institution.

Wilson, David.

1982 *Aerial Site Interpretation for the Archaeologist.* New
York: St. Martins Press.

Wilson, Gilbert L.

1934 *The Hidatsa Earthlodge.* Anthropological Papers,
vol. 33, pt. 5. American Museum of Natural History,
New York.

Wilson, Rex L.

1964 A Radiocarbon Date for the Macon Earthlodge.
American Antiquity 30:202–3.

Wilson, Robert C., and Kathleen A. Deagan.

1985 Dialogue: Charles H. Fairbanks' Role in the
Emergence of Southeastern Archaeology. In
*Indians, Colonists, and Slaves: Essays in Memory of
Charles H. Fairbanks*, edited by Kenneth W. Johnson,
Jonathan M. Leader, and Robert C. Wilson, 1–
10. Special Publication no. 4, Florida Journal
of Anthropology. Department of Anthropology,
University of Florida, Gainesville.

Winters, Howard D.

1981 Excavating in Museums: Notes on Mississippian
Hoes and Middle Woodland Copper Gouges and
Celts. In *The Research Potential of Anthropological
Museum Collections*, edited by Anne-Marie Cantwell,
James B. Griffin, and Nan A. Rothchild, 17–34.
Annals of the New York Academy of Science,
no. 376. New York.

Wittry, Warren L.

1977 The American Woodhenge. In *Explorations into
Cahokia Archaeology*, 2d. rev. ed., edited by Melvin L.
Fowler, 43–48. Illinois Archaeological Survey,
Bulletin no. 7. Urbana: University of Illinois.

Wobst, Martin.

1974 Boundary Conditions for Paleolithic Social Systems:
A Simulation Approach. *American Antiquity* 39:147–
78.

1977 Stylistic Behavior and Information Exchange. In
*For the Director: Research Essays in Honor of James B.
Griffin*, edited by Charles E. Cleland, 317–42.
Anthropological Papers, no. 61. Ann Arbor: Museum
of Anthropology, University of Michigan.

Wolf, Eric R.

1982 *Europe and the People Without History.* Berkeley:
University of California Press.

Woodruff, J. F., and E. J. Parizeh.

1956 Influence of Underlying Rock Structures on Stream
Courses and Valley Profiles in the Georgia Piedmont.
Annals of the Association of American Geographers
54:129–39.

Worth, John E.

1988 Mississippian Occupation of the Middle Flint River.
Master's thesis, Department of Anthropology,
University of Georgia, Athens.

1989 Mississippian Mound Centers Along Chickasawhatchee Swamp. *LAMAR Briefs* 13:7–9.

1994 Late Spanish Military Expeditions in the Interior
Southeast, 1597–1628. In *The Forgotten Centuries:
Indians and Europeans in the American South, 1521–*

1704, edited by Charles Hudson and Carmen Chaves Tesser, 104–22. Athens: University of Georgia Press.

Wright, Henry T.
1981   Technology and Economy: Recent Research on Early Hunters of the Central Great Lakes. Paper presented at the annual meeting of the Society for American Archaeology, San Diego, Calif.

Wynn, Jack.
1982   Cultural Resources Overview for the Chattahoochee-Oconee National Forests. Ms. on file, USDA, Forest Service, Gainesville, Ga.

Yarnell, Richard A.
1978   Domestication of Sunflower and Sumpweed in North America, In *The Nature and Status of Ethnobotany*, edited by Richard I. Ford, 289–99. Anthropological Papers 67. Ann Arbor: Museum of Anthropology, University of Michigan.

Zierden, Martha A.
1978   *The Hawkins Point Site (15-Bi-21) in Central Georgia Prehistory*. Florida State Univerity, Tallahassee. Submitted to Southeast Archeological Center, National Park Service, Tallahassee, Fla. Contract no. 500071207.

CONTRIBUTORS

DAVID G. ANDERSON is an archaeologist in the Southeast Regional Office of the National Park Service in Atlanta, Georgia. He is the author of numerous papers and monographs on prehistoric archaeology in various parts of North America and the Caribbean, including *The Savannah River Chiefdoms: Political Change in the Late Prehistoric Southeast,* based on his doctoral research. In 1990 he received the C. B. Moore award for excellence by a young scholar from the Southeastern Archaeological Conference, and in 1991 the Society for American Archaeology awarded him its dissertation prize.

DENNIS BLANTON is a codirector of the Center for Archaeological Research, Department of Anthropology at the College of William and Mary. He has published articles pertaining to southeastern archaeology in local journals as well as several edited volumes.

DANIEL T. ELLIOTT is a senior archaeologist with Garrow & Associates, Inc., a private consulting firm in Atlanta, Georgia, and is the secretary and a research associate for the LAMAR Institute, Inc., a nonprofit organization in Watkinsville, Georgia, created to foster archaeological research and public education about archaeology. He is also an archaeologist for the colonial German town of New Ebenezer in Effingham County, Georgia. He has written more than sixty archaeological research reports and has published numerous articles on southeastern archaeology in books and professional journals.

JAMES B. GRIFFIN is a retired curator of Museum of Anthropology and former professor at the University of Michigan. He has been active in interpreting America's prehistoric past for more than fifty years and has published more than three hundred articles. He is a member of the National Academy of Sciences and is a Smithsonian Institution Research Associate.

DAVID J. HALLY is an associate professor of anthropology at the University of Georgia. He has published numerous articles and monographs on the archaeology of the late prehistoric and early historic periods in Georgia. His current research focuses on the settlement patterns of Mississippian Chiefdoms.

GLEN T. HANSON is the director of technical operations for the Battelle Memorial Institute office in Albuquerque, New Mexico, and is a former associate director of research for the South Carolina Institute of Archaeology and Anthropology. He directed the Savannah River Archaeological Research Program from 1977 through 1989. His research has been published in the *American Antiquity, Southeastern Archaeology* and in various monographs and reports from the University of South Carolina.

CHARLES HUDSON is Franklin Professor of Anthropology at the University of Georgia. His most recent books are *The Juan Pardo Expeditions,* with Jerald Milanich; *Hernando de Soto and the Indians of Florida;* and *The Forgotten Centuries: Indians and Europeans in the American South, 1521–1704* (Georgia, 1994), coedited with Carmen Chaves Tesser.

RICHARD W. JEFFERIES is an assistant professor of anthropology at the University of Kentucky. He is the author of *The Archaeology of Carrier Mills: 10,000 Years in the Saline Valley of Illinois* and has written numerous papers on Woodland period mound construction and mortuary practices in the southeastern and midwestern United States. Jeffries is currently studying the development of interaction and exchange networks among Archaic period hunter-gatherers that once inhabited the North American midcontinent.

JESSE D. JENNINGS, Distinguished Professor of Anthropology Emeritus from the University of Utah, is perhaps best known for his work at Danger Cave and his Desert Culture concept that simplified and systematized the archaeology of the Desert West. Among his many monographs and articles, his text *Prehistory of North America* is most widely known. Although he retired in 1986, he occasionally teaches at the University of Oregon.

VERNON JAMES KNIGHT, JR., is an associate professor of anthropology at the University of Alabama. He is an archaeologist whose research and publications treat several areas and cultural periods in the Southeast. Among his recent publications is *The De Soto Chronicles,* coedited with Lawrence Clayton and Edward Moore.

LEWIS LARSON is a professor of anthropology at West Georgia College in Carrollton, Georgia. He received his master's and doctoral degrees from the University of Michigan. A state archaeologist for Georgia since 1972, Larson specializes in southeastern archaeology, southeastern ethnohistory, and cultural ecology.

JERALD LEDBETTER has had almost two decades of professional archaeological experience in the southeastern United States. His primary interests are the Paleoindian and Archaic periods. He is currently a staff archaeologist with Southeastern Archaeological Services, Inc., of Athens. Georgia.

LISA O'STEEN has been an independent archaeological contractor and zooarchaeological analyst since 1988. She has completed more than fifty archaeological and zooarchaeological reports and has published in *Early Georgia, The Profile, Current Research in the Pleistocene*, the *University of Georgia Laboratory of Archaeology Series, Paleoindian and Early Archaic Research in the Lower Southeast*, and *Current Archaeological Research in Kentucky*.

MARY LUCAS POWELL is the director/curator of the Museum of Anthropology at the University of Kentucky. Her bioarchaeological research has focused on associations between rank status and health in late prehistoric southeastern United States chiefdoms, most notably in *Status and Health in Prehistory, a Case Study of the Moundville Chiefdom*. She has also published numerous articles on the paleoepidemiology of precontact treponematosis and tuberculosis in the eastern United States.

THOMAS J. RILEY is an associate professor and former head of the department of anthropology at the University of Illinois at Urbana-Champaign. He is a specialist in prehistoric agricultural systems in eastern North America and in Oceania. He is currently conducting archaeological excavations at the Utica Mounds Hopewell site in Illinois and is completing an archaeological report on the prehistoric and historic remains recovered during excavations in Honolulu's Chinatown district. His three monographs and more than sixty articles include a study of ceramic sourcing for selected Mississippian sites in *Ancient Technologies and Archaeological Materials* and another on American Indians, ascarids, and the modern world parasites in *Perspectives in Biology and Medicine*.

GERALD F. SCHROEDL is an associate professor of anthropology at the University of Tennessee, Knoxville. He received his doctoral degree in anthropology from Washington State University. His research interests are focused on Mississippian cultures in the Southeast and on the ethnohistory and archaeology of historic period Native Americans, especially the Cherokee. He is the principal author of *Explaining Mississippian Origins in East Tennessee, Late Woodland Culture in East Tennessee, Overhill Cherokee Archaeology at Chota-Tanasee*, and *Overhill Cherokee Household and Village Patterns in the Eighteenth Century*.

FRANKIE SNOW is the director of the Science Learning Center at South Georgia College. A recipient of the J. R. Caldwell Award for outstanding contributions to southeastern archae-ology, he has written numerous articles about the prehistory of southern Georgia.

JOHN W. WALKER, who began work as a National Park Service archaeologist at Ocmulgee National Monument in 1958, retired in 1990. After 1961, with the exception of four years spent in Washington as the National Survey of Historic Sites and Buildings archaeologist, he was on the staff of the Archaeological Research Unit and of the Southeast Archaeological Center. In the latter position, he conducted, supervised, or contracted for almost all park-related archaeological research carried out in the southeastern United States.

GREGORY A. WASELKOV is an assistant professor of anthropology at the University of South Alabama and is currently directing archaeological excavations at the original site of French colonial Mobile. He is an editor, with Peter Wood and Thomas Hatley, of *Powhatan's Mantle: Indians of the Colonial Southeast* and also an editor, with Kathryn Holland Braund, of *William Bartram's Collected Writings on the Southeastern Indians* (forthcoming).

GORDON R. WILLEY is Bowditch Professor of Mexican and Central American Archaeology, Emeritus, at Harvard University. He is the author of various archaeological monographs treating of Florida, Peru, Panama, Belize, Guatemala, and Honduras. His most recent publications are *Excavations at Seibal, Department of Peten, Guatemala: General Summary and Conclusions* and the forthcoming *Ceramics and Artifacts from the Copan Residential Zone*, prepared in collaboration with former graduate student colleagues.

MARK WILLIAMS holds a Ph.D. degree in anthropology from the University of Georgia. He is president of the LAMAR Institute and an adjunct assistant professor of anthropology at the University of Georgia. He has conducted extensive excavations in both the Oconee and Ocmulgee river valleys in central Georgia and has published many monographs and papers on his work. He is a coeditor of *Lamar Archaeology: Mississippian Chiefdoms in the Deep South*.

STEPHEN WILLIAMS is Peabody Professor of American Archaeology and Ethnology, Emeritus, in the Department of Anthropology at Harvard University and Honorary Curator of North American Archaeology at Harvard's Peabody Museum. His archaeological research has focused on the Lower Mississippi Valley, and he has written and edited a number of books and articles on that region as well as on the larger southeastern United States. He is particularly concerned with the intellectual history of American archaeology, including the more bizarre side of the field represented by what he calls "fantastic archaeology," about which he has recently written a book for a popular audience.

INDEX

Civil Works Administration (CWA): excavations, 18–20, 21
Claflin, William H., Jr., 10
Claggett, Stephen R., 67, 68
Clovis points, 4, 20, 59; discovery of Macon Clovis, 55, 56, 57.
    See also Dalton points; Fluted points; Folsom point
Coastal Plain, 61, 66; Lamar chronology in, 147; meander-belt
    habitat, 160
Coe, Joffre L., 25, 66
Coevolution hypothesis, 102, 103–4
Cofaqui, 6
Coffee County, Ga., 62
Cofitachequi chiefdom, 176–77, 179
Coke, Cecil R., 18
Coke, Joseph B., 18, 21
Cold Springs site, 4, 71, 76–82
Cole, Fay-Cooper, 17
"Coles Creek" pottery type, 26
Collins, Henry B., Jr., 11, 17, 52
Colonists: European, 6; Spanish, 16, 21
Columbia County, Fla., 75
Columbia University-National Park Service survey, 27
Columbus Museum of Arts and Sciences, 31, 183
Comer, J. Anderson, 33
Complicated Stamped Complex pottery, 20
Conasauga River, 162, 163
Conference on Historic Site Archaeology (1969), 33
Connestee pottery, 74
Cook, Fred C., 148
Cooper, Allen H., 35
Coosa chiefdom, 176–77, 179
Coosa River, 162, 163; Lamar polity on, 170–71; Creek towns
    on, 182; drainage, pottery type assemblages in, 183–84
Coosawattee River, 162, 163; Lamar polities along, 169–70;
    Coosa chiefdom on, 176, 179
Coral: silicified, 64
Corbett, John M., 30, 32
Corn agriculture: 53, 54, 96, 97, 101, 102–3, 142, 153. See also
    Ridged fields
Cosgrove, C. B., 10
Cosgrove, Mrs. C. B., 10
Cosner, Oliver J., 32
Cotter, John L., 30
Council Chamber. See Macon Council Chamber; Macon Earth
    Lodge
Council houses: Creek and Cherokee, 157
Cowart's Landing site, 24, 25, 43, 131, 137, 145
Cowarts phase pottery, 178
Coweta (town), 191, 193
Coweta Creek site, 157, 158
Coweta Tallahassee site, 183
"Creek and Pre-Creek" (Fairbanks), 131
Creek Confederacy, 16, 182, 186, 194
Creek culture, 6, 19; pottery, 6, 181–89, 194; burial artifacts, 19;
    history of Lower Creeks, 21; Fort Hawkins and, 22; and black
    drink, 35; domestic structures, 90, 192–93, 195; migration
    legends, 130, 131, 137; change during early historic period,
    193–95. See also Lower Creeks
Creek phase characteristics, 186–89
Cultigens: European introduced, 153; Lamar, 153

CWA. See Civil Works Administration

Dallas culture: domestic structures, 154; burials, 164, 167;
    Creek culture and, 183
Dallas phase pottery, 185, 188
Dallas phase towns, 179
Dallas site, 138
Dalton and Palmer assemblages, 67
Dalton points, 59, 60, 61, 62, 64. See also Clovis points; Fluted
    points; Folsom point
Daniel, I. Randolph, 68
Datha, 176
Daub, 107, 111–12, 157, 164, 192
Davis, Dave D., 142
Day, H. Summerfield, 21
Deer, white-tailed, 151, 153, 160, 171
Deer Park site, 20
Deer scapula hoes, 103–4
Deerskin trade, 6, 195
Delabarre, Edmund D., 96, 104
Delta (Napier Complicated Stamped) pottery, 20
Dendrochronology, 13, 22, 23, 24, 39, 41, 42–43
Dent site excavations, 55
DePratter, Chester, 35, 54, 83, 175
Depression, the: archaeological projects during, 1, 8, 11, 38;
    Ocmulgee in period after, 28–35. See also Federal relief
    archaeology
Deptford Checked Stamped pottery, 76
Deptford complex, 76
Deptford Simple Stamped pottery, 20, 76
De Soto, Hernando, 6, 175, 176
De Soto expedition, 5–6, 54, 144, 147, 175, 194; C. Hudson's
    De Soto route reconstruction, 6, 35, 167, 171–72, 173, 175–80
De Soto Expedition Commission, 6, 19
Diagnostic hafted bifaces, 57–58, 61, 66
Diagnostic projectile points, 61, 62, 67, 69, 70
Dickens, Roy S., Jr., 74, 163
Diffusion and migration, 142
Diffusion hypothesis, 102–3
Dillahunty, Albert L., 332
"Dirt lodges," 106
Ditches, defensive, 91–93
Doerschuk site (N.C.), 57
Domestic structures: Creek, 90, 192–93, 195; Lamar, 153–59
Dougherty County, Ga., 60
Douglass, A. E., 39, 42, 43
Dugouts, 3, 19–20; interpretation as fortification ditches, 91–93
Dunlap Fabric Impressed pottery, 53
Dunnell, Robert C., 142
Dunwoody, W. E., 20
Dyar phase mound construction, 167
Dyar site, 132, 154, 157–58, 161, 171

Early Archaic culture, 4; projectile points, 35, 66, 67; artifact
    assemblages, 62, 63, 66–69; sites, 66
Early Holocene period, 59, 64, 66, 67
Early Lamar phase pottery, 147, 148, 149, 150
Early man research: in Georgia, 4
Early Mississippian ceramics, 140, 141, 142

Early Mississippi period. *See* Mississippi period
Earth-covered structures, 111, 114–15
Earth-embanked structures, 89, 106, 154, 157
Earth lodges, 5, 20, 21, 89; in Southeast, 54, 105–15. *See also* Macon Earth Lodge
East Alabama Archaeological Survey, 182
Eastern States Archaeological Federation, 64
Edge-field scrapers, 63
Effective Temperature/Technological Organization Model, 67
"Egg-stones," 63
Egloff, Brian J., 147
Elk scapulae hoes, 103
Elliott, Daniel T., 135
Elmore County, Ala., 107
Emergency Relief Administration (ERA), 1, 28
English colonists, 16, 21
English trade: with the Creeks, 6, 191, 193, 194, 195
Erection trenches, 78
Estatoe site, 157
Etowah Complicated Stamped pottery, 32, 149
Etowah Mounds, 51
Etowah Papers, The (Moorehead), 36
Etowah period, 157
Etowah pottery, 135
Etowah River, 162, 163; Lamar sites along, 170
Etowah site, 41, 43, 169; nineteenth-century research on, 8–9; Peabody Foundation research, 10; W. K. Moorehead and, 51; fortification ditches, 91; aboriginal house with daubed roof, 112; Mound C, 113; Mound B, 170
Eulrich site (Wisc.), 99
European artifact associations, 148
European colonists, 6
European cultigens: Lamar botanical samples, 153
European trade: and Creek culture, 191–92, 193–95
Evans, Donald, 35
Evelyn Plantation, 24
Ewers, John C., 26, 27, 30
Excavation assemblages: Georgia area, 59–60, 66
Exploration, 176; Spanish, 15, 175
Extinctions: Pleistocene era, 59

Fairbanks, Charles H., 25, 26, 27, 28, 31, 52, 53, 90, 145, 183, 192; Stallings Island site and, 10, 13; as CCC senior foreman archaeologist, 25–26, 46, 50; pottery descriptions of Georgia wares, 26, 27; at Hartford Mound site, 27; at Jackson site, 27; at Turnbull site, 27; survey of Houston County site, 28; on National Park Service staff, 28, 30–31; on colonial Spanish ceramics, 34; on Creek use of black drink, 35; on Macon Plateau culture, 53, 93, 131, 132; on earth lodges at Macon Plateau site, 89, 109, 111; on migratory origins of Macon Plateau, 131, 139; Chickamauga Basin excavations, 138; on Lamar culture, 145, 147; on Ocmulgee Fields ceramics, 181, 182, 185
Fall Line, 84, 132; Early Archaic band aggregation at, 68; Lamar mound sites and flood plain habitat below, 160–61, 163, 170
Faunal samples: Lamar, 151, 153, 158; coastal, 153
Faust, Richard D., 33, 34, 35
Federal Emergency Relief Administration (FERA) archaeology, 19, 20

Federal relief archaeology, 1–5, 11–12, 28, 34, 42; at Ocmulgee, 16–28, 38, 51, 144. *See also* WPA archaeology
Feng, Han-Yi, 21, 37, 40
FERA archaeology: at Ocmulgee site, 19; at Mile Track site, 20
Feronia locality, 62–64
Field agricultural practices, 96
Finkelstein, J. Joe, 26
Fischer, George R., 32, 34–35
Fish, Paul R., 83
Fish, Suzanne K., 83
Fishing camps, 163
Flint implements, 53, 55–57
Flint River, 60, 132, 178
Floodplain: sites, 68, 158; river, 84, 85, 130, 132, 162; loams from alluvial silts, 100; alluvial, in Coastal Plain, 160; in Valley and Ridge Province, 162–63; Qualla sites in, 163
Florida: fluted points in, 62
Florida Gulf Coast archaeological survey, 27
Florida Indians: missionized, 194
Florida State University, 31, 34
Flowers, Sylvia, 35
Fluted points: Macon Plateau, 53, 55, 56–57; in Virginia, 55; Big Kiokee Creek; 57; in Georgia, 57; Brier Creek area, 57, 60; SGA survey, 58–59; in Alabama, 62; in Florida, 62. *See also* Clovis points; Folsom point
Folsom point, 20
Foraging camps, 68
Ford, James A., 3, 17, 24, 32, 38, 51, 53; at Birmingham archaeological conference, 11; at Marksville site, 12, 17, 51–52; McKern Classification and, 13; at Macon Plateau, 13, 43; at Ocmulgee site, 18–20, 21, 23; on ceramic typology, 25, 44, 45; at Lamar site, 39; on Lamar culture, 145
Forests: "primary forest efficiency," 67; hardwood, 164
Fort Ancient phase, 103–4
Fort Apalachicola, 189
Fort Center site (Fla.), 75–76, 78, 82
Fort Frederica National Monument, 28
Fort Hawkins, 16, 22
Fortification ditches: Macon Plateau, 91–93. *See also* Dugouts
Fort Leslie, 184
Fort Toulouse site, 183
Fort Walton culture, 173, 178
Fort Walton-Lamar occupation, 73
Fowler, Melvin L., 94, 99
Francisco of Chicora, 176
Freeway routes near Macon: archaeological survey of, 35
French Broad River, 179
Fushatchi site, 183

Gallagher, James P., 100–101
Garden beds: in midwest, 99
Garden Creek Mound No. 1 (N.C.), 110, 111
Garden Creek Mound No. 2 (N.C.), 74
Gentleman of Elvas, 178
George, Walter, 30
Georgia: Paleoenvironmental setting, 59; Paleoindian assemblages, 59–60; Wallace Reservoir locality, 61–62; Coastal Plain Paleoindian settlement, 62–64; Early Archaic assemblages, 66–69

Late Paleoindian period, 59, 64
Late Paleoindian sites, 61, 62–63
Late Savannah period, 147
Late Woodland period: Mississippi period sites and, 5; culture, 5, 53; maize agriculture, 97; Texas site (Ill.), 99, 102; hoes, 103, 104; ceramics, 135, 141, 142; Hamilton peoples, 139, 140, 141
Lavender, Mr. (assistant to A. R. Kelly), 18
Lawson Field phase pottery, 185, 189
Lawson Field site, 25
Law's site, 194
Leake Mounds site, 28, 30, 82
Ledbetter, R. Jerald, 60
Ledford Island site (Tenn.): 157, 158, 165
Lee, Ronald F., 30, 50
Lester, Frank E., 18, 24, 26, 41, 43, 48, 52
Levees, 162, 163
Lewis, George S., 60, 63
Lewis, G. S., site, 66
Lewis, Thomas M. N., 38, 45, 53; at Ocmulgee site, 20, 52; in Chickamauga Basin, 138; ceramic evidence for cultural replacement, 139
Lexington Archaeological Conference, 27–28
Lifesey, Mr. (assistant to A. R. Kelly), 18
Limestone-tempered pottery, 142
Lindenmeier site, 55
Linton, Ralph, 97, 106
Lithics, 37; Archaic, at Macon, 12; raw material sources, 61, 62, 64, 68, 69
Little Egypt site, 163, 183; Lamar domestic structures, 155, 158; Mound A, 157, 158; Lamar polity, 167, 170; platform mound site, 169, 170; capital of De Soto's Coosa province, 176
Little River site, 132, 171
Little Salt Springs (Fla.), 57
Little Tennessee River, 176; Early Archaic sites, 66; Martin Farm site, 140; Dallas phase sites, 154, 179
Little Tennessee River valley, 67
Lockett phase: Lamar culture, 178
Logan, Wilfred D., 32
Louisiana State University, 25
Lower Creeks: towns on the Chattahoochee River, 15, 21, 182, 185; history, 21; and Spanish trade monopoly, 191–92, 193, 195. See also Creek culture
Lower Creek site (Ala.), 107
Lowe site, 60
Loy site (Tenn.), 112
Lucas, James, 15
Luckett, William W., 27, 28
Luna, Tristán de, 144, 167, 175, 176

McDonald site, 140
McDougal Plain pottery, 132
McDougal pottery, 98
McKee Island phase pottery, 183, 185
McKeithen site (Fla.), 75, 78, 82
McMurray, Carl D., 34
Macon Archaeological Society, 31
Macon Chamber of Commerce, 116

Macon Council Chamber, 13, 38, 39, 43, 45, 48, 88, 108. See also Macon Earth Lodge
Macon Earth Lodge (Mound 1 Lodge), 5, 23, 34–35, 38, 88–89, 98, 107–8, 110; CWA excavation of, 19, 21; Laboratory of Anthropology students at, 22; reconstruction of the, 23, 24; Macon Plateau period earth lodges, 27; radiocarbon date for, 33. See also Earth lodges
"Macon Earthlodge, The" (Fairbanks), 27
Macon Historical Society, 16–17
Macon Junior Chamber of Commerce, 17
Macon Plateau, Ga., 1, 38
Macon Plateau complex, 20, 53
Macon Plateau culture, 4–5, 41, 54; in situ development model for origin, 5, 140–43; A. R. Kelly on, 20, 43; classification of culture contact situations, 31; corn agriculture, 53, 96; migration model for origin, 130–37
Macon Plateau phase, 102; ceramics, 35; artifacts and pit features, 90, 91; subperiods of the South Plateau, 93, 94
Macon Plateau pottery, 20, 32, 33–34, 35, 41, 43, 48–49, 52, 90, 91, 93–94, 98, 131–37, 140–42
Macon Plateau site: excavations, 1, 52, 53, 97–99; dugouts, 3, 19–20, 91–93; Mound D (Corn Field Mound), 5, 18, 19, 31, 88, 90, 94, 95, 96, 97–99, 108; Mound C (Funeral Mound), 10, 18, 19, 26, 31, 33, 38, 49, 53, 87–88, 90, 92, 93, 95, 116–24, 131; Oglethorpe party at, 15; nineteenth-century observations, 15, 16; Mound A (Great Temple Mound), 18, 19, 23, 33, 38, 49, 85, 87, 93, 94, 95, 130; CWA excavations, 18–20; Mound D-1 Lodge, 19, 22, 88–89, 94, 98, 107–8, 110; Mound E (Southeast Mound), 19, 85, 88, 93, 95; Dunlap mound, 20, 32, 85, 88, 93, 94, 95; McDougal mound, 20, 32, 85, 88, 94, 95; Mound B (Lesser Temple Mound), 23, 33, 87, 93, 94; Creek Trading House, 28; gunflints from, 33; beginnings of excavations, 38; Laboratory of Anthropology field program, 39–41; long trench excavations, 42; CCC establishes camp, 43; G. R. Willey's stratigraphic survey, 43–45; pottery classification staff, 44; "pithouses," 50; discovery of fluted point, 53, 55, 56–57; Mississippian platform mounds, 71; community pattern, 84–95; Granary, 88, 90; Sub-Mound House, 88, 90; Terrace House, 88, 90, 97–98; Mound X, 88, 94; Mound D-2 structure, 89; houses, 90; nonmound, nonearth lodge structures, 90, 91; lodges, 90, 93; Stratified Village, 90, 93; Halfway House, 90, 98; origins, 130–37; and Hiwassee Island cultures, 138–43
Macon Telegraph and News, 16, 18, 19, 20, 21
Macon Thick pottery, 33, 131, 132
Macon Trading House. See Macon Trading Post
Macon Trading Post, 190–96: burials, 5, 90, 124–29; excavations, 6, 13, 20, 21, 91; Kelly-Swanton correspondence, 21; artifacts, 31; Ocmulgee Fields ceramics and, 181–82, 185
Macon Trading Post ceramic complex, 181
Madison County, Ala., 74
Mainfort, Robert C., Jr., 82
Maize cultivation. See Corn agriculture
Majolica pottery, 31
Mandan house type, 106
Mandeville site, 73, 82
Marksville site (La.): 11–12, 17, 51, 75
Marsh, Alan, 35
Marshall, Richard A., 31

Temple mounds. *See* Platform mounds

"Temple Mound II" cultures, 145

Tennessee, 103; burials, 165, 167; Late Lamar pottery in, 147; Qualla variant of Lamar pottery in, 173

Tennessee River, 12, 74, 102

Tennessee Valley Authority: establishment, 12

Terrestrial species: Lamar, 151, 153, 158, 160

Texas site (Ill.), 99, 102

Thatch-covered buildings, 107, 112

Theriault chert quarry, 60, 66

Thomas, Cyrus, 9

Thompson site, 163, 169, 170, 171

"Time Studies: Pottery and Trees in Georgia" (Willey), 25

Timucua Mission, 193, 194

Toa, 178, 179

Tobesofkee Creek, 22, 32

Toltec site (Ark.), 94

Tools: Paleoindian and Archaic, 55, 56, 60, 61, 62, 63, 64, 67; curated and expedient forms, 67; agricultural implements and coevolution, 103–4

Toqua site (Tenn.), 112, 154–55, 157

Trade: Spanish, with Lower Creeks, 191–92, 193, 195; European, and Creek culture, 191–92, 193–95

Trading Post. *See* Macon Trading Post

Trait-unit diffusion, 141–42

Treaty of 1805, 15

Tree Ring Bulletin, 43

Tree rings, 39, 42–43. *See also* Dendrochronology

Trend and Tradition in the Prehistory of the Eastern United States (Caldwell), 66–67

Tributary status, 176

Trimble, Lee S., 28

Trueblood, Mr. (WPA worker), 40

Tugalo phase pottery, 151, 153, 154

Tugalo site, 27

Tukabatchee site (Ala.), 153, 154, 187

Turnbull site, 27

Ulibahali chiefdom, 176

U.S. Department of the Interior, 32

U.S. Forest Service, 61

University of Alabama: excavations, 74–75, 182–83

University of Alabama Archaeological Survey, 182

University of Chicago, 51

University of Georgia: surveys, 27, 132; at Cold Springs site, 76–77

University of Michigan: 1938 conference, 45

University of Michigan Museum of Anthropology: Ceramic Repository, 25

University of New Mexico: field school at Chaco Canyon, 25

University of Wisconsin-La Crosse, 100

Urn burials, 164, 173

Valley and Ridge province, 161–63, 170

Valley View site (Wisc.), 100

Vega, Garcilaso de la, 114

Vescelius, Gary S., 75

Vining Simple Stamped pottery, 53, 135

Vinson, Carl, 17, 26, 30, 32; Congressional sponsorship for Ocmulgee National Monument, 19, 53

Virginia: fluted points in, 55

Voll, Charles B., 32

Wacissa River (Fla.), 57

Wagley, Charles, 21, 37–38, 40

Walker, John W., 31, 32, 33, 35, 51, 132; excavations of Macon mounds A and B, 85, 87

Walker, Winslow, 11

Wallace Reservoir Archaeology Project, 76, 83

Wallace Reservoir Early Archaic Model, 67–68

Wallace Reservoir locality, 61–62, 66

Walling site (Ala.), 74–75, 82

Walnut Creek, 1

Walnut Roughened pottery, 182

Waring, Antonio J., 8, 9, 10, 22, 27; on Southern Cult, 13; on discovery of Macon fluted point, 20, 55; on pottery typology, 44–45; on fluted points in private collections, 57

Water bottles: dog effigy, 52

Watersheds, Atlantic and Gulf: presence of tool forms from, 64

Wattle-and-daub structure, 157, 164, 192

Wauchope, Robert, 27, 30, 50, 57, 74, 113, 139, 145

Webb, William S., 12, 38, 45, 53; on Ocmulgee excavations, 20, 52; on Norris Basin sites, 20, 52, 105, 111, 112, 138

Weeden Island complex, 24

Weeden Island pottery, 26, 28, 33, 34, 74

Weiss Basin, 183

West, John T., 18, 20–21, 24, 25, 26

Whaley, Claude Lambert, 46

White, George, 16

Wickliffe site (Ky.), 33

Wilbanks site, 110, 112–13, 114

Wilder, Harris H., 96, 104

Wild plant species: Lamar, 153

Willey, Gordon R., 4, 47, 53, 131, 189; on Mississippian migration, 12, 131; dendrochronology and, 13, 23, 24, 39, 41, 42–43; Laboratory of Anthropology student at Ocmulgee, 21; assistant archaeologist for WPA Projects, 23, 41; stratigraphic surveys of Ocmulgee site, 23–25, 43–45, 48; "Recorded Surface Areas," 24; and Louisiana State University WPA laboratory, 25, 46, 50; at Leake Mounds site, 28, 30; early career in Macon, 36–46; at Stubbs Mound site, 39–41, 73; on pottery typology, 44–45; on Lamar culture, 144, 145

Williams, J. Mark, 35, 41, 53, 167, 179

Williams, Stephen, 32

Willoughby, Charles C., 10

Wilson, Gilbert, 106, 114

Wilson, Mrs., 50

Winchester, Tom, 48

Winters, Howard D., 103

Winterville site (Miss.), 10

Wisconsin, ridged-field systems, 96, 99, 101–2, 104; chert hoes in, 103; Oneota sites in, 103

Wobst, Martin, 68

Woodbury, Richard B., 27

Woodland platform mounds, 3, 4, 6, 73–76

Woodland pottery, 90, 135, 140

Woodruff, J. F., 161

Woods Island phase pottery, 183, 186
Woodstock pottery, 135
Woodward (CCC inspector), 48
Works Progress Administration archaeology. *See* WPA archaeology
World War II, 12, 28
Worth, John, 132, 178
WPA archaeology, 1, 11, 13, 71; Southeastern Ceramic Conferences and, 13; Ocmulgee site, 20, 23, 24, 43, 47, 48; Swift Creek site, 21; proposal for Irene site excavations, 22; G. R. Willey and Louisiana State University WPA laboratory, 25, 46, 50; Swift Creek-Adkins site, 39, 40; Stubbs Mound site, 41; A. R. A. R. Kelly's WPA pottery lab, 44

Wyman, Jeffries, 9
Wynn, Jack T., 135

Yamassee War, 185, 192, 195
Yuchi Town site, 183